Prague in Black

Prague in Black

Nazi Rule and Czech Nationalism

Chad Bryant

HARVARD UNIVERSITY PRESS

Cambridge, Massachusetts

London, England

2007

Library of Congress Cataloging-in-Publication Data

Bryant, Chad Carl.
 Prague in black : Nazi rule and Czech nationalism / Chad Bryant.
  p. cm.
 Includes bibliographical references and index.
 ISBN-13: 978-0-674-02451-9 (alk. paper)
 ISBN-10: 0-674-02451-6 (alk. paper)
  1. Nationalism—Czechoslovakia—History. 2. Germanization.
3. Czechoslovakia—Politics and government—1938–1945. 4. Bohemia
and Moravia (Protectorate, 1939–1945). I. Title.

 DB2208.7.B79 2007
 943.71′033—dc22   2006049653

For my parents,
Janet Bryant and William A. Bryant

Contents

A Note on Place-Names   *ix*

Illustrations   *xi*

Introduction   *1*

1   A Hopelessly Mixed People   *28*

2   The Reich Way of Thinking   *66*

3   Plans to Make the Czechs German   *104*

4   Heydrich Imposes Racial Order   *139*

5   Surrounded by War, Living in Peace   *179*

6   All the Germans Must Go   *208*

Conclusion   *253*

Place-Names in Czech and German   *271*

Abbreviations   *273*

Notes   *275*

Archival Sources   *365*

Published Document Collections 367

Acknowledgments 369

Index 373

A Note on Place-Names

The historian of Bohemia, Moravia, and Silesia—what I will refer to as the "Bohemian lands"—faces many choices when deciding to write about the region. One such choice involves place-names. In the Bohemian lands every location had, and for some people still has, two names. Czech-speakers referred to Brno, German-speakers to Brünn. One man's Olomouc was another man's Olmütz. Czech-speakers, German-speakers, and people who spoke both languages lived in most of the places mentioned here. I have chosen to use the Czech names throughout the text, not because Brno and Olomouc were more "Czech" than "German," but because the style is easier to read. I chose the Czech version of place-names simply because that is what most readers will encounter today. There are two exceptions to my rule. First, when quoting a German-speaker or citing a document written in German, I use the German place-name. Second, when a modern English equivalent, such as "Prague" or "Bohemia," exists, I use it instead of the Czech place-name. I trust the reader to remember that place-names, like so much in the Bohemian lands, were claimed by patriots on both sides, and that nearly every Czech place-name had its German equivalent. A listing of the Czech- and German-language versions of the places mentioned in the text can be found near the end of the book.

Illustrations

Europe, 1930   *xiii*

Europe, fall 1942   *xiv*

Europe, 1949   *xv*

German, Polish, and Hungarian populations in Czechoslovakia according to the 1930 census   *19*

Residents of Brno greeting Hitler upon his arrival in the city on March 17, 1939   *30*

Administrative districts of the Oberlandräte   *32*

Karl Hermann Frank (far right facing forward) and Konstantin von Neurath (second from right facing forward) escorting Konrad Henlein (second from left facing forward) to Prague's Veletřní palac during Henlein's first official visit to Prague on June 29, 1939   *35*

Emil Hácha before his Christmas radio address in 1939   *43*

Marchers at the funeral of Jan Opletal   *61*

The German army taking up position in front of the Vítkovice Ironworks in Moravská Ostrava shortly after the invasion   *79*

Edvard Beneš in England, 1942   *90*

Nazi Party Gaue in East-Central Europe   *124*

V symbols on Prague's Wenceslas Square in 1941   *133*

V signs on a Prague building   *134*

Heydrich shortly after his arrival in Prague   *142*

Two people marked with the yellow star   *150*

Medical examination record from a mixed Czech-German couple's marriage application file   *164*

Medical examination record from a mixed Czech-German couple's marriage application file   *165*

Moravec delivering an anti-Bolshevik speech in Pelhřimov, June 2, 1944   *181*

A transport of female forced laborers about to depart for Germany, January 25, 1944   *183*

Placard, signed by Frank, listing the names of people sentenced to death for "unfriendly behavior toward the Reich"   *187*

A street in Brno after an Allied bombing raid in August 1944   *227*

Czechs preparing to defend the Prague radio station   *233*

The first victims of the fighting near the radio station   *234*

Captured German soldiers outside Prague Castle   *236*

Germans in Prague awaiting their transport from the city, May or June 1945   *243*

Europe, 1930. Map by Philip Schwartzberg.

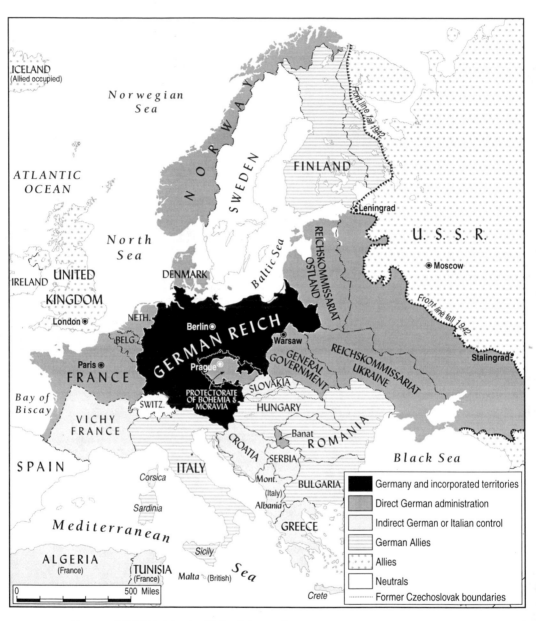

Europe, fall 1942. Map by Philip Schwartzberg.

Europe, 1949. Map by Philip Schwartzberg.

Prague in Black

Introduction

"Hitler Follows His Troops into Prague; Czechs Jeer the Nazis; New Regime Set Up," declared the *New York Times* banner headline on March 16, 1939. The morning of the day before, the *Times* correspondent reported, Prague residents awoke to radio announcements that the German army was marching toward the capital city. Every half hour thereafter Czech broadcasters warned the population to remain calm. Large snowflakes dropped from the sky as steel-helmeted soldiers marched through the city and took up positions in front of Prague's baroque palaces. German university students paraded around in Nazi uniforms. Other local Germans thronged the streets, screaming "Heil Hitler" and waving paper swastikas. Czechs, too, joined the crowds. On the side streets, men and women wept. The more daring tempted the invaders and threw snowballs at tanks and armored cars. Some Czechs wore Czechoslovak flags in their buttonholes. Isolated groups sang the national anthem. The Gestapo, relying on lists prepared beforehand, swept the city for "enemies of the Reich." Jews, many of them refugees who had already fled Nazi rule elsewhere, banged on the doors of foreign consulates, begging for visas. Some Jews committed suicide. As the sun set, people went home, mindful of the curfew announced earlier that day. "Prague streets, usually so animated, now completely empty and deserted," George Kennan, who was stationed in the American consulate in Prague, commented in his private notes. "Tomorrow, to be sure, they would fill with life again, but it would not be the same life that had filled them before; and we were all acutely conscious that in this case the curfew had indeed tolled the knell of a long and distinctly tragic day."[1]

1

A day after his troops entered Prague, Adolf Hitler, who had traveled by car from Berlin, announced the establishment of the Protectorate of Bohemia and Moravia. Only six months earlier, Britain and France had signed the infamous Munich agreement, which permitted Hitler's troops to occupy Czechoslovakia's largely German-inhabited Sudetenland. After Hitler's march on Prague, Britain and France promised to defend with armed force Hitler's next target, Poland. Germany and the Soviet Union signed a pact of nonaggression, and in September they attacked Poland from both sides. World War II had begun. At this point the Western historian's attention usually turns away from Czechoslovakia, only to return, if at all, in 1945 (when Allied troops liberated the country) or in 1948 (when Communist leaders grabbed control of the government). Yet remarkable events unfolded from 1939 to 1945 in the Protectorate, where seven million Czechs outnumbered their German rivals thirty-to-one.[2] About the size of Vermont and New Hampshire combined, the Protectorate was the first non-German territory to be occupied by Nazi Germany.[3] In the course of those six long years, Nazi rule utterly transformed the economy, political practices, and face-to-face relationships. It changed forever what it meant to be Czech or German. Events set in motion during the Protectorate years laid the foundation for today's Czech Republic, a nation-state that is almost entirely inhabited by Czechs.[4]

This study traces the origins, implementation, and ultimate effects of two grandiose, violent attempts at nation-making in western Czechoslovakia: one begun by the Nazi regime and one undertaken by Czechoslovak leaders after liberation. It also asks how Czechs and Germans continued to act nationally under Nazi rule, thus showing how Nazi rule forced patriots to reinvent what it meant to be "Czech" or "German." These struggles, in turn, require us to think differently about resistance and collaboration in Hitler's Europe. Exploring these themes also requires asking a common set of questions that troubled Czech patriots, Protectorate German patriots, Nazi leaders, and their Czechoslovak successors. What makes a person German, or Czech, and who gets to decide the matter? Definitive answers were never found, yet the process of making nations continued. Minorities were killed or deported. The region's ethnographic map was redrawn. To borrow from Ernest Gellner, what once looked like a painting by Oskar Kokoschka now resembled one by Amedeo Modigliani. In the process, a liberty perhaps unique to East-Central Europe—the right to choose a public nationality—was lost.[5]

After France fell, Nazi officials in Prague began devising plans to make the Protectorate, and the Czechs, "German." Planners estimated that half the Czech population would be expelled or killed; the other half was to be assimilated into a German national community that possessed a uniform national culture, the same and correct racial composition, and the same everyday way of life. As Wehrmacht troops marched deep into the Soviet Union, Nazi officials in the Protectorate began to identify potential Germans in the Czech population. Nazis and their accomplices murdered more than 78,000 of the Protectorate's Jews, as defined by the Nuremberg Laws. Only 14,045 survived the occupation years. Of the Protectorate's estimated 6,500 Roma (pejoratively known as Gypsies) only 583 returned from concentration camps after the war.[6] In the last years of the war Czechoslovak government-in-exile officials lobbied hard among the Allies in support of a "transfer" of Germans from postwar Czechoslovakia. At the Potsdam Conference they got their wish: Allied approval for an "organized" transfer of Czechoslovakia's Germans—but not before thousands had fled or had been forced across the country's borders. Before 1939, three out of every ten people living in the Bohemian lands counted themselves as Germans. Results from the 1950 census showed that Czechs made up almost 94 percent of the region's inhabitants.[7]

Nation-building required that state officials label individuals as members of one or another nation, or race, using an array of often contradictory criteria. Most confusing for Nazi and Czechoslovak officials, and hence creating the most documentation, were so-called amphibians—a term used by nineteenth-century patriots and the Protectorate's most influential social anthropologist to refer to people who could switch public nationalities or to people whose nationality was unclear. Only now becoming noticed by historians of East-Central Europe, amphibians were quite visible throughout the region before, during, and after World War II. Upper Silesians called them Water Poles (*Wasserpolen*); Hungarians called them Janissaries, recalling the Christian-born warrior elite of Ottoman times.[8] In prewar Czechoslovakia, patriots called them Germanized Czechs or Czechified Germans. Amphibians are important because Nazi and Czechoslovak officials saw them everywhere. After the war, the Czechoslovak minister of the interior estimated that one in every twenty-five "Czechs"—about 300,000 people—had been registered as Nazi citizens in the occupied Bohemian lands before liberation. Statistically speaking, then, every Czech in postwar Czechoslovakia had at least one distant relative who had become, in legal terms, a German. In one of the Protectorate's most ethnically mixed areas, the town of České Budějovice and its surroundings, about 11 percent of the so-called Czech residents had become Germans.[9] Fewer people in the Protectorate were identified as Jews (118,310) in 1939 according to the Nuremberg Laws; fewer gentile Czech *and* Slovak inhabitants of the Czechoslovak First Republic (roughly 70,000 people) perished during the occupation years.[10]

Amphibians expose the absurdity of reducing human diversity to simple nations, of placing individuals who were more than just Czechs and Germans into neat categories. Their sheer numbers aside, amphibians are also important for what they represent—the right and ability to chose a public nationality that existed in principle, if not always practice, before 1938. Indeed, people could and did "act nationally" in myriad ways before the occupation. In other words, they identified themselves as Czech or German by engaging in public practices tinged with national meaning.[11] At the most basic level people often acted nationally by speaking (or singing, or writing in) either Czech or German. Acting nationally meant creating and imbibing cultural products. By the late nineteenth century, one could act nationally by participating in a remarkable civil and political society that developed under Habsburg rule.[12] People expressed their national loyalties by belonging to clubs, marching in the streets, buying newspapers, voting for a political party, and participating in the census. Acting nationally sometimes meant shopping at either "Czech" or "German" stores, or even watching certain movies. Patriots of various stripes, all claiming to speak for the "nation," demanded expressions of national loyalty from the population as part of a wider effort to shore up national loyalites and pull amphibians over to their side. Through all this, however, nationality remained an individual choice made relatively free of state influence. For bilingual speakers in ethnically mixed regions it was a daily choice. At the same time, Czech and German anti-Semites worked to exclude Jews from their respective national communities. By the turn of the century, Jews, once the most adept at switching nationalities, saw their choices begin to dwindle.

Under Nazi rule, nationality, once something acted out in civil and political society, became something that state officials assigned to individuals. Jews, once designated as such by Nazi officials, found their fates sealed. Other Nazi officials—armed with X-ray machines, photographs of schoolchildren, and absurd confidence in racialist theories—sought out Czechs who could become Germans. After the war Czechoslovak officials, sometimes relying on methods and paperwork inherited from their predecessors, decided the fates of former Czechoslovak citizens of indeterminate nationality. They assumed the right to dictate the play of nationality politics—the mélange of actions endowed with political meaning all swirling around the choosing, imposing, or resisting of national identity. In their rush to put individuals into strict national categories, Nazi officials and postwar Czechoslovak leaders had little patience for amphibianism. Although it emerged from Nazi rule, and then again after the fall of Communism, Czechoslovakia's civil and political society would never be the same. Neither would notions about what it meant to be Czech.

Questions of nationality, however, were not left entirely in the hands of ideologues and government officials. Practices loaded with national meaning inherited from the past gained new significance under the Nazi occupation. Czechs and Germans acted nationally in new ways. Thousands of loyal Czechs took to the streets in 1939 to celebrate the reburial of Karel Hynek Mácha, a romantic poet who had died more than one hundred years earlier. Resistance fighters risked their lives to distribute underground pamphlets. As the war drew to a close, the Czechs collected jokes. Taking the perspective of patriots provides a new window on questions of "resistance" and "collaboration," terms weighed down by political baggage that often blur more than illuminate. Generations of scholars have attempted to define "resistance" and "collaboration" and then fit an array of motives and actions into these boxes. Asking how people acted nationally allows us to understand these motives and actions on their own terms. Conversely, tracing out Czech-Czech debates about what constituted resistance (*odboj*) and collaboration (*kolaborace*) reveals how the language of guilt intertwined with postwar attempts to punish Czech collaborators and expel the Germans. Rather than attempting to measure the extent and effectiveness of "resistance," we can examine instead how nationalists adapted their methods in pursuit of goals that, to them, were more important than sabotage or organized, armed attacks on the enemy. It helps us understand why Czech patriots after the war considered the postwar period the greatest triumph in the nation's history. Similarly, the actions of local German patriots do not fall neatly into categories of "resistance" or "collaboration." Tensions between "Protectorate Germans"—meaning self-ascribed Sudeten Germans who had been Czechoslovak citizens before 1939 but now found themselves within the Protectorate's borders—and "Reich Germans" simmered throughout the occupation years. Just weeks after the occupation had begun, Protectorate Germans began to chafe under the demands imposed upon them by the new regime. Thousands of Protectorate Germans refused to register for Reich German citizenship. Protectorate Germans in the SS vehemently opposed Nazi Germanization plans, even if few disapproved of massive expulsions.

In the Protectorate, national thought informed every action, every thought, every judgment. Individuals—both members of the state and objects of its rule—navigated in a world that had become consumed with questions regarding nationality. But individuals, not homogeneous and uniform nations, made history, if not always as they pleased, in response to particular events at peculiar times and places. Postwar mythmakers in Czechoslovakia and Germany determined, for different reasons, to remember the Nazi occupation and the postwar expulsions as the culmination of a long history of conflict between two homogeneous nations, the telos of a story with its own natural, internal dynamic. Czech mythmakers portrayed Czechs as victims or resistance fighters, Germans as traitors and perpetrators. Germans and Nazis were synonymous. When Czechoslovak German expellees and their organizations addressed the war at all, they tended to see themselves as victims of a chauvinistic Czechoslovakia, victims of Nazi rule, and then victims of the Czechs again. In darker moments, each side attempted to claim Jews as fellow victims. These myths, forged in some cases even before the war had ended, still resonate in Central Europe today. The time has come to ask new questions and to think beyond simple nationalist dichotomies.[13]

Perspectives

The emergence of valuable and penetrating scholarship on the Protectorate years has begun to undermine these politically charged myths. Drawing on this research, along with recent works on nationalism in the

Bohemian lands, Nazi-occupied Europe, "war as revolution," and the nation-building state, this study approaches common themes from different angles. By bringing together fields of scholarship often separated from each other, *Prague in Black* offers insights into issues that reach far beyond the boundaries of the history of the Bohemian lands.

After the fall of Communist rule in Czechoslovakia, and the opening of the archives, Central European historians of the occupation years rushed to "make up for lost time" and to fill "empty spaces" left blank by decades of Communist rule.[14] Indeed, there was much work to be done. Vojtech Mastny's impressive *Czechs under Nazi Rule* was published in 1971, before most Western scholars had access to archives on the other side of the Iron Curtain. Only volume 1 of Detlef Brandes's two-volume counterpart, *Die Tschechen unter deutschem Protektorat* (The Czechs under the German Protectorate), could rely on materials found in Prague's archives. Far-reaching in scope, both books concentrated on organized resistance groups and political collaboration. Few other works in English or German were available.[15] Historians in Czechoslovakia, of course, faced all the restraints of a Communist regime determined to shape how this politically sensitive topic was remembered and understood. Work on politically fraught topics such as the Nazi occupation emphasized atrocities committed by the Nazi regime, the activities of Communist partisans, the heroic role of the Soviet Union, and the 1945 uprisings.[16] Only during a brief period of liberalization in the 1960s could historians dare to challenge the Marxist paradigm and address topics such as the non-Communist resistance, Edvard Beneš's Czechoslovak government-in-exile in London, and life under Nazi rule.[17] Since 1989, fresh examinations of non-Communist resistance movements have complemented groundbreaking studies on collaboration.[18] Historians have investigated previously taboo topics such as culture, university life, and the fate of Czechoslovakia's Jews and Roma.[19] More general works have greatly enhanced our understanding of high politics and the structures of state rule.[20] Many other topics only hinted at by my sources still await a historian: the Nazi euthanasia program, religious life, and the fate of the Protectorate's Polish minority, to name just a few. Similarly, the chosen boundaries of *Prague in Black* prohibit close discussion of the Reichsgau Sudetenland, the largest of the German-inhabited units integrated into Nazi Germany following the Munich agreement. Nor can it claim to address in detail the important issue of

Czech-Slovak relations during the war, the Nazi satellite state of Slovakia, or the partial expulsion of the Hungarians from Slovakia after the war. While not claiming to offer a synthesis, I have attempted to synthesize recent works of scholarship dealing with the Protectorate. Though historians have recently written valuable studies of wartime Slovakia and the Gau Sudetenland, no general history of the Protectorate— whether in English, German, or Czech—has been published since the 1970s.[21]

Nor does the Protectorate need not be studied in a temporal vacuum. I have also followed in the footsteps of English-speaking historians whose studies of national identity, gender politics, and postwar retribution trials have placed the Protectorate years within the flow of the Bohemian lands' history.[22] In asking how people acted nationally within the context of state institutions and laws, I have drawn insights and questions from scholarship on national identity in the Bohemian lands before 1938, and the final decades of Habsburg rule in particular. The last years of the Nazi occupation are only beginning to receive the attention they deserve, and there has been remarkably little interest in the society that emerged after liberation in 1945.[23] After 1989, scholars have examined the development of the Czechoslovak government-in-exile's expulsion plans, the radicalizing effect that the domestic resistance had on those plans, and how the collapse of the Nazi regime created the necessary conditions for the "wild transfer" of 1945. A thick line, however, still separates much of the scholarship on the Protectorate from scholarship on the postwar expulsions from Czechoslovakia.[24]

Drawing on literature outside the history of the Bohemian lands places the Protectorate and its aftermath within the flow of modern European history. Transnational causal linkages appear. Looking outside the region reveals, at the same time, what distinguishes events here from events elsewhere in Europe. The Protectorate was a Nazi project, which necessitates situating the Protectorate within the context of Hitler's Europe. Reich Germans dominated within the state administration, the SS, and, to a lesser extent, the Nazi Party in the Protectorate. Recent scholarship on Nazi Germanization across Europe can help explain why the Protectorate, like parts of Poland, Ukraine, Alsace, Lorraine, Luxemburg, Slovenia, and other regions of Europe, became a target of Nazi plans to make whole lands, peoples, and economies German. It also helps us understand difference and causality. Germanization, at least the way Nazi leaders understood it, was a European project first undertaken in Poland. Why were Nazi Germanization plans in the Protectorate approved but only half-heartedly enacted, whereas authorities in western Poland deported tens of thousand of Jews and Poles by 1941? How did massive plans for expulsion and resettlement farther east influence Germanization policies in the Protectorate? How did Nazi authorities in Poland and elsewhere make determinations about nationality?[25] The answers to these questions shed new light on the interplay between ideology and pragmatism in Nazi Europe. As Chapter 3 demonstrates, the decision-making process in the Protectorate was a product of both improvisation on the peripheries of Nazi rule and directives from the center. Decisions emerged as a result of both compromise and competition among agencies with overlapping competencies. The European context, and the experience of marking nationality in the Protectorate, reveal the singularity of the Holocaust while uncovering causal relationships between the Final Solution and Nazi Germanization plans.[26]

From the outbreak of war until 1943, governments transplanted more than thirty million Europeans, most of them from East-Central Europe. From 1943 to 1948, another twenty-one million were on the move. Like the Bohemian lands, Poland emerged as a homogeneous, national unit. Only in Romania did a significant German minority remain after the war. The experience of World War II, Jan Gross noted as early as 1989, accelerated change; it did away with old ideas, old politics, and old economic structures; and it laid the groundwork for Communist rule in East-Central Europe. Forced migrations counted among the most radical and heart-rending of these transformations, which, as historians have suggested, together constituted a revolution of sorts in the region.[27] Similarly, Hitler's Germany and postwar East-Central European regimes were not alone in assigning nationality to individuals in an effort to extract "dangerous" elements, to eliminate difference, and to create nations or, in the case of the Soviet Union, nationally homogeneous republics.[28] They shared characteristics with other modern states that, as Norman Naimark writes, identified, counted, and expelled whole populations in order to create nation-states, which many Europeans came to see as the only legitimate and workable form of government. Social Darwinist rhetoric legitimated the project. War often provided the context.[29]

States, as Naimark understood, are not singular, uniform actors.[30]

Moreover, in the Bohemian lands national homogenization did not follow a straight line from ideology to implementation, from modern nationalism to the modern nation. Protectorate Germans in the SS were not alone in opposing plans for making millions of Czechs into Germans. Economic and military considerations, including the need to keep armaments factories manned by Czech workers running, at times halted radical Germanization measures. Plans to murder the Bohemian lands' Jews, however, played out to their horrible end. Nor was the path to the expulsion of the Germans a straight one. A host of individuals outside Czechoslovak state structures played important roles. The Czechoslovak government-in-exile had to balance demands from radicalized members of the domestic resistance for the complete expulsion of Germans with Allied resistance to such plans. Nazi policies of exclusion provided the justification, and often a model, for Czech patriots and Czechoslovak officials after the war. The Czechoslovak government, in turn, played a leading role in making the postwar expulsions throughout Eastern Europe possible. Its leaders created the context necessary for the "wild transfer" that followed liberation. In both cases the actual marking of nationality was a local event, which in its last phases was undertaken by local officials on the ground using a confusing array of criteria. In fact, if we look top to bottom, from within the Protectorate and outside it, we see myriad individuals pushing policy and policy implementation in various directions at various at times, often with unintended consequences. Many of these people's thoughts and actions stemmed from years of nationality politics peculiar to the Bohemian lands, whose history from 1939 to 1948 emerges as both European and unique.

As this study moves forward in time, it adopts a variety of changing perspectives. This approach requires drawing on several sets of primary sources. The view "from above" comes from various government documents created or received by the Reich Protector's Office in Prague, the central administrative apparatus in the region. In addition to internal documents generated within the Reich Protector's Office, this collection includes correspondence to and from Protectorate leaders and Berlin officials, Nazi Party leaders, regional administrators, military officers, and collaborationist Czech politicians. The view "from below" draws on three sets of sources that describe the moods and actions of the general population—police reports from the SS's Intelligence Service (Sicherheitsdienst), situation reports penned by local Nazi administrative officials, and underground correspondence between Protectorate inhabitants and the Czechoslovak government-in-exile based in London. Telegrams sent by Communist agents to their superiors in Moscow, economic reports, letters written by ethnic Germans after the war, diaries, and memoirs complete the list of primary sources. Taken together, these sources reveal numerous divisions within state and society. Conflicts between party officials, bureaucrats, and SS men, as well as between Czech patriots at home, officials in London, and people simply trying to muddle through, form an integral part of the story. Published radio broadcast transcripts and a wealth of secondary literature add a view from "the outside"—from London, the eventual home of the Czechoslovak government-in-exile, and from Moscow, home of Czechoslovakia's Communist Party in exile. Connections, divisions, and causal linkages emerge.

While not eschewing moral judgments completely, in *Prague in Black* I have described few heroes, few straight lines, many tragic absurdities, and many more unintended outcomes. I have sought to understand a tragedy. The book is, then, primarily about loss. The sheer numbers of dead (sixty million Europeans) and displaced (fifty-one million more) that World War II and its aftermath produced are still difficult to comprehend.[31] The memories of disgraceful wartime behavior and the destruction of the Jews still haunt thoughtful Europeans. In the Bohemian lands, as elsewhere, politics, economics, and cultures changed forever as a result of World War II. Throughout East-Central Europe diverse societies became nationally homogeneous. A little less than ten years after the Munich agreement, Czechoslovak Communists grabbed control of the government in Prague. The history of the Bohemian lands, and indeed world history, entered a new era. But the old era had already been swept away.

Historical Background

Like many of their counterparts in the Habsburg monarchy, whose ruling family obtained the Bohemian crown in 1526, the Czech national movement began as a cultural project. Early nineteenth-century nationalists, drawing on the philosophy of Johann Gottfried Herder and others, viewed each nation as an organic, individual whole with its own history, personality, fate, and language. People naturally belonged to one or another primordial tribe and became conscious of their place in the national organism through language and history. For Czech patriots in particular, language and other national symbols provided the "proof" that the nation existed, and from the early nineteenth century on they jealously guarded the symbols that made up Czech culture, feeling that they embodied the nation's existence.[32] By the turn of the century, thanks to the development of a highly literate audience of consumers, being a good Czech meant reading books and any of the hundreds of Czech-language newspapers and periodicals available for sale.[33] For middle-class Czechs it meant attending performances at the National Theater in Prague and other venues. It meant admiring the producers of culture: intellectuals who, in another Eastern European tradition, wrote to and for the nation. Patriots throughout the nineteenth century believed that language pulsed through the heart and soul of the nation. It was in the realm of culture that the Czechs could establish a place among the nations of Europe.

German-speakers predominated in Silesia and the mountainous territories that rimmed the edges of Bohemia and Moravia. Other German-speakers lived in cities such as Prague, Brno, Jihlava, and Olomouc, while still more were scattered throughout the countryside. Like their Czech counterparts, early German nationalists in the Bohemian lands drew important lessons from Herder about language and culture. Language also played the crucial role of differentiating Germans from Czechs, part of a larger process in which the two rival national movements defined themselves in opposition to each other.[34] The German national movement, however, had to contend with several, often troubling, complications. Eighteenth-century reforms made German the common administrative language of the Habsburg monarchy. Following the 1867 *Ausgleich* (Compromise) with Hungary, the Bohemian lands belonged squarely within the independently governed Austrian (or, more properly, Cisleithanian) half of the monarchy. Yet most of Europe's German-speakers lived outside the borders of the Habsburg realm, a hodgepodge of nationalities that appeared increasingly unworkable, and illegitimate, in an age of emerging nation-states. German patriots, like their Czech counterparts, shared a strong sense of belonging to a certain place, or *Heimat*. German loyalties were thus pulled in three directions. German-speakers could be Bohemian Germans, Austrians, and Germans.[35]

By the late nineteenth century, acting Czech, and acting German, came to include participating in a remarkable civil and political society that developed under Habsburg rule. Following a devastating economic crisis in 1857 and military defeat at Solferino in 1859, Habsburg rulers slowly acquiesced to pressures for reform from Austria's German liberals, who for the next two decades remained the dominant political force within newly established, but limited, representational institutions in Vienna and much of the Bohemian lands. Citizens became equal under the law, civil marriage was introduced, and an independent court system was established. Imperial law granted its citizens considerable rights to freedom of assembly, which proved crucial for the development of national movements in Austria.[36] Between 1868 and 1871, for example, about 1.5 million Czechs attended national camps, or *tábory*— mass public meetings for political debate that recalled supposedly similar gatherings during the Hussite period. Among the most successful clubs emerging from the 1860s was the gymnastics organization and "Czech national army" Sokol, which counted over one thousand clubs and more than 119,000 members by 1912. Its national rival, the German-Austrian section of the German Turnverein, counted more than 103,000 members in 1914. About a third of its members lived in the Bohemian lands.[37]

Acting nationally also meant voting for a national party. As the century advanced, Habsburg rulers gradually widened the franchise, culminating in the introduction of male suffrage for the Austrian-wide parliamentary elections of 1907. The first victims were German liberals, whose political fortunes declined as the Bohemian lands entered the age of mass parties and mass politics. In the elections of 1911 voters could choose among thirteen Czech parties that included clerical-conservatives, liberals, "Realists," socialists, and Christian Socialists—most of which possessed mirror-image German counterparts.[38] Associations and labor organizations organized under party umbrellas. The parliament in Vienna, although a weak representative institution prone to obstructionist tactics, served as an important forum for opinions ranging across the political spectrum. The stakes were especially high at the provincial, district, and communal levels, where competition for resources combined with competition over national symbols in a highly urbanized and industrialized society.[39] Parties at the local level vied for control over the regulation of businesses, welfare institutions, hospitals, and a host of other local institutions. In theory, locally elected elites shared power with district governors appointed by Habsburg rulers in Vienna. In practice, most district governors kept their distance from day-to-day governance. Just as important as elections were censuses, taken decennially after 1880, which directly affected the allocation of state resources. At election and census time the national colors appeared more prominently, as patriots marched, electioneered, and sang on the streets. A peculiar mixture of centralization and federalism allowed the tiniest administrative regions to become sites of the most intense, and meaningful, "battles" among nationalities. Borderlands and language islands where the boundaries between the two nations blurred formed the "frontlines."[40]

By the turn of the century the vocabulary of war pervaded nationalist rhetoric. Mass politics combined with a Europe-wide shift toward Social Darwinist thinking to create an atmosphere of desperate competition among nationalists. Nations, Czech and German patriots contended with violent words, were organisms locked in a life-and-death struggle for survival. Population numbers, economic success, and political power were some of the many measures by which patriots gauged the relative strength of their nation. And in nearly every case, the Czechs were "winning." Industrialization pulled thousands of Czechs into traditionally German regions and urban spaces. Especially in the cities, the Czech population, as measured by annual censuses after 1880, was steadily growing, and at a quicker pace than the German numbers. Even in Vienna, the heart of "Germanness" in the monarchy, nearly one-fifth of the city's population in 1900 had come from Czech-speaking regions.[41] A growing Czech banking industry established financial independence from its Viennese German counterparts. After 1884, Czechs assumed control over chambers of commerce in Prague, Plzeň, and Budějovice, leaving the Germans with only Liberec and Cheb.[42] In 1906 Czech parties gained a foothold within Budějovice's city council. Czech representatives took control of Olomouc in 1910. Czech politicians gained control of municipal affairs in Prague in the 1880s. Prominent symbols of Czech middle-class success—the National Theater, a Czech University, and the Municipal House, adorned by artists versed in the art nouveau style of the day—dotted the cityscape. Large demonstrations to celebrate national holidays brought thousands out into the streets. In 1892, the aldermen removed German-language names from some of the city's street signs. To add insult to injury, the lettering was now in red and white, the Czechs' national colors, instead of the traditional German black and yellow.[43]

At the local level, "professional nationalists"—journalists, association leaders, politicians, and others—imbued nearly every aspect of daily life with national colors.[44] The demands became particularly intense in mixed regions during times of political agitation. Marching, electioneering, engaging in boycotts, and even speaking a language were some of the many ways of being counted at a time when the relative strength or weakness of the nation was measured in numbers. Associations encouraged widescale boycotts that targeted small shop owners and large businesses alike. The associations published guides that listed shops as being either Czech or German; many owners hung signs in their shop windows declaring themselves to be "pure Czech" or "pure German." Czech patriots targeted firms owned by members of German associations or businesses that did not hire Czech workers.[45] Patriots claimed children for the nation, harassing parents into sending their offspring to Czech- or German-language schools. They constructed private schools to ensure that each child could obtain a properly national education. The largest German school association had one hundred thousand members in 1880, a number that doubled by 1910. By 1887 its Czech rival had twelve thousand members, funded and operated twenty-six private schools, and subsidized forty-one others. By the turn of the century ten thousand Czech children were enrolled in private schools.[46] The League of North Moravian Germans (Bund der Deutschen Nordmähren) planned to insert Germans in Czech areas so that "not another square foot from the region that our ancestors inhabited would be lost to the opponent."[47] Small victories at the local level translated to small national victories. In the process increasing numbers of people, especially in areas where Czechs and Germans lived side-by-side, were drawn into the game.

The intensity with which patriots fought for individual loyalties betrayed a paradox. Patriots portrayed the nation as eternal, unified, and homogeneous. They contended that each individual "truly" belonged to one or another nation. Yet they realized that national consciousness had to be forged, and that national loyalties had to be won. The "nation" was not the only entity to which people proclaimed their loyalties.[48] Although prominent Czech and German nationalists adhered to Protestantism, the vast majority of the Bohemian lands' inhabitants declared themselves to be Catholics.[49] Habsburg citizenship did not require national distinctions. The emperor and dynasty remained important symbols in the public realm and within schools, even if nationalism and modernity had diminished the potency of those symbols. Powerful landowning nobles dabbled with nationalist language, but in the end most chose loyalty to the empire over loyalty to any one nation.[50] Nobles were not alone in being indifferent to nationality. Many in the Bohemian lands refused to accept national labels. Other people consciously chose to move between Czech and German camps. Czech nationalism provided a voice and place for industrialization's losers—peasant farmers, estate managers, self-employed craftsmen, and owners of small- to medium-sized businesses who in 1910 constituted more than 40 percent of Czechs studying at Prague's Czech University.[51] Modernization produced legions of Czech-speaking citizens and consumers, to whom bureaucrats, entertainers, bankers, merchants, and producers had to appeal, in Czech.[52] Habsburg civil servants, while nominally anational, had ample incentives to identify themselves as Austrian Germans.[53] Czech- and German-speaking parents exchanged children for a summer or school year, believing that bilingualism would open up professional opportunities for their offspring.[54]

Patriots demanded that national loyalties be paramount, if not all-consuming. They declared the days of in-betweenness over and were determined to pull amphibians to one side or the other. Still, people were more than just Czechs and Germans. And for many people nationality represented a choice—a choice that hypernationalism required but could not make permanent.[55] Of course, choice did not exist for everyone. Education, language skills, and a whole array of local pressures made, and kept, many people Czech or German. In 1905 middle-class Czech and German leaders hammered out the Moravian Compromise, which required that Czech and German voters register into one of two cadastres and henceforth vote only for their own national parties. The Compromise, which applied only in Moravia, also empowered local school boards to ensure that children attended the "correct" national school system. Nor was nationality politics played on an even playing field. Czech politicians accused German employers in northern Bohemia and Brno of pressuring Czech immigrant workers at census time into choosing German as their everyday language. Until 1912 imperial law prevented women from joining political associations. Unequal under the law, women's voting rights actually became more restricted in the last decade of the monarchy's existence.[56]

Choice existed in greater degree for some people than others. The choices available to some people changed over time, as the case of the region's most persecuted group demonstrates. Although the Bohemian lands' Jews counted among the most secularized in Europe, distinct Jewish institutions such as congregations *(Gemeinden)* survived into the modern era. Twenty-five Moravian cities maintained separate Jewish municipalities.[57] In the postliberal era, many Jews were bilingual, meaning that they could easily move between Czech and German communities.[58] Jews had long identified with German liberalism, but they could also associate with socialism, the Czech national movement, and the small but influential Zionist movement by the turn of the century.[59] Election campaigners courted Jewish voters, who could swing elections in mixed towns like Brno and Budějovice.[60] By 1890, however, renewed anti-Semitism and increasingly racial understandings of nationality worked to exclude Jews from the German and Czech national communities. Many Czech patriots saw Jews as a variant of the hated Germans, even though half of Bohemia's Jews, and 20 percent of Moravia's Jews, declared Czech to be their language of everyday use in the 1900 census. Economic boycotts in small towns and villages drove Jewish establishments out of business.[61] Most Sokol and Turnverein unions refused membership to Jews.[62] Because Hebrew and Yiddish were not listed under the census category "language of everyday use," even the choice of Jewish nationality was not available to them. (More than eighty-five thousand people in the Bohemian lands, a little more than 1 percent of the total population, identified themselves as Jews according to religion in the census of 1910.)[63] At a time when national belonging had become all-encompassing, Jews found themselves excluded and included and in-between.[64]

In June 1914 a Serbian nationalist shot dead the heir to the Habsburg throne, Archduke Franz Ferdinand, thereby setting in a motion a chain of events that led to World War I and the eventual collapse of Europe's four continental empires. In the aftermath of the war, a swath of smaller countries filled the territory between Germany and the Soviet Union. All became increasingly intertwined in Germany's economic and diplomatic power politics. Before the outbreak of World War II all but Czechoslovakia had disposed of democratic procedure in favor of various forms of dictatorship. All the new states, supposedly founded on the principle of national self-determination, had within their borders large, vocal national minorities, who could claim internationally sanctioned, collective legal rights. Czechoslovakia was among the most heterogeneous countries in the region and had the largest ethnic German community outside Germany and Austria. (According to the 1930 census, Czechoslovakia was home to more than three million Germans, who made up 22 percent of the country's total population[65]). By attaching sections of pre-1918 Hungary to the Bohemian crownlands, Czechoslovakia also included a large number of Ruthenes, Hungarians, and Slovaks, who, the newly minted term "Czechoslovak" aside, greatly differed historically, culturally, and economically from the Czechs (Fig. I.1).[66]

In one interwar era Czech-language dictionary the word "nation" (or *národ*) had two entries. The first entry defined a nation as a "community of people with the same language, culture," and their own state. The second entry referred to a community within a state "where another nation has predominance," in other words, the dictionary explained, "the German nation among us."[67] German leaders, their appeals to join Austria rejected by the Allies, played no role in the creation of the Czechoslovak state and its constitution. Czechoslovak legions, composed of prisoners of war, *Sokolovci*, and others who had volunteered to fight alongside Allied armies, patrolled the state's new borders. Trains to Brno now pulled into Masaryk Station. In Prague, the main train station was renamed after President Woodrow Wilson. "Czechoslovak" became the official language of the Republic. German bureaucrats unable to speak Czech lost their jobs, while Czechs "colonized" government positions in Slovakia. Nostrification laws aimed at establishing Czechoslovak economic independence enriched Czech banks at the expense of their Viennese competitors, thereby allowing them to gain greater influence in commerce and industry throughout the country. German patriots complained that the Czechoslovak state encouraged the establishment of Czech schools at the expense of German ones. With the help of the state, Czechs infiltrated "German" land behind the nationality borders and swamped German-language islands. A revolutionary land reform divided up nobles' property to the advantage of Czechs, and state-sponsored resettlement schemes inserted Czechs and Slovaks into German- and Hungarian-dominated areas.[68]

These measures were possible because a small number of powerful Czech politicians predominated within the government. In the republic's four elections fifty parties ran for seats in the powerful bicameral parliament. Especially during the early years of the republic's exis-

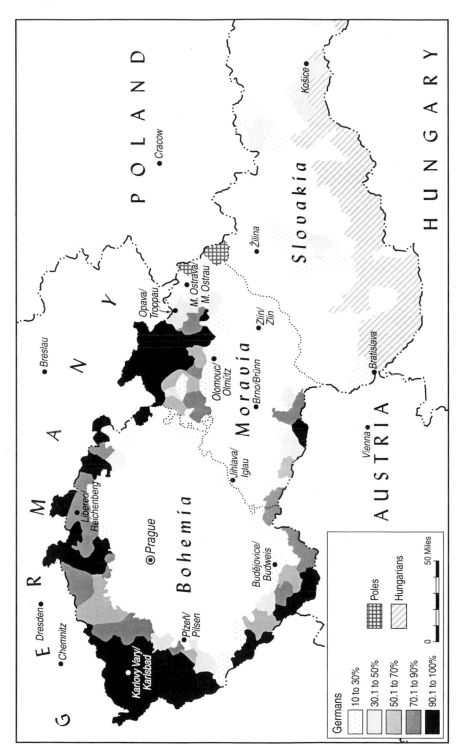

Figure I.1 German, Polish, and Hungarian populations in Czechoslovakia according to the 1930 census. Map by Philip Schwartzberg.

tence, however, the assembly followed the dictates of the five Czech party leaders whose followers commanded a slight majority in parliament. Meeting informally, the powerful five (or *"pětka"*) dictated policy from Prague and staffed all levels of government with party faithful.[69] Local and provincial governments were reorganized on the French model. Centrally appointed district chief administrators (*hejtmany*), provincial presidents, and their appointed assemblymen lorded it over weak, popularly elected commune, district, and provincial representatives. President Tomáš Masaryk had considerable powers, too, including his own intelligence service, which spied on all political party activity. He and others in the Prague castle (*Hrad*), where the president had his offices, could appoint and dismiss the government and rule directly in case of an emergency. Masaryk's prestige and position as sole arbiter among parties allowed him to foist favorites off on coalition governments.[70]

Yet it would be unfair to portray Czechoslovakia simply as an undemocratic state governed for and by Czechs to the detriment of its minorities.[71] Habsburg law codes, administrative institutions, and educational systems that had survived World War I allowed citizens to enjoy equal protection under the law and to act nationally within civil and political society.[72] Citizenship remained based upon the principle of *jus soli*, meaning that citizenship was granted to those born within the state's territorial boundaries. Nationality, ethnicity, or heritage was irrelevant to citizenship.[73] In many respects civic and political rights for individuals expanded. Every vote was direct, secret, and, unlike under Habsburg rule, directly proportional. Although still subject to unfair citizenship laws and other forms of official discrimination, women obtained the same voting rights as men.[74] International treaties guaranteed Germans, Jews, and other groups collective rights as a minority. In areas where they made up at least 20 percent of the population, for example, Germans had the right to obtain an education and deal with state authorities in their own language. (Only 10 percent of all Germans lived outside areas with this minimal population requirement.[75]) In the 1925 elections Sudeten Germans voted overwhelmingly for "activist" parties that accepted the government's legitimacy. In 1926 Czech leaders rewarded middle-class German parties with cabinet positions in the Czechoslovak government.[76]

Amid all the changes that the establishment of the Czechoslovak Republic brought, nationality politics took familiar forms. Czechs and

Germans acted nationally in ways inherited from the past. In fact, although little research into associational life under the First Republic has been done, there are indications that public participation in civil and political society increased. By 1936, 1.4 million people of various ages belonged to one of eight gymnastics clubs. The Sokol had 3,255 unions and 2,680 summer training grounds. Its German rival, the German Gymnastic Association (Deutscher Turnverband) had 1,187 unions with 626 summer training grounds. Parties campaigned for women's votes. Newspapers aimed at a female audience increased in volume and distribution. Liberal groups formed to ensure that equal rights, as guaranteed by the constitution, were observed. The most prominent of these liberal women's associations counted 27,000 members in 1935. Catholic activists in Moravia, too, organized their own women's clubs, which had strong ties to the pro-Catholic People's Party and its newspapers.[77] New forms of media mixed with old-style nationality politics. In September 1930, for example, Czech protesters tore down German-language movie posters and threatened German and Jewish theater owners. "We don't want any German kitsch; we want Czech films," a crowd chanted as they burst into a showing of the musical comedy *Delikatessen*, interrupting German heartthrob Harry Liedkte's singing and dancing.[78] Approximately 13,000 people attended a national demonstration in Moravská Ostrava organized by the National Democratic Party, its women's organization, and its youth clubs before the 1930 census. German newspapers in the Hlučin region, which had been part of Prussia before World War I, set up information booths to help locals through the census process and to agitate for a higher German count.[79]

Nationality remained a choice for many people. In Moravia, national school boards could still assign children to the "proper" school, but the cadastres established after the Moravian Compromise were undone.[80] Patriots continued to court and deride "Germanized" Czechs and "Czechified" Germans who chose their nationality according to convenience.[81] Thanks to lobbying by Zionist groups and Masaryk, who had been sympathetic to their cause before World War I, individuals could claim Jewish nationality. The government's decree providing guidelines for the 1921 census declared that respondents could choose their nationality according to "their own conscience and according to the truth." Only in cases of "clear impropriety" could the census commissar change the response. Curiously, neither the Czechoslovak constitution nor the 1921 decree defined the word "nationality," although "nationality" replaced "language of everyday use" on census forms. Not until 1930 did the Ministry of the Interior, which conducted the census, define "nationality," when it was declared "as a rule . . . to be determined by mother tongue." An exception was made for Jews, few of whom spoke Hebrew or Yiddish. The choice of nationality, however, remained with the respondent.[82]

The Great Depression and the rise of Hitler's Germany changed once again the tone of nationality politics in the region. Paradoxically, the "state people" appeared to be fragmenting. Cautious and often secret compromises within the *pětka* and *Hrad* turned many Czech voters away from larger political issues. Younger Czechs in particular had reason to feel disconnected from politics in Prague. The average age of parliament members in 1935 was 45.6 years. Without the German representatives, the number jumped to 65.4 years.[83] Prominent artists, writers, and critics embraced cosmopolitan modernism and attacked the unthinking, romantic, bourgeois Czech historicism of their fathers. Public intellectuals, including Masaryk, engaged in heated debates on the mission, nature, and history of "Czechness." When Masaryk died in 1937, cultlike admiration of him survived. Yet his successor, Edvard Beneš, lacked the charisma and prestige required to serve as a unifying, respected figure within an increasingly fractious political environment. The Depression left one million people unemployed and hit the working classes particularly hard. Before 1939, one Czech writer commented after the war, most workers "lived on the border between a very modest life and destitution. If just one thing happened, an illness in the family or [the birth of] another child, that border was crossed." And, he added, this situation referred to the people lucky enough to have work.[84] Political leaders remained committed to the protection of cartels and to laissez-faire economics, while limiting government aid to the poor to small-scale relief campaigns.[85] The Communist Party obtained 10 percent of the vote in 1935.[86] On the right, clerico-conservatives and young fascists joined a growing antidemocratic, anti-Beneš camp.

Czechoslovakia's Germans, who assumed the common label of Sudeten Germans after World War I, were hit particularly hard by the Depression. Many of their industries relied heavily on exports to Germany, and their industries had failed to modernize. A disproportionate number of Czechoslovakia's unemployed were Sudeten Germans.[87] Social insecurity and constant chafing under Czech rule, however, proved a uniting force. Throughout Europe, national rights and individual rights had become indistinguishable; individuals, wrote the influential Viennese political thinker Othmar Spann, were mere *Teilganzheiten,* parts of a larger, organic whole.[88] By 1938 nearly all German political organizations and parties crowded under the umbrella of the Sudeten German Party, now 1.3 million people strong. Only the German Communists and Social Democrats remained independent.[89] Led by Turnverein leader Konrad Henlein, the Sudeten German Party openly promised to return its compatriots "home to the Reich." Nazi Germany's remarkable economic recovery, combined with chauvinistic, nationalistic, and anti-Semitic propaganda, drew many Sudeten eyes across the border. In the municipal elections of May and June of 1938, which were, admittedly, marred by numerous irregularities, more than 85 percent of German votes cast went to the Sudeten German Party.[90]

On November 5, 1937, Hitler met with top military leaders and Foreign Minister Konstantin von Neurath—a man who would later assume the top position in the Protectorate. On this day Hitler determined that he would invade Austria and Czechoslovakia. "The aim of German policy," he stated, "was to make secure and to preserve the racial community and to enlarge it." The absorption of these countries into the Nazi Reich, he argued, would arrest the decline of Germandom (*Deutschtum*) and free up crucial foodstuffs for Germany, an aim that would require expelling two million people from Czechoslovakia and one million from Austria. Crucially, Hitler concluded, military strategy demanded the destruction of Czechoslovakia. Czechoslovakia's well-trained army and its alliance with France complicated other plans for conquest in Eastern and Western Europe.[91] Hitler's plans were eventually realized, in large part thanks to the eager cooperation of the Sudeten German Party, whose members had long enjoyed funding from various Weimar and Nazi agencies. In the course of the 1930s, Nazi ideologues among Sudeten German leaders either won over or eliminated their party rivals, many of whom, like Henlein, originally espoused a more spiritual, "Catholic," and dreamy vision for united Germandom, without "soil and blood" racism. Henlein's deputy and rival, Karl Hermann Frank—another man who would play a leading role in the Protectorate—was certainly taking orders from the SS by 1937. Henlein, almost alone at the top, threw his lot in with Nazism. Several weeks after Hitler privately announced his intentions to invade Czechoslovakia, Henlein suggested to the Führer that his party could be a "factor in National Socialist Reich policy." Hitler did not respond. The time was not yet right.[92]

Shortly after Nazi Germany's annexation of Austria in March 1938, Hitler set in motion plans for the destruction of Czechoslovakia. Henlein, reporting on a three-hour meeting that he and Frank had with Hitler, summed up the strategy imparted to him by the Führer: "We must always demand so much [of the Czechoslovak government] that we can never be satisfied." The next month, at his party's annual congress in Karlovy Vary, Henlein demanded political autonomy for the Sudeten Germans and openly declared his party's loyalty to Nazi ideals. European fears of another world war mounted, as Germany and Czechoslovakia seemed destined for war. In early September Beneš's government relented to pressure from Britain and France and agreed to accept the Sudeten German Party's calls for political autonomy. Henlein responded with another demand: that Germany annex Czechoslovakia's German-speaking territories. Beneš's government banned the Sudeten German Party and its shock troops. Hitler announced the creation of a Sudeten German Freikorps, a paramilitary organization. Its ranks quickly filled with more than ten thousand Sudeten Germans who had jumped the border. Twice in the ensuing weeks British prime minister Neville Chamberlain flew to Germany. During the first meeting Chamberlain agreed to Germany's annexation of portions of the Sudetenland in return for military restraint, an agreement that the British and French governments pressured Czechoslovakia to accept. At the second meeting Hitler declared the timetable for German occupation to be unacceptable. The transfer of territories would take place on October 1, even if it meant unleashing the German armed forces. The Czechoslovak government declared a general mobilization on September 23, 1938, as did the British government four days later. German military formations marched through Berlin; army divisions massed on the border. War seemed certain.[93]

Instead, in the waning days of September, Hitler, Chamberlain, Italian "duce" Benito Mussolini, and French prime minister Édouard Daladier sat around a table in Munich's newly constructed Führerbau and decided how best to carve up Czechoslovakia. In the early morning hours the three leaders, without consulting representatives from Czechoslovakia, conceded to Hitler's demands for immediate annexation. The Beneš government capitulated, thereby sparking violent protests throughout Prague.[94] Enormous celebrations greeted incoming Wehrmacht soldiers as they marched into the Sudetenland.[95] Over the next six months Gestapo and SS Intelligence Service men and fanatical members of the Sudeten German Freikorps arrested over ten thousand "enemies of the Reich," many of whom were eventually sent to the Dachau concentration camp. Germans attacked synagogues and Jewish businesses, a wave of violence that culminated in the "Kristallnacht" pogroms that rocked Nazi-controlled Central Europe one November night. Aryanization measures and implementation of the Nuremberg Laws followed soon thereafter.[96] An estimated twenty to thirty thousand Jews, the large majority of the region's mostly German-speaking Jewish population, fled to the interior, along with more than 160,000 Czech nationals and thousands of German antifascists.[97] Hitler named Henlein the top Nazi Party leader and *Reichskommissar* (roughly, "viceroy") of what eventually became the Reichsgau Sudetenland, formed from territories along the northern and western borders of dismantled Czechoslovakia. Three other Nazi Party regional administrative units, or *Gaue,* absorbed what remained of the Sudetenland. All the occupied territories were fully incorporated into the Greater German Reich. With the acquiescence of the Axis powers, Hungary grabbed portions of southern Slovakia, and Poland snatched the Těšín region of Silesia.

Democratic Czechoslovakia ceased to exist. Beneš resigned and left the country. The National Assembly of the so-called Second Republic, renamed Czecho-Slovakia to appease Slovak nationalists, introduced censorship and a rigid two-party system. A combination of anti-Benešites, antidemocrats, and clerico-fascists took over government offices. The Second Republic's president and his government ruled by decree. The Communist Party was banned, and the labor unions were melded together into one pliant organization. The ruling National Unity Party refused membership to Jews, Poles, Germans, and Magyars, and the government dismissed or pensioned off Jewish state employees. German newspapers, theaters, and the German university in Prague purged Jews from their institutions. Czech organizations, such as the Sokol, did the same. Hospitals removed Jewish doctors at the behest of the Federation of Czech Physicians. In its short existence, the Second Republic sent between twenty thousand and twenty seven thousand Jews—many of them refugees from the Sudetenland—into second exile. More exclusionary practices were being prepared, but time ran out for the government before they could be enacted.[98]

The Second Republic's foreign policy consisted of compliance with

Hitler's demands, but that did little to ensure its survival. The Munich agreement had left Hitler feeling cheated of his triumphant march into Prague and the destruction of Czechoslovakia. The rump state that survived after 1938 still had sovereignty over many of Czechoslovakia's valuable industries. Occupying Bohemia and Moravia would open the way for projecting economic influence to the southeast, and the state's northern borders would provide strategic military bases from which to launch attacks on Poland and farther east. Germans living in the interior demanded to be reunited with Sudeten Germans now in "Germany." On March 10, 1939, responding to rising tensions with Slovak leaders, the Prague government sent police into state offices in Bratislava, arrested the Slovak prime minister, and dismissed the cabinet. Hitler, who had convinced the Slovaks to demand independence, had an opening. A day later Hitler's army marched on the rest of Bohemia and Moravia. Poland and Hungary grabbed more territory from Slovakia, which became a satellite state to Nazi Germany. The Bohemian lands, Hitler stated, rightfully belonged to the Reich; he bragged that the occupation would be remembered as one of his greatest accomplishments.[99] Czech patriots feared repression. Local Germans, one Nazi Intelligence Service agent observed, "counted on an immediate about-face in all areas of their lives," and their patriots dreamed of reversing the long-running trend toward Czechification.[100]

Thus, an era of nationality politics in the Bohemian lands appeared to have come to an end. From the late nineteenth century until 1938 people acted nationally within the framework of a civil and political society protected by the state. They marched on the streets before censuses and elections; they voted; they engaged in boycotts; they raised money for schools; they engaged in vitriolic public exchanges; they spoke Czech or German. Patriots led "battles" for wealth, political power, territory, and individual loyalties. Only in rare cases did state officials assign a nationality to individuals, and even then the label was not permanent. Although patriots insisted that membership in the nation was "natural," edging more and more toward ethnic and racial understandings of nationhood, they understood that for many people nationality represented a choice—a choice that for some, like the Jews, became increasing fraught with uncertainties. Patriots demanded that their followers not just be national, but that they act nationally in public in order to demonstrate the "strength" of the nation.

Nazi leaders in the Protectorate eventually undid civil and political society, imposed strict censorship laws, and killed Jews. Czech industries and banks came under the control of the new "German" regime. The language of public administration became German. The Nazis dispensed with notions like equality under the law and introduced terror and fear as weapons of political control. State officials attempted to rewrite the rules that had governed nationality politics in Bohemia and Moravia for over a hundred years. They were determined to dictate who was, or could be, a German, Czech, or Jew. Anyone identified as a German, or potential German, was to be made into a loyal Nazi. The rest would be deported or murdered. The inhabitants of Bohemia and Moravia, however, would continue to act nationally in ways inherited from their past, even if their practices took place within a radically different context. In fact, for those familiar with nationality politics in the region, the first year of Nazi occupation in the Protectorate of Bohemia and Moravia seemed like an unlikely return to the nineteenth century. And, once again, it appeared that the Czechs were "winning."

A Hopelessly Mixed People

Emil Hácha, president of Czecho-Slovakia, arrived in Berlin shortly before midnight on March 14, 1939. Much had already happened that day. At the urging of Nazi leaders in Berlin, Slovak leaders had declared independence shortly after noontime. While Hácha was traveling to Berlin the SS unit Adolf Hitler occupied territories in the industrial region of Moravská Ostrava. In Berlin, a Nazi government representative escorted Hácha to his hotel room. More than an hour later Hitler finally agreed to meet Hácha in the Reich Chancellery. When Hitler appeared, Hácha rushed to speak first, assuring the Führer that his government would look favorably on Bratislava's demands. "[T]he fate of Czechoslovakia lies in the hands of the Führer and it believes that in his hands the nation will be well looked after," Hácha declared. Hitler shocked Hácha with his response. The German army had orders to march into the Bohemian lands of Czecho-Slovakia beginning at 6:00 A.M. that morning. Hácha, he said, had two choices. In the first scenario, Czech resistance to occupation provoked massive destruction. In the second, German forces entered unopposed, and the Führer would permit the Czechs "their own dignified (national life), autonomy, and guaranteed national freedoms."[1] According to Hitler's secretary, Hácha sank into his armchair. He looked as if he had turned to stone. So shaken was the Czecho-Slovak president that, at one point, a doctor had to revive him with an injection.[2]

Following Hitler's ultimatum, Hácha was led to another room where he telephoned Prague with orders for the military to avoid any shows of resistance. "Everything must be calm, totally calm!" he begged Prime Minister Rudolf Beran. "Let it happen, otherwise it will be horrible!"[3]

When he returned, Hitler presented him with a document to sign: "The Czechoslovak President declared that, in order . . . to achieve ultimate pacification, he confidently placed the fate of the Czech people and country in the hands of the Führer and the German Reich. The Führer accepted this declaration and expressed his intention of taking the Czech people under the protection of the German Reich and of guaranteeing them an autonomous development of their national life as suited to their character."[4] The badgering of Hácha continued. "I'm in a tough position," Luftwaffe chief Hermann Göring threatened. "It would pain me enormously to have to destroy that beautiful city [Prague]. But I must be certain that the English and French know that my air force is at 100 percent. They still refuse to believe it, and I'd like to give them some proof to the contrary!"[5] Hácha signed. At 4:30 in the morning Hácha broadcast a radio message to the population to remain calm. Nazi troops entered cities across the Bohemian lands to cheering crowds of local Germans. That evening Hitler and several leading Nazi figures entered Prague, ahead of Hácha. The next day, the Führer announced the creation of the Protectorate of Bohemia and Moravia. On March 17 he and his entourage paraded through Olomouc and Brno before heading to Vienna (Fig. 1.1). Hitler would not return to the Protectorate again.[6]

The Czechoslovak project appeared to have come to an end. The Reich assumed control over foreign affairs and defense in the territories, although the Czech government remained in power and attended to a limited number of domestic matters. German military rule gave way to the authority of the newly established Reich Protector's Office, the center of power in the Protectorate. Yet the play of nationality politics continued, following oddly familiar patterns. Czech patriots would, in fact, later remember the first half year of the occupation as one of the nation's finest moments. Czechs, drawing from practices borrowed from the past, acted nationally with an energy and unity rarely seen after World War I. Protectorate German patriots complained that the occupation had worsened their economic, social, and cultural standing vis-à-vis the Czechs. As in years past, Czechs and Germans continue to mix. Patriots employed an array of tactics to sway amphibians to their side. Here, too, the Czechs seemed to be "winning." Nazi leaders, confused and cautious, unwittingly provided new opportunities for Czechs to express national solidarity. In his March 16, 1939, announcement, Hitler promised that the Czech government would attend to domestic matters and that the Czechs would enjoy a vaguely worded "autonomy." Two days before, in Berlin, Hitler had also promised Hácha that his government would enjoy "the fullest autonomy," adding that the Czech nation would enjoy an independence "greater than any that had existed under Austrian rule."[7] Many Czechs, and perhaps Hácha, took him at his word. In fact, many local inhabitants interpreted the occupation as a return to the Habsburg era and acted accordingly.

Figure 1.1 Residents of Brno greeting Hitler upon his arrival in the city on March 17, 1939. (Reproduced by permission of the Vojenský ústřední archiv Fotoarchiv.)

The New State

In the first month of the occupation the army remained the Protectorate's supreme civil authority. In April a civil administration, largely the design of State Secretary of the Ministry of the Interior Wilhelm Stuckart, came to power. In its first incarnation, the ruling apparatus mimicked prewar Czechoslovakia's three-tiered administrative pyramid. At the top of the pyramid was a Reich protector, who, Stuckart emphasized, "is . . . the viceroy in the Protectorate. . . . He alone embodies the Reich in all areas of state and governmental life in the Protectorate." Below the new Reich protector, and the Reich Protector's Office, the Bohemian representative body was eventually dissolved, and its Moravian counterpart was reduced to an administrative arm within the Reich Protector's Office. The third and final level consisted of thirty-five *Oberlandräte*, whose numbers were reduced to nineteen by summer 1939, then to fifteen before the end of 1940 (Fig. 1.2). Each Oberlandrat was responsible for the local German administration, the German police, citizenship registration, and Czech-German relations within his fiefdom. All laws and ordinances from the center had to pass through him, as did all correspondence between local administrators and officials in Prague.[8]

The first Reich protector was Konstantin von Neurath. Born into an old Swabian aristocratic family, he had spent more than twenty years in the diplomatic service before being assigned to Bohemia and Moravia. Neurath once compared his approach to diplomacy in terms borrowed from his experience as a devoted hunter. Rather than having the animals driven toward him, as a common practice held, Neurath preferred following the prey's tracks, learning the prey's behavior patterns, and waiting for it to betray itself. He rarely pulled the trigger. Following stints as first secretary to the German embassy in Constantinople and then ambassador to Rome and London, Neurath became German foreign minister a year before the Nazis seized power and remained at the post until 1938. His strong sense of duty and natural shyness meant that he was not someone who would challenge radical Nazi leaders within Hitler's inner circle. Although he privately dismissed Hitler's ideas about *Lebensraum* (living space), and thought less of the Führer's demagoguery, Neurath enthusiastically supported the remilitarization of the Rhine and the annexation of Austria. He was known abroad for being well mannered, cultured, and respected—one reason Hitler appointed

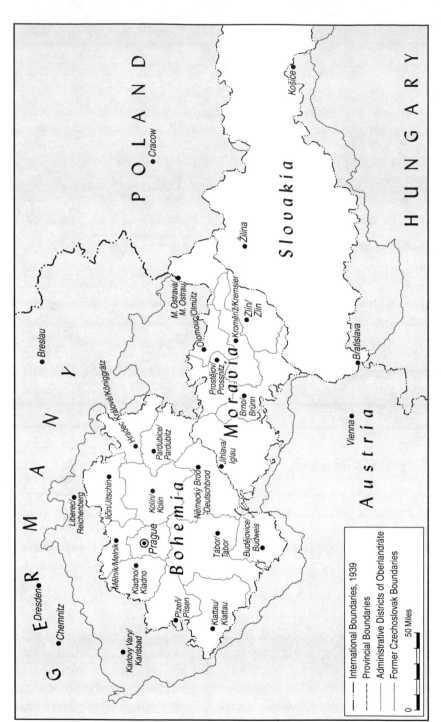

Figure 1.2 Administrative districts of the Oberlandräte. Map by Philip Schwartzberg.

him Reich protector. These same qualities aroused suspicion among many committed Nazis. "Neurath is well-known for a being a soft-peddler. The Protectorate needs a strong hand to maintain order there," Josef Goebbels complained to Hitler after Neurath's appointment as Reich protector. "This man has nothing in common with us. He belongs to an entirely different world."[9]

Stuckart's decree to the contrary, Neurath's power was limited. As in Germany and elsewhere in occupied Europe a mishmash of agencies vied for power and influence. By the end of the year the army still controlled the war industry, press, propaganda, civil defense, and conscription. The Justice and Finance ministries answered to their superiors in Berlin. The railway system, the post, German institutes of higher education, the radio station, and the Foreign Office were also linked administratively to Germany. Hermann Göring's Economic Ministry lorded over vital sectors of the Protectorate's economy. Treason cases could be tried in Nazi Germany's infamous People's Court. The Nazi Party took up the concerns of local Germans. Six days after the occupation began, Hitler divided the Protectorate's territory among four preexisting Nazi Party *Gaue* that cut across Protectorate boundaries from Austria, Bavaria, and the Reichsgau Sudetenland. Although hampered by administrative chaos, four *Gauleiter,* or Gau leaders, retained a representative in Prague and influential contacts in Berlin. Jealous of the Reich protector's powers, they began plotting to undo the Protectorate structure almost from the first days of the occupation.[10] Neurath's most powerful rivals, however, came from the ranks of the SS. Members of its information-gathering agency, the Intelligence Service, answered to their own boss in Prague, and then to the agency's founder in Berlin, SS Obergruppenführer Reinhard Heydrich. The Intelligence Service headquarters and jurisdictional regions mirrored those of the Oberlandräte. Although subordinate to the Oberlandräte, local police (*Kreispolizei* and *Ortspolizei*) were at the service of the Gestapo, which, along with the Criminal Police (*Kriminalpolizei*), answered to the SS's Intelligence Service. The Intelligence Service had virtually unlimited power to spy and arrest as they pleased. The information they generated traveled to the highest levels of power in Prague and Berlin.[11]

In the Protectorate, the senior SS official was Karl Hermann Frank, who was also the Protectorate's state secretary, the new regime's second highest position. Frank could hardly have been more different from

Neurath. Born in 1889 to a family of committed Pan-Germanists in Karlovy Vary, Frank served in the Austrian army during World War I and had spent a year studying law in Prague before quitting to work at a number of small, badly paid jobs. A loyal member of his local Turnverein, he joined Henlein's Sudeten German movement in 1934 and quickly rose to become its propaganda chief. Through the Nazi regime's official body for ethnic German propaganda and financial support, Frank illegally siphoned funding to the Sudeten German Party while cultivating relationships with Heydrich and his immediate superior in the SS, Heinrich Himmler.[12] Hugo Jury, the Protectorate's most ambitious Gauleiter, feared being in the same city as Frank, such was the latter's reputation for bureaucratic knife-fighting and vicious rages.[13] Whereas tact and compromise characterized Neurath's public announcements, Frank's public persona was that of a radical Sudeten German chauvinist. "The Protectorate means nothing less than a defense," a journalist for *Der Neue Tag* (The New Day) quoted him as saying that, "a special form of defense from within and without: defense of the *Volkstum* [nation] and defense of order, defense of *Raum* [space] against constant destroyers of peace, and defense of constructive energy against parasites."[14] Kennan wondered what motivated this "half-educated" man who had risen to such great heights of power, unsure "whether his ruthless zeal is the result of political ambition or a self-righteous belief in the innate sinfulness of the Czechs"[15] (Fig. 1.3).

The new leaders quickly established their rule, and ensured domestic peace, thanks in large part to SS-engineered political terror that aimed to eliminate existing and potential enemies while frightening the rest of the population into submission. The Gestapo and the Intelligence Service could take into "protective custody" any individuals they deemed dangerous to the nation or state and deport them to a concentration camp. So-called enemies of the state could have their property confiscated.[16] As soon as the occupation began, the Gestapo arrested more than 4,600 Communists and refugees from Germany. Three-fourths of the detainees were released after promising loyalty to the new regime, although the remaining victims, most of them refugees from Austria and Germany, were sent to concentration camps. The arrests, numbering in the thousands, continued throughout the spring and summer. The reasons for arrest varied wildly. Gestapo officers based in Německý Brod, for example, arrested at least seven men in the two weeks leading up to

August 1. Four had disparaged German rule in a local pub. A fifth predicted aloud that Edvard Beneš would some day return and that neighboring Czechs would destroy German Jihlava. A sixth man had tried to steal guns and then pretended to be a Gestapo officer. The last man, in another pub, also claimed to be a Gestapo officer. He was simply showing off to the other guests, the real Gestapo concluded.[17]

Until the outbreak of World War II, however, Neurath's tone won the day. Officially sanctioned newspapers like *Prager Abend* (Prague Evening), for example, recalled a mythical one thousand years of cohab-

Figure 1.3 Karl Hermann Frank (far right facing forward) and Konstantin von Neurath (second from right facing forward) escorting Konrad Henlein (second from left facing forward) to Prague's Veletržní palac during Henlein's first official visit to Prague on June 29, 1939. (Reproduced by permission of the Česká tisková kancelář.)

itation among Czechs and Germans. The Reich protector allowed Czech patriots a remarkable amount of room for maneuver. The priority of Nazi officials in the early months of their rule was to gain control over the country. Among high officials, the "Czech question" remained on the margins of discussion while practical administrative questions dominated.[18] Before his attack on Poland, Hitler still hoped for a last appeasement from Britain and France. "Von Neurath was the only possibility," Hitler reassured a doubtful Goebbels. "The Anglo-Saxon world valued him as a man of distinction. His appointment will have the effect of calming the international situation after my desire not to take the Czechs' national life will become known."[19] Stuckart had hoped that other nations might find the idea of becoming protectorates appealing.[20] Investigators from the Deutsche Bank noted that, given the right administrative decisions, Protectorate industries could play a key role in the German economy. The Bohemian lands' famous armaments industry could do much to strengthen Germany's military might. Furthermore, a radical policy might disrupt relations with important trading partners in southeast Europe.[21] New figures assumed new positions within a new state and had many reasons to proceed cautiously. On the ground, old players continued to practice old-style nationality politics.

"Apolitical Politics"

In spring and summer 1939, one Czech publicist recalled after the war, "our culture mobilized its strengths."[22] Nineteenth-century musical classics like "Má vlast" (My Homeland) played to packed halls during Prague's annual musical festival in May. Concert-goers throughout the country sang the national anthem at random intervals. In response, Nazi authorities issued a decree the next month forbidding Czechs from singing national songs in restaurants, wine bars, and other public spaces.[23] Although the cultural section of the Reich Protector's Office kept a watchful eye over the production and distribution of films, theaters showed the same number of Czech-language films as they had in 1938. German films were often boycotted, with Czechs choosing Hollywood productions instead. Attempts by Nazi propagandists to insert newsreels before Czech films provoked popular opposition. Film operators had to interrupt a Hitler speech because of the whistles, stomping, and yelled insults from the audience. Czech film operators deliberately ran the propaganda reels at high speed or blurred the picture.[24] Bookstores stocked reprinted Czech classics by nineteenth-century nationalists like František Palacký, Jan Neruda, and Alois Jirásek, whose books readers snatched up in increasing numbers. For every Protectorate inhabitant, 1.3 new books rolled off publishers' presses. Czech readers could also choose from 48 daily newspapers and 164 weeklies. The Intelligence Service constantly spotted instances of anti-German prose in these publications. They complained that, in the first year of the occupation, authorities had shut down only two newspapers.[25]

Typically, Intelligence Service agents exaggerated the dangers posed to Germandom and Nazi rule in order to justify more repressive measures. The media, of course, was by no means free. A special section of the Reich Protector's Office employed Czech-speaking censors from the Second Republic to read over every press article three times: first the article manuscript, then the proofs, and then the printed page before distribution. Journalists could not comment on German troop movements or engage in polemics with Nazi publications.[26] Nor did all media promote Czech nationalism. Newspapers still mirrored their former party affiliations. Many writers penned mundane, apolitical pieces. But the Nazi regime did prove surprisingly tolerant—even to the point of allowing well-known, unabashedly nationalist writers to continue to write and publish.

Ferdinand Peroutka, a liberal publicist and prominent member of the Hrad group, was one such writer. Arrested by Czech police shortly after the occupation, Peroutka was released six days later. Under the watchful eye of the Gestapo and its helpers he continued to produce challenging Sunday opinion columns for *Lidové noviny* (The People's News). "Few among us are those who now think about things other than his membership in the nation," Peroutka wrote in an article entitled "We Are Czechs." "Few among us," he continued, "presume that we live in a time in which our heritage is not in danger, a heritage handed down by our predecessors. Whoever thinks differently must be looked at in amazement, either for his obtuseness or his strong nerves."[27] During the interwar period Peroutka had defended Tomáš Masaryk's state and Czech liberalism. Under the Protectorate, he argued, Czechs, regardless of their political views, needed to unite if they were to have any influence: "[I]n this Central European space, only a totality can negotiate with a totality."[28] "We know that in the nineteenth century the Czech nation raised itself more as a result of apolitical than of political politics," Peroutka wrote later that summer, as Czech influence among Nazi leaders seemed on the wane. "The time has come for us to repeat this old and proven achievement."[29] Just years earlier he had called nineteenth-century nationalism a period of collective adolescence that needed to be outgrown. Now, however, he called on his co-nationals to fight for small advantages, especially in the realm of culture.[30]

Peroutka's legacy was *Přítomnost* (Presence), a weekly review founded in 1924 with a personal donation from Masaryk. Following the invasion Peroutka continued to contribute articles to *Přítomnost,* but the weekly's editorship went to Milena Jesenská, an unlikely proponent of Czech nationalism. Before 1938 she made her living writing for various interwar publications and ran in a number of Prague circles—the Devětsil avant-gardists, German-Jewish writers around Max Brod, and the Communist Party, which she quit in 1937 in opposition to the Moscow trials. Like so many writers, Jesenská became a patriot only after the occupation had begun. "Trifles become big symbols," she wrote for an article in *Přítomnost* shortly after the occupation had begun. "And since it is woman who wields in her hand the trifles, she reigns over the big symbols. Czech song and the Czech book. Czech hospitality. The Czech language and the old Czech customs. Czech Easter eggs, little Czech gardens, and clumps of Czech roses." "It is our communal duty to be good Czechs," she wrote in another article. Being a good Czech, she argued, meant uniting the nation, encouraging the nation, and ensuring that "each of us be truly filled with that national spirit that has endured throughout history."[31]

"Good Czechs" continued to act as such outside the realm of high culture as well. Clubs continued to play an active role in national life. One Intelligence Service report dedicated eleven pages to describing the dangers posed by organizations like the Czech Aviation Club and the National Auto Club. Of particular concern was the Sokol movement, which, the report claimed, counted one-eighth of the Protectorate's population as members. Out of public view, various underground organizations began to take form. The Communist Party of Czechoslovakia, although forcibly disbanded after Munich, survived the March 15 arrests and maintained contact with party organizations abroad. Various members of the ruling prewar political parties who communicated with Beneš and his loyalists abroad organized under the group Politické ústředí (Political Central). Former army officers, many of whom had been forced into early retirement, banded together within the Obrana národa (Defense of the Nation), while Social Democratic intellectuals, blue-collar youth, and students organized as well. The prospects for armed resistance and sabotage were bleak. Shortly after the occupation had begun, agents from Germany's War Economy and Armaments Board quickly secured the Czechoslovak army's entire supply of weapons and ammunition. The Protectorate regime demanded that privately owned guns be turned in to the police. The threat of Gestapo arrest hovered over society. No help would come from abroad.[32] Instead, the underground organizations concentrated their efforts on producing and distributing underground publications. Twenty underground publications circulated throughout the Protectorate before war began.[33] The most well known, *V boj* (In Battle) was under the influence of the Politické ústředí and was published in several Protectorate locations. (One of its contributors was Milena Jesenská.) Its first of twenty-seven issues published in 1939 consisted of a speech given by President Beneš at the University of Chicago. The second issue contained an extended debate surrounding a *Saturday Evening Post* article about *Mein Kampf.*[34] The Communist underground managed two issues of *Rudé právo,* which called for "national unity" among Czechs, regardless of class or political beliefs, and "passive resistance, strikes, boycotts of fascist agents and Czech traitors, [and] great demonstrations of national intentions."[35] Although internally these groups discussed future forms a Czechoslovak government might take, shoring up national loyalties in the present remained their primary, and unifying, concern.[36]

Often inspired by official and unofficial writings, Czechs from all sectors of society—not just intellectuals, politicians, Communists, and the military—acted Czech in ways that would have been familiar to patriots from previous eras. Prague houses remained decorated in the blue, red, and white colors of the Czechoslovak flag throughout the month of May. Around ten thousand people marched past the romantic poet Karel Hynek Mácha's coffin at the National Museum. Others left flowers at the memorials to Mácha, other nineteenth-century national heroes, and the unknown soldier.[37] An estimated eighty thousand met in Moravská Ostrava for a celebration of Czech mothers. In Brno Czechs boycotted the public transportation system to protest the introduction of bilingual service in the streetcars.[38] In Prague between thirty thousand and forty thousand people participated in a demonstration at the statue of Jan Hus on Old Town Square. As locals knew quite well, both the Hus of history and the twentieth-century rally were filled with symbolic potency. Czech patriots remembered the fifteenth-century priest as a man who attempted to introduce Czech into the Mass and codified the early Czech language, thereby initiating revolutionary reforms that provoked medieval Catholic Church leaders to have him burned at the stake. Nineteenth-century Czech patriots had drawn parallels between his brave stand against the Church and contemporary resistance to Catholic Austrian rule. Czech historians pointed to the Hussite period as proof that the nation, and national consciousness, predated the nineteenth century. In 1915 Masaryk, no doubt seeking to position himself as a successor to Hus, chose the five-hundredth anniversary of Hus's death to declare his intention to create an independent Czechoslovakia. That same day, Czech leaders unveiled the Hus memorial in Prague. Habsburg leaders forbade any public celebration, but Prague citizens defied the ban and surreptitiously laid thousands of flowers at the base of the statue. Ten years later, in 1925, at an officially sanctioned rally centered around the monument, Czechoslovak leaders celebrated Hus's death and the Czechs' "resistance" to Austrian rule during World War I. In 1939, as in 1925, Czechs were commemorating many things: a medieval national hero, the nation's long existence, and the creation of Czechoslovakia. They were reenacting popular opposition to previous forms of "German" rule.[39]

Other celebrations pointed to a newfound solidarity among patriots and Catholic leaders that had not existed before 1938. Shortly after the proclamation of Czechoslovak independence in 1918, mobs had ripped down the Marian Column in Old Town Square. Attacks on Catholic monuments across the country had continued into the 1920s, which often provoked counterprotests from local Czech Catholics. Masaryk associated Catholicism with the Habsburg monarchy; he claimed for Protestantism all the positive qualities of his imagined Czech nation. Yet the majority of Czechs remained Catholic, and by 1925 the Catholic People's Party had become the third largest in parliament. In 1925 Czech Catholic newspapers used the Hus celebration to remind voters that their political leaders were overwhelmingly Protestant, and all-too-often anti-Church.[40] In 1939, however, as one Intelligence Service agent fretted, Catholic leaders not only had "cautiously taken up the task of encouraging national loyalty among the Czechs" but also were co-organizing gatherings with secular, patriotic, and traditionally Protestant organizations like the Sokol. Religious processions, which had been poorly attended in the past, transformed into mass demonstrations of national loyalty. Nearly ninety thousand people participated in a pilgrimage that ended near Terezín, the future site of the Protectorate's only concentration camp. Across the border in the Reichsgau Sudetenland, just as many participated in a pilgrimage in the west Bohemian town of Domažlice that ended with a "stirring, national speech" given by a Catholic representative. The Sokol and its Catholic counterpart, Orel, declared July the "month of Czech religious festivals," during which at least four gatherings honoring Catholic personae took place.[41] Religious events had the added advantage of not being too overtly patriotic. In August the Oberlandrat in Olomouc, for example, permitted three religious processions co-organized by Czech leaders associated with Hácha's government. He forbade a rally by Czechoslovak legionnaires and forwarded the list of proposed speakers to the Gestapo. Intelligence Service agents and Oberlandräte, however, still saw the hand of patriots everywhere. And Czechs—whether meeting in clubs, buying books, watching certain films, marching, or singing—seemed to be celebrating, not bemoaning, their national existence in unison.[42]

The Czech Government

Within the new state, too, Czech loyalties survived, as did remnants of the conservative Second Republic. The autonomy that Hitler promised Hácha, however, proved to be quite limited. According to the Führer's March 16 decree, Czech autonomy had to be exercised "in harmony with the political, military, and economic needs of the Reich."[43] By the summer all laws and provisions created by the Czech government, as well as appointments within the government, required Neurath's approval. Each Czech department was supervised by a corresponding department within the Reich Protector's Office. Still, before the outbreak of war, Neurath's men interfered very little in the functioning of the Czech government, which still maintained its own police, legal system, and courts. Mechanisms for voicing "Czech" concerns survived. The Czechs retained public, if compromised, political figures who claimed to speak to and for the nation. Members of the Czech government, like the population, acted Czech in ways borrowed from the not-so-distant past.[44]

The man who had signed his country away to Hitler stood as state president of the autonomous government. Emil Hácha had been an Austro-Hungarian civil servant and later chief justice of the Supreme Administrative Court until Munich. Then, following Beneš's departure in 1938, the National Assembly, seeking someone who appealed to various hues on the political right, elected him president. Sixty-seven years old in 1939, Hácha suffered from cerebral sclerosis, which had begun to deteriorate his mental abilities, and his heavy smoking kept him awake at night. He also had a second life as a poet. While president of Czecho-Slovakia he secretly published fifty copies of his own poetry, sweet words (presumably) intended for his recently deceased wife.[45] Later that year he found himself in Hitler's office, barely coherent and ruthlessly cajoled into signing away his country to German rule. One popular joke conveyed the popular impression of his being a pliable tool of the Nazis: "When Hácha was in Berlin they had to take him out for something to eat. He sat next to Göring, who gave him the menu. Hácha took the menu in his hands and asked where he should sign."[46] For his part, Hácha saw himself as a hapless, even unwilling martyr for the nation. He described his thoughts that fateful night to Czech writer Karel Horký, who visited the president a month after the Nazi occupation had begun:

> I said to myself: who am I, Emil Hácha? From this matter-of-fact point of view I am quite an ordinary person who will return to dust like everyone else. The nation didn't sign it, only, understand me, an unfortunate individual, only this unhappy Hácha. And so it happens, that this isn't for us a blemish of historic proportions. . . . In short, only a personal blemish. By God's mercy, I as an old man have taken this on and have come to terms with it. . . . And still, as you know, [the statue of] Saint Wenceslas is still standing in its place, Charles Bridge is standing, too, the Castle district was not blown "into the air" and hundreds of thousands of our young people are still breathing and living.[47]

As state president under Nazi rule, Hácha was tolerated by his government and Nazi rulers as a sad figure who nonetheless enjoyed a degree of respect among Czech patriots and the general population. A conservative Catholic, he welcomed anti-Semitic measures and the undoing of democratic structures. He challenged, to no avail, the introduction of the Gestapo and the dismantling of the Czechoslovak army. He maintained contact with several underground organizations and Beneš loyalists abroad. He announced to Protectorate radio listeners and confidants his belief that the Bohemian lands belonged within the Central European—that is, German—sphere of influence, yet in public he strained to remain a visible, public voice for the Czech nation. For these reasons, joking aside, he found public acceptance for representing and protecting the nation in a time devoid of national heroes, when Czech politics had swung to the right, when patriotism mattered more than political and ethical principles (Fig. 1.4).[48]

Hácha was not the lone holdover from the Second Republic. With a few exceptions, the composition of Hácha's cabinet changed very little after March 1939.[49] Alois Eliáš, a former Czechoslovak legionnaire, maintained contact with underground movements and served as Hácha's communications link to Beneš's men abroad. Other men, like Minister of

Figure 1.4 Emil Hácha before his Christmas radio address in 1939. (Reproduced by permission of the Česká tisková kancelář.)

Justice Jaroslav Krejčí, were enthusiastic supporters of Nazi rule. Most in the cabinet, however, followed Hácha's lead in acting as good bureaucrats returning to life under German state rule. In total, ten thousand German officials watched over 400,000 Czech officials, and, by nearly all accounts, the bureaucracy continued to run smoothly until the end of the war.[50] Nor did many in the Czech government lament the destruction of the First Republic; they proudly stood against the values Peroutka held dear. Pro-German, pro-Catholic, anti-Masaryk, antidemocratic, antisocialist, and intolerant Czech nationalists before the occupation, they had already undone Czechoslovak democratic structures under their watch, one reason that coordination with the Nazi regime proceeded so smoothly.[51]

The only political challengers to Hácha's conservative regime in 1939 were the Czech fascists, political outliers before 1938 known for their boisterous, rabble-rousing nationalist demonstrations. The rivalry between Hácha's government and Czech fascists came to a head two months after the occupation had begun. Two fascist groups took over the streets of Brno and, to a lesser extent, Prague, molesting pedestrians and beating up Jews. Some hoped to re-create Kristallnacht in the Moravian capital and to create a "Czestapo." Other leaders spoke of creating an independent, fascist Moravia. After days of inaction, Hácha, with the silent blessing of the Reich Protector's Office, ordered the Czech police to disband the hooligans, who screamed in protest: "You Benešite wretches, you're going to protect the Jews? For twenty years you betrayed the nation, and now we're in charge!" Several leading fascists later formed the Český svaz pro spolupráci s Němci (Czech League for Cooperation with the Germans), but after the summer of 1939 the fascists' role in the Protectorate was reduced to working as informants for the Gestapo, which they did in large numbers. Hitler, Neurath, and Frank continued to threaten Hácha with a Czech fascist takeover, leveraging even more concessions from the elderly jurist.[52]

Despite, or possibly thanks to, his antidemocratic views, his willingness to work with Nazi leaders, and his cabinet's anti-Semitism, Hácha's government enjoyed a mild degree of popularity. In fact, in the spring of 1939 his government received a popular vote of legitimacy while encouraging a mass-based, remarkably successful show of Czechness. Soon after dissolving all political parties in March, Hácha organized the National Solidarity Movement, which was modeled after the Nazi Party. Its program was tinged with anti-Semitic rhetoric, calls for more state control over the economy, and close ties to the Nazi Party. Hácha became the movement's *vůdce*, a direct translation of the German word *Führer*. Most of its active members were students, but its membership was open to any male. (Fascists boycotted the group—and Jews and women were forbidden to join.) During the registration campaign, movement organizers registered 2,130,000 people—between 98 and 99 percent of the estimated population of eligible Czech males.[53]

The registration was more than just a vote of confidence. Indeed, the registration looked suspiciously like a census—an event that had traditionally been the arena for Czech-German nationality conflicts. Patriots pressured fellow Czechs to join. (Nazi authorities, before they understood what the registration signified and seeking more legitimacy for their puppet government, coerced concentration camp inmates into signing up.) For patriots, the meaning of the campaign was clear. Peroutka even joined Hácha in urging Czechs to register. "The original, observable chaos and later fear of [Gestapo] informants and uncertainty has changed to courage and hope," wrote one correspondent to London. "The nation is coming together, not only in the National Solidarity Movement, which the majority did only to avoid losing our national existence, but individuals are coming together and one begins to feel as if [the nation] has a backbone again. All of this is evidenced in Prague and in the countryside." He was hardly alone in believing Czech national feeling had never been so united. "The Czechs are closely uniting and concentrating," Frank warned immediately after the registration-cum-census. For the new regime, however, the Czechs were only half the problem.[54]

Germans and Other Germans

On March 14, 1939, Eugen Fiechtner, a state administrator from southwestern Germany, reported to Vienna, where a Ministry of the Interior official from Berlin briefed him and other future Oberlandräte on their new assignments. Filled, as he later remembered, with "dark foreboding and great worry" about his "assignment in an unknown land," he took a taxi to Jihlava that evening. The local military leader in Jihlava, he soon noticed, knew nothing about civil administration, yet there was no sign of popular unrest. The next day Fiechtner met with local German leaders, who detailed the plight of the local German population, which seemed on the verge of extinction.[55] In 1880, 17.2 percent of Jihlava's population gave "Czech" as their language of daily use. In 1921, after the establishment of the Czechoslovak Republic, 46.2 percent gave "Czech" as their nationality, and by 1930 Czechs had become a majority within Jihlava, gaining control over local government and administration.[56] Jihlava had produced some of the Sudeten Germans' most radical voices, including Arthur Seyss-Inquart, a leading Nazi activist in Austria whom Hitler later appointed as the top civil administrator in the Nazi-occupied Netherlands. Of Jihlava's German inhabitants, 97 percent voted for Henlein's party in 1938.[57] Expectations—and tensions—were running high among the local German population, Fiechtner's guides told him. Protectorate Germans demanded schools, administrative positions, and economic betterment, preferably at the expense of local Czechs. The guides also demanded that measures be taken to subdue the Czechs. In the days preceding the occupation, Jihlava had almost exploded. Czech patriots had entered a German theater, rounded up the Germans, and took them to the local gymnastics club, where, following a long and strange tradition in Czech history, the victims were tossed out the windows. The next day a shoot-out with Czech police left a local German landlord and hunter dead. Patriots, including Seyss-Inquart, visited his grave. Fiechtner felt obliged to visit the dead man's widow.[58]

Local Germans were quickly disappointed. The economic turnaround was slow in coming. By summer 1939, as elsewhere, Czech patriots in Jihlava seemed to be more confident than ever. Fiechtner's relationship with local German patriots deteriorated. The new Oberlandrat filled local administrative posts with civil servants he knew from Germany. Paid in Reichsmarks, they emptied local stores of goods. One of Fiechtner's subordinates went into a clothing shop and appropriated boxes full of women's underwear for his sister's boutique in Germany. (Fiechtner reassigned him to a post in the Reich.) Worst of all, Fiechtner consorted with Czech bureaucrats who welcomed Nazi rule as a return to Austrian times. He often went hunting with a Czech friend. Arrogant, inconsiderate, and economically prosperous, Reich Germans—that is, Germans from Austria and, more often, the lands of pre-1938 Germany—had entered a different world. After the war, a group of local patriots remembered the disappointing state of affairs: "The Reich Germans who came to the Jihlava language island only very rarely had an understanding of the nationality battles between Germans and Czechs. One often heard remarks like 'The Czechs aren't so bad' and 'We get along with them well.' They simply didn't realize that the Czechs knew quite well how to ingratiate themselves with the Reich Germans, and, through their obliging behavior, drove a wedge between Reich Germans and the local German residents."[59]

German-German tensions were not relegated to Jihlava. Throughout the Protectorate the enthusiasm local Germans felt for the new regime quickly faded after the occupation had begun. Czech patriots continued to play out old battles within a new context. The new regime seemed powerless or, worse, unconcerned. Sokol leaders repeated timeworn phrases like "to each his own" and "buy only Czech products." German and German-friendly shopkeepers, especially those scattered throughout the predominantly Czech countryside, were often forced out of business. Authorities ordered all "Made in Czechoslovakia" labels removed from manufactured goods, but Czechs boycotted anything with "Made in Germany" on it. Bending to popular pressure, many firms added their own English-language label: "Made in Bohemia formely [*sic*] Czechoslovakia." Whereas Czechs could tap into the growing black market, Protectorate German farmers complained that they lacked feed for livestock, feed that their Czech neighbors somehow managed to obtain.[60] Protectorate Germans became the victims of small, petty acts of Czech "terror." In Německý Brod, a Czech shopkeeper refused to sell butter to a German woman. In Chrudim a shoe salesman made German customers wait five or six weeks for damaged shoes to be repaired. Czechs waited only ten days. During the June Corpus Christi celebration in Olomouc, marchers told German participants that *"Hakenkreuzers"* were not welcome. The few Germans who continued into the church learned that only Czech songs would be sung. Czechs threw rocks at an SA man, beat up Hitler Youth, and spit on a German girl attending a Pentecost celebration. They sullied Nazi Party announcement boards, sometimes repeating the act after the boards were repaired, and stole *Hakenkreuz* flags.[61] Czechs who consorted with Germans were isolated as well. Even movie stars fell victim. Goebbels, for example, was ordered by the Führer to break off a two-year adulterous affair with Czech-born sex symbol Lida Baarová. In Germany, Goebbels escaped relatively unscathed, but in her homeland Baarová soon became persona non grata.[62]

These incidents were just a sampling, Intelligence Service agents reported. Furthermore, the presence of the new "German" state seemed to have put Protectorate Germans at a disadvantage versus the Czechs in their long-standing nationality conflict. Many of the Protectorate Germans' "best men" (read: most nationalistic) were lost when they joined the SS, the Nazi Party, and other Nazi organizations that took them outside the Protectorate. During the first year of the occupation, the production of German-language books, unlike that of Czech-language books, sank. Although the Deutsche Kulturverband (German Association of Culture) had managed to construct about sixty new schools before the end of the 1938–1939 school year, even after "borrowing" desks and chairs from Czech schools, many buildings remained empty. German schools lacked German teachers. Expectations for a quick economic turnaround were disappointed, too. Teachers, Protectorate Germans complained, did not earn a living wage, especially when one took into account the membership dues required by patriotic organizations. The new regime had done nothing to remedy a severe housing shortage. Nazi officials tied the Czechoslovak crown to the German mark at a rate of ten-to-one, although the actual rate should have been six- or seven-to-one. The result was higher inflation rates in the Protectorate. Meanwhile, wages remained the same, further reducing workers' purchasing power. In search of a living wage, many Protectorate Germans and Czechs took up jobs in Germany.[63]

Resentment among Protectorate Germans toward their Reich German co-nationals grew. Protectorate Germans began to realize that these "other" Germans were, contrary to pre-1938 propaganda, quite different from themselves. Things are done differently here, one Intelligence Service agent wrote, "so it happens that sometimes German officials carrying out their duties and in dealing with ethnic Germans [*Volksdeutsche*] lack an important sense of empathy, so that unfortunately there have arisen in some places sharp tensions between Reich and ethnic Germans."[64] Reich women complained of local Germans being disorderly and lazy.[65] The army would sometimes take goods from local Germans without paying the bill—a "good business deal," one Protectorate German commented sarcastically. In Prostějov the army accused Protectorate Germans of selling them subpar goods at outrageously high prices.[66] That Reich Germans had managed to obtain almost all the most powerful and lucrative positions within the Protectorate added to the resentment. In general, despite Frank's efforts, Neurath and Stuckart staffed high-level government positions with Reich Germans. Some Protectorate Germans were able to find important government positions, but, on the whole, Protectorate Germans occupied lower-level positions within the government. Reich Germans even took over the top positions in schools, the focal point of Sudeten German politics and emotional intensity before the occupation. By 1940 Reich Germans chaired or directed more than half the departments in Prague's German University.[67] Protectorate Germans did fill positions within the Sturm Abteilung (literally, "Assault Divisions," but better known as Brown Shirts or the SA) and the Nazi Party. In the neighboring Reichsgau Sudetenland, where Gauleiter and Reichskomissar Konrad Henlein held the top position, Sudeten Germans in the Nazi Party wielded considerable power. In the Protectorate, however, local Germans in the party, and the SA, were for the most part reduced to agitating for pro-German, pro-Nazi demonstrations of loyalty among the local population. The ranks of the Intelligence Service contained a high proportion of Protectorate Germans, most of them bilingual students and university professors who had been members of the Sudeten German Party. They produced, and encouraged, a continuous stream of grumbling among power-hungry Protectorate Germans. And because Reich Germans headed most government agencies, the newcomers were held responsible for failed expectations and new problems.[68]

Just as the Czechs were uniting and concentrating, the German Volk seemed to be splintering. Reich Germans felt underappreciated. Protectorate Germans felt like "second-class Germans." "Dissatisfaction among the Germans," one correspondent wrote to Beneš, "is even greater than among the Czech population."[69] The tensions never abated. In March 1940, for example, a local Intelligence Service agent reported that Reich Germans in Jihlava were buying from Czechs, not local Germans, because Czech shops were cleaner and their goods were cheaper. Concerned, the Reich Protector's Office asked Oberlandrat Fiechtner to confirm the report. He did, adding that Reich Germans in his office were put off by a general unfriendliness and lack of comradeship among the locals, especially among shopkeepers. (The hotels were too expensive, too.) The boycott was intended to "teach these German shopkeepers what one should expect from a German shopkeeper." The official in charge sent a note to the Nazi Party asking for financial support and "education." Twenty years later, Protectorate German patriots from Jihlava were still smarting about the affair. Maybe the Czech restaurants had nicer table-cloths, they conceded, but this was because their German competitors had little money after long years of battling with the Czechs.[70]

German, Not German

While Czechs and Protectorate Germans acted nationally in ways bor-rowed from the nineteenth century, the Nazi regime began to lay the foundations for a society divided on national and racial lines. The new state initiated measures to separate Jews from Germans, and Germans from Czechs. Building upon measures initiated by the Second Republic, the Reich Protector's Office added its own decrees intended to segregate Jews from the rest of society. For the first time since the Moravian Com-promise of 1905, the government assumed the right to determine who was a German or a Czech. Both tasks proved easier in theory than in practice. In fact, Nazi rulers unwittingly created a mechanism by which many gentile amphibians could choose their nationality. Once again, the German national movement seemed at a disadvantage vis-à-vis its Czech counterpart.

Only two days after the occupation had begun, Hácha's government drew up a long list of measures aimed at excluding Jews from public life and expropriating their property. In May the Czech government sent Neurath more detailed plans for anti-Jewish legislation.[71] Neurath re-sponded by taking control of the creation of anti-Jewish legislation. The Reich protector decreed that all Jews employed in public administration and the courts had to be dismissed, as did translators, consultants, stockbrokers, and many other professionals. Neurath's office forbade Jews from teaching in German schools. Across the Protectorate, thanks to initiatives by local German police, restaurants and other public places posted signs like "Jews not allowed to enter."[72] In July 1939 the Reich Protector's Office reduced the number of Jewish religious congregations outside Prague to fourteen. Each newly consolidated congregation an-swered to the main Jewish Congregation in Prague; the council, in turn, took orders from Adolf Eichmann's newly established Central Office for Jewish Emigration.[73] Under the direct supervision of the Intelligence Service, and working with bureaucrats from Neurath's office and leaders from the Jewish Religious Congregation of Prague, Eichmann's men ob-tained full control over all matters related to Jewish emigration. Almost nine thousand Jews, most them refugees from Germany and Austria, had emigrated before Eichmann's men had taken their posts in July. By the end of the year, another ten thousand Jews had left the Protectorate for other parts of Europe, the United States, Palestine, and elsewhere.[74]

Neurath also wrested from the Czech government the right to determine who was a Jew. His definition, announced in a July decree, relied on criteria laid out in the Nuremberg Laws, which, along with the Reich Citizenship Law, defined Jews and *Mischlinge* (those with "mixed Jewish blood") according to various past and present personal characteristics. A Jew, in the eyes of the Protectorate regime, had either three Jewish grandparents or two Jewish grandparents and one of several indications of belonging to the Jewish community. Ironically, these so-called racial laws had nothing to do with race. Religion was the sole determinant of the laws, for it was membership in Jewish religious organizations and birth records that left the paper trail for officials to trace Jews or for others to prove they were not Jews. As Hitler had stated in his March 16, 1939, decree, the Nuremberg Laws clearly stated that Jews could not be citizens of Germany. In 1939 the only organizations that held detailed lists of Jews, however, were the Protectorate's Jewish religious congregations. Many people whose parents had belonged to a Jewish congregation were not members themselves. For the moment, then, thousands of Jews defined as such by the Nuremberg Laws escaped being labeled.[75]

Reich Protectorate officials, who ruled over Nazi Germany's first non-German population, faced another daunting task: to separate Reich German citizens from the rest of the former Czechoslovakia's non-Jewish citizenry. This, too, was a continuation of policies set in motion before the occupation, for the Second Republic had allowed Germans to claim Reich citizenship.[76] Reich Protectorate officials had also drawn upon laws already on the books in Germany. In his March 16 decree Hitler had borrowed language from the Nuremberg Laws to declare that non-Jews in the Protectorate would be divided into two groups—Germans with full benefits (and obligations) of Reich citizenship and *Staatsangehörige des Protektorats* (members of the state of the Protectorate) outside the *Volksgemeinschaft* (racial or national community). In August "member of the state" became "member of the Protectorate," hereafter referred to as "Protectorate national." Reich Protectorate officials hoped to discourage Czechs from thinking of the Protectorate as their state.[77]

Further decrees from the Ministry of the Interior and the Reich Protector's Office set forth procedures for registering Reich citizens. In the eyes of many officials, however, the legislation contained a glaring flaw. Reich citizenship—unlike the designation Jew—often required a conscious choice, and action, by the subject. Before the occupation and under pressure from Hitler's Germany, Hácha's regime had allowed ethnic Germans to opt for either Czechoslovak or Reich citizenship. That principle remained intact after the occupation. Only members of the former Sudeten German Party automatically became Reich citizens after March 15, 1939. Others were required to register with offices under the direction of the local Oberlandrat, who was to work with the mayor and party members. Oberlandräte announced the program in local papers. Officials working for the Oberlandräte and Nazi Party members distributed applications to known Germans. Willing Germans had two weeks to fill out a short application that asked, among other things, for the applicant's mother tongue, membership in past military and national organizations, and an assertion that none of the applicant's grandparents were Jewish. The applicant was then to submit the form to the local branch of the Oberlandrat's administration. If approved, the applicant would receive a pass from the local office.[78]

Jews occasionally applied for Reich citizenship. Fiechtner and the Oberlandrat in Brno processed their applications and provided dozens of local Jews with citizenship papers. Following reprimands from officials in Prague and Berlin, they annulled their decisions. There are indications, however, that the practice of granting citizenship to Jews continued. In a September 1939 circular to leading officials in the Protectorate and Berlin, Frank stated that Jewish Mischlinge could, in rare cases, be granted German citizenship. Jews who obtained German citizenship, whether Mischlinge or "full Jews," protested one Reich Protectorate official the following year, had better chances of gaining immigration papers from foreign governments. The procedures were unclear.[79]

Another problem related to the Reich Citizenship Law, however, obsessed officials throughout the Protectorate. Many so-called Germans refused to submit their applications for Reich citizenship and, in doing so, refused to be counted as Germans and faithful Nazi subjects. Other supposed Germans did not receive an application and simply let the matter drop. In Brno an estimated one-sixth of the estimated German population had failed to register by March 1940. In Zlín, far from any substantial German population, the number was one-third.[80] "We had undoubtedly reckoned that all ethnic Germans would press to become Reich Germans. This reckoning—and it cannot fail to be appreciated—was a mistake. . . . We must say that in this respect the ethnic Germans have disappointed [us]," an official in the Reich Protector's Office opined.[81] Oberlandräte, army generals, and officials within the Reich Protector's Office all acknowledged the problem. In the mixed city of České Budějovice, Frank was even driven to give a speech in which he forcefully reminded fellow Protectorate Germans "that you are representatives of the Reich."[82] Officials in the Reich Protector's Office proposed schemes to bypass the registration process, but all were discarded as impractical.[83]

There were many reasons not to become a citizen. Some Protectorate Germans refused to register out of protest against the regime and Reich German rule. One German-speaking woman in Prague, for example, told the Oberlandrat's Office that she could never register for Reich citizenship. She had promised her recently deceased son, presumably a Czech patriot, that she would always identify herself as a Czech.[84] Others feared the consequences of becoming a Reich citizen. The Nazi Party pressured Reich citizens to join Nazi organizations and participate in public shows of loyalty to the regime. As Frank told the Oberlandräte, Czech "terror" dissuaded potential Germans "fearful of repression from the Czechs." Czech-organized "social boycotts"—petty, face-to-face exclusionary tactics—hit "scattered Germans" in small communities particularly hard, as did economic boycotts in areas with few German customers. One war veteran, Ignatz Daniel, told officials that he would register as a German only if the state would cover the eventual losses that his tobacco shop would incur. His parents, he added, were Moravians.[85] Another fact made the whole application process all the more distasteful: Czechs staffed many of the offices where potential Reich citizens were told to hand in their paperwork.[86]

The citizenship decrees created two legal worlds, each with its own set of advantages and disadvantages. Protectorate nationals, most of whom were Czechs, were subject to Czech laws and were tried in Czech courts, unless the crime was deemed "political." Germans were tried in German courts, where punishment for certain crimes, such as listening to Radio Moscow, was often harsher. Germans received slightly higher rations and could be promoted within the bureaucracies more easily. Protectorate nationals, on the other hand, were spared the duties of citizenship, most notably work duty and the draft.[87] In July 1939 Neurath's regime instituted mandatory one-year work duty for certain segments of the local Reich German citizenry. Despite reports of ill treatment at the hands of Reich Germans in Germany, Neurath's office decided in August to make all local Reich citizens between the ages of sixteen and twenty-five eligible for work duty.[88] Young Protectorate Germans, unlike their Czech counterparts, were also subject to the draft. In March 1939 the army's highest officer warned that the lower ranks' handling of newly arrived Austrian and Sudeten German troops could result in a loss of trust in and aversion to the Reich. But complaints from ethnic Germans continued throughout the war.[89] Proportionally, Sudeten German casualties had been greater than those of any group within the Habsburg monarchy, as well as within Germany as a whole, during World War I, so the population had good reason to fear joining another war effort.[90] No wonder, then, that most of the registered Germans in Brno were more than forty years old; only 12 percent were between the ages of twenty-one and thirty.[91]

The failure to register Germans was no small matter. The army's ability to tap the population's human resources was being compromised.[92] Germans were also needed to staff low-level administrative offices, management positions in armaments factories, and Nazi Party cells. In addition, just as the National Solidarity Movement's registration was seen as a census, Reich citizenship registration was interpreted as a Protectorate-wide head count. The German numbers looked bad. It had become sadly clear, the Brno Oberlandrat wrote, "that the basis of national character [Volkstumsbasis] is qualitatively and quantitatively on the decline, and in a short time will be doomed." He pointed to a common trend among "language islands." In 1910, Brno's 201,500 German-speakers made up 66 percent of the city's population. By 1930, thanks to "Czechification measures and emigration," this number had dropped to 21 percent. Now the number was 17 percent, although the "real" number of ethnic Germans stood between 19 and 20 percent. In the Prague region, registered Germans amounted to a mere 2 percent of the total population.[93] Nazi rule had done little to reverse the trend toward complete Czechification. In fact, it appeared to have accelerated the process. "The Czech infiltration in the areas of nationality struggles has made startling progress," one Intelligence Service agent wrote. "[T]he German language islands . . . seem endangered."[94] There simply was not enough "German strength" to provide reliable workers, soldiers, administrators, and mothers to hold back the Czechs.

The citizenship fiasco pointed to an aspect of life in Bohemia and Moravia that baffled and worried officials: Czechs, Germans, and Jews were hopelessly mixed. Czech words infiltrated the German language. Much was made of the fact that two Germans workers in Jihlava greeted each other with a Czech "na zdar"—one of countless instances of Germans speaking Czech on the streets. Party members suggested that locals be shipped to the Reich, where they could improve their language skills. Protectorate Germans in youth organizations had trouble understanding their Reich superiors. Girls forced to join their local Nazi organizations seemed timid in expressing their Germanness in public and were known to avoid required activities to spend time with Czechs instead.[95] The Oberlandrat in Pardubice suggested that boarding schools be built to isolate German students from Czech influence.[96] The true nationality of some people was unclear. An "intermediary stratum" of people of "German descent" with "frail national" allegiance inhabited the real and imaginary borders separating Czechs and Germans. Amphibians continued to move between national groups. Many supposed Germans who received citizenship applications protested (in German) that they spoke only Czech. Adults belonged to both German and Czech nationalist organizations. In several cases men with important positions within the Nazi Party or as SA Brown Shirts had signed up with the National Solidarity Movement. One local warden for the Nazi Party was also treasurer of his chapter of the National Solidarity Movement. The citizenship law, while introducing bureaucratic procedure and creating a legal divide between Czechs and Germans, still allowed for choice among nationalities and for overlapping public identities.[97]

Most disconcerting for Nazi leaders was the "problem" of mixed marriages, which usually meant a loss for Germandom. The Reich Protector's Office estimated there to be ten thousand mixed Czech-German marriages in the Bohemian lands just before the Munich agreement.[98] More than one-sixth of the almost three thousand marriages concluded before the German magistrate during the first year of the Protectorate's existence involved Czech-German couples.[99] (In general, the number of marriages had jumped sharply. More than 78,100 Protectorate inhabitants married in 1939, up from about 56,600 the year before.[100]) Intermarriage, of course, doused German (and Czech) nationalism. Members of mixed families were less likely to register as Germans, as were children of

Czech-German couples. What bothered Nazi officials more, however, was their inability to control this intermixture. Marriages are among the strongest of social bonds and hence the most difficult to alter after the fact. Marriages were also crucial to the imagined future of the German nation. The marriage question lay at the crossroads of two thrusts of Nazi rule—to establish the primacy of the state over all aspects of daily life and to solve social and cultural problems through biological means. In the Protectorate, much of the process lay outside the state's control. In 1939 Nazi officials did not even legislate against sexual relations between Czechs and Germans. Indeed, while Neurath claimed in summer 1939 that the Nuremberg Laws' prohibition on German-Jewish marriages was in force, no law prevented Jews from marrying Czechs.[101]

In terms of nationality politics, the citizenship dilemma was making a bad situation worse. With so many male Reich citizens being drafted or assigned to work duty in the Reich, few German bachelors remained.[102] German women who married non-Germans lost their Reich citizenship, weakening an already weak German presence in the Protectorate. The Brno Oberlandrat claimed to know two thousand German women prevented from registering.[103] On the other hand, a large number of Czech women were marrying German men and entering, without an application process, into the German Volk. In Plzeň more German men married Czech women than German women between August 1939 and February 1940. In Prague almost one-third of the 177 marriages that involved at least one German contracted from March 1939 to the end of the year were between German men and Czech women.[104] Parents, hoping to gain influence for themselves, actively encouraged Czech girls to meet German policemen. Czech shopkeepers, acting upon rumors that in the future only German businesses would be allowed to operate, hoped that if one of their offspring married a German, they could save the family business.[105]

As with the Nuremberg Laws—and the pre-1938 census law—the Protectorate's citizenship law had assumed that the father or husband, the family's authority figure, determined the nationality of the family. The opposite turned out to be true. At least four hundred German men had, in the year following July 1, 1939, married Czech women who could not speak a word of German.[106] In Olomouc the Oberlandrat estimated that 70 to 80 percent of the men in the SA there had married women who "barely speak a word of German." The women then raised the children as Czechs, the fathers being at work all day.[107] In Brno, thirty-seven Germans (including three from the Reich and one from Austria) married Czech women within one three-month period. More than half of these men were members of the Nazi Party or other prominent Nazi organizations. Of these Brno women, only five were fluent in German, meaning that the rest, the Oberlandrat opined, were a loss to Germandom.[108] Children of Czech mothers and German fathers were becoming Czechs, the Plzeň Oberlandrat wrote, because "the ethnic Germans are as a rule not proud or tough enough in their relationships with their Czech wives."[109] But the simple fact was that the mother, as Milena Jesenská had intimated, usually determined the nationality of the children, whether she was German or Czech.

Farce to Tragedy

On September 1, 1939, Germany and the Soviet Union invaded Poland from both sides. SS, SA, and German police patrolled the Protectorate's northeast border, taking special care to secure the region's valuable industrials plants. Young Germans in Jihlava attacked Czech passersby and tore down National Solidarity Movement posters. Order was restored only after the SS, acting on a request by Fiechtner, stationed patrols throughout the city. The Intelligence Service moved against its imagined enemies. It ordered that all Polish citizens of the Protectorate register with the local police within twenty-four hours. Male Polish citizens—with the exception of ethnic Germans, Poles deemed necessary laborers, and Ukrainians whose nationality was "indisputable"—were shipped to camps in Germany.[110] Nazi officials also moved against itinerants and so-called Gypsies. In May 1939 a Protectorate decree had forbidden all inhabitants to travel in large groups. In November another decree gave itinerants two months to find a permanent residence, and the next year they were required to remain in their current location. Police arrested any individuals without a permanent abode and assigned them to labor camps. Only "ethnic Germans" were spared. Many itinerants ended up in camps at Lety and Hodonín, which were erected in summer 1940. Between September 1940 and December 1941 the camps held 732 inmates labeled "wandering Gypsies" or "tramps"—a whole array of people accused of being beggars, gamblers, idlers, and loafers, along with a minority of self-defined Roma and Sinti.[111]

A long procession of decrees from Neurath's office moved to segregate Jews even further from the rest of society. Movie theaters posted signs, in Czech and German, prohibiting Jews from entering. The Reich protector forbade Jews from leaving their homes after 8:00 P.M. Police disconnected telephones and confiscated radios in Jewish homes. In spring 1940 all Jews and Mischlinge as defined by the Nuremberg Laws—regardless of religion or self-identification—learned that they had to register with their local Jewish religious congregation. These people also had to register at local police stations and have their identification cards stamped in red with a capital J. By mid-1940 the Jewish religious congregations had registered almost ninety-two thousand people. Roughly five thousand names had been added since the spring, bringing to fifteen thousand the number of people who did not profess to be Jewish by religion, but whom the Nazi regime labeled as Jews. The stated goals of Eichmann's office, which lorded over the Jewish religious congregations, remained unchanged: to encourage, even coerce, Jews to leave for other countries. The outbreak of war, however, closed doors around the world to Jewish émigrés. As the succeeding chapters will explore, Nazi officials in Prague and elsewhere then began to experiment with other "solutions" to the "Jewish problem."[112]

As soon as the war had begun, newspapers and placards across the Protectorate announced that any act of resistance, broadly defined, would result in a death sentence. Gestapo agents and their minions arrested prominent Jewish leaders throughout the country. A separate wave of arrests swept up several thousand intellectuals, priests, Communists, and Social Democrats, all part of a wider attack on the Czech national movement. Nazi authorities shut down *Přítomnost* shortly before the war began and on September 1 arrested Peroutka, who spent the rest of the war struggling to survive in the Dachau and Buchenwald concentration camps. (In 1942 Nazi officials offered him the position of editor-in-chief of the collaborationist version of *Přítomnost*. He refused and was returned to the concentration camp.) Gestapo agents also seized Milena Jesenská, who died in Ravensbrück five years later. The army and the Gestapo immediately assumed the right to censor all media. After a few months a special section of the Reich Protector's Office reasserted control over the task. Each daily and weekly was assigned two Czech censors. The number of forbidden topics increased, and the head German censor summoned editors to weekly "press conferences," which were actually marching orders. Newspapers devolved into organs of Nazi propaganda.[113]

Shows of Czech national loyalty, however, continued. On September 28, 1939, Czech religious leaders, politicians, and patriots staged an event to honor St. Wenceslas, medieval king and patron saint of the Bohemian lands. Ten years earlier thousands crowded the streets to honor the millennial anniversary of the saint's martyrdom—the third largest demonstration in Czechoslovakia's brief history. A powerful symbol that combined Catholicism and Czech national loyalty, St. Wenceslas perhaps meant even more in 1939 than he had in 1929. As king of Bohemia, Wenceslas had made political compromises with more powerful German rivals in order to ensure peace in his realm. Legends abounded that when the Czech nation entered its darkest hours, Wenceslas would return as its savior. In 1939, Catholicism and national loyalty mixed more easily than they had a decade before. The 1939 celebration began with prominent Czech leaders, including Hácha, attending morning Mass in St. Vitus Cathedral, a Prague landmark first established by Wenceslas that also housed his remains. In the afternoon, religious leaders carried those remains from St. Vitus, followed by hundreds of people carrying banners from various national organizations. More than ten thousand people lined the streets to watch the procession. Meanwhile, in another part of town, locals quietly laid flowers at the base of the St. Wenceslas statue on the square bearing his name. A small crowd began to gather. At 6:15 P.M. five women sang a hymn to the saint until police rushed in to quiet them. Fifteen minutes later the crowd sang the Czechoslovak national anthem. Police rushed in again. The back and forth continued several times until the police forcibly dispersed the crowd and arrested five men—four of "Czech nationality" and one identified as a Jew, whom police held for five days before releasing.[114]

A similar event honoring St. Wenceslas took place in Brno, one of many demonstrations of national loyalty that arose in the city despite threats and arrests by Nazi authorities. Women in Jihlava clothed themselves in Czechoslovak national colors one day after the German attack on Poland. In Brno and Olomouc opera-goers packed theaters to watch the national classic *Libuše*, giving roaring ovations at the appropriately patriotic moments. Underground publishers reached the remotest villages. Some Czechs dared to write threatening letters to local Nazi Party officials. Others tore down Reich protector decrees posted in public.

Even after Polish forces had surrendered on October 6, 1939, Prague cit-izens boycotted the public transportation system, thanks in part to a well-coordinated, massive leaflet campaign. On October 28 and 29 demonstrators filled the streets to celebrate Czechoslovakia's Independence Day. Weeks later, crowds commemorated the Bohemian nobles' defeat at White Mountain. Protesters even went public to honor the founding of the Soviet Union, which had just helped to destroy Poland. Oberlandräte, most notably those in Moravia, suggested that the situa-tion did not pose a danger. Frank and Intelligence Service agents, how-ever, wrote that the autumn demonstrations had emboldened loyal Czechs. The national movement, they maintained, was gaining mo-mentum.[115]

On November 15, 1939, students flooded the streets to commemorate the death of Jan Opletal, a young Czech whom German police had killed the previous month during the Independence Day demonstrations (Fig. 1.5). A German car carrying Karl Hermann Frank's chauffeur barged through the crowd. Enraged protesters responded by overturning the car and engaging its passengers in fisticuffs. Frank and Neurath flew the chauffeur to Berlin the next day, where they presented the driver, and his wounds, to Hitler. With Hitler's approval, the Gestapo responded to the disturbances by arresting twelve hundred students in Prague and Brno. As the sun came up, they shot nine dead; the rest were sent to a concen-tration camp. (In an irony characteristic of life in the Protectorate, eight of the nine murdered students had recently pledged to work toward a better Czech-German understanding, and one was even deputy chairman of the Czech Union for Cooperation with Germans.) All Czech institutions of higher education were immediately closed. Frank, who along with Intelligence Service agents had been demanding harsher measures against the Czechs, had gotten his wish. In fact, he had taken a plane back to Berlin ahead of Neurath to ensure that he oversaw the crackdown.[116]

Popular demonstrations of nationality, for the most part, came to an end. *V boj*, although shut down for several months, eventually resumed publication, Czechs in Prague heckled down Germans singing Nazi hymns, and approximately 100,000 people sang national and Catholic hymns during a January pilgrimage in Moravia that had been explicitly forbidden.[117] But these were isolated incidents. Intelligence Service agents, SS leader Heinrich Himmler, Oberlandäte, and the Reich Protector's Office agreed that the November arrests had frightened most of the population into submission. Fiechtner reported that Czech students returning from slogans to Jihlava found their anti-German slogans ignored by the Czech locals. When illegal pamphlets called for a March demonstration in honor of Masaryk's birthday, no one showed up. Across the Protectorate, some of the most aggressive acts of resistance consisted of nighttime attacks on Nazi posters.[118] Hácha's government was reduced to an administrative role, and the National Solidarity Movement became irrelevant and was ignored. Public life, and the ways that Czechs acted nationally, had changed.[119]

Divisions among the Czech population reappeared. The arrests signaled an all-out attack against Czech intellectuals and so-called intelligentsia, by which Reich officials often, but not always, meant professors, teachers, students, bureaucrats, officers, doctors, and lawyers. As in

Figure 1.5 Marchers at the funeral of Jan Opletal. (Reproduced by permission of the Vojenský ústřední archiv Fotoarchiv.)

Poland, Nazi leaders hoped to decapitate Czech national feeling by arresting those who spoke to and for the nation. The mantra was repeated throughout the regime's ruling structures and especially within Intelligence Service reports. As a result, this vaguely defined group was hounded until the end of the war. Jesenská, for example, was just one of the one hundred twelve editors and editorial staffers who perished in concentration camps during the war.[120] While some members of the so-called intelligentsia continued to publish underground newspapers and collect information for the allies, others slid into apolitical lives. Most Czech professors, while prevented from teaching, quietly went about their research.[121] The Reich Protector's Office informed Berlin that even the most loyal Czechs, although internally bitter, had adopted a wait-and-see attitude.[122] Before the war had begun, Gestapo agents had relied on local Protectorate Germans, Czech fascists, and stunts by agents provocateur for information. A small number of politically ambitious Czechs met Reich elite in Prague's most famous "gossiping circle" at the Hotel Ambassador. Now, however, informants from all sections of society offered their services.[123] Intelligence Service agents even suggested that in the countryside Czechs were glad to be under German rule, and that national feeling had faded into a less dangerous kind of local patriotism.[124] Stalin's nonaggression pact with Hitler devastated Communist true believers. Directives from Moscow now urged followers to fight a class, not a national, struggle.[125] In what would become a cliché among German authorities, reports from all quarters claimed that workers, in particular, cared little for politics and nationality struggles. The key to maintaining calm among the workers, and thus encouraging industrial productivity, was to keep wages and the supply of basic goods at reasonable levels—a strategy that Protectorate leaders would follow until the very end.[126]

Gordon Wright once wrote that the various forms of Nazi rule in Europe "took on a heterogeneous patchwork character; it appeared to be the work of a pure pragmatist rather than a systematic planner."[127] Nazi treatment of subject populations varied as well. In the Protectorate, Nazi rulers abstained from the violence they later visited upon Poland, Serbia, and other regions of Eastern Europe. For their part, the Czechs did little to "trigger" Nazi violence. Just before the Munich agreement young men across the country had enthusiastically rushed to mobilization; when

Beneš announced Czechoslovakia's capitulation in 1938, thousands took to the streets in protests. But, unlike in Yugoslavia, there existed among the Czechs little tradition of armed resistance and partisan warfare. Arms had been seized. Military officers and willing patriots had no time to organize; no call to war spurred them to fight.[128] Given the cynicism of the Second Republic era and the country's weakened defense system, it is doubtful that many would have taken up arms in 1939. Hácha, like Beneš, begged the population to remain peaceful. At first the occupation seemed like a return to living under "German" rule, which many Czechs welcomed. Hácha was not alone in celebrating the demise of democratic rule; the memory of Austrian rule was still fresh, and many knew how to "deal with" the Germans.[129] On the regime's side, too, more was to be gained from compromise than from violence. In the months before the outbreak of World War II, Hitler had hoped that a show a good faith in the Protectorate would mollify the Allies one last time. Caution ruled the day as administrators attempted to come to grips with their newly acquired, mostly Czech-inhabited territory. Lack of armed resistance, diplomacy, and administrative confusion tempered Nazi actions until the outbreak of World War II. Finally, as the next chapter discusses in greater detail, Göring and others had begun to integrate the Protectorate's economic structures with Reich ones. Domestic tranquility meant profits and increased armaments production necessary for military adventures elsewhere.

As a result, old-style nationality politics, transmitted from the near and distant past, continued. There was much from the nineteenth century to recall. Peroutka heralded the return of "apolitical politics," by which he meant turning to the press, literature, film, theater, and radio "to strengthen Czech national consciousness through the cultivation of Czech culture and language."[130] Modernism gave way to nineteenth-century historicism and nationalism. Jesenská was not alone in replacing cosmopolitanism with traditional Czech values.[131] Loyal Czechs sang, wrote, and published; they marched, boycotted German shops and goods, and participated in a "census" organized by the National Solidarity Movement. Munich, and the first year of occupation, marked for many a return to the "small Czech" nationalism of the late Habsburg era—small minded, local, Manichaean, distrustful of outsiders, and anti-German.[132] As before, Czech patriots acted nationally and encouraged others to do the same. Of course, "symbolic resistance" existed

throughout occupied Europe. But Czech "symbolic resistance" was a peculiar defense of national feeling, national symbols, and national heritage using methods inherited from a specific past. In fact, to many it
seemed as if history had looped back upon itself.

In 1939 protecting Czech cultural autonomy and acting Czech in various ways united patriots regardless of their political stripes. The political ideologies of the interwar period had left a bad taste in the mouths
of most Czechs. Western democracies had betrayed Czechoslovakia,
whose living symbols were either now dead, safely abroad, or eventually
thrown into concentration camps. The Soviet Union, a beacon of hope
for idealistic Communists and Pan-Slavic patriots, had signed a pact
with the devil to snatch territory from helpless Poland. With time, antidemocratic conservatives became tools of Nazi rule. Fascists resembled
Nazi rulers in their ideologies, while their actions bespoke an anarchic
ruffianism. The events of 1938–1939, the occupation, and the presence
of a "German" state united a previously fragmented population with
"apolitical politics." How one represented and protected the nation at
the level of daily life would become the standard by which actions were
to be celebrated or condemned. For patriots, protecting the "nation"
trumped any political, individual, or ethical concerns. Being a "good
Czech"—not a democrat, Communist, antifascist, or even loyal friend—
became the baseline for all ethical behavior in a world increasingly
viewed only through the lens of nationalism.

And, as before, German rivals seemed to be losing in their ongoing
nationality battles with the Czechs. So-called Germans refused to register as Reich citizens, thus passively counting themselves as Czechs.
Protectorate Germans continued to speak a language "infected" with
Czech words. The new "German" state worsened matters. The best men
left the region, economic recovery was slow in coming, and local Germans were rewarded with work duty and the draft. The citizenship law
stripped German women in mixed marriages of their Reich citizenship;
yet Czech women, by marrying German men, could enter the German
Volk and then, to add insult to injury, raise more Czechs. Decrees from
the Reich Protector's Office created legal chasms separating Czechs,
German, and Jews. Nazi rulers successfully began to segregate Jews from
the rest of the population. Yet the lines separating the three groups were
anything but clear. Many people could still choose among nationalities.
Some people, by belonging simultaneously to Czech and German organ-

izations, counted twice. Especially in language islands like Brno and Olomouc many people were unaware of their national heritage or inhabited an "intermediary stratum" that hovered above cultural boundaries. All this was abhorrent to Nazi ideologues and local German patriots, who would soon attack these "problems" with a ruthlessness never before seen in the history of Bohemia and Moravia.

The Nazi Reich, Frank warned a crowd in České Budějovice in June, "was no Austria-Hungary."[133] Following Germany's attack on Poland, the Nazi grip on society began to tighten. Gestapo officers arrested thousands. Censorship intensified, and the fear of denunciations began to make itself felt. The shooting of students, one Intelligence Service agent wrote, "in one blow destroyed the Czechs' delusion that the previous leniency of the German authorities was attributed to weakness." More than ever, Czechs saw that "their fate lay not with internal but foreign politics that will be decided with the war's end."[134] Loyal Czechs would have to act nationally in different ways. Nazi rulers promised to defend and strengthen Germandom at the expense of the Czechs, and in the process they would refashion the state's role in nationality politics. In the past, local and federal governments that ruled Bohemia and Moravia had taken an interest in the ongoing nationality struggles between Czechs and Germans, but their interest was tempered both by rule of law and raison d'état. Instead of providing rationality and order to the field of play, as previous rulers in the Bohemian crownlands had attempted to do, the Nazi regime was now determined to dictate play. And the German national movement, finally, would become ascendant.

2

The Reich Way of Thinking

In late spring 1940, after months of tense *Sitzkrieg*, Hitler launched his attack in the west. A little more than two months later, France, for many Europeans the shining symbol of culture and democracy, was utterly defeated. A French collaborationist government established itself in Vichy. Nazi soldiers occupied Norway, Denmark, Belgium, the Netherlands, and northern France. Germany annexed Luxembourg and Lorraine directly into the Reich; Alsace remained legally separate but became, de facto, part of the Reich. From the Pyrenees to the northern tip of Norway to the eastern coast of the Baltic Sea, Nazi rule dominated the continent. In southeastern Europe, a host of countries had joined the Axis alliance and become drawn into Germany's increasingly constrictive economic system. A new era in European history seemed to be at hand.

Nazi Germany's victories on the battlefront had immense consequences for the Protectorate of Bohemia and Moravia. Among many Czechs, tense anticipation leading up to Germany's attack on France gave way to great nervousness, and then to further political malaise. In 1939 Czech jokesters had referred to the Protectorate as *"protentokrát"* (for the time being), but after the fall of France it seemed as if Nazi rule was here to stay.[1] The national unity that had characterized the first months of the occupation disappeared, replaced by accusations of opportunism, cowardice, and treachery. The Gestapo launched a new wave of arrests, further decimating domestic resistance groups. Just as disturbing, from the point of view of Czech patriots, the Nazi regime now seemed determined to reverse a hundred-year trend toward the Czechification of Bohemia and Moravia's politics, culture, and economy. Protectorate German patriots relished the idea of finally turning the tables on their Czech neighbors.

To many patriots, it seemed that a new chapter in the long history of Czech-German nationality politics had begun. Yet the second year of occupation completed a radical break with the past. Following the student murders in November 1939 few Czechs dared to act nationally in public. Equality under the law was undone. Terror, more and more, shrouded everyday life. Two more developments radically altered the course of history in the region. First, by the end of 1940 the Protectorate had been fully integrated into a wider, Nazi-designed "linked economy" that stretched across Europe. Protectorate factories had become vital suppliers of the German war effort. Economically speaking, the Protectorate had become almost one with Germany, and a key component within an industrialized core of German-dominated territories in the middle of Europe. Meanwhile, outside the Protectorate, one of the last remaining symbols of interwar Czechoslovakia, Edvard Beneš, established himself as the unquestioned leader of a government-in-exile in London. He borrowed methods from the past to lobby British and American officials to recognize his government. As Beneš had done during World War I, he sought international commitments to support a restored Czechoslovakia following an unlikely German defeat. By summer 1940, however, Beneš began to consider a second, decisive break with the past: the expulsion of Germans from Czechoslovakia. Pushing him, at every step, were increasingly radical and desperate voices from home.

Germanization and the Nazi State

In April 1940 Oberlandrat Molsen of Olomouc detailed to officials in Prague a disturbing trend in his region: Germandom was dying out. While visiting one small town east of Olomouc, he had learned that only twenty people had registered as citizens of the Reich. During the 1921 census five hundred had counted themselves as Germans. In 1890 the town's mayor was German. There were few German schools. The economic situation of the local Germans was dire. Molsen had chosen this town to make a larger point about the fate of "scattered Germans" in his region. And, as Molsen knew, the numbers for the city of Olomouc, his region's capital, looked bad, too. Before World War I, Germans had controlled the city council and outnumbered Czechs approximately thirteen thousand to eight thousand. But in 1919 Czech officials incorporated two towns and eleven villages, giving the Czechs a majority and, hence, control of city government. Even within the original town's boundaries the census counted about fourteen thousand Czechs to about eight thousand Germans, and by 1930 the number of Olomouc Germans fell below 20 percent, which led to the loss of their minority status.[2] The language island appeared to be on the verge of extinction, yet there was still hope for Germandom in the Olomouc region, Molsen wrote to Prague just before the fall of France. Olomouc and its surrounding towns, he argued, needed German mayors and an influx of German bureaucrats to ensure German rule. A decades-long trend toward the Czechification of local culture, economy, and population could, with financial support from the Reich Protector's Office, be reversed. As the executor of these proposed measures, Molsen was seeking to strengthen his hand in the region. His measures promised to entrench Nazi rule there. "Small-scale" work to advance German economic, cultural, and political interests at the expense of the Czechs promised to benefit the Oberlandrat, local Germans, and Nazi leaders in Prague. Like many of his fellow Oberlandräte, Molsen had learned the benefits of speaking the language of nationality politics in the Bohemian lands.[3]

A little more than a year later, Molsen bragged, Germans were ascendant in Olomouc. They administered Olomouc, the region's next five populous towns, and five German-dominated, agriculturally vital villages. Below Molsen, Germans filled the most important positions in his regional administrative pyramid. The building that once housed the city's oldest Czech *gymnázium* (college-track high school) was filled with German students. Molsen had opened eleven new German schools since the beginning of the occupation. Over that same period the number of German teachers in his region jumped from eighteen to forty-eight, the number of students in German schools from 536 to 1,493. He refurbished the library and revived Olomouc's German Theater, which had been out of business for the last twenty years.[4] During the 1939–1940 season the city's leading Czech theater put on 647 performances, 106 more than the previous year. Then the Gestapo arrested its director, his company, and three other local theater companies. The Czech Committee for Cooperation with the Germans, when not distributing articles from SS publications, filled the void with musicals like *The*

Busch Circus from Berlin.[5] After the Gestapo arrested the Czech director of Přerov's electrical plant, Molsen replaced him with a German, who in turn fired top-level Czechs to make room for more Germans—just one example, Molsen wrote, of how he had strengthened the Germans' hand in the local economy.[6]

Much had changed since summer 1939. Germany's defeat of Poland and the arrests of Czech students in autumn 1939 had squelched most public displays of Czechness. By May of the following year, German patriotism was at an all-time high. The Wehrmacht's victories in the west, one Intelligence Service agent observed, "did much for the self-assurance of the German people," even among "scattered Germans." Protectorate Germans displayed their loyalty to the regime more openly. They raised more flags, collected more spare metal, and gave more to various "charity" organizations.[7] Another, crucial change had taken place. Beginning in spring 1940 Protectorate leaders took a new interest in Protectorate Germans and *Volkstumsarbeit* (nationality work). In March 1940 representatives from various departments within the Reich Protector's Office began having weekly meetings to discuss nationality work in the Protectorate. Two months later the Reich Protector's Office began to demand monthly reports from Oberlandräte on the general situation in their jurisdictions, including reports on activities related to *Volkstumspolitik* (nationality politics). Shortly thereafter, leading officials representing the various departments used the reports penned by the Oberlandräte to design measures to shore up Protectorate Germans' loyalty to the regime and promote German patriotism.[8] By the middle of May, proposals emerged that would have pleased any Protectorate German patriot. Industries, shops, cultural and social institutions, and government agencies were to be placed in the hands of Germans. The number of German schools was to be increased. The German language would dominate public life and public institutions. Special attention was to be paid to "scattered Germans" in the Czech countryside. Throughout the Protectorate, officials in the Reich Protector's Office predicted, the number of Germans would rise, and the number of Czechs would fall.[9]

Protectorate Germans had the full force and finances of the state behind them. The Reich Protector's Office established a special *Volkstumsfond*, or "nationality fund," to support Germans and German activity in the Protectorate. A special committee in Prague named by the Reich protector decided which individuals or institutions received funding. Ober-landräte provided the committee with detailed budgets and wish lists. They, too, distributed the funds. In the second half of 1940 alone three million Reichsmarks were distributed through the fund.[10] Although all had the stated goal of improving the local Germans' economic and cultural "strength" vis-à-vis the Czechs, there were few limits to what the money could buy. The Oberlandrat in Zlín used the money to build a public health office, four German libraries (with two more planned), a meeting hall, and a secondary school. Oberlandrat Fiechtner planned to offer financial rewards to newly married German couples in Jihlava. Thanks to Volkstumsfond monies, Germans across the Protectorate attended the theater more often and bought more German-language books. Other monies subsidized the Nazi Party's official newspaper. The fund paid for radios to spread Nazi propaganda. Even swimming pools, nurseries, and "German" tourist spots received support.[11]

Intelligence Service agents noted that the construction of new schools was among the most significant political and national measures taken by the Reich Protector's Office in 1940.[12] These cultural "victories" over the Czechs took place thanks in large part to Volkstumsfond monies. At the end of the 1938–1939 school year there were only 179 German elementary, junior high, and high schools in the Protectorate. That figure had more than doubled by the time the 1941–1942 school year had begun. The number of students attending German schools in that period rose from 17,196 to 33,800.[13] Oberlandräte bragged that the school openings were a matter of local prestige that impressed German patriots of all stripes. In less densely populated areas, "scattered" German children could at last gather together for a proper "German" education.[14] Many of these gains came at the expense of the Czechs. The Reich Protector's Office shut down Czech schools, many of which were converted to German schools. The number of students attending the Czech schools below the university level dropped from 1,000,730 to 931,283 over the same period mentioned above.[15]

Meanwhile, German control over local administration and public spaces spread. By the end of 1940 every Protectorate city with more than twenty-five thousand inhabitants had a German government commissioner who was in charge at city hall. German government commissioners controlled about 125 small districts around the language islands of Brno, České Budějovice, Moravská Ostrava, Olomouc, Jihlava, and Prague.[16]

Under the First Republic, Czech had been the official language of state correspondence. Bureaucrats who failed to prove proficiency in the state language were dismissed. Neurath decreed that all governmental correspondence had to be written both in German and Czech or only in German. All public servants and functionaries had until March 1942 to prove competence in German. Czech bureaucrats spread rumors that their ranks would be cut by one-third.[17] Local state officials initiated measures to establish the primacy of German symbols in public spaces. In Plzeň, the local Czech beer garden became a *Volkspark* (people's park). In Prague, city officials tore down all traces of the First Republic, including some building facades. Paris Street became Nuremberg Street; Richard Wagner Street replaced Hoover Street. Victory Square became Wehrmacht Square. Neurath's office decreed that public signs, even street signs and shop windows in solidly Czech areas, had to be in German and Czech. German-language names, significantly, had to be listed first.[18]

It appeared, too, that the German population numbers were improving. One optimist within the Intelligence Service pointed out that Germans who in 1939 "out of fright or ignorance" had refused to apply for Reich citizenship now felt confident enough to do so.[19] As of the end of September 1939 less than 188,000 Protectorate inhabitants had applied for German citizenship. By July 1940, however, Oberlandrat offices had received more than 212,000 citizenship applications. By November of that year 8,000 more had applied for citizenship, and the numbers kept growing.[20] From May to November 1940 the German population in the Brno region went up by one-third. Fiechtner complained that, following the fall of France, he lacked the personnel to handle the rush of applications.[21] Officials from the Reich Protector's Office and most Oberlandräte hailed the increase in applications as a success. Germandom was growing in strength. The trend toward Czechification had been reversed. Nazi rulers appeared to have gained bodies for the economic, military, and political machinery of the regime.

There was, as many Intelligence Service agents pointed out, a flip side to this optimism. Many applicants hardly seemed to be German. In the Tábor region only three-fourths of registered Germans could speak German. In the Kolín region the number was 60 percent.[22] An Intelligence Service agent reporting from the České Budějovice region during spring 1940 saw only "rubbish" among the new registrants, pointing out that many had Czech last names and could hardly speak German:

In Pflugschar near Neuhaus [Mr.] Opořil, a man with twenty-three previous burglarly convictions, poses as a German and wrongly denounces Jews with whom he had previously done business. In Mokrilom near Budweis a certain Habermann pretends to be a German, and one who does not speak a word of German and has eighteen previous perjury, burglary, fraud, pan-handling, and other various convictions. In Budweis itself there is a man with twenty-four previous convictions of various sorts who has gone over to Germandom. At the regional office for compulsory work duty in Pardubitz fourteen inmates alone have claimed allegiance to Germandom and sometimes have voluntarily signed up for the army. All the same, most have been convicted more than twenty times, in one instance fifty-four times.

In most such cases the local Oberlandrat's office was able to rescind the Reich citizenship of these criminals. Still, the whole matter was embarrassing, and some of the "asocials" and criminals did manage to cross the legal divide, hoping for more lenient sentences from German courts.[23] Other "new Germans" were obviously unstable, as the report from a Czech bureaucrat testifies:

Dr. Hudec, administrative commissioner [in the Ministry of the Interior], is a Czech, who one fine day arrived at the office and greeted everyone with a "Heil Hitler." His colleagues thought that it was a joke and made fun of him, but Hudec announced, with all seriousness, that he was now a German and that he wished his colleagues to greet him with "Heil Hitler." When it became apparent that he meant it seriously, no one spoke to him; Hudec was totally ruined, and had to be carried away to [the insane asylum] at Bohnice.[24]

On the whole, however, Czechs despised "new Germans" for, as the Oberlandrat in Zlín described, their tendency to display their new nationality "in a boisterous and distasteful manner." The Czechs also rightfully feared them to be Gestapo agents.[25]

Not all "new Germans" were criminals or "asocials," both labels that the Intelligence Service often applied to many of its ideological enemies. With Nazi rule firmly entrenched throughout the continent, becoming a German seemed a logical choice to many respectable amphibians. Post office and railway bureaucrats, along with other state officials, applied for German citizenship in order to be eligible for promotions and better pay. Efforts to reduce the size of the Czech bureaucracy encouraged others to become German in order to save their jobs.

Reich citizens and Protectorate nationals received separate ration cards. Although both received roughly the same rations, German card-carriers received priority when it came to receiving the dwindling allotments of fat, milk, meat, and fruits. Local party leaders handed out extra rations of flour, margarine, and coal to Germans. Protectorate nationals could purchase vegetables only after 10:00 A.M., allowing Reich citizens to get the first pick. Germans gained businesses and apartments stolen from Jews. Still more became Germans in order to reap the benefits of belonging to the Nazi Party and other Reich organizations.[26] Similarly, material motivations often caused parents to send their children to better-funded German schools. A "German" education promised better career opportunities after graduation. As a result, Czech-speakers filled the newly built German schools. Oberlandrat von Watter in Prague became obsessed with the problem, dashing off monthly diatribes to his superiors in the Reich Protector's Office. Czech students outnumbered Germans in the schools, he wrote. Even the so-called Germans could barely speak the language correctly.[27]

The situation caused by people being neither exactly German nor Czech was confused even further by the Protectorate's citizenship law that had been hastily constructed the year before. According to Ministry of the Interior guidelines, one could become a citizen simply by claiming to be a German, as long as this Germanness "can be confirmed through certain factors such as language, education, culture, and so on." Only Jews, because of their "foreign blood," could not become citizens. Although the guidelines stated that the inclusion of persons with non-German heritage should be kept to a minimum, they also stated that applicants with "part or totally different family backgrounds, for example, Czechs, Slovaks, Ukrainians, Hungarians, or Poles," could become German citizens.[28] With such an open-ended definition of what made a German, it was little wonder that many "undesirable elements" passed through the application process.

The process of selecting among the applicants, in turn, depended upon the individual, subjective judgments of the various Oberlandräte. Many so-called Czechs, Molsen wrote, "in their racial and ethical worth do not appear to be that bad, often because they do not know to which side they should belong, due to the fact that their parents belonged to both nationalities."[29] Oberlandräte like Molsen, and many within the Reich Protector's Office, saw amphibians as a means to strengthen Germandom and Nazi rule in the Protectorate. Amphibians added to his population numbers. They also provided reliable administrators. In the city of Olomouc, for example, Commissioner Czermak had been previously known as a Czech who went by the name of Čermak. As of November 1, 1940, Molsen and his counterpart in Brno had issued citizenship papers to 86 percent of their applicants. In Jihlava, Oberlandrat Fiechtner, who had few friends among Protectorate German patriots, handed out citizenship papers to 90 percent of applicants. The acceptance rate was no doubt higher, since applications that were still being processed figured into the "not accepted" numbers. Not all Oberlandräte, however, shared Molsen's positive views of amphibians. The Oberlandrat in Pardubice had granted citizenship to less than half of the applicants.[30] Oberlandrat von Watter of Prague, who openly worried about perfidious Czech influences and the dangers of Slavic blood, approved only six of every ten applications. Perhaps he thought his anti-Czech diatribes would win him some needed respect among die-hard Nazis. Von Watter owed his position to the fact that he was Reich Protector Neurath's nephew.[31]

Protectorate leaders slowly reformed the procedures by which individuals could enter the German community. In June Frank declared that Czech-speaking children could make up no more than one-quarter of the students in any German class. The decision as to which Czech-speaking children would be admitted was left to local state and party officials.[32] In September the Reich Protector's Office revamped the process by which individuals entered the German legal community. Both the local Oberlandrat and Nazi Party *Kreisleiter* (district official) had to approve the application for citizenship.[33] Still, the decision to apply for citizenship remained in the hands of the individuals involved. And Protectorate nationals chose to send their children to German schools. In each case, the individual—not the state—initiated the selection process. Furthermore, the final decision lay in the hands of local officials, who in turn had their own agendas. Political interests, and the criteria by which to judge future citizens, multiplied. The Reich Protector's Office told Oberlandräte and local party officials charged with judging the applications to look at "moral conduct," "political conduct," "personal achievements," "racial characteristics," and "German blood." The criteria remained hopelessly vague. What constituted having "German blood"? No guidelines were laid out. Even though the Germans were ascendant, what a "German" really was remained unclear.

As with so many issues, Protectorate Germans and Reich Germans remained divided on many and often contradictory issues revolving around citizenship. Intelligence Service agents, most of them patriotic Sudeten Germans and Nazi ideologues, openly resented amphibians. The Protectorate's relatively open-ended citizenship criteria allowed "Czechs" and self-serving amphibians to become Germans when it became most convenient to do so. Just like loyal Sudeten German patriots, "new Germans" obtained all the benefits of being Reich citizens, including career advancements. On the other hand, Protectorate Germans still resented the many obligations that came with citizenship, like the draft and work duty. Anyone faking ill health to avoid these commitments was arrested or assigned to hard labor.[34] The draft, especially, reduced the number of Protectorate German men in the region. Party members charged with leading the various Nazi organizations within the Protectorate were severely overextended. In several cases newly built schools could not open because of a continuing shortage of teachers. The number of Sudeten Germans attending university dropped severely, and a number of teaching positions at Charles University remained empty. There was also a shortage of German doctors.[35] Reich Germans' favorable comments, such as "The Czechs are not so bad" and "We get along with them quite well," further enraged Protectorate German patriots, who accused the Czechs of trying to drive a wedge between Sudeten Germans and powerful Germans from the Reich. Neurath was even driven to issue a decree forbidding German officials in Prague from accepting invitations to Czech social and family events.[36]

Similarly, as Protectorate Germans pointed out, what posed as Germanization was actually Nazification, or just bald measures designed to benefit Reich Germans. Thirty-four Nazi organizations—from professional organizations, to the German Red Cross, to the German Auto Club—had established themselves in the Protectorate. Many replaced indigenous clubs and charged onerous dues.[37] Reich Germans stood at the top of administrative pyramids, and their numbers were growing. By June 1940 the population of Prague was increasing by one thousand people per month, chiefly from the influx of Reich Germans employed within a burgeoning civil service. Bureaucrats, soldiers, police, and businessmen considered the Protectorate a plum assignment. Far from the front, their lives were not in danger. Vacation spots in the Reich suffered as annoying Reich German tourists decided instead to visit the Reichsgau Sudetenland and the Protectorate. "The Bohemian dumpling, the Pilsner beer, and the excursion to Prague are all too tempting," a report to German Social Democrats abroad explained. They were no doubt tempted, too, by the knowledge that an unfair exchange rate meant that their reichsmarks bought more in the Protectorate. To many Protectorate German patriots, it was clear that this "German" regime was actually part of a "Reich German" regime, or better said, a "Nazi German" regime, whose tentacles had spread across Europe. Nowhere was this more evident than in the realm of economics.[38]

Großraumwirtschaft

A day after Nazi troops marched on Prague, Hermann Göring announced to officials in Bohemia and Moravia that the Protectorate's economy would be integrated into the "German economic space." In the interest of a smooth transition, Göring continued, his offices would assume control over economic matters in the Protectorate.[39] These were not empty words. From his position as plenipotentiary of the Four-Year Plan, Göring wielded both direct and indirect power over heavy industry and the acquisition of raw materials within Germany and beyond. His men controlled the Ministry of Economics and the Hermann Göring Works, a massive semistate, semiprivate enterprise that gobbled up industries deemed crucial to the German war effort. He and his minions allocated labor, supervised price levels, managed industrial investments, regulated contract orders, and established trade relations. Following the anti-Jewish violence that accompanied Germany's annexation of Austria, Göring established more formal, "legal" mechanisms for the robbery of Jewish property. By 1939 Göring had become the unquestioned master of economic policy making in Nazi Germany.[40]

Göring, like so many Nazi leaders, worked to realize a peculiar set of ideological visions. Within Germany, Nazi control over a "managed economy" promised to allow national, not private, interests to prevail as the country geared for war. For the areas outside Germany, Göring shared with many German businessmen, bankers, and Ministry of Economics technocrats a grand vision for a German *Großraumwirtschaft* (greater economic space) that spread across Europe. They imagined a continentwide "linked economy" of strictly regulated and managed cartels, investment practices, prices, wages, production goals, and avenues of trade. German businesses would sweep across Europe. Food- and raw material–producing areas on the peripheries of Europe would be linked to the industrially rich center in a system designed to enrich Germany and tool it for war. Economic autarky promised to protect Germany against blockades and raw material shortages. Economic power would go hand in hand with war in redrawing the political map of Europe.[41] Göring also had foreign policy ambitions. As he had confided to a visiting Englishman in 1937, the German conquest of Europe would follow two stages. In the first stage, Germany would swallow up territories inhabited by German minorities, creating an industrialized Central Europe linked economically to the dependent, raw material–producing states of southeastern Europe. In the second phase, after years of economic exploitation and rearmament, Germany would be prepared to expand its empire at the expense of the Great Powers of Europe. Germany would reduce France to a vassal state and exclude Britain from European affairs. The main goal of this expansion, however, lay in the East, where German troops would destroy Bolshevism and establish Nazi domination over the region.[42]

While foreign minister, Neurath on several occasions complained that Göring meddled too much in foreign affairs, visiting foreign officials and speaking on behalf of Germany. Göring was intimately involved in the decision making behind Germany's annexation of Austria and the Munich agreement, although Hitler made the decision to occupy Prague without him. Göring, like many army generals, feared that Germany was not yet prepared to fight a European war. Hitler thought otherwise and thus excluded Göring from most foreign policy decisions made after 1938, including the decision to attack Poland.[43] Even after Germany's invasion of Poland, however, Göring retained immense powers over economic policy making throughout Nazi-dominated Europe. Göring's expansionist goals, unlike Hitler's, did not stem primarily from ideas about race and space but from the more traditional fount of German *mitteleuropäische* (Central European) thinking about territory and resources. Securing raw materials and establishing a strong, industrialized Germany in the middle of Europe remained his first priority.[44]

Although Czechs outnumbered Germans in the Protectorate, it, like Austria and the occupied Sudetenland, fit squarely within Göring's industrialized Central Europe. Czechoslovakia had inherited one-fifth of the land, one-fourth of the population, but three-fourths of the Habsburg monarchy's industrial producing capacity after the monarchy's dissolution in 1918. Interwar Czechoslovakia was the world's tenth largest per capita producer of industrial goods. Now 70 percent of Czechoslovakia's industry lay in the Protectorate. As Göring was well aware, Czechoslovakia had been the seventh largest supplier of armaments in the world. Its arms were among the best in Europe, and its workers among the most highly trained on the continent.[45] Within days of the occupation, Göring, with the help of the Dresdner Bank and the Gestapo, set in motion efforts to acquire for the Göring Works control over enterprises deemed vital to the war effort.[46] By the end of 1940 the Göring Works—using government loans, coerced stock sales, and other means—controlled 50–60 percent of the shareholding value of the former Czechoslovakia's heavy industry.[47] The Göring Works obtained majority ownership of the Protectorate's two largest armaments manufacturers—the Škoda Works in Plzeň and the Czech Armaments Works in Brno—along with machinery plants, the railroad connecting Vienna to Moravská Ostrava, and various coal-mining enterprises. It held in trust the Vítkovice Mining and Ironworks Company, which Göring predicted would become an "industrial pillar of the Reich in the east" (Fig. 2.1). Göring even had the gall to appoint his brother, Albert, to the top management position of the Poldina hut' Iron and Steel Works near Kladno.[48]

Other measures modeled on Göring's policies in Germany, but emanating from within the Protectorate, further revamped the Protectorate's economic structure. Following the German model, the Czech government in spring 1939 organized enterprises in the Protectorate into one of several central associations, which coordinated the planning, production, and distribution of goods and raw materials in the Protectorate. Czechs retained their businesses, but membership in an association was compulsory. Months later, the associations were all headed by Germans appointed by the top official within the Economics Section of the Reich Protector's Office, Walter Bertsch.[49] Under Bertsch's leadership, associations allocated government contracts and set production quotas. They played a key role in retooling the Protectorate's economy for war production. By 1940 the Central Association of Industry had assumed nearly complete control over orders and production in the Protectorate. Candy and chocolate factories in Olomouc had to limit their production while local iron and steel works refitted their production processes to make tanks and grenades. Pharmaceutical plants now made vitamins for

German troops.[50] An agency in Neurath's office claimed the right to supervise price levels. Any price increase required the approval of the Reich Protector's Office's. Only the state could buy products in bulk from summer 1939 onward. Following Germany's attack on Poland, the Czech government introduced a rationing system. Food tickets became the only way to get textiles, shoes, and a widening array of basic foodstuffs. The only free market that remained was black.[51]

The Reich Protector's Office coordinated with several Reich ministries on foreign trade and worked to enmesh the Protectorate within Ger-

Figure 2.1 The German army taking up position in front of the Vítkovice Ironworks in Moravská Ostrava shortly after the invasion. (Reproduced by permission of the Vojenský ústřední archiv Fotoarchiv.)

many's economy. In October 1940 the Protectorate entered the Reich's Customs Union. By the end of 1940, 80 percent of the Protectorate's imports and 71 percent of its exports involved exchanges with the Reich. By contrast, in 1937 only 15 percent of Czechoslovakia's imports and exports had been with Germany.[52] Nazi leaders like Göring also viewed the Protectorate as a way of strengthening their grip over the economies in southeastern Europe. Rattled by the depression and disenchanted by free trade on the world market, Hungary, Yugoslavia, Bulgaria, Romania, and other southeastern European states signed a series of trade agreements with Nazi Germany before World War II. According to the agreements, southeastern European raw materials and agricultural products were exchanged, at fixed prices and fixed exchange rates according to fixed quotas, for German industrial goods and a small percentage of transit goods as well as hard currency through a central clearing house in Berlin. Although some managed to wriggle out of their increasingly onerous agreements before the war, the rise of German power in 1939 and 1940 brought southeastern Europe even more tightly into Germany's Großraumwirtschaft system.[53] The Protectorate lands and the contacts established by Czechoslovak industrialists and businessmen constituted an important conduit through which German businesses could reach valuable markets and resources in the southeast, a fact duly noted by the Deutsche Bank in 1939. In 1937, 62.1 percent of Romania's imports came from Germany, Austria, or Czechoslovakia. For Yugoslavia and Bulgaria the numbers were 58.1 percent and 60.8 percent respectively.[54] Through the Czech Armaments Works, the Göring Works obtained influence over mines and steel complexes in Romania—just one example of how the accumulation of stockholdings and outright takeovers allowed Göring to extend Germany's economic tentacles across the continent.[55]

The Protectorate, a top official in Göring's Four-Year Plan office predicted in April 1939, should be prepared to "contribute its share to the building up of an integrated and harmonious Großraumwirtschaft."[56] Indeed, by the end of 1940 Göring's vision seemed to have become reality, and not just in the Protectorate. Göring saddled France and other occupied countries in the West with special levies. Existing stocks were appropriated, industries put under German "trusteeships," and Jewish-owned firms and businesses simply taken over. Germany imposed trade agreements modeled after those with southeastern European states before the war on weakling collaborationist governments and satellite states. By 1943 three-quarters of the iron and steel produced in Belgium was under German contract. The same fraction of all the iron ore mined in France went to Germany.[57] In Hungary, crude oil output rose from 42,000 tons in 1938 to 842,000 tons in 1943, 50 percent of which traveled to Germany.[58] In Slovakia, the Göring Works, the Dresdner Bank, the Deutsche Bank, and corporations like IG Farben AG directly controlled all of Slovakia's oil fields and coal mines, three-quarters of its chemical industry, and half of its metal industry by 1942.[59] The Protectorate, too, had become woven into the new economic order. Tons of food products arrived in the Protectorate from new members of the Nazis' international, increasingly intertwined continental economic system. Bacon and bacon fat came primarily from Yugoslavia. The Netherlands provided other livestock products. Romanian producers shipped seeds used to make margarine. Norway sent fish oil.[60] At the same time, the Protectorate had become an integral part of an industrialized Central Europe. By the end of 1940 half of the Protectorate's foreign capital investment was from the German Reich, six times more than in 1937. Another third was English capital that was now in the hands of trusteeships run mainly by the Göring Works.[61] Almost a third of all the raw steel and rolling mill products made during the war by Göring Works' holdings came from the Vítkovice Mining and Iron Works.[62] By spring 1941 roughly a third of the chemical industry, all the major steel- and iron-producing factories, and all the oil refineries were, according to Bertsch, in "German hands."[63]

The Protectorate of Bohemia and Moravia had become an economic component of the German Reich, an Intelligence Service report concluded in 1940, ruefully adding that Reich German, not Protectorate German, interests had been served first. Economic decision making, it charged, emanated from Germany from "economic circles within the Reich that remain under the influence of West German industrialists," who were thought to exploit the Protectorate for their own gain.[64] Göring was no doubt meant to be a target of this attack, and for good reason. Bertsch, head of the Economics Section within the Reich Protector's Office, reported directly to the Ministry of Economics in Berlin, which in turn reported to Göring.[65] There is little doubt that Bertsch and those in his office not only cooperated with Göring's men but also shared their vision for a new economic order in Europe. At the same time, Neurath and Frank do not appear to have disapproved of these policies. As Hitler had made clear in 1939, Neurath had the authority to set economic policy in the Protectorate. In fact, the economic integration of the Protectorate achieved much more than helping Nazi leaders like Göring realize geopolitical dreams while enriching German banks and big businesses: it shored up "German" rule and made the economy more "German." Occasionally, and despite claims from the Intelligence Service to the contrary, the measures enriched the local German population. Nowhere was this confluence of interests exposed more clearly than in the case of the state-sponsored robbery of the Protectorate's Jewish population.

"Wild Aryanization [in the Protectorate] is to be prevented," Göring announced on March 16, 1939. "I will decide upon the timing, degree, and tempo of any measures at de-Jewification."[66] Four days later Göring declared that Jewish property could not be sold, transferred, or given away without his approval.[67] "Aryanization" encompassed a whole range of measures to enrich Germans at the expense of Jews, measures that Göring attempted to control and regulate beginning in 1938.[68] In fact, Göring's tactics depended in large part on the robbery of Jews, which in turn depended on aid from the Gestapo and SS. The Dresdner Bank and the Deutsche Bank, the main conduits through which large Jewish capital holdings were absorbed, swallowed up Prague's two largest banks. Threats from the Intelligence Service forced the banks' Jewish board members to resign.[69] Jews were "persuaded" to sell their stocks and other assets to the Göring Works at prices well below market value, often in return for exit visas. In other cases, simple takeovers sufficed.[70]

The "wild Aryanization" feared by Göring never happened.[71] Aryanization did, however, take place beyond his direct control. Two days after the establishment of the Protectorate the Czech government began drafting measures for the expropriation of Jewish property and, to the dismay of local Oberlandräte, began assigning Treuhänder (literally, "trustees") to Jewish firms.[72] In June Neurath's office issued a decree that claimed for the Reich Protector's Office the sole authority to issue decrees relating to Aryanization. Bertsch's office was responsible for the implementation of most of these measures. Neurath repeated Göring's declaration that no Jewish property could be sold, transferred, or given away without permission. All valuables, such as gold and pearls, had to be registered with special offices created by the Reich Protector's Office. Only the Reich protector had the right to assign Treuhänder, a responsibility that in practice fell to the Oberlandräte.[73] In 1940 Neurath's office accelerated the process. Decrees that year required Jews to sell their valuables to a special public purchasing agency and to deposit stocks and other paper assets in a foreign currency bank.[74] A second cascade of decrees declared a whole range of business ventures—film production, textile and shoe manufacturing, and then pubs, insurance companies, and banks—off limits to Jewish owners.[75] Germans, with the help of "Aryanization loans" from German banks and subsidies from the German Reich, could purchase these businesses. More often, however, the regime simply liquidated the Jewish firms.[76] Oberlandräte, the Gestapo, and the SS worked together to force owners of small businesses to sell at "Jewish prices" well below market value.[77] Fiechtner, like his fellow Oberlandräte, never raised a single protest against Aryanization measures. Only rarely did he or other Oberlandräte complain of interference from other agencies.[78] In autumn 1940 local Nazi Party officials obtained the right to judge the "political reliability" of potential Treuhänder. It appears, however, that unlike in Germany, Austria, and the Reichsgau Sudetenland, the Nazi Party had been largely excluded from the process, though not without protest.[79]

In the end, Aryanization benefited a wide range of constituencies: the Göring Works, German industrialists, the Dresdner Bank and Deutsche Bank, the Reich Protector's Office, Oberlandräte, the Gestapo, and the Intelligence Service, to name just a few. There was a lot to go around, and Germans from all walks of life profited. By 1941, Aryanization measures enabled the seizure of savings deposits, cash, foreign exchange, and securities valued at nearly 1.8 billion crowns. Six billion crowns' worth of moveable and immoveable assets were eventually distributed, almost exclusively, to Germans.[80] George Kennan estimated that by October 1940 more than 120,000 Reich Germans had relocated to Prague, many of whom had been fortunate enough to be named Treuhänder. "They are, in the most literal sense of the term, the carpetbaggers of the occupation," he wrote.[81] Sudeten Germans benefited even more from various Aryanization measures. Molsen claimed that 188 of the 195 Treuhänder in his region were Germans from the Protectorate. In just eight months, he continued, local German Treuhänder had siphoned at least 2.5 million crowns from local Jewish businesses.[82] During the second phase of Aryanization, when Jews were forced to sell off their small businesses and manufacturing operations, Sudeten Germans were again the prime beneficiaries. One detailed study of 255 "Aryanization loans" in the Protectorate, provided by the Kreditanstalt der Deutschen, which had been the largest German banking institution in Czechoslovakia, shows that four out of every five of the beneficiaries were Germans from the Bohemian lands. Most of the perpetrators were middle-class employees and civil servants for whom Aryanization provided social advancement and economic independence.[83] By March 1941 Molsen had overseen the transfer of 135 small businesses into the hands of Sudeten Germans. Another 49 had been almost equally divided among Reich Germans and Czechs.[84]

In April 1940 Bertsch's office released a report bragging of its accomplishments. Thanks mainly to Aryanization measures, Germans now owned more textile, glass, and paper factories than ever before. Aryanization not only encouraged Germans to take up residence in the Protectorate but also provided local Germans with "a more stable existence." The "strengthening of German influences" in the economy, the report concluded, has had a "favorable effect" on nationality politics.[85] The assessment was perhaps a bit rosy: although diverse Germans benefited from the crime, Reich and Protectorate Germans bickered over the spoils. Local Germans complained that Reich Germans obtained all the best businesses. Textile factories under German "trusteeship" closed because they lacked raw materials. Courageous Jews would sometimes refuse to hand over control of their businesses.[86] Reich Germans accused local Germans of incompetence and of running perfectly fine businesses into the ground. The Treuhänder in the Moravská Ostrava region, the local Oberlandrat claimed, were nothing but dolts, drunks, and swindlers.[87]

Muted

Reich German leaders could at least claim that robbing the Jews of their property and a whole slew of other measures advanced a long-standing effort to reverse the "Czechification" of the economy. Yet the Protectorate had also become an integral part of Nazi Germany's economic order. It was also a system that depended upon Czechs, many of whom benefited as well. There was much about which Czech patriots at home and abroad could fret in 1940. Bureaucrats remained in their positions, faithfully serving the state. Farmers continued to produce goods at levels high enough to avoid widescale hunger. Czech businesses, large and small, fell victim to aggressive German takeovers. Yet most Czechs remained in control of their enterprises, playing key roles in the functioning of the new economy. Czech industrialists made handsome profits as they worked within, not against, the German system.[88] In 1941 Czechs still held 84 percent of the top managerial positions in the Protectorate's industries and continued to cultivate ties with their southeastern European partners.[89] When no suitable Germans could be found, Oberlandräte occasionally assigned Czechs to act as Treuhänder. In Prague, where the local Oberlandrat was known for his anti-Czech attitude, 96 of the 1,109 Treuhänder in mid-1940 were Czechs. Outside Prague, and especially in areas with few German inhabitants, the number of Czech Treuhänder might have been higher.[90] Although only Germans could purchase Jewish property with the help of "Aryanization loans," some of these "Germans" had previously identified themselves as Czechs.[91] When the Reich Protector's Office dissolved Jewish enterprises, the decreased competition for resources and customers resulted in higher profits for Czech and German owners of small businesses.[92]

Perhaps most critical to the functioning of the German-coordinated system were the Protectorate's 730,000 industrial workers, more than 310,000 of whom worked in the metal-manufacturing and -finishing sectors.[93] "As a whole," an Intelligence Service agent summing up the events of 1940 wrote, "the armaments industry in the Protectorate has no reason to worry about the Czech worker." One reason was that workers "hope[d] for social betterment through the Reich."[94] When Hitler came to power in Germany, the number of unemployed in Czechoslovakia was about one million. In November 1942 the Reich Ministry of Economics and Labor counted only twenty-three unemployed in the Protectorate.[95] Although long lines for food and chronic shortages angered Protectorate inhabitants, no one starved. Although less generous, Czech rations were comparable to those of their German neighbors, as well as of anyone living in the German Reich. Workers involved in heavy industrial labor received higher wages and higher rations than their Czech counterparts in other professions.[96]

Economic security was certainly one, but not the only, reason that Protectorate industries continued to hum. Factory workers and miners had taken part in the 1939 marches and demonstrations, but strikes had been rare. The few strikes that had taken place came to an abrupt end after Germany attacked Poland.[97] German police arrested or murdered strike organizers and Communist functionaries, sometimes in front of the workers. Another massive wave of arrests followed the war in the west. Gestapo agents shot dead seven workers in the Plzeň Škoda Works, seven in the Brno armaments factory, and twenty in Moravská Ostrava's Českomoravská plant.[98] Even work slowdowns or calling in sick could earn beatings, as in one factory where Nazi bosses took every second worker from his position and "beat him black and blue." As a result, workers kept each other in line.[99] Nor, to be fair, was there much agitation from leaders abroad. Former Czechoslovak president Beneš was silent on the issue of strikes and sabotage.[100] After the fall of France, the Czechoslovak Communist Party, having abandoned hopes of worker revolts in Germany and still hamstrung by Stalin's pact with Hitler, called on workers to support a vaguely worded "fight for people's freedom using half measures."[101] Thus, Protectorate industries made significant contributions to the German war effort. Coal miners pulled 16.7 million tons of coal from the earth around Moravská Ostrava in 1940, up from less than 12 million tons in 1939.[102] Not until June 1940 did Reich Protectorate authorities find a single act of sabotage in an armaments factory that year.[103]

"The nation realizes that it is a part of the Reich; it wants to be an integral element of the Reich, and it wants to work towards [that end]," the chairman of the National Solidarity Movement told members gathered in Prague's Lucerna Theater shortly after the fall of France.[104] Economically speaking, he seemed to have gotten his wish. Czech economic dominance had been eroded, business and industry either controlled, if not owned outright, by Germans. Meanwhile, a thin membrane of Nazi rulers and officials held tight a population of Czech laborers who— cowed, coordinated, and sometimes worse—continued to work for the Reich. At the same time, Nazi officials realized that the German economy and Germany war machine depended upon the Protectorate, and especially its workers. In 1941 Protectorate industrial workers accounted for 7 percent of the industrial workforce in Germany, Austria, and the occupied Bohemian lands combined.[105] A precarious balance had been struck. As an armaments factory official in Moravská Ostrava wrote, Czechs were working efficiently but refused to join the German Workers' Front. The lesson to be learned, he concluded, is "where the boundaries are, [and] how far one may go to enlist people" without provoking protest.[106] A mixture of coordination, control, repression, and material rewards kept the Protectorate's economy running smoothly.

The developments in the economic sphere spoke to a further weakening of the Czech national movement. Like the Czech worker, Hácha's government had, in a way, been coopted and coordinated. When in spring 1940 Frank threatened Hácha with the execution of the two thousand Czech university students held in concentration camps, Hácha offered the *Sieg Heil* to Hitler and signed an oath of allegiance to the Führer—symbolic acts of compliance that he had eluded the previous September. In return, two hundred students were immediately released. The damage to his credibility, however, had been done. [107] Members of Hácha's government became more openly "activist" as they "tried to outdo themselves in assurances of loyalty" and initiated a propaganda campaign to "reeducate the Czech nation in the Reich way of thinking," as one Intelligence Service agent wrote. The machinery of government functioned smoothly until the end of the war.[108] The only challenge to Hácha's government came, once again, from the Czech fascists, who at one point attacked Prague's National Solidarity Movement chapter and wounded thirty-four Czech police officers. Hácha was able to prevent fascists from gaining government positions. Their more moderate adherents, however, entered a reconstructed, pro-German National Solidarity Movement and added to the ranks of collaborationist organizations like the Czech Committee for Cooperation with Germans.[109] Czech fascists registered for Reich citizenship in increasingly large numbers. They then used their Gestapo connections to blackmail their way into lucrative positions within police and state institutions.[110]

Public displays of Czech national loyalty were few. Dvořak and Smetana concerts continued to draw crowds, as did other performances in "houses of culture" throughout the Protectorate, but little of value appeared in newspapers and magazines. Scores of journalists had been arrested; committed "activists" wrote articles according to strict, officially dictated guidelines. As a result, total sales of these items dropped by at least 25 percent over the course of 1940.[111] University doors remained closed to Czech students; scholars continued to publish in obscure journals, engage in personal squabbles, and quietly conduct research in official institutions like the Czech Academy of Arts and Letters.[112] Although patriotic clubs like the Sokol and Orel still existed, other Czech organizations had begun working with Reich ones; one contribution drive by Czech charities added 3.8 million Reichsmarks to the coffers of the German Red Cross.[113] Czech symbols disappeared from public view. In

1940 German officials began removing Masaryk monuments that had been scattered across the country. Czech patriots, most likely Sokol members, rescued other Masaryk statues and buried them.[114] Patriots could only shake their heads at the predominance of German words in public spaces. One common joke told the story of an old man from the countryside who had just arrived in Prague by train. *"Hauptbahnhof— Hlavní nadraži!"* announced the loudspeaker, telling him that he had arrived at the main train station. On the tram came the words *"Wenzel-splatz—Václavské náměstí"* (Wenceslas Square, in German and then Czech). The old man rushed to the square's statue of St. Wenceslas, clasped his hands together, and called out: "St. Wenceslas, prince of the Czech lands, what do you make of all this!?" The knight balanced his lance in his hand and quoth: *"Dreck—hovno!"* [Crap—crap!]"[115]

Organized underground resistance had been dealt a series of heavy blows throughout 1940. In April fifteen hundred people suspected of belonging to resistance organizations were arrested.[116] In the coming months, Gestapo agents rounded up thousands more, most of them lesser-known Social Democrats and Communists. Orders from Moscow demanded that Communist propaganda emphasize class resistance, not national resistance. Yet few Czechs paid attention to their leaflets or to Moscow radio broadcasts.[117] Within the democratic resistance, desperation forced the three major non-Communist resistance groups to combine their efforts and accept centralized rule under an umbrella organization, the Ústřední vedení odboje domácího (Central Leadership of Home Resistance), or ÚVOD. Many in the democratic resistance still saw shoring up national consciousness as their primary task. *V boj* resumed publication, and pamphlets still circulated throughout the Protectorate. After the fall of France, however, the tone of the pamphlets changed from wild optimism to grim caution.[118]

Czechs uninvolved with resistance movements also confronted violence, or at least the threat of violence. Following Germany's victories in the west, SA men in Brno and Olomouc attacked Czech- and Jewish-owned businesses. Later they broke into Czech homes demanding to see the residents' Hakenkreuz flags.[119] More disturbing, however, was the threat of Gestapo arrest that shrouded everyday life. As retribution for the killing of two German customs officials in Domažlice, Frank had one hundred of the town's inhabitants shipped to the concentration camp at Flossenbürg in Bavaria.[120] Troublesome Czechs—and Jews and

Protectorate Germans—could, without a trial, be arrested, deported, and executed. Gestapo and Intelligence Service agents continued to hound members of the so-called intelligentsia, and resistance organizations continually lost members to arrest. Fear of the Gestapo and its growing network of informants spread.[121] The editor of one weekly in Olomouc was moved to publish an article warning against a repeat of the history of Judas's betrayal of Jesus. We run across people, the article wrote, who "betray the friend, the comrade . . . they sometimes also betray the most precious thing: their mother language and their nation." *V boj* published a poem calling on Czechs to "keep quiet" as part of national resistance. "The nation is fighting the manly fight; and its silence is a powerful weapon as explosive as a large grenade," it wrote.[122] That is exactly what most Czechs did—with the exception of a dwindling domestic resistance movement and Czechs safely abroad.

Home and Abroad

Among the democratic resistance, one report to London stated, not even the "greatest pessimists" had expected France to collapse so quickly.[123] Yet optimists among them found hope in the Italians' bumbled invasion of Greece that autumn and in the growing chill in the relations between the Soviet Union and Germany. Great Britain's new prime minister, Winston Churchill, promised to fight to the bitter end, even as his country withstood an intense bombing campaign. From just outside London, where he had moved to avoid the Blitz, former Czechoslovak president Edvard Beneš established a government-in-exile. As he cultivated diplomatic contacts, Beneš relentlessly pursued three goals—the international recognition of his government, the annulment of the Munich agreement, and promises to restore Czechoslovakia along its former borders after the war. World War II, which much of Europe had tried so desperately to avoid, meant something different to Czech patriots. Only with war could Germany be defeated and Bohemia and Moravia liberated. At home and abroad many Czech patriots hoped that Beneš, who had helped convince Entente leaders to create Czechoslovakia from the ruins of the World War I, could work his magic once again.

The last of ten children born to parents in a small central Bohemian town, Beneš was sent to study in Prague before entering the Czech branch of Charles University in 1904 to study philosophy. In the years before World War I he traveled throughout western Europe, studying at the Sorbonne and in Dijon before landing in England in 1911. There he focused on sociology and political science, and with the help of his brother, Vojta, published a number of dry, methodical academic books. "Science," meaning careful, rational judgments based on truths exposed by empirical evidence, enchanted Beneš. Policy, he wrote, should be based on science and "according to the demands of new circumstances." To Beneš, "politics," a sociologist close to him reported, needed to be "completely matter-of-fact, totally sober, analytical, [and] free from unnecessary emotion."[124] Tireless, rational Beneš might have just as well been speaking of himself (Fig. 2.2). "He is a machine for thinking and working, though with human weaknesses," commented one of his closest aides in London, Jaromír Smutný, who marveled at "the absence of everything human in his character."[125]

Beneš was a masterful networker. Thanks to his brother, Vojta, he cul-

Figure 2.2 Edvard Beneš in England, 1942. (Reproduced by permission of the Česká tisková kancelář.)

tivated relationships with Masaryk's Realist Party before World War I. Soon after the war began he offered several of his articles to the Realists' newspaper, *Čas*, pledged four thousand crowns to help Masaryk's growing resistance movement abroad, and provided him with intelligence gleaned from a Czech working for the Minister of the Interior in Vienna. Beneš's intelligence network expanded as he recruited more followers. Soon he became one of Masaryk's most trusted confidants. In 1915 Beneš, who faked a limp to avoid military service, fled Austria-Hungary to Switzerland and then to Paris, where he became Masaryk's representative. Thoughtful, informed, and manipulative, he won over newspaper editors, Foreign Office secretaries, and seasoned diplomats. Beneš also won over Allied supporters thanks to the heroics of the Czechoslovak legions—pawns in a larger political game over sovereignty and borders in postwar Eastern Europe.[126] Just before the war's end the Allies recognized Masaryk and Beneš's national council as representatives of a still nonexistent Czechoslovakia. Patriots at home marveled at their achievements. "Wilson or anyone else would never say anything which Masaryk or Beneš did not underwrite," National Socialist leader Václav Klofáč announced, with a fair amount of exaggeration, upon returning to Prague in 1918. "The authority of these people is simply amazing." "If you saw Dr. Beneš, and his mastery of all global questions . . . you would certainly take your hat off," the well-known liberal politician Karel Kramář chimed in. "Imagine, the same Beneš who came to Switzerland with his little rucksack."[127]

As Czechoslovakia's longtime foreign minister, Beneš worked to strengthen ties with France and Great Britain, placing deep confidence in the postwar system of international treaties and his abilities to operate within them. "Nobody," the *London Times* wrote in 1940, "could use the League of Nations more skillfully for the maintenance of the status quo. Nobody fought with greater effort to preserve the artificial French system than did Edvard Beneš." The system in which he placed so much faith betrayed him. As president, a position he assumed in 1935, Beneš seemed powerless in the face of the rise of the Sudeten German Party, and in 1938 he found himself outmaneuvered at Munich. It was Beneš who gave the order for Czechoslovak troops to stand down, after which he volunteered his resignation and congratulated Hácha as the new president of truncated Czecho-Slovakia. Followed by a handful of loyalists, he emigrated to London, to the United States as a chaired

professor of sociology, and then, after the establishment of the Protectorate, back to London. From there, Beneš forged a national council that
claimed to represent Czechoslovakia abroad and to have the right to organize and direct the Czechoslovak army in France. He ruthlessly silenced his many rivals and withstood challenges from the Slovak National Council, which had, until France's defeat, been based in Paris,
and demanded more Slovak autonomy. Beneš, a former right-wing
Czechoslovak parliamentarian abroad complained in April 1940, "wants
to establish a personal dictatorship. . . . [He] can stand *instruments* only,
not fellow workers. The tragedy is that he has not changed the *manner*
of his work, and perseveres stubbornly in his domestic and foreign
policy mistakes." World War I made Beneš. Munich nearly destroyed
him. World War II promised redemption.[128]

Restoring his creation, the Czechoslovak state, and seeing the Munich
agreement annulled became Beneš's single-minded obsession. Deeming
everything after Munich "illegal," Beneš argued that in the absence of
proper elections and a proper parliament after 1938, he remained
Czechoslovakia's president. In 1940 he assumed the right to issue far-
reaching presidential decrees—forty-three of which were issued in exile
and ninety-eight in Czechoslovakia after liberation.[129] In May 1939 he
notified the French, British, and U.S. governments, as well as the League
of Nations, that the signatories of Munich had failed to uphold their
commitments, hence making the Munich agreement null and void.[130] He
demanded that Czechoslovakia be restored along its former borders and
that his government have jurisdiction over Czechoslovak finances, citizens, and its army abroad. He encouraged legions of legal experts to back
up his case for the legal continuity of Czechoslovakia. The president-in-
exile repeated for foreign audiences arguments first made during World
War I to explain why his country needed to be restored intact. Without
the mountain ranges ringing Bohemia, the mostly Czech-inhabited regions in the interior and its major industrial centers, he argued, Czechoslovakia would forever remain defenseless in the face of German aggression.[131] His pleas fell on deaf ears. To the French and British governments,
Beneš remained a painful reminder of their betrayals and false belief in
appeasement, and they feared any further commitments for the future.
The British Foreign Office, in particular, viewed Czechoslovakia as a
hopeless mélange of nationalities. Still, "just like the last war: persistent,
patient, slow, [with] daily work, thousands of lobbying activities, conver-

sations, memoranda, and so on," Beneš wrote to his brother, he and his entourage hoped to repeat his past successes and, with the support of the Great Powers working within an international framework, return to a renewed Czechoslovakia.[132]

The Czechoslovak "president" had many advantages on his side. His international reputation had been bloodied, yet it survived, especially within British circles. He was a known entity, and eventually the British government preferred working with one man rather than a mixed group of quarrelsome exiles. As he told Franklin Roosevelt, the Czechs and Slovaks needed "a certain national symbol," a role that only he could play. Thousands of young men and professional officers slipped across the Slovak border or made it to Switzerland after accepting work assignments in Germany in order to fight the Germans in France.[133] Following the collapse of France, Beneš's organizational heroics allowed many to escape across the Channel. Months later Czechoslovak pilots loyal to Beneš's government-in-exile fought alongside the British in the victorious air war over the skies of England. Not surprisingly, Czechoslovakia's four thousand troops abroad—as well as at least some former Czechoslovak citizens among the three thousand German antifascist fighters in Great Britain—remained deeply loyal to Beneš.[134] Men eager for battle were not the only Protectorate inhabitants to escape abroad. Hácha's minister of agriculture, for example, hopped the border with the help of a friendly train engineer and made his way to London.[135] As Beneš consolidated his rule, thousands of Czechoslovak exiles—and especially members of the government-in-exile's burgeoning bureaucracy—became legally and financially dependent upon him.[136]

Beneš and those around him also possessed the means to speak directly to Czechs at home. The British air force and its balloons dropped thousands of propaganda leaflets over the Protectorate in early 1940—paper bombs that obsessed Protectorate officials and police.[137] BBC radio transmissions, however, reached more people, more often. A London informant estimated at the beginning of 1941 that one million Protectorate inhabitants owned radio receivers of various wavelengths.[138] The Czechs act friendly toward us, Oberlandrat Schultz of Pardubice allegedly said, "but in the evening just before 6:30 one hears on the streets and the squares nothing other than 'Bye, I have to go home'" as they all hurry home to hear London radio.[139] The broadcasts, and in particular the speeches by Jan Masaryk, the son of Czechoslovakia's first president and now Beneš's foreign minister, helped many Protectorate inhabitants battle disillusionment and uncertainty. Listening constituted a way of acting Czech, as did spreading reliable news about foreign events to friends the next day. Crucially, it established bonds between Beneš and many loyal Czechs. "The decisive means of communication (between London and the Protectorate) remains the radio. The rumors that arise among the population and even the mood of the Czechs can in most cases be traced back to radio broadcasts of the previous day," Neurath's office concluded in April 1940.[140] "People everywhere are listening to the London broadcasts, and everything that the radio says is immediately known throughout the Protectorate," a London informant confirmed.[141]

Listening also constituted a determined, although "passive," form of opposition to the regime. On September 1, 1939, Neurath decreed that anyone deliberately spreading news deemed harmful to Germany or the Germans could be imprisoned or killed. Tuning in to foreign broadcasts became illegal in January 1940. But as the Reich Protector's Office acknowledged, locating radio-listeners was nearly impossible. Indeed, after the fall of France, Neurath's office seemed to lose interest in the foreign broadcasts.[142] Only in winter 1941 did Nazi officials send everyone who owned a radio receiver a gold-colored plate with the words "Listening to foreign broadcasts is punishable by death." From then on, people could purchase radios only at local administrative offices. Workers carried various radio parts in their pockets. When all the parts came together, they could listen to foreign broadcasts. Listeners who shared apartment buildings with Germans devised special earphones to reduce the possibility of being heard. "Churchillkies," radios rigged to pick up short-wave radio signals, sold on the black market for sixteen hundred crowns. Until the end of the war, even the most draconian Nazi measures could not break up the one-sided conversation between London and the Protectorate's inhabitants.[143]

Beneš also greatly benefited from his contacts with a small group of prodemocracy members of the resistance and from their knowledge about events at home. At the request of London, correspondents commented on radio programs, speeches, and the strength of various radio frequencies. Underground publications and stickers attached to phone booths announced the time and radio frequency of the Czech-language BBC broadcasts.[144] Increasingly, however, ÚVOD members and Beneš's government came to see intelligence as an equally valuable contribution to the war effort. Beneš's government received thousands of "reports from home," which consisted of letters sent by courier and post, and of interviews with those who had escaped the Protectorate. His government's intelligence network also pulled in information from ÚVOD and from its contacts in the Czech government in the Protectorate.[145] Two-way radio transmissions provided the primary communications link between the democratic resistance in the Protectorate and Czechoslovak leaders in London. Using equipment supplied by the British, ÚVOD established radio transmitters, Sparta I and Sparta II, which beamed almost six thousand messages to London from April 1940 until May 1941, when they were discovered by Gestapo agents.[146]

These various "reports from home" served many purposes. The messages described, among other things, troop movements, economic measures, the Protectorate regime, and the mood of population. In addition to reading the messages for information about events and public opinion in the Protectorate, Beneš's government, after careful screening and editing, used the messages to construct propaganda.[147] Also through ÚVOD, Beneš was able to maintain contact with Alois Eliáš, a former legionnaire who was now Hácha's second-in-command, and through him with Hácha and the rest of the Czech government (code-named "family"). (Gestapo agents knew of Eliáš's activities, which included helping others escape abroad, but the regime decided, for the time being, to permit the relationship to continue.)[148] Finally, ÚVOD' messages provided Beneš with much-needed assurances about his legitimacy at home. "Your authority among the whole nation is great," one message soothingly reported.[149] Part of the nation, another message said, was "spontaneously" against the Czechoslovak president-in-exile, and another part consisted entirely of Czechs who aided the Germans, but Beneš was the unquestioned leader of the resistance movement and a man "with whom the majority of the nation agrees."[150] The assurances went both ways. Beneš continually predicted the imminent defeat of Germany. Neither judgment seemed based on much empirical evidence.

Although ÚVOD and the government-in-exile were linked by radio waves, a chasm opened between ÚVOD and Beneš over the course of 1940 and into 1941, exposing differences that would cause the president-in-exile to rethink his future plans for Czechoslovakia. Many members of ÚVOD complained that officials in London had little understanding of the hardships that they faced. For his part, Beneš shared the view that the small domestic resistance should not put itself at further risk or provoke more measures against the population. To the general population, the message coming from BBC transmitters was clear: "Remain peaceful and calm."[151] But the head of Czechoslovak intelligence, František Moravec, and another important link between London and the underground, General Sergej Ingr, often chided the domestic resistance for lacking the courage to do more. The British wanted to see acts of violence that aided the war effort. "Your pains, your suffering, Germanization, the plundering, German bestiality—all of it is temporary and slight" in comparison to the catastrophes suffered by other Europeans, one of their messages lectured. "We assume that you will be able to defeat this view that our nation is not at war," ÚVOD responded angrily. "It is not our fault that we cannot conduct war with the units we used to have. Your activities abroad, and ours at home, heavy losses of life and property, full prisons and concentration camps are proof of such war activities. . . . Is it too little for the Allies?"[152]

Two different experiences—one abroad, one at home—also exacerbated the differences between Beneš the pragmatist and idealists within the resistance. The arrest, torture, and execution of their comrades—combined with the helplessness of their position and the Germanization measures—radicalized many members of the democratic resistance. The disaffected members spewed venom toward Hácha's compromising government and demanded that "all culprits, Czech and German . . . be punished" after the war, and that "public life . . . be cleansed of everyone who cares about himself more than the nation."[153] Correspondents demanded that London broadcast the names of Czechs who worked for the Gestapo or applied for German citizenship and warn them that the tables would turn some day.[154] Resistance fighters also spoke wildly of radical, postwar transformations in politics, the economy, and society. Although the resistance members realized that for the moment Great Britain remained their only hope, they had little faith in the West and liberal democracy. Hácha's government and its bureaucracy, said many on both the left and the right, must be purged; old parties and their old party leaders must be undone, replaced by an ill-defined "national unity" under Beneš's leadership.[155] Privately Beneš agreed, and he often spoke vaguely of a postwar revolution. World War II, he said, "will be a continuation, and in many cases the completion, of what had been started in the First World War. Great changes will take place in our country, not only economic but political."[156] He was sympathetic to many of ÚVOD's pleas for nationalizing big industry. He envisioned reducing the number of political parties, ensuring that a socialist bloc would be the strongest. Yet, fearful of upsetting Beneš's relations with the British, his interlocutor warned ÚVOD to tone down its revolutionary rhetoric.[157]

Nowhere were the tensions between the London exiles and the domestic resistance more apparent than with regard to the "German question" and the future makeup of Czechoslovakia. As Václav Kural reminds us, it was ÚVOD resistance fighters who first, and most fiercely, called for not only social revolution but also the expulsion of every German from postwar Czechoslovakia.[158] They claimed to be speaking for the nation. They justified their demands by pointing to the betrayals that led to Munich, Germanization measures, and the arrest and torture of their comrades. They also believed that expulsions constituted a legitimate form of nation-making, a notion that did not come from thin air. Indeed, their demands were very much in step with European thinking at the time. Before 1914 German, Russian, Ottoman, and Balkan governments had expelled thousands in order to validate national and territorial claims, and the Great War further convinced many in Europe that the problem of intractable and dangerous national minorities could best be "solved" by shifting, and sometimes killing, whole populations. During World War I the Ottoman Empire expelled and massacred most of its Armenian population; after the war almost a million Greeks were expelled from Turkey, on their way out of the country passing Turks from Greece heading in the opposite direction. Five years after the war's end the international community sanctioned the Greco-Turkish "population exchange" agreed upon in the Lausanne Treaty, which provided later "exchanges" with a model and a source of legitimacy.[159] From 1935 to 1938 the supranationalist Soviet Union arrested, deported, or executed about 800,000 people in an attempt to realize the principles of the nation-state within the empire.[160] In 1940 Beneš's Polish counterpart in London, too, demanded massive German expulsions following the hoped-for liberation.[161] Europeans lived in an age of population transfers and genocide when governments, in extreme moments, used violence and modern technology to create nationally homogeneous societies, ridding nation-states of troublesome, unassimilated

minorities. In the interwar period the morality of shifting whole populations was a matter of debate, not a given. Even the British Royal Commission, for example, saw in the Greco-Turkish case a potential model
for easing ethnic conflict in Palestine.[162] Throughout the war members
of the Czech underground, too, took note of the Lausanne Treaty when
speaking of expulsion plans.[163]

The European context made the expulsions thinkable, yet the road to
the postwar expulsions was neither straight nor predetermined. In their
reports to London, Czechs who were not members of the resistance rarely
made mention of calls to expel the Germans. In 1939 most of the democratic resistance as well as Communists at home and abroad still distinguished "good Germans" from Nazis.[164] "We must not aim for the physical destruction of Germany, but only to destroy the Nazi executioners,
industrial rulers, and capitalists. Our ally is the anti-Hitler opposition:
workers, a large percentage of the soldiers, Catholics, and others. Really,
not every German is the same," a group of young, left-wing intellectuals
declared in summer 1939.[165] "Nationalism leads us to the chauvinistic
delusion that would cause us to desire the extermination of all Germans," the underground newspaper Český kurýr warned. Elsewhere it
cautioned against "hysterical, chauvinistic" rantings.[166] A leading
Czech Social Democrat abroad, Jaromír Nečas, reminded Czechs in
summer 1940 that "among Germans there are many anti-Nazis," and he
called for a united front that included both.[167] On orders from Moscow,
whose government was still under the obligations of the Stalin-Hitler
pact of 1939, the underground Communist newspaper Rudé právo told
readers that "Hitler's clique is not the German nation." Instead, the
German nation (meaning the workers and peasants) was the "nation of
Liebknecht and Luxemburg," and the paper emphasized the Czechs'
long association with Austrian Germans.[168] Dispatches from Moscow to
the Protectorate demanded that Czech functionaries establish underground ties with their German comrades.[169] In fact, these dispatches
were in German, the language of the Comintern.

Although resistance fighters and communists alike were distinguishing between "good" and "bad" Germans, talk of expulsion hung in
the air as early as 1939. Several influential members of the underground—predominantly former military officers, Czechoslovak political
leaders, and even some Social Democratic intellectuals—were calling for
resettlement schemes aimed at creating nationally homogeneous political

units within Czechoslovakia. They also supported a partial expulsion of guilty Germans from postwar Czechoslovakia. All Germans who failed to prove "pro-Czechoslovak activities," estimated to be two million people, would have to go, one report to London demanded.[170] Beneš, too, wavered on the issue of massive expulsions and resettlement schemes as he toyed with numerous plans for postwar Czechoslovakia. Just before Munich and again in 1939 he proposed that a number of Germans be expelled from Czechoslovakia as compensation for territorial losses. Later he conceded to Czechoslovakia's leading German Social Democrat in London, Wenzel Jaksch, that rumors of mass expulsions, spurred by reports from the Protectorate, were floating around his offices, but he dismissed the plans as "foolishness." Both men later agreed in principle to Beneš's plans to decentralize the government, to create several purely German cantons along the borderlands, and to move people in order to eliminate language islands and other mixed communities. So-called Nazis would be shipped to Germany.[171] The lines separating the cantons, and the lines separating Czechoslovakia from its neighbors, remained to be drawn. "The question causing debate is one of borders," Beneš wrote to his brother. "But we will again have Germans and again have Slovaks."[172] For Beneš the state, and the old state borders, remained paramount.

But among the democratic resistance a significant shift in thinking occurred as a result of the frustrations and terrors that followed the fall of France. Now all Germans, and especially Sudeten Germans, were guilty of crimes perpetrated by the Nazi regime. More and more members of the resistance demanded that all Germans be expelled from a future Czechoslovakia. A tense back-and-forth between London and the home resistance ensued. ÚVOD leaders warned Beneš that among the rank and file the calls for violent, widescale revenge were growing. Beneš's proposal that Sudeten German Social Democrats join the State Council, which functioned as a weak "parliament-in-exile," provoked outraged responses from ÚVOD members, to which Beneš, mindful of his international standing, chided them for being unreasonable:

We cannot hold onto unrealistic hopes that we can simply destroy or wipe out three million Germans, as some of us naïvely believe. However, it is possible, and necessary, to count on the departure or expulsion of hundreds of thousands of compromised Nazis and the forced displacement of hundreds of thousands more [from the Czech-dominated interior] to the three German cantons, Austria, or Germany proper. But, such a displacement is unlikely to involve more than a total of one million. . . . The first question posed by any politically influential Englishman is "What do you want to do with your Germans?" And if the Americans decide to tamper with these things it will be even more difficult. All the same it is generally believed that we were wronged at Munich and that will help us greatly and allow us to formulate a program that is clear, firm, and for us advantageous, a program that is victorious but not one that is too unrealistic.

The response from home was swift and aimed at a particularly sensitive nerve—Beneš's fears that he lacked legitimacy at home. "We will beat [the Hitlerlites] so hard that the three damned cantons you thought up and for which the people will tear you to pieces will be somewhere near Berlin," one lieutenant colonel radioed. "We will see you in a Czechoslovakia without cantons." Cooperating with Sudeten Germans abroad and the Czech government in the Protectorate, others warned, could "make [your] return impossible." No one would be able to prevent Czechs from attacking Germans.[173] By mid-December 1940 both sides had cooled off. Beneš seemed more willing to compromise, partly thanks to the British, whose attitudes toward the Czechoslovak Germans had hardened, no doubt as a result of the Blitz. Beneš's relations with Jaksch became strained.[174] Then ÚVOD restated its position: a restored Czechoslovakia with pre-Munich borders and a substantially reduced number of Germans. It added demands no doubt inspired by Aryanization measures: the seizure of German property and the removal of Germans from positions of influence in the economy.[175] Among ÚVOD soldiers, "Germans out" remained the rallying call.[176]

Despite pre-Christmas promises to the State Council that "we shall not abandon our citizens of any nationality," Beneš conceded to ÚVOD in summer 1941 that the "maximum" solution would be restoration of Czechoslovakia along its pre-Munich borders and the complete expulsion of the Germans. But the domestic resistance, he warned, should be ready to accept a "minimum" solution, which included loss of territory and the expulsion of a mere one million Germans.[177] The resistance organization never accepted this compromise. While Beneš saw only a restored Czechoslovakia, his contacts in the Protectorate could imagine only the "maximum" solution. At the time all these visions seemed far off and perhaps a bit unrealistic. Nazi Germany dominated much of continent. Germans had almost complete control in the Protectorate, and the majority of Czechs passively accepted their role in the system. Now, more than ever, Czechs came to believe that their fates lay in the hands of foreign politics and the course of the war.[178] But unbeknownst to most of them, their fates, and the fates of their German neighbors, were already being decided amidst the crisscrossing of radio transmissions.

"We will remember 1940 as a time of profound humiliations and the ruthless strangulation of our nation," the underground newspaper *Český kurýr* wrote on the last day of 1940. Germans had almost complete control over the levers of state administration. Czech bureaucrats who could not speak German could lose their jobs. German leaders waged on all-out attack on Czech culture. Clubs were shut down. Czechs were still forbidden to attend university. Czech schools closed, replaced by German ones. Public signs had to be in German and Czech, with the former always on top. Germans assumed control over banks, heavy industry, and other sectors of the economy. In a little more than a year, *Český kurýr* concluded, the Nazi regime had done more to Germanize Bohemia and Moravia than post-1848 Habsburg absolutism could accomplish in ten.[179] As did many local Germans and Czechs, the editors of *Český kurýr* understood Nazi rule as yet another chapter in a long history of Czech-German nationality politics—small-scale battles for political, economic, and cultural superiority often centered on the borderlands. Amphibianism thrived, yet most chose to become "new Germans." The flow of history had apparently been reversed. Germans, it seemed, were ascendant.

Yet the early years of the Protectorate, and especially the months that followed the fall of France, also constituted a radical break with the past. Nationality politics, once centered on battles played out in civil and political society for political, cultural, economic, and demographic dominance along the borderlands, had been co-opted by the Nazi state. Just as significant, old economic structures and practices were undone as Göring and officials within the Reich Protector's Office pulled the Protectorate into Nazi Germany's Großraumwirtschaft. Reich German banks absorbed Czech ones. Reich German capital flowed into the Protectorate's economy, allowing Reich German enterprises to gain control of Bohemian and Moravian ones. The Göring Works used a variety of tactics, including bald threats of violence, to absorb the Protectorate's heavy industry. The Reich Protector's Office not only marked Jews but then robbed them, or allowed others to rob them. The Protectorate had become an integral part of an industrialized Central Europe within a vast, European "linked economy." When the customs barriers were finally lifted in October 1940, the Reich Protector's Office boasted that the event "represented an impressive milestone in the incorporation of the Protectorate of Bohemia and Moravia into the Greater German Reich."[180] Local Germans, and many Oberlandräte, concerned themselves foremost with Germanization goals that harked back to the nineteenth century. Neurath's office and Oberlandräte claimed that the transformations benefited all Germans, yet they were taking part in a Reich German project. Göring, loyalists like Bertsch, and Neurath's office had Nazified the Bohemian lands' economy according to a blueprint first designed in Berlin. The Protectorate, in many ways, had become one with Germany.

The fall of France also marked another turning point in the history of the Bohemian lands. Beneš, the most potent symbolic link with the First Republic, solidified his standing as the leader of a government-in-exile that could speak directly to the population. As he had done during World War I, Beneš lobbied British officials to support his plans for the establishment of Czechoslovakia. This time, however, the voices coming from home had a different tone. They demanded social reforms that would produce a different Czechoslovakia. By summer 1940 members of the domestic resistance were united in calling for the complete expulsion of the Germans from any future Czechoslovakia—a demand from which they would never retreat. Witnesses to Nazi-promoted Germanization and new forms of violence, they refused to distinguish any further between "good" Germans and "bad" Germans, between Reich Germans and Protectorate Germans. Although he embraced various forced resettlement schemes, Beneš espoused a pragmatism that clashed with a radicalized nationalism at home that he never quite understood. The tug-of-war would continue until summer 1945. In 1940 Czechs both at home and abroad, however, had crossed an important line. In the past Czech patriots employed a range of tactics to create and secure individual loyalties, to pull amphibians from one side or another. Now Czech loyalists determined to move whole populations in order to create national units without minorities.

Members of the Czech resistance were not alone among Europeans in seeing expulsions as a legitimate means of creating an ethnically homogeneous nation-state. While ÚVOD radioed its demands to London, Nazi leaders to the north of the Protectorate were driving hundreds of thousands of Poles and Jews eastward to make room for German settlers. Underground newspapers included detailed reports of the mass expulsions taking place in Poland, leading many Czechs to wonder if Nazi leaders had similar plans in store for them.[181] Indeed, in early spring 1940 Czechs in Prostějov near the former Polish border spread rumors to the effect that the Nazi regime planned to expel the Czechs eastward, spurring numerous people in the Prostějov region to apply for German citizenship.[182] The rumors turned out to be true. In October 1940 Hitler approved a plan, crafted by Neurath and Frank, to make half the Czechs into Germans and to expel the rest. The stated goal was to make the Protectorate entirely German—not just a part of a Großraumwirtschaft but a German Lebensraum filled entirely with Germans. Once again, this was a Nazi, not a Protectorate German, project, made both possible and impossible by Göring's successful economic transformations. Ironically, most influential Protectorate Germans vehemently opposed the plan, yet they unwittingly set in motion forces that led to its implementation.

3

Plans to Make the Czechs German

After the fall of France, Germans were ascendant in the Protectorate of Bohemia and Moravia. The region was fast becoming an integral and productive part of Germany's Großraumwirtschaft. Outward shows of Czech patriotism were rare. Behind the scenes, in the waning summer months of 1940, Neurath and Frank submitted two similar, and equally remarkable, memoranda to Hitler. In them they proposed making half the Czechs German and expelling the rest. The goal was total Germanization of the Bohemian lands, or, in Neurath's words, "that this space be stuffed with German people." Both men appeared to have turned their backs on old methods of "small-scale" work on the borderlands. Instead of holding and then pushing back the Czech demographic, political, cultural, and economic advances, they would simply wipe the Czech nation from the map. The very meaning of "Germanization," and with it the methods and goals of nationality politics in the Bohemian lands, would never be the same.

But why devise and execute a plan for total Germanization of the peaceful, productive Bohemian lands at all? Why plan for expulsions that were guaranteed to disrupt the economy? Why bother trying to make half the Czech population into loyal Germans? These questions are all the more puzzling, since Neurath and large sections of the Protectorate's administrative apparatus opposed large-scale expulsions. Moreover, Frank and many Protectorate German agents in the Intelligence Service found the idea of making the Czechs into Germans repulsive. If we view the Protectorate within the context of Nazi-occupied Europe, it becomes clear that Frank and Neurath's plans were not, as some historians have argued, a direct product of the Czech-German rivalry in the Bohemian lands. Instead, the plans were part of a continent-wide Nazi program of demographic and national engineering. The answer to the puzzle lay with vague, abstract, and powerful ideas dear to Nazi ideologues; events in Poland; a Gauleiter without a capital; and the radicalization of Nazi leaders in 1940. Other forces released by a resurgent Czech patriotism in 1941 then brought the executor of total Germanization plans, Reinhard Heydrich, to Prague.

Volk and Lebensraum

National Socialism, historian Martin Broszat wrote early in his career, was less an ideology than a "hodgepodge of terms picked up from all over," or as one contemporary wrote, "a grandiose vagueness" that gave its leaders much room for maneuver.[1] But there was at least one word, as Broszat pointed out, that remained central to Nazi politics and propaganda—the word "Volk." Its linguistic relatives could be chapter headings for a book on the various aspects of National Socialism: its people (*Volksgenossen*), their community (*Volksgemeinschaft* or *Volkskörper*), their place (*Volksboden*), the political movement (*Volksbewegung*), and the dissemination of ideas (*Volksaufklärung*). Its seeming omnipresence aside, the word "Volk" did possess meaning, if not several overlapping meanings.

Throughout the nineteenth century "Volk," a common term among liberal, Catholic, and Social Democratic politicians, was used to mean the "people," as opposed to the state and ruling elites. Under the Weimar Republic, National Socialists and right-wing students hijacked the word, employing the notion of Volk as the true, noble people to criticize and sap legitimacy from "those up there." As Cornelia Berning observes, right radicals defined "Volk" as something "earthy and natural as opposed to class," something that embodied for them a new way of comprehending and organizing the world. While the great nineteenth-century ideologies maintained that all humans were equal but divided by social categories, *völkisch* thinking saw the human race as fundamentally divided into categories whose peoples possessed varying degrees of worth. The Volk, again citing Berning, was a "historical [entity], destined by fate, a particular idea of blood and land" that suggested that history itself could be viewed as a continuous struggle among various

Völker. A healthy Volk needed to be purged of "foreign" elements, the mentally ill, homosexuals, "asocials," and, most of all, Jews, who were condemned as parasites and the embodiment of everything Nazi ideology despised most. And, of course, the Volk was "German," perhaps the slipperiest of words in the Nazis' vocabulary.[2]

Most important, as Broszat pointed out, a healthy Volk was homogeneous, united, and clearly circumscribed by boundaries separating it from its rivals. In one sense it referred to a politically united nation, but "Volk" suggested more. The primacy of the Volk collapsed the individual's thoughts and fate into that of the whole. Individuals, in fact, were little more than "parts of the whole." And, unlike their nineteenth-century predecessors, Nazis claimed that the expression of the Volk's will was found in its rulers, above all in the Führer. The state not only provided a political roof for the Volk but was its expression.[3] If, as Ernest Gellner writes, nationalism sought to make political and national units congruent, then National Socialism took this belief one step further. State and society, political and national (and racial) units, were to become one. In reality, of course, the Volksgemeinschaft and the Volk were just fictions, but these words suggested very real consequences. Not only did the Volksgenossen often use these terms instrumentally. Many Nazi officials were determined to make this fiction reality.[4]

The Volk inhabited an expanding or contracting "living space," or Lebensraum. The word "Lebensraum" marked a break from traditional political science and international law, suggesting that political borders were fluid and subject to the relative weaknesses or strengths of the states and Völker that were locked in a Darwinian battle for space. Part of the verbal repertoire among right-wing extremists in Wilhemine Germany, "Lebensraum" became a catchword across the right side of the political spectrum after World War I just as the word "Volk" began to be identified with a racially pure, organic whole. An expanding Lebensraum promised to restore Germany's national pride. The additional space would provide land for small-scale farmers who, untainted by urbanization and industrialization, would preserve all that was good and "German." German farmers would also raise agricultural production, allowing Germany to avoid the crippling shortages that had afflicted the population during World War I.[5] Finally, expanding borders also promised to provide space for a supposedly burgeoning population, a release from the national claustrophobia from which many Germans suffered.[6]

In the eyes of many nationalists, Germany was, borrowing from the widely popular political novel by Hans Grimm, a *Volk ohne Raum* (a Volk without space). Hitler made the acquisition of Lebensraum central to his foreign policy objectives. References to the "need for space" and Germany's rightful Lebensraum abounded, first in *Mein Kampf* and even more often in his unpublished "second book," written in 1928. "Politics is the carrying out of a Volk's struggle for existence," he wrote. "Foreign policy is the art of securing for a people the necessary quantity and quality of Lebensraum." "I have taken it upon myself . . . to solve the German problem of space," Hitler told his senior commanders in February 1939. "Note that as long as I live this thought will dominate my entire being." "Germany needs 1,320,000 square kilometers of Lebensraum," the Nazi propaganda sheet *Völkische Beobachter* proclaimed with suspicious accuracy, comparing the Volk's spatial growth to a small child's balloon that expands in the direction of least resistance.[7]

Nazi radicals, and most proponents of territorial expansion and population transfers before them, believed that the direction in which German Lebensraum was to expand was eastward. There, the *Völkische Beobachter* contended, a "filthy, yes indolent" Polish people "has no right to live where Germans belong."[8] Indeed, Poles and the Eastern Prussian lands remained the focus of German nationalist, and then Nazi, passions before World War II. Degrading phrases that hinted at the Poles' supposed disorganization and ineptitude (*polnische Wirtschaft, polnischer Reichstag*, literally "Polish economy" and "Polish parliament") suffused everyday speech. Max Weber's first important empirical work studied the displacement of German peasants by cheap Polish labor in eastern Prussia, which led him to call for "systematic colonization of German peasants on German soil" to hold back the "Slavic flood." Vociferous members of the Pan-German League drummed up protest against the intrusion of an "inferior" Polish culture, a disloyal minority, and, again, cheap Polish labor. Plans for the Germanization of schools and courts of law, and even wild talk of "national engineering" and "national redistribution," came to little, however. Schemes to entice German settlers to move to lands appropriated from Polish landowners attracted few takers. In the heady days following the treaty of Brest-Litovsk with Bolshevik Russia in 1918, German leaders drew up plans to resettle two million people in the East, but the end of the war prevented their implementation.[9]

World War I proved to be a watershed. Images of Germanizing the East flourished anew in Germany, this time within a wider, European context of "population transfers" and in the shadow of a humiliating defeat. German administrators and German generals stationed in the Ottoman Empire (including Neurath, who was then a councillor at the German embassy in Turkey) were well aware of deportations and massacres that left 1.5 million Armenians dead. "Who still talks nowadays of the Armenians?" Hitler asked rhetorically just before Germany attacked Poland.[10] When proposing the removal of Germans from Italian-controlled South Tyrol, Hitler cited the "success" of the Greco-Turkish "population exchange" and the internationally sanctioned Lausanne Treaty of 1923. For many Germans the war also added new ideological layers to visions of the East. The East was a place where German blood had been spilled; it was territory—13 percent of prewar Germany's land with 10 percent of its prewar population—stripped away and handed to the Poles by the Allies. More ethnic Germans waiting to come "home to the Reich" lived throughout the East. There, too, lived millions of Nazism's most disparaged bogeymen: the Jews. Beyond Poland lay its greatest political threat: Communism. Buoyed by "scientific" backing, the three aims of Hitler's Germany—the restoration of German national pride, the destruction of the Jews, and the defeat of Communism—could all be realized in the mythical East.[11] Finally, the experience of war, both on the front and at home, radicalized and intellectually transformed a whole generation of young, well-educated men who came to share common notions about the Volk, Lebensraum, the East, and population transfers. As idealists in the 1920s, they joined any number of right-wing political groups in the Weimar Republic before coming to dominate the SS. They included men like Reinhard Heydrich, chief of the SS's Intelligence Service and master of a whole array of security and criminal justice organs, and Heinrich Himmler, the head of the SS. These young men promised to transform Europe, and especially the East. "These new provinces," Himmler promised, "will be Germanic, blond provinces."[12]

Bohemia and Moravia, not Poland, came under German control first. In *Mein Kampf,* Hitler, having learned his racialist nationalism in fin-de-siècle Vienna, spewed much of his venom at the Czechs.[13] In 1937 he told then foreign minister Neurath and top military officials that, in the interests of extending Germany's Lebensraum, he intended to absorb both Austria and the Bohemian lands into Germany. The takeover of the Bohemian lands, he predicted, would result in additional foodstuffs for five to six million Germans. He declared that two million Czechs would be expelled and vaguely alluded to "the elimination of the Czechs."[14] Indeed, Alfred Rosenberg and other Nazi "experts" argued that demographic realities demanded that Czechs *and* Poles be expelled eastward to make room for healthy and productive German peasants, and by 1937 agricultural experts within the Nazi Party had drawn up secret plans to settle Germans in Bohemia and Moravia as part of a larger project of Germanizing the space.[15] "Bohemia and Moravia have belonged to the Lebensraum of the German Volk," Hitler's decree establishing the Protectorate stated.[16] Yet after the occupation of Prague, Ian Kershaw writes, even Hitler showed "remarkably little interest in the Czechs" after the peaceful occupation of the Bohemian lands. Instead he looked directly eastward from Berlin.[17]

Like so many Nazi leaders, Hitler turned his attentions to Poland in summer 1939. His hatred of the Poles was no doubt stoked, among other things, by the latter's diplomatic stubbornness. Despite a nonaggression pact in 1934 and spoils awarded after the Munich agreement, the Poles refused, in 1939, Hitler's offers to become a satellite state in a German-dominated Europe.[18] Other circumstances and structures further mitigated against expulsion plans in the Protectorate and opened the way for violence in Poland. In the East, first after the attack on Poland and then following the invasion of the Soviet Union, the chaos of war permitted massive expulsions, resettlement schemes, and genocide in the name of realizing ideological dreams. War did not come to the Protectorate; nor did it radicalize the political atmosphere as it did in Poland. In the Protectorate, members of the SS had less influence than in occupied Poland, hindering plans to move populations at will. Less radical leaders, like Neurath and the Oberlandräte, still held sway. Protectorate Germans, who thought more in terms of small-scale battles for territorial gain, predominated in the Intelligence Service. Western Poland, Alsace, and Lorraine had all been part of Bismarck's Germany, but not Bohemia and Moravia. The former Czechoslovakia possessed a more amorphous, more confused position within Nazi ideology. Perhaps most crucially, the Czechs, and the Bohemian lands, rarely elicited the same violent reactions that Poles provoked.[19] Thus, until the end of the war Poland remained the focus of Nazi energies and hatred, the place where visions of a racially homogeneous Volk expanding its Lebensraum could be realized. Yet Germanization policies in Poland and the Protectorate would remain intimately intertwined, and Protectorate leaders found themselves inevitably drawn into the maelstrom.

Expulsions and Short-Term Plans

Population schemes in the first year of the Protectorate's existence were relegated to the Land Office, a First Republic agency that had redistributed property following the government's land reform and had played a pivotal role in the Czechification of German borderlands. Under the Protectorate, Germanization measures taken by the same Land Office, now controlled by the Nazis, amounted to little. Shortly after arriving in Prague the Land Office's top official, SS man Curt von Gottberg, had promised quite openly that within ten years no land or property would remain in Czech hands. (Neurath, fearful of domestic repercussions, quickly dashed off a letter to Berlin demanding that von Gottberg be removed should such statements again leak to the public.) Von Gottberg's office absorbed Jewish property, state forests, and Czech-owned farmland, most of it earmarked for the construction of German settlements to connect German-inhabited areas to each other.[20] He was, however, unable to fulfill promises to link previously isolated language islands to each other and wider Germandom. Von Gottberg had counted on the arrival of 150,000 SS families, war veterans, and ethnic Germans from South Tirol and southeastern Europe, but almost five years after his arrival only a small fraction of that number had actually settled in the Protectorate. Economic integration and the establishment of administrative control remained paramount in the Protectorate. Poland, Hitler told Neurath, would receive priority when it came to ethnic German settlements. By the end of 1939 von Gottberg left the country in disgrace. The reasons are unclear. Perhaps he fell victim to bureaucratic intrigues by Neurath and other rivals. Rumors of financial impropriety swirled around his departure. His replacement, a civil servant from the Reich Ministry of Food, thought little of expulsion plans and promptly set out to purge the Land Office of SS men.[21]

To the north of the Protectorate, Germans in Poland executed fifty thousand people by the end of 1939, an orgy of violence perpetrated by ethnic German vigilantes and military personnel, including Waffen SS units and Heydrich's newly created SS Einsatzgruppen and Einsatzkommandos. "Fundamental cleansing" of "Jews, intelligentsia, clergy, [and] nobles" from western Poland, as Heydrich called it, eventually gave way to coordinated population policies.[22] The western third of Poland was divided among the two previously existing Gaue of East Prussia and East Upper Silesia and the newly created Reichsgaue of Danzig–West Prussia and Wartheland. All were headed by Nazi Party Gauleiter and incorporated directly into Germany. The middle third of Poland, or the General Government, was originally meant to be another protectorate. Instead, it devolved into a dumping ground for Poles, Jews, and Gypsies from western Poland. Later it became home to the regime's most murderous extermination camps. (The Soviet Union occupied Poland's eastern third according to terms agreed to in the Molotov-Ribbentrop Pact.) Göring quickly claimed the right to issue decrees related to economic policy in occupied Poland. Through the newly created Main Trustee Office East he claimed jurisdiction over all Jewish and Polish property. His real power, however, became diluted over time. The top Nazi leader in the General Government, Hans Frank, managed to prohibit the Main Trustee Office East from operating in his realm. The region's dominant figure, however, was SS head Heinrich Himmler.[23]

Just days after World War II had begun, Hitler told Reichstag deputies that Nazi Germany would "create a new ethnographic order; i.e. to resettle nationalities" within "better lines" in Poland, resulting in the "ordering of the entire Lebensraum according to nationality."[24] Hitler gave Himmler the job of settling Germans in the incorporated territories, filling German spaces with Germans and expelling the rest. As Reich Commissar for the Strengthening of Germandom Himmler hovered over a wide range of SS, state, and party organizations. One of the regime's most radical voices possessed, in theory, virtually unlimited power to fill the German Lebensraum with Germans and to expel non-Germans eastward. Himmler's right-hand man, and head of the SS-controlled Central Immigration Office and Central Resettlement Office, was Heydrich.[25] Treaties with the Soviet Union in 1939 and 1940 provided for the resettlement of thousands of Germans from the Baltics, Soviet-occupied Poland, and finally Bessarabia and Bukovina, former Romanian territories annexed by the Soviet Union. Thousands of Reich German administrators and volunteers, including many middle-class women eager to aid resettled ethnic Germans and to Germanize homes and local cultures, rushed into the newly occupied territories. The stage was set for dreams about the Volk, Lebensraum, and the East to be realized. According to a first "short-term plan" developed by Himmler and announced by Heydrich in November 1939, eighty thousand Poles and Jews were to be expelled eastward to make room for forty thousand Baltic Germans from the Soviet Union. Nazi authorities exceeded the goal, expelling almost eighty-eight thousand people eastward.[26]

The expulsions also inspired Nazi officials throughout Central Europe to begin searching for ways of realizing a second ideological dream: a "solution" to the "Jewish problem." Shortly after being named Reich commissar, Himmler expressly stated that his first priority would be to expel *all* Jews from the newly incorporated territories. Although exact numbers are difficult to ascertain, officials and vigilantes certainly targeted Jews for murder and expulsion.[27] In September 1939 Protectorate Oberlandrat Fiechtner dashed off a report to Prague complaining that Aryanization in his district had come to a halt. Gestapo agents had told the region's Jews that they had three weeks to evacuate Jihlava. It would be impossible, Fiechtner complained to Neurath, to find enough Treuhänder in time. The expulsions from Jihlava never happened. A month later, however, Adolf Eichmann's office rounded up and deported several thousand Jews from Vienna, Katowice in Poland, and Moravská Ostrava in the Protectorate to a "retraining camp" in Nisko, near the western edge of the General Government's Lublin district. From here many of the victims were marched to the eastern parts of the General Government.[28]

Grandiose, vague intentions crashed against the complications of moving whole populations like pieces of furniture. The Nisko project was complicating Himmler's other expulsion and resettlement schemes. Heydrich's Reich Security Main Office ordered Eichmann to abandon his deportation plans, and many of Moravská Ostrava's Jews were shipped home.[29] Himmler saw his plans in Poland bogged down by competition and overlapping jurisdictions within the SS and among the army and state ministries. With the exception of the Reichsgau Wartheland, where Nazi officials managed to expel more than 260,000 people between December 1939 and January 1941, Gauleiter put up dogged resistance to SS interference in their realms.[30] The planning was shoddy. Gauleiter Albert Forster of Danzig–West Prussia, locked in a battle with Himmler's SS for control of the deportation and resettlement schemes, complained to Goebbels of the "hair-raising organizational abuses during the evacuation of the Baltic Germans. These cry out to high heaven."[31] Ethnic Germans arriving from the East had to suffer both arrogant Reich German behavior and cold weather while huddled in makeshift winter camps. Polish sabotage and demands by the army led to a shortage of trains necessary to move Poles and Jews eastward. Many died along the way, cramped in small train cars. The army and economists close to Göring worried about the lack of workers and decreased production numbers. Deadlines passed, and a sense of failure loomed over SS officials. "Himmler is presently shifting populations. Not always successfully," Goebbels noted in January 1940.[32]

Victory in France sparked another wave of enthusiasm for measures to rid Europe of the Jews and for total Germanization plans, and not just in Poland. Among top Nazi leaders and demographic engineers the idea of expelling the Jews to the French colony of Madagascar became hotly discussed, although this plan, too, would eventually crash against reality, in this case the war with Britain.[33] In May 1940 Himmler penned a memorandum entitled "Some Thoughts on the Treatment of Alien Populations in the East," in which he laid out his plans for the "screening and sifting" of the inhabitants of the incorporated Poland and the General Government. Later that month, flush with the sight of British and French troops cornered at Dunkirk, Hitler met with Himmler and gave his approval to the memorandum. Shortly thereafter, a second "short-term plan" led to the expulsion of 158,200 more Poles and Jews from the incorporated territories to the General Government. Ethnic Germans from the General Government and parts of the Soviet Union traveled westward.[34] On September 25 Hitler told his top civilian administrators in the former French territories of Alsace and Lorrraine that both territories were to be "German, purely German" within ten years. Less than two months later Nazi officials expelled approximately seventy thousand people from the territories to Vichy France. More than seventy thousand who had escaped Alsace ahead of the Wehrmacht were forbidden to return.[35] Internal and external pressures to make the Bohemian lands entirely German weighed on the Protectorate leadership.[36] Finally, in October Hitler would approve Frank's and Neurath's plans for complete Germanization of the Protectorate. In the meantime a remarkable shift in Nazi policy had taken place. Poles, Czechs, and other non-Germans (but not Jews) could now become German, join the Volk, and inhabit its Lebensraum, provided that populations were properly "screened and sifted."

Making the Czechs German

The Protectorate, once ignored, began to attract the attention of Berlin's most powerful figures as the first short-term plan was coming to an end. Chief of the Reich Chancellery Heinrich Lammers, one of Hitler's closest advisers, began demanding monthly reports on the economic and political situation in the Protectorate. Party officials in the Protectorate began sending monthly reports to their superiors in Berlin. SS leaders, in particular, took a keen interest in the Protectorate, which had been excluded from Hitler's October 1939 decree allowing Himmler to reshape populations in Poland. In February 1940 Frank promised Heydrich a report on nationality politics in the Protectorate. (As head of the Intelligence Service Heydrich was no doubt already well informed.) Gestapo and Intelligence Service agents now sent regular reports to the SS's Race and Settlement Office. That summer five-member groups of students from Germany, Austria, and the former Czechoslovakia descended upon České Budějovice, Brno, Olomouc, and Jihlava. Their purpose, in the words of the Reich Protector's Office, was to "register the biological and social structure of each piece of property in the area," taking note, among other things, of the geography of Czech-German property, credit records, and the condition of the farmland. The raw data were to be used, presumably, to begin planning expulsion and resettlement measures aimed at building "population bridges" connecting German-inhabited areas.[37]

Pressure for German settlers and so-called population bridges arose from below as well. Throughout 1940 Nazi officials in Prague and Brno were especially vehement in their calls for German emigrants. The Brno Oberlandrat was worried about the lack of German workers in his region. Oberlandräte proposed settling Germans and building army bases along lines running from Vienna to Wrocław, Olomouc to the north, and along the Bohemian-Moravian border from Silesia down to Austria.[38] Measures first enacted by the Land Office in 1939 briefly gained new impetus. Protectorate officials provided financial incentives for Germans who had fled the First Republic in the 1930s to return. In April 1940 the regime claimed all the property of the former Czechoslovak state for the settlement of Germans from abroad. In July

1940 Frank told the Land Office to begin inventorying property for further settlements or for sale. By September 1940 Nazi officials in Jihlava, Olomouc, and Vyškov had removed more than eighty-six families from their homes to make room for Germans from Eastern Europe.[39] As in Poland, the settlement planning was shoddy. When, in September 1940, just four thousand German "returnees" from Bessarabia arrived at České Budějovice and Tábor, the Oberlandrat in charge had prepared accommodations for only fifteen hundred of them. The cost of housing and feeding the Bessarabian Germans strained the Oberlandrat's finances. The emigrants were filling up hotels, summer homes, and schools. The local Nazi Party chieftain endangered relations with the Church when he suggested that the new arrivals be housed in various Catholic institutions.[40]

Enthusiasm for population bridges, however, soon waned. Meanwhile in Poland, and in some ways more so in the Protectorate, economic and demographic realities inspired a remarkable shift: Germanization plans now included the expulsion of un-Germanizable "foreigners" *and* the assimilation of potential Germans. Himmler faced a simple arithmetic problem. "In 50–80 years 20 million German settlers should be living in the great settlement area in the East, and of these, 10 million farmers with eight to ten children each," he bragged to SS officials in Poznán in 1940.[41] But he knew that the number of Germans being resettled thanks to treaties with Italy and the Soviet Union numbered in the hundreds of thousands. Only about two million ethnic Germans lived in southeastern and northeastern Europe combined.[42] Even plans to give land to war veterans and encourage emigration from the Reich would fail to realize such absurd projections. Worse, by January 1940 it had become clear that the Reich, rather than being overpopulated, lacked bodies. Especially wanting were agricultural workers, and in that time officials began sending Poles to work as slave laborers in the Reich, some of whom had first been transplanted from the occupied territories into the General Government. By 1944, 1.7 million Poles—and almost 6 million other "foreign" civilians and prisoners of war—were working in the Reich.[43] The Nazis' claims that the Germans were a Volk without its space ("Volk ohne Raum") became more difficult to justify once new territories were annexed to the Reich. In fact, the opposite soon proved to be true. The Reich now began to include much space but not enough (German) Volk.[44]

Priorities, as well as certain ideological principles, would have to be modified. Before World War II Hitler had been adamant in stating that assimilation leads to a biological weakening of the Volk. "Germanization," he wrote in *Mein Kampf*, "can be applied to soil and never people." The Nazi movement, he declared in his unpublished "second book" before the war, "knows no Germanization . . . but only the expansion of our own people. The movement will never see subjugated, so-called Germanized Czechs or Poles as a strengthening of the nation or of the Volk." The only option, he continued, would be "either to isolate these racial elements in order to prevent . . . contamination . . . or . . . to remove them entirely."[45] Facing a lack of German bodies for his German Lebensraum in Poland, however, Himmler determined that at least some members of non-German minorities would have to be made German. The SS leader's May memorandum called for the "re-Germanization" of racially suitable Poles, Ukrainians, Belorussians, Kashubians, and other non-Jewish minorities, adding that "the basis of our considerations must be to fish out of this mush the racially valuable, in order to bring them to Germany for assimilation." The rest of the population would be driven into the General Government, where they would become a leaderless mass of workers.[46] That summer the first "re-Germanizable" Poles were transported to Germany, where they were assigned to work in factories, on farms, and in the homes of well-placed SS and Nazi Party officials.[47] On September 12, 1940, Himmler circulated a memorandum declaring that a "maximum of one million" people from western Poland—out a total population of almost nine million "foreign Völker" inhabiting the region—were to be Germanized. Racial experts from the SS's Central Emigration Office were to test all candidates for "the recovery of German blood" from the "standpoint of race, health, and politics." At first a simple plan to make room for Germans by expelling and murdering non-Germans, Nazi Germanization plans now included a third element: the Germanization of racially suitable foreigners using the techniques of what Himmler termed "racial weeding out."[48]

A similar logic was at work in the Protectorate, where talk of Germanization as assimilation began to swirl in spring 1940. As Hitler had made clear, the Bohemian lands belonged squarely within the Germans' Lebensraum. Before coming to power he had said that any Germanization of the Czechs was impossible, and as late as 1937 he spoke only of expelling at least a portion of the population. Yet in the Protectorate, as in

Poland, officials quickly concluded expulsions alone would be impossible if Bohemia and Moravia were to become entirely German. Frank, in his Germanization proposal to Hitler, ticked off a long list of arguments against expelling all the Czechs:

a) [T]here is no area where they can be settled; b) there are no Germans who could immediately fill up the vacated area; c) this highly civilized heartland of Europe, with its easily disrupted economic and transportation systems, will not stand any upsetting of its function or a vacuum [of people]; d) human beings are capital of the Reich and we cannot do without the force of seven million Czechs in the new Reich; e) the probable shock on the other nations of the South East would be undesirable.[49]

Neurath was more blunt: "The most radical and theoretically most perfect solution of the problem would be the complete expulsion of all Czechs from the country and its settlement by Germans. This solution, however, is impossible because there are not enough Germans for the immediate occupation of the territories which belong in the foreseeable future to the Greater German area. [Expelling all the Czechs] would leave the fields fallow and the cities deserted."[50] There simply would never be enough colonists to replace the Czechs.[51] The war effort, and the Czechs' contribution to that effort, made the total expulsion of the Czechs impossible. The Protectorate was due to enter the Reich Customs Union in October. The Protectorate had become intricately entangled within the economic, industrial, and commercial webs of Germany's Großraumwirtschaft. As Frank wrote elsewhere, the war provided high officials with new opportunities to realize ideological goals, and, on the other hand, tempered more radical solutions to the "Czech problem."[52] The Czechs could not go. Nor, in the view of many proponents of total Germanization, could Bohemia and Moravia—a German space with a German regime, German economy, and German history—remain inhabited by non-Germans. Thus, the Czechs would have to become Germans. Ideological principles were to be modified, thanks to a useful interpretation of racial mixture.

Racists from Arthur comte de Gobineau to Houston Stewart Chamberlain, from Adolf Hitler to contemporary right-wing extremists in Europe and the United States, have shared one belief: racial mixing brings decline. One need only look at the Protectorate Germans to see that, their Reich German rivals deviously explained. For instance, the Ober-landrat in Jičín described the Germans in his area as "sickly" looking and wondered if they could make a biological contribution to Germandom at all. Biological decline, his Plzeň colleague suggested, might explain why Protectorate Germans could not raise their children as Germans. The infusion of "foreign elements" endangered the German Volk; yet, others argued, mixing had the opposite effect on "foreign" peoples. Thanks to centuries of mixing with Germans, the Slavs, and the Czechs in particular, seemed to possess that magic substance that made Germans special and superior. Mixing threatened to destroy the Germans, but it also made Czechs into potential Germans.[53]

Indeed, the ideological ground for making Czechs into Germans had been tilled before 1940.[54] Much of the work was done by scholars based at the German University in Prague, a leading center for research on "racial hygiene" in Nazi-occupied Europe. In the first two years of the Protectorate's existence, few scholars were more influential than Karl Valentin Müller. Born in northern Bohemia just before the turn of the century, Müller had received his doctorate in social anthropology from Leipzig University and had studied at Dresden University before coming to Prague's German University in 1939. Once there, he founded a "social-anthropology and biology of nations" department and assumed a post as Frank's special adviser on racial affairs.[55] In a new journal committed to studying nationality and race, *Deutsche Volksforschung in Böhmen und Mähren* (roughly, German Volk-Research in Bohemia and Moravia), Müller made a long-winded, jargon-laden, but highly influential case for large-scale assimilationist measures. He accepted as an opening premise that racial mixing could be faulted for the weakening of German blood. And like his predecessors, he believed the the evil force was modernization, or, more precisely, urbanization, which threw together various races while stripping them of their ties to the land. But, he stated, this historical development also meant that those with whom the Germans have mixed, most notably the Slavs, have in turn gained in biological terms. Urbanization, he argued, had had another consequence—it infected city dwellers with modern ideas, such as Czech nationalism, which separated Czechs and Germans culturally while, ironically, mixing them biologically. Quoting the historian and Czechoslovak foreign minister Kamil Krofta, Müller contended that at the end of the eighteenth century, when the Czech language and culture was about to die out, Germans outnumbered Czechs five-to-three. Now that ratio was reversed. German blood, however, remained and formed the basis of a person's fundamental being. To cinch his case he quoted other Czech writers, including the positivist historian Josef Pekař: "In the course of hundreds of years we have quite often mixed with Germans, have absorbed much German blood, have fundamentally altered our racial character." He even quoted Peroutka, who was, by this time, languishing away in a concentration camp: "Our nature and our character have not always followed in a clear line. . . . It is my belief that we are in our ways much more similar to the Germans than we want to admit."[56]

Through summer 1940 Müller continued his research into the Germanizability of the Czechs. With each month his ideas found increasing acceptance among academics and Nazi officials in the Protectorate. Following Müller's first article in *Deutsche Volksforschung in Böhmen und Mähren,* a number of studies attempting to identify and describe the "national geography" of the region found their way onto the journal's pages.[57] The Oberlandrat in Prostějov claimed that the Czechs' blood, thanks to intermixture with German blood, was "some of the best in the whole Slavic area." Oberlandrat Molsen conceded that mixing had dulled German nationalist feeling in his region; yet mixing had created so-called Czechs who "in their racial and ethical worth do not appear to be that bad." Lacking assimilationist measures, a "worthy section of the [German] population would be irrevocably lost," he wrote.[58] "One is continually amazed at the number of blond-haired people with intelligent faces and pleasing bodies," Neurath wrote in fall 1940. The regime needed only to separate the "racially unusable" elements and, along with the anti-Nazi Czech intelligentsia, "toss [them] aside." In making the same argument, Frank quoted Müller's arguments and statistical data almost verbatim. Czechs and Germans were so mixed, he concluded, that they were "racially on the same level."[59]

The Politics of Germanization

Ideas about the Volk and its Lebensraum—tempered by economic and demographic realities, political pressures from outside the Protectorate, and the language of racial mixing—made the creation of Frank and Neurath's proposal possible. Yet in summer 1940 there were still many structural barriers to the creation of a Germanization plan in the Protectorate. Other ideological options remained. In April 1940 the head of the Racial-Political Department within the Nazi Party sent a twenty-six-page pamphlet entitled "Racial-Political Guiding Principles Regarding Politics with Foreigners in the German Reich" to the Reich Protector's Office. Addressing the "Polish and Czech questions," he repeatedly emphasized the dangers of "untrue *Umvolkung*," meaning "the sole penetration into völkisch life by assuming the language, political biases, and cultural forms of another Volk while being able to grasp and hold onto the spiritual principles of his way of life and his own *Volkstum*." With the acquisition of new territories in the East, he continued, the possibility that most Slavs would be only superficially assimilated posed a potentially lethal danger to the German Volk. Such a development "would in the long run destroy and dissolve our spiritual and creative strength and allow the spirit of our Volk to become 'Slavic.'"[60] Shortly after the invasion of Poland another racial expert warned his colleagues and German leaders that "bastardized" Germans in the East could weaken "German national strength [*Volkskraft*] and cultural abilities," adding that the Reich Germans did not need a "bastard people with Polish character and Polish cultural ineptitude."[61]

A second danger was that Czechs and other Slavs benefited from German blood, and that its combination with "Eastern" blood could produce a potent and dangerous mixture. Hitler was just one of many Nazis who had contended that mixing with Slavs spelled doom for the Germans. In 1930 Alfred Rosenberg claimed that the Hussite Wars were begun by Czechs who possessed a large portion of Alpine-Dinarian blood. Their fatal mistake was to rally the racially inferior Czech masses to revolt against the Catholic Church. (Rosenberg claimed that the skull of Jan Žižka, the most brutal of generals during the Hussite Wars, betrayed his Eastern or half-Asian racial origins.) During the Munich crisis, the infamous Nazi propaganda sheet *Der Stürmer* (literally, "the one who storms") employed these claims to stir up fear of the Czechs. Separate articles by Sudeten German agitator Rudolf Jung and a leading racial expert argued that the combination of "Eastern" or "Jewish" trickery with German blood made the Czechs extremely dangerous to the German Volk, especially when the Czechs were united. Opponents of "screening and sifting" had ample ideological ammunition on their side.[62]

Nor did total Germanization find many adherents among Protectorate Germans who had dedicated their lives to fighting, not assimilating, the

Czechs. Although many true Nazi believers existed among them, Sudeten German patriots radicalized by World War I generally spoke a different language than men like Heydrich and Himmler. Their battles for Lebensraum consisted of piece-by-piece struggles for land and property on the Czech-German borderlands. They proudly bore the label of bearers of culture (*Kulturträger*) charged with educating the backward Slavs, or they fashioned themselves as warriors on the front lines trying to hold back Slavic incursions. Sudeten German interwar historians, inspired by Viennese professor Othmar Spann, consistently harked back to a mystical medieval German empire that included the Bohemian crownlands. Indeed, Henlein and many of the early Sudeten German political activists had espoused a "spiritual" understanding of Germanness—that to be German meant to feel German, to be one with the larger Volk.[63]

Protectorate Germans in the Intelligence Service warned their Reich German superiors that Czechs would never "feel" German and that "only fear of the Reich's instruments of power keeps the Czechs in a position of external loyalty." Worse, Czechs were well versed in feigning obedience and playing dumb in order to obtain certain benefits while still engaging in "passive resistance" to the regime—"playing Schwejk," the "good soldier" in Jaroslav Hašek's popular novel. Czechs were so good at "playing Schwejk," in fact, that Reich Germans had been fooled into believing that tensions between the two nationalities were entirely the fault of Sudeten German chauvinism. Giving the Czechs rations on par with Germans, exempting them from the draft, and even fraternizing with them had been enough. To make them part of the German Volk after nearly a century of nationality battles seemed unconscionable.[64] Frank's hatred of the Czechs had been quite public. In 1939 Frank had envisioned a Bohemia and Moravia dominated by Germans and German interests and favored expelling members of the Czech intelligentsia, but he did not envision expelling or assimilating large numbers of Czechs, who instead "must rediscover their true mission in the Central European area."[65] Heydrich, upon receiving Frank's proposal, could not resist a sarcastic comment: "To start, we must take note of the surprising fact that SS-Gruppenführer Frank, who up to now had demanded a radical politics of destruction toward the Czechs, has suddenly [come out in favor of] far-reaching if not complete assimilation of the Czech element."[66] Although their politics had much in common,

Reich and Protectorate Germans envisioned territory, nation, and their ultimate political goals quite differently.

Neurath's transformation was no less remarkable than Frank's. Hardly a committed Nazi ideologue, the aristocratic conservative had urged caution and compromise with the Czechs in the face of Frank's chauvinism. Below Neurath on the administrative pyramid, Oberlandräte warned against radical action that could spur resistance, hurt the economy, and disrupt the smooth functioning of their local administrations. Although many Oberlandräte favored the creation of German population bridges, they also favored "small-scale work" that would, gradually, reinforce language islands and push back the language borders. "In time of war there are not only limitations on financial possibilities, but . . . the question of securing people—that is, the necessary flood of new German blood," Fiechtner wrote in September 1940. "There exists the danger," the Oberlandrat in Zlín warned, "that a grounded reality will be left behind to be replaced by an excursion into the realm of fantasy."[67] The Foreign Office in Prague agreed with the "integration of the Bohemian-Moravian space into the Greater German Reich" but urged a more gradual approach: "In one or two generations the Czech Volk will be relegated to the status of historical curiosity (like the Bretons in France, [or] the Wends in Lausitz)." For inspiration they looked to Bismarck's policies toward Bavarian particularists.[68] Indeed, vast resistance to total Germanization plans existed within and at the very top of Protectorate structures. In April the leading Protectorate officials had agreed that a "solution" to the "Czech problem" would have to wait until the end of the war.[69]

Not ideology but interagency rivalry, which created an internal, radicalizing dynamic, eventually brought Frank and Neurath to their total Germanization proposals in September 1940. The unlikely trigger for these events came from a petty Gauleiter without a capital, Hugo Jury. Jury, like Hitler, was a product of turn-of-the-century German chauvinism in Central Europe. Born in Moravia, he obtained a medical degree at the German university in Prague. After World War I he moved to St. Pölten in Austria, where he specialized in the treatment of tuberculosis, a disease he had contracted while a medic on the front lines. He had been personally acquainted with the Pan-Germanist party leaders Georg von Schönerer and Karl Hermann Wolff, and in 1931 he joined the Nazi Party in Austria, which earned him a two-year prison sentence.

In 1938 he joined the SS, and that May Hitler named him head of a newly created Nazi Party administrative unit in Austria, the Gau Upper Danube. A year later Hitler stretched the boundaries of his and three other Gaue across the Protectorate's borders. Jury's jurisdiction now included much of Moravia, including his home town.[70]

The ambitious lung specialist was soon disappointed, however. Gauleiter had little influence in the Protectorate. Party members helped build schools, register Germans, and agitate against the Czechs at the local level, but their superiors were forbidden to engage in any form of governance, including anything that involved the Czech population. Because party administrative boundaries cut across Protectorate borders, bureaucratic confusion reigned. Nor, until 1940, could Gauleiter present a unified front in Prague. Austria, much of occupied Poland, and most of the Sudetenland had been divided into Reichsgaue, where men like Henlein had near dictatorial powers over Nazi Party and state administrative apparatuses. In summer 1939 party members and other Nazi officials had openly questioned the viability of the Protectorate, but by the end of the year Hitler quashed such suggestions, telling Neurath that, for the moment, the Protectorate would remain in its current form.[71] Injury heaped upon insult for Hugo Jury. Although his offices were based in Vienna, Vienna was its own Gau (Fig. 3.1). Thus began his campaign to obtain a base of operations in Brno. In Brno he could have a proper capital, enjoy heightened prestige, and, he argued using language dear to Himmler and other SS population planners, form a "dynamic center" from which he could Germanize Moravia. "What was German will once again become German," he proclaimed in the Protectorate's official propaganda sheet.[72]

In 1940, just as support for total Germanization began to gain momentum, a political storm, conjured up around questions regarding the Protectorate's viability and its leaders' ability to Germanize their realm, reached fever pitch.[73] Jury was among the most vocal. As the newly appointed head of the Party Liaison Office in Prague, he obtained a foothold within the Reich Protector's Office. He also had contacts in Berlin, among them Deputy Chief Martin Bormann, one of a handful of men who had Hitler's ear. In summer 1940 Jury prepared for Berlin a memorandum. The fault of the Protectorate, he told his readers, was that it preserved the unity of the Czechs. (Here he was not alone. Even Frank's second-in-command had warned that the Protectorate might become a "Czech reservation . . . a compact Czech mass where a feeling of strength,

Figure 3.1 Nazi Party Gaue in East-Central Europe. Map by Philip Schwartzberg.

and with it the thoughts of its own state, is imminent.") Better to split the chauvinistic Bohemian Czechs from their more apathetic Moravian countrymen, improve the German numbers, and break up the unity of the Czechs. Now was the time to act. The fall of France and the "approaching defeat of England" had given the Reich a new independence to achieve ideological goals. To the northeast, "clear lines had been created" with the destruction of Poland; but the Protectorate, a "wedge of Slavdom deep in the heart of Germany," remained. Drastic changes, he conceded, could not be expected during the war, but a preliminary decision could do much for future political, governmental, and scientific planning in the area. By the end of August Jury was prepared to send to Berlin a detailed plan for the reorganization and Germanization of Bohemia and Moravia. But Neurath and Frank got the Führer's attention first.[74]

Openly stating his knowledge of the Gauleiter's intentions, Neurath's missive to Hitler claimed that the Protectorate could achieve the "clear and unambiguous goal" of Nazi rule in Bohemia and Moravia: "its complete incorporation into the Reich" and "the inhabitation of this area with German men and women." Only the Protectorate, he and Frank argued, could offer a centralized, unified approach to the Germanization of the Czechs. Germanization policies needed to emanate from Prague, the region's cultural and political capital.[75] On October 1, in Berlin, Hitler met with Neurath and Frank. He told the two men that, at least until the end of the war, the Protectorate would not be dismantled. He also agreed with Neurath and Frank that, although half the Czech population would be expelled, the other half might be assimilated into the German Volk. Both tasks would be carried out through the Reich Protector's Office.[76] Jury continued to dream of a more powerful Gau and to fix his sights on Brno. In 1943 he taunted Frank: "As you perhaps know, the Führer was in my Gau three weeks ago. I used the opportunity to touch on the question of my Gau's capital, and received from the Führer . . . an assurance that Brno will be the Gau's capital in the future."[77] It never came to pass.

Hitler seemed to have changed his opinions about the Germanizability of the Czechs and Poles. Although he still considered Czechs a dangerous influence on the German Volk, in 1942 calling them a "foreign body" that must be completely removed from Bohemia and Moravia, in 1941 and 1942 he lauded the Czechs' work ethic and discipline. And in 1942 he stated that up to half the Czechs had Nordic blood.[78] Heydrich became even more intimately involved in Germanization plans in the Protectorate. Several weeks before Hitler's decision about the Protectorate, and one day before Himmler's September memorandum regarding re-Germanization in Poland, Heydrich dictated to his secretary a response to Frank and Neurath's proposal. The future of the Protectorate lands, he argued, depended upon what percentage of the Czech population was un-Germanizable. Although he argued that the term "Protectorate" should be replaced with "reservation," he concluded that the current structure should remain in place "until the whole space can be cleared of the remaining [un-Germanizable] Czechs."[79] Not long after sending the memorandum to the head of the SS's Race and Settlement Office, Heydrich dispatched an SS racial expert to conduct a study of the Protectorate's population. Drawing on information from interwar conscription records, Dr. Walter König-Beyer wrote a forty-two-page report for Heydrich and top Protectorate officials, affirming Frank and Neurath's claims that over half the Czech population could be assimilated. "From a racial point of view," his calculations of height, weight, eye color, and other physical characteristics determined, the Czech nation was not a "foreign body" in relation to the Germans. Instead, making the Czechs German was necessary not only in order to take control of the Bohemian and Moravian territory but also for "the rewinning of racially valuable German blood predominant in the Nordic and Dinarian race." Beyer claimed that most Czechs were no more than Germans who spoke another language and possessed a "false" historical consciousness. They could, and must, be made Germans, he concluded. König-Beyer, in fact, contended that the Czechs possessed more "German blood" than did their Sudeten German rivals, who had been weakened by a long history of living in cities, mixing with Jews, and even falling under the evil influence of foreign-blooded Jesuits.[80]

The debate about whether or not the Protectorate would be completely Germanized was over. Other questions remained unanswered. Heydrich wondered what would become of the un-Germanizable Czechs. Allowing them to remain in Bohemia would compromise the goal of making this "space" German, yet no dumping ground, like Poland's General Government, existed.[81] In his meeting with Neurath and Frank, Hitler declared that "mongoloid" types and the Czech intelligentsia could not become Germans. Both groups, along with anyone who resisted assimilation, would either be "eliminated" or expelled.

How these people were to be selected, and who, precisely, was to do the selecting, was unclear. Nor was it clear what made a German.[82] Frank's second-in-command, Kurt von Burgsdorff, agreed with the principle that racially worthy Czechs were to be "absorbed into the German Volk" while the racially inferior and politically unreliable should be expelled or "rendered harmless," but he warned against "objective" racial testing. Such a "purely theoretical separation" of Czechs and Germans, and its attendant "process of assimilation [Umvolkung]," he wrote, is easy in the abstract but "most difficult when it comes to practical implementation." Instead, other methods that transformed cultural symbols, raised wages, and brought Czechs "into the rhythm of German life" would prove more effective.[83]

Timing and pace were issues as well. "What we are dealing with here," Burgsdorff argued, "is a process that demands generations [of work] and requires careful preparation."[84] Twice in 1941 officials in the Reich Protector's Office eschewed suggestions that "Czech" children with German Reich citizenship be required by law to attend German schools. To require so, one official warned, risked a political backlash. The schools should attract students based on their own merit. Besides, he argued, children "will be rushing into German schools after the war."[85] In autumn 1940 Germany remained at war with Britain, and in October Wehrmacht troops entered Romania. The threat of war with the Soviet Union loomed. Thus, keeping the Protectorate economy functioning and maintaining productivity in Protectorate factories mitigated against radical Germanization measures. Indeed, as the chairman of the Federation of Industries in Prague observed, expelling the Czechs would be tantamount to committing an act of self-mutilation:

> The Czech nation, which inhabits the area of the Protectorate of Bohemia and Moravia as a coherent whole, is not simply a sum of individuals but rather an organism, which simultaneously constitutes an integral part of the Greater German and future European economic area, in which it has to fulfill special functions. . . . This is the main reason for the fact that it is not possible simply to deport the Czech nation in its entirety, as the resulting vacuum could have very unfavorable consequences for the whole of the Greater German Reich. The process of Germanization must rather proceed in such a way that the work of the entire organism will not be disturbed in any way, neither in the field of politics, culture, or ethics, nor in the field of the economy.[86]

Oberlandräte had spent the entire year shoring up their own power and improving relations with the local Protectorate German population. Like many powerful figures within the Reich Protector's Office, they still supported "small-scale national work" in favor of disruptive population engineering plans.[87] Oberlandräte and party members still determined who was allowed to enter the German Volk. Within the Reich Protector's Office radical Protectorate Germans around Frank demanded more repressive measures against the Czechs, but moderates around Neurath still held sway.[88] Neither seemed interested in making the Czechs into Germans. Gradualism, and perhaps the shelving of total Germanization, seemed to be winning the day again. From the outside, too, pressure for the total Germanization of the Protectorate subsided, but only temporarily.

Acting Czech and Going Hungry

Within the framework of a third short-term plan devised in December 1940, Heydrich hoped to deport one million inhabitants of incorporated Poland to the General Government. Only 238,500 were deported before the operation bogged down in March when Himmler's Reich Commissariat issued a stop order on all deportations. Officials needed the trains for another grand project: the attack on the Soviet Union, which began in June 1941.[89] Nazi leaders steeled themselves for a battle with two ideological enemies, the Communists and the Jews.[90] The SS's power and influence grew, too, and not just in the East. In September 1941 Hitler appointed Heydrich acting Reich protector in Bohemia and Moravia. Riding another wave of enthusiasm following military victories, Heydrich promised to revive and execute Germanization plans for the Protectorate. He also inflicted upon its inhabitants a terror heretofore unimaginable in Bohemia and Moravia. Ironically, however, Hitler's reasons for appointing Heydrich had less to do with Germanization policy than with a need to quell popular unrest in the Protectorate. Energized by Germany's attack on the Soviet Union, its inhabitants were acting Czech again—a development quickly seized upon by Protectorate Germans keen to depose Neurath. A pathetic party leader, Hugo Jury, had triggered the development of Germanization plans in the Protectorate. Beneš, Czech patriots, and Protectorate Germans in the Intelligence Service now set in motion events that brought Heydrich, a determined proponent of total Germanization, to Bohemia and Moravia.

Months before Germany launched its attack in June, rumors of war with the Soviet Union were rife in the Protectorate. At the end of 1940 Neurath warned Oberlandräte to expect dramatic changes in German-Soviet relations by spring, a message that the regional leaders then passed on to those below them. That same month, Nazi Party propaganda launched a new wave of verbal attacks against the Soviet Union. Czechs, they said, should fear the Soviets; Germans should fear the consequences of losing the war. Frank told a crowd of loyalists that he would rather see total destruction than the reestablishment of the Czechoslovak state and a free Czech nation.[91] Shortly thereafter he threatened a new wave of repression against former Czechoslovak legionnaires, bringing Czech patriotic anger, one London informant reported, "near the boiling point." Although widescale terror and arrests did not follow, arrests of top Sokol leaders continued throughout the spring.[92]

Arrests aside, the rumors sparked a renewed sense of optimism among Czechs in London and in the Protectorate. Beneš relayed a message to Eliáš that by April the United States would certainly enter the war, thereby eventually drawing in the Soviet Union. Germany would fall, he predicted, by spring 1942 at the latest. Members of ÚVOD also stared eastward, divining Soviet intentions from the course of events abroad. The German and Italian occupation of Greece and Yugoslavia in April 1941 surely meant that a German attack on the Soviet Union was imminent. Eventually ÚVOD began to gather more concrete indications of German plans and, just as with the attack on Great Britain the previous year, predicted the Germans' intentions. Correspondents noted large numbers of trains heading to Poland; the Military Cartographic Institute in Prague, another claimed, was copiously printing maps of Soviet territory. The attack was certain, others said, even if the date was not. On June 20 Beneš relayed a message to one of the underground's vital spies in the German military's counterintelligence service, Paul Thümmel, begging for news of a concrete date. Two days later German tanks were racing eastward toward Moscow.[93]

The attack electrified resistance movements, many Protectorate inhabitants, and, most of all, Beneš. "[He] now has only Russia on his mind," Foreign Minister Jan Masaryk told his colleagues. "We must hold him, so that he won't fly off to the sky."[94] In summer 1940 ÚVOD had established regular contacts with a Soviet attaché in the Prague consulate just before Beneš's agents began sharing intelligence information with their Soviet counterparts in Istanbul. Before the attack Beneš had sent a high-ranking military mission to Moscow. If information about the Germans' attack plans was shared with the Soviets, it did not seem to have had an effect on Stalin. These contacts, however, did lay the groundwork for a strong relationships between the Czechoslovak government abroad and Stalin's Soviet Union. In July Stalin joined Great Britain in fully recognizing Beneš's government. Beneš's eyes remained fixed on Moscow until the end of the war.[95]

With his eye on this prize, and eager to protect Czechoslovakia's image among powerful Allied circles, Beneš shifted his position toward the Protectorate's Czech government and popular resistance in his homeland. He first sought to distance himself from Hácha, whose anti-Communist declarations and quisling appearance threatened to compromise Beneš's legitimacy among the Soviets. He suggested to Eliáš and Hácha that they should resign. Better, he said, that "the worst riff-raff takes the leadership, as in Croatia, or if the Protectorate and its autonomy are completely suppressed" than to have respectable Czechs cooperating with Germans. He told ÚVOD, for the first time, that important position-holders in the Protectorate would be purged after the war. To the chagrin of Beneš and ÚVOD leaders, Eliáš responded that he was needed to prevent further bloodshed. Hácha did not respond at all. Beneš, who had preached calm before the attack, now demanded that Czechs do their part for the war effort. He told resistance organizations to step up their activities: "It is necessary to pass from theoretical plans and preparations to deeds. . . . In London and Moscow, we have been bluntly reminded that the disruption or at least a substantial reduction of the war industry in the Czechoslovak territory would at this very moment hit the Germans severely. . . . Our situation would definitely appear in an unfavorable light if we . . . [did not] at least keep in step with the others." That autumn, the British and the Soviets began dropping parachutists into the Protectorate. The British intelligence service began training Czechoslovak army troops in guerrilla warfare. Czechoslovakia's reputation abroad, crucial to the renewal of his state, had become Beneš's blinding obsession—a goal that would justify sacrificing thousands of his countrymen.[96]

The Czechoslovak Communist Party breathed new life, too. "Our time has come," one Communist leaflet began. "Fascist barbarians out of our fatherland! Carry out all kinds of sabotage! Prepare for a general strike! Everything for the victory of the Red Army and for the freedom of our homeland!" Now, instead of advocating class struggle, *Rudé právo* called for a united, national fight against fascism that included "the Sokol warrior, the Benešite, the democrat, the socialist, the communist, the worker, the farmer, the student, men, women, and youth."[97] *Rudé právo, V boj,* and other underground pamphlets called for acts of sabotage and work slowdowns, and it seems that Czechs responded. Railway cars were set on fire, train tracks were destroyed, and telephone wires were cut. Arsonists near Hradec Králové set 100,000 liters of fuel ablaze. The Armament Inspection Board counted ten major strikes and twelve walkouts between August 10 and September 10. The board also reported 31 cases of sabotage in July; from August 20 through September they found 115 cases in which train air brakes were severed. According to ÚVOD agents, in the early summer months the Protectorate's industrial output dropped by a third.[98]

So-called new Germans, fearful of the revenge that Czechs might visit upon them following a German defeat, suddenly began, in the words of one Intelligence Service agent, "to sway."[99] Symbolic resistance revived. Czechs found ways of acting Czech. Assemblies being largely forbidden, they met in large numbers and dressed in national colors for Mass, parish festivals, and funerals. Graffiti artists painted slogans on buildings. Russian jackets were in style. During one night in June someone climbed the forty-five-meter-tall smokestack at the Siemens-Martin Plant in Kladno and attached a large red banner.[100] Most disastrous for Nazi propagandists, however, was Goebbels's ill-conceived attempt to co-opt the V symbol from Churchill and the British propaganda machine. V stood for (Allied) "victory," and Goebbels feared the sight of V's dotting public spaces and underground literature across Europe (Figs. 3.2 and 3.3). V, Goebbels decided, would instead refer to the fictitious German pagan god Viktoria or Caesar's "veni, vidi, vici" and ordered Nazi-constructed V's placed everywhere. In the Protectorate, Goebbels's semantic acrobatics flopped. Quipsters created whole sentences that played with the letter V, like "Věřit ve vítězství vélkého vůdce je velká volovina" (To believe in the victory of the great Führer is absolute rubbish). Wilhelm Dennler, a German bureaucrat in Prague who had been learning Czech, wrote in his memoirs:

At the moment all over the Protectorate there is a flood of V-symbols, on clothes and ribbons, painted in white on house doors, monuments, on street asphalt in all localities up and down the land, everywhere. However, the fact that the German word for victory ["Sieg"] can be translated into the English word "victory" and in Czech "vítězství" means that the propaganda is all too easy to make light of. And in order to choke off any doubt among the Czechs, loudspeakers in movie theaters and on the streets day in and day out blare: "The Reich is winning on all fronts."
The Czechs are laughing.

V could also stand for "verloren," the past tense form of the German infinitive meaning "to lose." Graffiti artists would add the letters *en* to Nazi *V*s, spelling out the Czech word "ven," meaning "get out." Thus, when Czechs held up their index and middle fingers to make a V, perhaps saluting a Nazi soldier or greeting a neighbor, they were not, as Goebbels had intended, expressing an unreal wish for Nazi success. They meant "victory," "vítězství," "verloren," and "ven."[101]

The crescendo to this wave of patriotism came during the week of September 14 in the form of a mass action inspired by the "to each his own" calls from the past—a massive boycott of official newspapers, which had since 1940 been heavily censored and under the control of Czech collaborationists. London radio had called the boycott, and Czechs responded. Sales in Prague dropped 70 percent; elsewhere sales fell 25 to 50 percent—a figure that was probably even higher for publications not sold by subscription.[102] Coffeehouse servers refused, even when asked, to bring newspapers to their customers' tables. Bundles of newspapers were not even opened; on public transportation people read only books.[103] "Your measures against newspapers very successful. Thanks," an informant from Prague told London. "Morale among us is excellent," another wrote; "optimism and resolve to resist firm."[104] Although the form had changed, Czechs were acting Czech again in the few ways available to them. A triangular relationship between London, underground movements, and the general population—forged in 1940—had now been solidified. Beneš seemed to have got his wish.

The picture, of course, was more complicated. We should not assume that German workers excluded themselves from these activities; in at least once case, party leaders had to reprimand their co-nationals for fraternizing with Czechs and Poles in their factory.[105] The extent of these activities—strikes, underground pamphleteering, and boycotts—is difficult to measure. Gestapo agents were on the lookout for signs of increased resistance and might have been boosting their own achievements by exaggerating the number of arrests. Seeking to satisfy Beneš, ÚVOD members had their own reasons to exaggerate. The Intelligence Service, as we will see, had its own motives for reporting a rise in Czech activities.[106] Czechs, and especially Czech workers, might have had other, more material reasons to express discontent. Entrance into the Reich's customs union and war in southeastern Europe drew away many of the Protectorate's basic goods. The shortages, as well as shopkeepers determined to

Figure 3.2 *V* symbols on Prague's Wenceslas Square in 1941. (Reproduced by permission of the Česká tisková kancelář.)

play by the old rules of supply and demand, stymied efforts by the Reich Protector's Office to hold prices in check; this effect in turn led to higher inflation and a drop in real wages. Beginning in winter 1940–1941 Czechs could no longer obtain some basic goods like fruits and raisins. Only women who were sick, pregnant, or in childbed could obtain rice. To Frank's horror, a black market dealing in goods unavailable with ration cards blossomed.[107] After the attack on the Soviet Union, the economic situation only worsened as goods went to the eastern front. Food coupons brought smaller quantities of basic goods like potatoes. Fruits, vegetables, meat, fat, butter, and shoes were nearly impossible to obtain, particularly so in the cities. Economic hardship, not politics, was the prime motivating force behind the Czechs' unrest, the chief of the regular police for the Protectorate wrote in early September. German victories in

Figure 3.3 *V* signs on a Prague building. (Reproduced by permission of the Česká tisková kancelář.)

the East caused many disappointed Czechs to lose interest in the war. The shortages, however, had become increasingly acute.[108] Nazi leaders had good reason to worry. During World War I, food shortages inspired over 564,000 workers in the Bohemian lands from the beginning of 1917 to October 1918 to participate in over 288 strikes. Strikes and protests throughout Central Europe, many Germans believed, had spelled doom during the last years of war.[109]

Whatever the motivations for these actions or their level of intensity, the psychological effect of Czech "resistance" was real. From the first day of the attack on the Soviet Union, Frank and Neurath promised to take measures against anyone threatening "peace and order" in their realm. The Protectorate's industries were vital to the war effort. Domestic disruptions behind the lines, officials knew, threatened to sap other resources and energies.[110] As the actions multiplied, foreboding turned to paranoia within Nazi circles. Mass demonstrations and a nationwide strike were supposedly being planned for Czechoslovak Independence Day, October 28. Göring's sister-in-law, domiciled in Plzeň because her husband headed the city's important Škoda Works, left for Switzerland in a specially protected train car. Gestapo agents and local authorities seemed touchier than before. Anti-Hitler graffiti on the highway between Poděbrad and Mladá Boleslav prompted the cancellation of all Czech cultural and sport activities in the surrounding areas. Czech cinemas were closed, and all restaurants and pubs had to close by 10 P.M., unless they primarily served Germans. In Prague, a group of Germans, including SS-man Georg Koch, confronted a local warehouseman, František Pražák, in front of his house. Koch asked something in German, to which Pražák responded, "I don't understand. Speak Czech." Koch then took out his revolver and shot Pražák in the stomach; the wounds eventually killed the eighteen-year-old Czech. Nothing, of course, happened to Koch.[111]

Czech "resistance" brought about the end for Neurath's rule. Forces working against him were coming from below and at all angles. At the local level, rivalries between Oberlandräte loyal to the Reich protector, Intelligence Service agents, and party leaders were intensifying. As the summer of 1941 progressed, the latter two had been gaining influence over competencies previously reserved for the Oberlandräte. Beginning in September 1940 citizenship decisions required consultation with the local Kreisleiter. The next year all decisions concerning mixed Czech-German marriages included party and Intelligence Service officials. If the marriage involved a party member, the decision fell solely to the Nazi Party.[112] Despite Neurath's vehement protests to Berlin, party members, not Oberlandräte, dispensed Volkstumsfond monies and received the gratification of local Protectorate Germans beginning in summer 1941. Oberlandräte complained bitterly to Neurath's office that overlapping competencies led to confusion and a lack of common direction and purpose.[113] Rivalries between Protectorate and Reich Germans bogged down administrative functioning and widened chasms all the way to the top. Protectorate Germans, who tended to rally around Frank, called for radical measures against the Czechs. They also hoped that replacing Neurath with their fellow Protectorate German would lead to career advancements.[114]

Intelligence Service reports detailing Czech "chauvinism" and making remarks critical of local Oberlandräte, and by extension of Neurath's state apparatus, constantly made their way up the administrative pyramid. In Prague, the head of the Intelligence Service crafted summaries detailing Czech resistance that included statements critical of Neurath. Reinhard Heydrich, in turn, made sure that the reports reached Hitler's desk.[115] Hitler seems to have been convinced, declaring later that Neurath's "good and peaceable nature now seemed more like weakness and stupidity."[116] On September 16, 1941, Neurath, Frank, and members of the Gestapo, Intelligence Service, and military counterintelligence met in the office of the Reich protector. Gestapo agents, and especially Frank, called for "draconian measures" against the Czechs, including the death penalty for anyone found engaging in industrial sabotage. Neurath refused. Frank now had his chance.[117]

Frank met with Himmler and Hitler on September 22 to discuss the situation in the Protectorate. Neurath arrived in the afternoon of the next day, missing a meeting among the newly arrived Goebbels and Himmler, Heydrich, Frank, and Hitler. Neurath was told that he would be taking a sick leave, and he returned to Prague to gather his things. The new acting Reich protector, Reinhard Heydrich, arrived in Prague on September 27, 1941. Kiev had just fallen to German troops, and a new wave of euphoria was sweeping up Hitler, SS leaders, and other Nazi rulers.[118]

"Policies toward Slavs," John Connelly writes, "appear as constant improvisation, in which opportunity and ideology shaped one another."[119]

This was particularly true in the Protectorate, where a compromise among demographic realities, economic needs, and ideological demands—legitimized by scientific research and accelerated by bureaucratic rivalries—resulted in plans for the complete Germanization of Bohemia and Moravia's land and people. If total Germanization policies were to prevail, and if the Protectorate, already integral to Germany's Großraumwirtschaft, were to become part of its Lebensraum, basic ideological principles had to be reworked. There were simply not enough Germans to work the factories, staff the administrative posts, and till the soil. If the Czechs could not go, then they had to become Germans. As late as June 1939 Hitler was heard saying, during a conversation about the upcoming Winter Olympics, that "he would never have thought that Czechs would participate in sports under the German banner, and he thinks even less about making Czechs into Germans."[120] A little more than a year later he approved Neurath and Frank's proposal, which promised to do just that. Timing and the dynamics of war added even more ingredients to the concoction. From Poland, where the war provided Himmler, Heydrich, and other ideologues with the opportunity to realize Lebensraum dreams, pressures for total Germanization emanated across the continent. Yet the SS's influence in the Protectorate was weaker than in Poland. War had not come to the Bohemian lands, where armaments factories continued to make vital contributions to the German military machine. For the moment, as Frank had stated, the demands of fighting a war beyond the Protectorate prevented the immediate realization of ideological goals within the Protectorate. Although driven by Jury's intrigues to promise total Germanization, both Neurath and Frank could return to earth after the Protectorate had been saved. Plans for racial testing and large-scale expulsions appeared to have been put on hold.

In fall 1941 Heydrich became acting Reich protector. It appeared that Neurath and Frank's half-heartedly constructed plans for total Germanization would actually be realized. Yet Heydrich, soon the uncontested master of the Bohemian lands, faced a dilemma familiar to Nazi leaders throughout Europe: how to balance ideological aims and immediate wartime needs. As the executor of expulsion and assimilation policies, he also faced a number of vexing methodological and definitional questions. Himmler had called for a "racial weeding out" of potential Germans, yet it was not always apparent what "race" really meant. There were many, often competing opinions about what characteristics should prefigure membership in the Volk, and what methods for locating and marking potential Germans were most effective. Heydrich attacked the "Jewish problem" with ruthless energy and efficiency, but the "Czech problem" seemed much more complicated. Hanging over the whole project was a question that had befuddled Nazi leaders since the beginning of the occupation: What makes, or can make, a German?

4

Heydrich Imposes Racial Order

Days after his arrival in Prague, newly appointed acting Reich protector Reinhard Heydrich addressed a gathering of Reich Protectorate officials, Oberlandräte, party officials, and members of the SS in Prague's Černín Palace. The contrast to Neurath's style was immediately obvious. Heydrich reminded his audience of his position as head of the Intelligence Service and the role of the SS as the party's "shock troops," who ensured domestic security and the realization of Nazi ideas. Interspersed were hateful references to Jews and a constant flow of words common among his imagined warrior class—"fight," "battle," and "blood." He pictured for his audience a Europe rid of the Jews, who, in a variation on the Madagascar plan, would be shipped to Russia's Arctic regions. A growing, vibrant German Lebensraum in the middle of Europe would swallow up "Germanizable" inhabitants and expel the rest: "The future of the Reich after the war's end depends on the ability of the Reich and the ability of the people of the Reich to hold, to rule, and if necessary to fuse these [newly acquired] areas with the Reich. It also depends upon the means, as much as is possible, [in which we] deal with, lead, and fuse with these people." "These people" included the Norwegians, Dutch, Flemish, Danes, and Swedes, who thanks to "bad political leadership and the influence of Jews" had forgotten their Germanic roots and would be assimilated by being treated like Germans in the Reich. In much of former Poland and farther eastward, in a second imagined space, Germans would rule over a subject population as during the old days of medieval "colonization." Because of a lack of German bodies, the area could not be completely settled, he said, but its raw materials needed to be exploited. A third space, which included incorporated western Poland, would form an "Eastern wall" facing the Slavic world. Germans must inhabit the lands behind this wall, while "piece by piece, step by step, the Polish element [will be] tossed away."[1]

The Protectorate was included behind this "Eastern wall." "Gentlemen," Heydrich said, "the final solution [for the Protectorate] must be the following: that this space [*Raum*] must once and for all be settled by Germans." Bohemia and Moravia had always been a part of the German sphere of influence, a "bulwark of Germandom," a "sentry facing East," thanks in no part to a long history of "stabs in the back" by Czech patriots. To this end, Heydrich demanded not only a "total picture" that would allow him to "get a feel for the racial and völkisch character of the entire population" but also an inventory of "people from this space who are Germanizable." The "old ways" of "making this Czech garbage into Germans" must be abandoned in favor of testing based on racial characteristics: "These are clear, fundamental ideas that we must accept as our guidelines. And when [Germanization] happens—that is a question the Führer must decide. But the planning and collection of raw data can begin immediately." Making Bohemia and Moravia entirely German was Heydrich's stated "long-term goal." He also announced a second, "short-term" goal: "I need peace in this space." Industrial sabotage and the activities of resistance groups must be brought to an end, he said. They have brought, "to the shame of the Reich, a dangerous form of unrest to this space."[2]

This chapter traces Heydrich's moves toward his "short-term" and "long-term" goals. Heydrich not only quelled resistance and kept Protectorate factories running. He nearly closed off all avenues by which Czechs could act Czech in public. Not until after liberation would the constraints be lifted, with tragic consequences for local Germans. In the Protectorate, as in Europe, Nazi leaders made the fateful leap of deciding to "solve" the "Jewish question" by murdering nearly every one of them. Meanwhile, despite confusion about what made a German, Nazi officials began to implement the Germanization plans concocted in late 1940. The tensions among ideology, demographic realities, and economic necessity that led to the creation of Germanization plans in the Protectorate would constrain and contour their implementation. Ambiguity would turn to absurdity, and the meaning and ascription of nationality would be changed forever.

Spaces Closing In, Ties Being Severed

Reinhard Heydrich was born in Halle, Germany, in 1905 to a struggling middle-class family. A son of Bruno Heydrich, a committed völkisch nationalist and vehement anti-Semite, Heydrich joined one of the most radical Freikorps formations in Germany after World War I. In 1922 he enlisted in the navy, rising through the ranks to the Communications Section of the naval staff at Kiel. Eight years later an honor court discharged him for making improper advances toward the daughter of the Kiel naval dock superintendent, who also happened to be good friends with the navy's highest officer, Admiral Erich Raeder. Thus, unemployed at the peak of the Depression, Heydrich joined the Nazi Party and managed to secure an interview with Himmler, who had been looking for someone able to establish an agency to gather intelligence on fellow Nazi Party members. Heydrich, with his knowledge of military intelligence and love of British spy novels, seemed the perfect choice. From this starting point Heydrich built the Intelligence Service, which later expanded its competencies to include spying on whole populations, gathering intelligence, and interpreting popular attitudes. In 1939 he became director of the Reich Security Head Office, which provided an organizational roof over the Intelligence Service, the criminal police, and the criminal justice office. When Hitler named him acting Reich protector in 1941, Heydrich was one of the most powerful men in Nazi Germany. His Intelligence Service had been spying on Czechoslovakia before the war, at which time Heydrich established a close relationship with Frank. As a member of the SS, he promised to increase the organization's growing power in the occupied East. As director of the Central Emigration Office and Central Resettlement Office within Himmler's agency for population engineering, no one was better placed to implement the Nazis' Germanization policies.[3]

Heydrich thrived on intrigue. He had played a leading role in the "night of long knives," which in 1934 eliminated the SS's main rival, the SA, as a power and provided a pretext for arresting others deemed enemies of the Reich. As part of this operation, Heydrich ordered the murder of SA leader Ernst Röhm, the godfather of his oldest son. Rumors of a Jewish background, though untrue, followed Heydrich throughout his life, even after racial experts from the Race and Settlement Office confirmed his Aryan background. His high-pitched voice seemed out of place, since it came from a seemingly perfect Aryan makeup—tall, blond, and athletic. (His navy comrades had nicknamed him "billy goat.") Himmler, employing an intriguing mix of metaphors, called Heydrich a "living card index, a brain which held all the threads and wove them all together."[4] Adolf Eichmann later said that he "often let words slip through the fence of his teeth more quickly than one might have liked."[5] Whatever Heydrich's personality or his mental abilities, there can be no mistaking his actions. Heydrich consistently pushed Nazi rule toward radical "solutions" to various "problems," toward the realization of vague goals laid down by his only superiors in the Reich: Himmler and Hitler (Fig. 4.1).[6]

Figure 4.1 Heydrich shortly after his arrival in Prague. (Reproduced by permission of the Česká tisková kancelář.)

Upon arriving in Prague, Heydrich immediately set out to realize his short-term goals of pacification and productivity. He began by terrorizing the population. Within days of his arrival buildings across the Protectorate were splattered with red posters listing the names of people—ninety-two in the first three days of Heydrich's rule—sentenced to death by newly established summary courts. The summary courts allowed only three possible verdicts: the death sentence, shipment to a concentration camp, and release. Heydrich later claimed that by February 4, 1942, summary courts had brought in four thousand to five thousand people.[7] Many of those not executed boarded one of five transports to the Mauthausen concentration camp that winter. Only 4 percent of the Czech prisoners in Mauthausen survived the war.[8]

Domestic resistance groups suffered a near fatal blow. In March 1942 German police moved on Thümmel, Beneš's double agent in Prague. More than fifteen hundred victims had belonged to "legal" national organizations, such as the leading patriotic organization Sokol, which was finally dissolved soon after Heydrich's arrival. The sweeps, which targeted former Czechoslovak military officers and members of the so-called intelligentsia, nearly wiped out organized resistance in the Protectorate. Its leaders arrested, ÚVOD ceased to exist, although smaller, now uncoordinated, cells still survived. Gestapo agents shut down one of ÚVOD's radio transmitters, and patriots could manage to operate a second only sporadically. Only the Communist resistance survived, even though it, too, suffered a number of arrests. Strikes and work slowdowns disappeared overnight. Isolated acts of sabotage continued, but few managed to hit vital targets like telephone and telegraph lines and factories in heavy industry. A whole array of Czech and German police organizations guarded railway lines. To go near them required a special permit. Railway workers were forbidden to bring pocketknives to work.[9]

The terror did more than just debilitate the resistance movements and halt sabotage. It paralyzed all of society. Plates attached to radios reminded their owners that listening to foreign radio broadcasts was punishable by death, one of a growing number of offenses that could lead to an individual's execution.[10] Although paling in comparison to events in Poland, the speed and viciousness of Heydrich's repression were unprecedented in the history of Bohemia and Moravia. And Heydrich made the most of the terror by increasing the "optical effect" of the arrests and executions. Radio announcers blasted news of the arrests, newspapers detailed the trials of prominent individuals, and lists of the executed were posted throughout the Protectorate. In late autumn the first wave of terror subsided. From November 30, 1941, to May 27, 1942, Nazi authorities announced only thirty-three executions. Still, as one London informant reported, "people [kept] clear of any public actions, associational life, discussions and conversations, and the majority [avoided] relations altogether. . . . [All Czechs are] clenching their teeth." National pride still existed, a second London informant reported, but "everyone is a bit more thorough, straightforward; like people who fear for their lives, they're seeking a sense of clarity."[11]

Other "optical effects" aimed at placating workers and separating them from the rest of society. In the course of Heydrich's rule workers received ration increases, better welfare services, free shoes, and, for a time, Saturdays off. Displays of friendship and generosity complemented these real benefits. The media made much of Heydrich's meeting with chosen labor representatives on October 24, and that same day food confiscated from black marketeers was distributed in factory cafeterias. Many measures were deliberately aimed to divide Protectorate nationals along class lines. Heydrich retooled the formerly Czech-run National Union of Employees to mirror the German Labor Front. Its "Strength through Joy" campaign, using equipment and property confiscated from the Sokol, organized sports events, movies, plays, concerts, and musicals for workers. Still, wage increases failed to keep up with inflation. Perks for workers could not hide the fact that shortages persisted. By spring 1942 Protectorate office officials and Intelligence Service agents took note of widescale grumbling among workers. But sabotage had stopped, and there were no indications that the grumbling translated into any meaningful decreases in productivity.[12]

Heydrich applied the same combination of terror and "optical effects" to demand even more subservience from Hácha and his government. To this end, he ordered the immediate arrest of Alois Eliáš, Hácha's prime minister and ÚVOD's contact in the Czech government. Gestapo agents, and the highest Nazi officials, had known of Eliáš's communications with London for some time, and the People's Court wasted little time in sentencing him and Prague's mayor, Otokar Klapka, to death. Eliáš's humiliating "confession" made the front pages of collaborationist newspapers across the Protectorate. Klapka was executed on October 4, 1941. Hácha begged for Eliáš's life, and although Hitler spared him, Eliáš remained in prison as a hostage meant to keep Hácha and the rest of the Czech government under control.[13] As for the rest of the Czech government, Heydrich demanded order and coordination. Each Czech ministry became directly responsible to its counterpart within the Reich Protector's Office. (The lone exception to this rule was the Ministry of Enlightenment, which was headed by the overeager collaborationist Emanuel Moravec, a former Czechoslovak legionnaire and political pragmatist known for his weekly pro-Nazi radio addresses.) A November decree allowed Heydrich to discharge or transfer "politically unreliable" civil servants, regardless of age. In only a matter of months Hácha and those around him were little more than Czech-speaking Nazi bureaucrats and mouthpieces.[14]

With ÚVOD's leaders arrested, Eliáš now a hostage, and the Czech government compromised, Hácha had two options. Half of his cabinet voted that he resign; the other half voted that he stay on. After a meeting with Heydrich, Hácha chose the latter, and the die was cast.[15] "Citizens, do not listen to the heckling talk of the exiles . . . who by asking us to follow their radio allurements can only bring us great catastrophes," Hácha stated during a radio address in November. "At stake is no longer merely the fate of individuals but the fate of your children and the whole nation." Czechoslovak BBC broadcasts from London responded by calling Hácha a traitor, to which the beleaguered president replied: "Mr. Beneš does not see, as I do, the tears of the mothers and wives who address their desperate pleas to me because their sons and husbands fell into disaster after having been seduced by deceptive radio broadcasts. He is in a position to permit himself illusions, to build castles in the air, and to paint alluring pictures of the future. . . . For us, there is no way but to face reality with resolution and to act soberly in accordance with bare facts."[16] Hácha, like his government, had now been subdued, and he continued to live out a tragic existence until the end of the war. "The so-called Protectorate government and its president are a government no more," Beneš said in reply to Hácha's attack.[17] The gap between the two leaders, as well as between Beneš and Protectorate inhabitants, would only grow wider.

Destroying the Jews and Gypsies

Just as victory in France inspired Nazi expulsion and resettlement plans in 1940, similar bursts of optimism following the attack on the Soviet Union spurred a radicalization of policies toward the Jews. Until March 1942 Nazi officials at various levels stationed at various agencies throughout Europe entered what Christopher Browning calls a phase of "initiation, experimentation, and preparation" that ended with the industrialized, systematic murder of Jews at killing centers.[18] Impulses for mass murder, radicalized by war and born of an ideology that combined anti-Semitism with anti-Bolshevism, emanated from the peripheries. In the newly won eastern territories, Germans, with the willing aid of local nationalists, hooligans, and careerists, had free rein to commit unimaginable atrocities. They also began to search for the "solutions" to the "Jewish problem."[19] Impulses that eventually led to the Holocaust also emanated from the center. From Berlin and then Prague, Heydrich played a key role in radicalizing Jewish policy. He coordinated bureaucratic structures and ordered the deportation of some of the first victims, including Protectorate Jews. A European process was to have devastating local effects in the Protectorate.

Following early German victories, Hitler announced to a number of his top officials on July 16, 1941, his wishes to create a Garden of Eden in the East using "all necessary measures—shootings, resettlements, etc."—to realize his utopian visions. Two weeks later Heydrich obtained from Göring authorization to make "all necessary preparations" for "bringing about a complete solution of the Jewish question within the German sphere of influence." The paper concluded with a request that Heydrich prepare an "overall plan" for the "final solution" to the "Jewish question." Indeed, Nazi leaders had created a "problem" that demanded new "solutions." As German armies raced eastward, the number of Jews that came under Nazi control multiplied daily. At the same time, under the cover of war and drunk with military victories, ideologues could begin to pursue more radical measures aimed at eliminating the Jews. Shortly after Hitler's "Garden of Eden" declaration, Himmler multiplied the number of men attached to SS Einsatzgruppen—mobile units operating behind the front lines charged with the task of "cleansing" the area of partisans and other "enemies"—and organized local Lithuanians, Latvians, Estonians, Belorussians, and

Ukrainians into police auxiliary units. The so-called pacification of areas behind the front lines included pogroms, encouraged by German authorities, and routine killings of Jews and other civilians by German police, the SS, and soldiers. By the end of 1941 Germans and their minions had murdered 500,000 to 800,000 Jews, about 2,700 to 4,200 per day.[20]

That autumn a second wave of planning followed the encirclement of Leningrad and the fall of Kiev, which had ended a short period of German-Soviet stalemate on the eastern front. Nazi leaders again considered expelling the Jews eastward. On either September 23 or 24, perhaps during the same meeting in which Hitler appointed Heydrich acting Reich protector, Goebbels noted in his diary that the "Führer is of the opinion that the Jews are to be removed from Germany step-by-step. The first cities to be cleared of Jews are Berlin, Vienna, and Prague." Less than two weeks later Hitler declared that although military priorities created "a great shortage of transportation," the Jews of the Protectorate, along with those in Berlin and Vienna, "must disappear." On October 10 Heydrich, chairing a meeting in Prague, announced that Hitler demanded that "all Jews be removed from this German space by the end of the year," and that "all pending questions [regarding the Jewish policy] must be solved immediately. Even the transportation question must not present any problems." "I have decided," he stated the next day, "to go through these stages also in the Protectorate as quickly as possible."[21]

Beginning in mid-October and running until February 21, three short waves of deportations sent sixty thousand Jews from the Protectorate, Austria, Germany, and Luxembourg to ghettos behind the eastern front.[22] As in 1940, however, Heydrich and other planners faced the problem of where to expel the Jewish population. Local officials in the East complained of already being overburdened. German troops were not advancing quickly enough to make deportation to the Arctic regions feasible. After Heydrich considered several possibilities, the Prague head of the Intelligence Service secured an army base near the town of Terezín. The Czech inhabitants were evacuated, and more barracks were built to accommodate the new population. Later, Protectorate Jews were joined in Terezín by elderly Jews, certain disabled and highly decorated German-Jewish war veterans, and "prominent" Jews whose disappearance might excite world opinion. In summer 1941 Nazi officials counted 88,686 Jews in the Protectorate. By April 1945 Nazi officials had shipped 77,603 Protectorate Jews to Terezín.[23]

Ghettoization, war, and deportations set the context for industrialized killing. On January 20 Heydrich convened a meeting of Nazi notables at Wannsee, near Berlin, where, coded in various euphemisms, they agreed upon the destruction of every Jew in Europe. Heydrich began by running through a brief history of Nazi Germany's attempts at the expulsion of the Jews "from the Lebensraum of the German Volk." German victories in the East have opened the way for massive deportation, Heydrich stated. He then added: "These actions are to be regarded solely as provisional measures, but practical experiences are already being collected [in the East] which will be of great importance as the final solution of the Jewish question approaches."[24] Off the record, the Nazis' top brass discussed various methods of mass murder being tried on an experimental basis in the East. Nazi leaders like Himmler worried that the Einsatzgruppen killings threatened the mental health of the murderers. The uncontrolled nature of the executions threatened to create further unrest in the East. They were inefficient, and they threatened to drain important resources.[25] As of 1939 Nazi personnel had, on Hitler's order, already killed a number of physically and mentally handicapped people with carbon monoxide piped through specially designed vans and gas chambers. In the weeks leading up to the Wannsee Conference some of the same personnel had overseen the use of trucks to gas Jews with carbon monoxide in and around Chelmno. Beginning in August or September of 1941 Nazi officials in Auschwitz had murdered Soviet prisoners of war, and then Jews, with Zyklon B. After Wannsee, in February 1942, the head of SS construction arrived at Auschwitz to build a large crematorium. At about the same time camp officials were making a peasant hut into a gas chamber. In the next few months personnel who had operated gas vans and chambers for the euthanasia program were reassigned to death camps such as Sobibór and Treblinka.[26] In April 1942 the SS loaded one thousand Jews in Terezín onto rail cars, which left Terezín for Sobibór one month after construction of the extermination camp had been completed.[27]

Today the walls of the Pinkas Synagogue in Prague are covered with the names of 77,297 individuals, "full Jews" as well as Mischlinge as defined by the Nuremberg Laws, murdered by the Nazis and their henchmen. Before being murdered, however, the vast majority had been identified as Jews. Unlike in the chaotic East, in the Protectorate the murder of the Jews followed cool, bureaucratic procedure and depended on a card file, Habsburg-era institutions, and a workable definition of what constituted a "Jew." In June 1939 Neurath declared that Jews would be defined in accordance with the Nuremberg Laws, and in spring 1940 he decreed that all Jews register with their local Jewish congregation—a process overseen by Adolf Eichmann's Central Office for Jewish Emigration in Prague, a branch office of a section tied to Heydrich's Reich Security Main Office. Beginning October 1, 1941, Eichmann's office ordered the Jewish Religious Congregation of Prague, by now terrorized into almost complete compliance, to begin the process of registering anew every Jew in the Protectorate. In December branch offices extended the registration process. In Prague thirty-seven congregation members worked almost ceaselessly, and under threat of being deporting themselves, at times registering two thousand people per day. Using information from the registration applications—names of the registrant's relatives, the individual's relationship to these relatives, the relative's registration numbers and birth dates, and names of relatives who lived with the individual being questioned—Eichmann's office and various police organs tracked down Jews who had until then refused to count themselves as such.[28] Denunciations also proved crucial in identifying others as Jews. The Czech-run newspaper *Aryan Struggle* (*Árijský boj*) ran a special section for denunciations called the "Floodlight." Its aim, among other things, was to "shame" Czechs who continued to maintain relations with Jews. The Jewish newspaper *Židovské listy* (*The Jewish Pages*) ran a campaign entitled "They're Registering Themselves" (*Hledají se*) and, in 1942, began running the names of unregistered Jews, encouraging readers to turn them in.[29]

Once assigned, the categories were inescapable. Once marked publicly, the Jews were doomed. Decrees dating back to 1939 had isolated them professionally, economically, and socially. As of 1940 their identifications were stamped with *J*'s and they carried their own ration cards. A September 1, 1941, Ministry of the Interior decree required all "full Jews" six years of age or older to wear a yellow star, about the size of one's palm, with the word "*Jude*" (Jew) centered in black letters (Fig. 4.2). The star was to be sewn on the left front of their clothing. Only "full Jews" in certain mixed marriages were exempt. "No Jew, under those conditions," Raul Hilberg concludes, "could hide without first ridding himself of the conspicuous tag, the middle name, the telltale ration card, passport, and identification papers. . . . The vast majority wore the star, and wearing it, were lost."[30]

Before each transport Eichmann's office chose around twelve hundred names from its immense collection of files. Members of the Jewish Religious Congregation of Prague visited the doomed individuals at night, providing detailed instructions on reporting to the assembly point.[31] Heda Kaufmannová describes the moment she heard that her mother was on the transport list: "I moved around—no, I ran, I ran like greased

Figure 4.2 Two people marked with the yellow star. (Reproduced by permission of the Česká tisková kancelář.)

lightning, with my thoughts fixed precisely and exactly on the fury of things which might be able to set things right. Everyone else acted as if their switches had been turned off. There existed only packing, unsystematically, long thought of in advance. Checked off things from a list, nothing to be forgotten, worked with rational people who helped."[32] In June 1943 the last transport of "full Jews" left Prague, carrying the roughly four thousand members of the now dissolved Jewish Congregation of Prague and their families.[33] Some Jews managed to obtain fake identification papers or to survive in hiding thanks to the efforts of a small number of courageous "Aryans." By 1945, however, only 424 Jews had managed to survive the occupation in hiding.[34]

Along with the Reich Citizenship Law, the Nuremberg Laws defined Jews according to various past and present personal characteristics that, ironically, had nothing to do with race. Religion was the sole determinant, for it was membership in Jewish religious organizations and birth records that left the paper trail for officials to trace "Jews," or for others to prove that they were not "Jews."[35] Gray areas, of course, persisted, such as when the requisite paperwork was unavailable. As late as 1943 there were still 1,081 "disputed cases" in the Protectorate, although some of these "cases" were people whom Nazi leaders could not find.[36] Similarly, Nazi leaders had, since the inception of the Nuremberg Laws, struggled with the concept and ultimate fate of Mischlinge, or Jews of "mixed Jewish blood." The 1935 law created two "degrees" of Mischlinge. The first degree consisted of Jews with only two Jewish grandparents who were not married to "full Jews" and were not members of a Jewish congregation. Second-degree Jews had only one Jewish grandparent. In the Protectorate, as in Germany, Mischlinge were spared many of the discriminatory measures aimed at "full Jews," including the wearing of the yellow star. They could become either Reich citizens or Protectorate nationals. The euphoria that surrounded the search for a "final solution," however, threatened to draw in the Mischlinge. At Wannsee, Heydrich spent considerable time outlining a procedure that aimed at the destruction of the Mischlinge. First-degree Mischlinge, he said, should be considered Jews unless they (1) were married to "persons of German blood" [and] if the marriage has resulted in children or (2) have received an exemption permit from a top Nazi authority. But in return for being spared evacuation, the first-degree Mischling would have to submit to "voluntary" sterilization if he or she was to remain in the Reich. A second-degree Mischling was to be considered a Jew if (1) both parents were Mischlinge; (2) he or she had an "exceptionally poor racial appearance" that distinguished him or her as a Jew; or (3) he or she had an arrest record or "feels and behaves like a Jew." The conference ended without any clear decision. The minister of the interior, Wilhelm Stuckart, feared the administrative complexity involved, favoring instead complete sterilization of the Mischlinge population, which seemed impractical as well. Participants at a second meeting, on March 6, 1942, chaired by Eichmann, again failed to agree on a common "solution." Stuckart suggested that "deporting the half-Jews would mean abandoning that half of their blood which is German." Within thirty to forty years, the Mischlinge category would no longer exist.[37] In the Protectorate, Heydrich followed a policy of exclusion toward the Mischlinge. In May 1941 the Reich Protector's Office ordered that all Mischlinge who applied for Reich citizenship undergo racial testing. A year later Heydrich ordered that racial experts test all Mischlinge who had obtained Reich citizenship.[38] A Reich Protectorate Office decree that month prohibited Protectorate nationals from marrying Jews. First-degree Mischlinge could marry Czechs only with the permission of the Ministry of the Interior. The fate of the Mischlinge in the Protectorate, as in Germany, thus remained unclear.[39]

Jews, as defined by the Nuremberg Laws, left a paper trail that allowed Nazi officials to place them into complicated, constructed, yet relatively firm categories. Defining and then finding "Gypsies" followed a different path. The destruction of the community continued nonetheless. In the year leading up to Heydrich's arrival police had rounded up hundreds of "wandering Gypsies" or "tramps," meaning that "Gypsy" was a sociological category that included a whole array of "asocials." Heydrich and the SS inserted racial criteria into the definition of "Gypsies" and hence widened the net. In October 1941 the acting Reich Protector stated his wish to evacuate all the "Gypsies." The next spring he ordered that their identification cards be marked with a Z. (*Zigeuner* is the German word for "Gypsy.") A July 1942 Protectorate decree drew a line between "Gypsies," "Gypsies of mixed background," and "wanderers of the Gypsy type." Local police, without possessing any training to distinguish among categories, were to place in the first two categories anyone with dark hair and brown skin. In total, 6,500 Protectorate inhabitants fell into these categories. At least 3,000 died in the Gypsy camp at Auschwitz-Birkenau, and

533 died in special camps in Lety and Hodonín in the Protectorate. Countless others considered "asocial" or "unfit to work" died in concentration camps throughout East-Central Europe.[40]

Many of the victims had already been marked as early as 1927, when a First Republic law required every "wandering Gypsy" above the age of fourteen to obtain a special identification card. Upon entering a town, "wandering Gypsies" had to register with local authorities, who told the itinerants how long they could remain.[41] With such documentation it would not have been difficult for Nazi officials to locate "wandering Gypsies." The majority of Gypsies, however, were marked and arrested by people among whom they lived. Although these procedures were technically under the jurisdiction of the SS, the Reich Protector's Office required local authorities to photograph, fingerprint, arrest, and sometimes even deport their "Gypsies." Nazi authorities declared August 2, 1942, "Gypsy registration day," with registration a task that the German criminal police and Czech gendarmes were to carry out.[42] Individuals in the Protectorate persecuted as Gypies remember being registered and arrested by German police and Gestapo agents. Most often, however, they recall that "their" local Czech police performed the duty. A schoolmate who had shared the same bench with Eduard Holomek informed the family that they would be sent to a concentration camp. Božena Vladová né Heráková was betrayed by a member of her own Roma community. When her father complained to the Czech police, the officer simply responded: "Don't be angry Mr. Herák; we have to do our duty; you know that these are horrible times; if someone reported that we let you go then we'd all be done for."[43]

What Makes a German?

Jews and Gypsies were not the only victims targeted for destruction in Hitler's Europe. The war in the East, Himmler told Heydrich and others in June 1941, "is a question of existence; thus it will be a racial struggle of pitiless severity, in the course of which twenty to thirty million Slavs and Jews will perish through military actions and crisis of food supply." By spring 1942 more than two million Soviet soldiers in German captivity, along with countless other gentile noncombatants, had died.[44] At least one million civilians and prisoners of war in or from the Reichskommisariat Ukraine died.[45] In Belarus, a territory home to 10.6 million inhabitants in 1939, 2.2 million civilians and prisoners of war perished during the German occupation.[46] The June 1941 attack on the Soviet Union also gave new life to Lebensraum dreams. That same June Himmler ordered his leading population planner, Professor Konrad Meyer, to produce an expulsion and resettlement plan for the East. On July 15 Meyer presented his *Generalplan Ost* (General Plan East), which called for the Germanization of wide swaths of Poland and its eastern border regions. A day later, Hitler, when speaking about the creation of a "Garden of Eden" in the East, demanded that the Baltics, the region around Leningrad, Belorussia, Ukraine, and the Crimea be settled by Germans. Heydrich's Reich Security Head Office then produced its own plan. Between 80 and 85 percent of the Poles, 65 percent of West Ukrainians, and 75 percent of Belorussians—together with thirty-one million "racially unworthy foreign peoples"—would be expelled, mostly to Western Siberia. The Reich Security Head Office acknowledged that Germany lacked sufficient numbers of German colonists and that the war made massive transfer schemes difficult. Eliminating the Jews remained the priority. Still, in July 1941 Himmler approved plans for the Germanization of the Lublin district of the General Government. In September 1942 in Zhytomyr, in Ukraine, he announced plans to create German settlements in the East, a "string of pearls" to protect Germans from the "Asiatic hordes."[47]

Heydrich's speech in Černín Palace was laced with the latest ideas, including new visions for the Baltics, emanating from Hitler and various SS agencies. ("The best racial elements are found among the Estonians," he stated with absolute certainty, "because of the Swedish influence— then come the Latvians with the Lithuanians being the worst of all."[48]) Armed with "scientific" knowledge about racial selection, Heydrich confidently imagined boxes into which individuals might be placed. "Racially good" and "well-intentioned" Czechs, Heydrich announced, would certainly become Germans. "Racially bad" and "ill-intentioned" Czechs would be "removed" to the East. Racially inferior Czechs with good intentions would be sterilized and then settled deep in the Reich. "Ill-intentioned" but "racially good" Czechs would be convinced to become Germans or "stood up to the wall." Two-thirds of the population would immediately fall into one category or another. The remaining, less easily labeled people in the middle would be sorted out in a few years.[49] Left unsaid, however, was how racial experts and others would place Czechs into one of these categories. Unlike the labeling of Jews and Gypsies, testing for Germanizability involved whole populations, not isolating "enemies" to be pushed to society's peripheries. By 1942 the mind-boggling complexity and multiplicity of peoples in Eastern Europe had led many racialists to declare that the "Slavs" were not a race. No unambiguous definition of what made a German existed, however. Nazi legal experts had defined "German member of the state," "citizen of the Reich," "[legal] member of the German Volk," "ethnic German," "German abroad," and many more terms, but rarely, if ever, did they decide what made a German.[50] "Race" promised Nazi officials positive, concrete criteria based on biological precepts that could determine what made, or could make, a person German. Yet, like the word "German," it was equally unclear what "race" really meant.[51]

When testing SS candidates, Race and Settlement Office racial experts, although looking at height, health, and origin, only gave their approval to men "of good conduct" who, among other things, "led a decent life and performed their duty in their profession."[52] When testing Polish foreign workers who had had sexual intercourse with local Germans, the same racial experts were reminded to take in an "impression of the worth of the candidate's entire personality," which could negate a positive judgment based on bodily characteristics alone.[53] The SS Police leader for the General Government's Lublin region, Odilo Globocnik, had his own views on how re-Germanizable Poles could be spotted. Blue eyes, blonde hair, Nordic-shaped heads, and large bodies counted, as did orderly houses and personal cleanliness. Possession of "German" objects such as chests, spinning wheels, and printed documents supposedly betrayed a forgotten German heritage. Most important, however, were names. "Szprynger" most likely had been a German "Springer," "Gryn" formerly a "Grün." No matter that "Globocnik" had a suspiciously Slavic ring to it.[54] To Nazi demographers West Ukrainians seemed more Germanizable than East Ukrainians, who had mixed with various Soviet peoples and had, they no doubt believed, imbibed Soviet ideas as well.[55] Behavior, mental disposition, socialization, and other observed characteristics, as Heydrich had made clear, were mixed with so-called racial markers by observers deciding upon Germanizability. A candidate's values and social interaction, not physiognomy, sometimes betrayed his or her "racial" essence. As the criteria multiplied, race hardly seemed to matter at all, which was good news for many Nazi leaders. The roly-poly, near-sighted, and often sickly Himmler would hardly have been judged a pure German according to strictly racial criteria, a witness at Nuremberg testified.[56]

Highly subjective definitions mixed with overlapping political competencies and competing political objectives to create further confusion, as a return to the incorporated Polish lands and the German *Volksliste* (list of Germans) demonstrates. The Volksliste began as means by which Gauleiter Greiser of Wartheland registered German citizens in his fiefdom. In his September 1940 memorandum calling for the Germanization of incorporated territories, Himmler decreed that ethnic Germans in all the territories had to apply for slots on the Volksliste, an order sanctified with a decree from the Ministry of the Interior six months later. Himmler's version of the Volksliste divided entrants into four categories. Ethnic Germans "active in nationality battles" filled category I, whereas category II was for ethnic Germans who had "retained their Germanness" but had not engaged in patriotic activities. "People of German heritage who over the years have become attached to Polendom," but who might become worthy Germans, belonged in category III, along with "splinter groups" like the Kashubians and non-Germans married to Germans. Category IV was for "renegades": people with German blood who acted politically on behalf of Polendom. Categories I and II automatically received Reich citizenship. SS race experts, Himmler said, would test anyone in categories III and IV. Although the details changed over time, generally speaking most people in categories III and IV obtained "German nationality" that was subject to revocation. They were spared the threat of deportations to the East and other horrors visited on the rest of the population, but a category III individual could be drafted into the Wehrmacht.[57]

In practice, however, Gauleiter Forster of Danzig–West Prussia and Gauleiter Fritz Bracht of Upper Silesia resisted SS attempts to conduct racial tests on most of their candidates. Forster, perhaps eager to realize Hitler's vision for "a blossoming, German Gau with joyful people," had entered six-tenths of his Gau's population onto the Volksliste by 1944.[58] Bracht, too, kept standards low in the former Polish territories annexed to his Gau in 1939, entering more than half the population into the Volksliste over the same period of time. He sought to maintain industrial production, but historical prejudices came into play as well. Applicants from former Austrian Silesia had a much higher chance of gaining a spot on the list than their counterparts from the former Russian territories. In the Reichsgau Wartheland, however, where SS racial examiners could operate most freely, only one of every eight inhabitants had a place on the Volksliste by 1944.[59] The madness was not restricted to incorporated Poland. At least three agencies claimed the right to plan the ethnic reorganization of the occupied East.[60] As the war dragged on, Ministry of the Interior officials made it quite easy for residents of Alsace, Lorraine, and Luxembourg to become German. As of 1942 candidates needed only two German grandparents and had to join or be conscripted into the SS. In Kiev, five thousand rubles could buy a spot on the Volksliste, which Reichskommissar Erich Koch introduced in September 1942.[61]

"What should the ideal Nazi look like?" one joke in the Protectorate asked. "For the protection of the race and in the interest of the nation's population, he must have as many children as Hitler. He must be racially pure like Leni Riefenstahl. A slim, resilient frame like Göring. He must speak truthfully like Goebbels. And be true to the cause like Hess."[62] In the Protectorate, where even the vague outlines of the Volksliste had not been implemented, various savants and experts alike pronounced judgments on who shall become Germans. Influential academics and Jury had argued that Moravian Czechs, traditionally less nationalistic than their co-nationals in Bohemia, promised to be more Germanizable.[63] Academic research coming from Prague muddied the waters even further. For example, neat homes on the fertile lands of central Moravia led one researcher to conclude that the region's Czechs had Germanic origins. By the end of the war—and six thousand pages of research later—few, if any, common conceptions had emerged from Prague's researchers or among Nazi leaders in general.[64] Oberlandräte and local party leaders disputed SS racial experts' judgments, claiming a more in-depth knowledge of the individuals involved. Oberlandrat von Watter of Prague told Heydrich that many German citizens in his district had only "traces of German blood." The proof, he said, was that they felt "drawn into Czech cultural circles," were not married, and did not produce children. The "asocials," of course, did not possess any "German blood" because they were former convicts and prostitutes. In fact, rather than relying on "objective" racial testing, von Watter was using a reverse logic. Because one's constitution, patriotism, and virility were inherited, he could determine biological makeup by examining the subject's outward behavior.[65]

In fact, in the Protectorate Nazi officials, Heydrich among them, performed a strange logical twist. Aware that a high percentage of "riffraff" had obtained German citizenship, many came to argue that the best candidates for assimilation were the most determined Czech patriots. "For myself," one party leader told Heydrich, "I am of the point of view that the children of these fanatical Czechs of the past twenty years are much more valuable subjects for Germanization than these unprincipled scoundrels who change their view from day to day." Czech patriots, he suggested, would either choose to become Germans or be shot.[66] Heydrich told Bormann that nearly all of the most prominent Czechs carried German blood, adding, with a mixture of shock and admiration, that the current Sokol leader had a "pure German father and pure German mother."[67] The mother of Alois Eliáš, he told Hitler, seemed, from her outward appearance, to be a German. Jaroslav Krejčí's "beautiful blue eyes," Heydrich decided, meant that the newly appointed Czech minister of justice certainly had a German background. Both Eliáš and Krejčí were, in their own ways, determined Czech patriots. They were principled, youthful, vigorous, healthy, and energetic, and they demonstrated an independent streak. Heydrich, however, considered Hácha "incapable of Germanization," since he "is always sick, arrives with a trembling voice and attempts to evoke pity that demands our mercy."[68]

"When we utter the word 'race' we are sounding the leitmotiv of National Socialism and the National Socialist state," one of Nazism's leading legal experts, Helmut Nicholai, told a group of German lawyers in 1933. "There is absolutely nothing that we, that the new state, does not consider or appraise under the aspect of race."[69] Nazi Germany was, of course, a racial state. Nazi thinking was, at its core, racist. Yet when Nazi leaders asked what made a person German, they were also required to ask what words like "racially valuable," "German blood," "Nordic race," "German race," and even "race" itself really meant. Potential Germans, various officials and experts argued, could be spotted by their blue eyes, pleasing bodies, height, girth, or well-shaped heads, yet often it was nonphysical characteristics that betrayed a German interior camouflaged in false Czech consciousness. Clean houses, spinning wheels, class, virility, sexual morality, and social behavior were criteria for membership. The most willing Germans among the Czechs, the "unprincipled scoundrels" and "rubbish," were the least suitable candidates. Czech patriots—dedicated to their cause, healthy, and independent—

would make the best Germans. "Race" was thus much more than a biological concept. The language of race simply gave a form of legitimacy to policies of inclusion and exclusion largely based on nonphysiological attributes.[70] When put into practice, when asked to construct strict criteria and forced to face the reality of human agency and human diversity, Nazism seemed more like an ideological system with a hollow core. Yet the process of identifying Germans, in the Protectorate and elsewhere, continued unabated. Logic, consistency, concrete principles, and a common definition mattered little, if at all.

Testing and Registration

Racial testing for potential Germans had begun before Heydrich's arrival in Prague in September 1941. At Himmler's request, Frank, the head of the Race and Settlement Office, and Prague's Intelligence Service chief made preparations for testing Czech schoolchildren in January 1941. As German troops marched into Soviet territory, health experts from the Reich Protector's Office gathered German medical officers and their assistants for required lessons in the science of racial selection. Unlike in Poland, however, few people in the Protectorate were actually subjected to racial tests. Economic concerns held sway. The Reich Protectorate Office's main concern had been underground resistance movements and industrial sabotage. Moreover, Germanization measures involving large-scale expulsion and settlement had few devoted proponents within Protectorate structures. Polycracy, rather than contributing toward a radicalizing dynamic, threatened administrative drag.[71]

Heydrich, however, was genuinely determined to realize the complete Germanization of the Protectorate. His ability to drive and contour Nazi Germanization policies was unparalleled in Europe. His Reich Security Head Office had racial experts in nearly every corner of Europe. Heydrich filled research centers in Prague with trusted SS-men, many of whom influenced or directly participated in racial testing in Poland and regions farther east. SS Sturmbahnführer Erwin Künzel, who had established the Race and Settlement Office in Poznán and Łódź before arriving in Prague in February 1941, established nine branch offices in the Protectorate by the end of the year, eleven by July 1942. Himmler's Reich Commissariat for the Strengthening of Germandom assumed full jurisdiction over race and settlement policies in the Protectorate, where Heydrich's authority over such matters was uncontested.[72] In the Reichsgau Sudetenland, the SS wrested control of ethnopolitical matters from Henlein and his Sudeten German Party comrades at the end of 1940. From this point on, all Germanization measures were intricately tied to institutions in Prague, and then to Heydrich.[73]

In the Protectorate, Heydrich moved energetically to eliminate administrative drag. He curbed the independence of the Oberlandräte by assigning each of them an SS Führer. He also shut many of them down, reducing the number of Oberlandräte from fifteen to seven. By June 1942 only offices in Prague, Budějovice, Plzeň, Hradec Králové, Brno, and Jihlava remained, and all employed experts from the Race and Settlement Office. One-sixth of the Protectorate's civil servants, in Heydrich's words, were "freed up for military service." Before Heydrich's tenure had begun, 9,362 Germans worked in the Reich Protector's Office and 4,706 were assigned to Czech agencies. By the end of 1942 these numbers had been reduced to 738 and 1,146 respectively. Kurt von Burgsdorff was transferred to Cracow. Oberlandrat Fiechtner was drafted into the army and captured by the Soviets. After the war he returned to Stuttgart.[74] Heydrich also employed a variety of tactics to reduce the influence of the party. The Reich Protector's Office, not the party leadership, would be in charge of the distribution of Volkstumsfond moneys. During his speech in Černín Palace, he demanded that party leaders no longer operate solely in the interests of their individual Gaue. ("With four different methods working beneath mine, I cannot rule the Czechs," he stated.) In that same speech he singled out the Reich Protector Office's most determined rival, Hugo Jury, for disrupting his plans and later sent out a circular to that effect. He undercut Jury's political support, making one of his loyalists, Gustav Schulte-Schomberg, effective ruler of the central party offices in Prague to which all four Gauleiter were responsible. Heydrich also removed Jury's most vociferous supporter in Moravia, Horst Naudé, from a state post in Brno and brought him to Prague, an act for which Naudé was to remain grateful. Other Nazi Party officials were simply removed from their posts.[75]

Heydrich's racial experts descended, virtually unimpeded, upon forced laborers, schoolchildren, and finally the general population. One of Heydrich's first acts, however, was to correct shocking "mistakes" from the past. Oberlandräte, Heydrich fumed, had allowed "racially imperfect and asocial elements" to become Germans, pointing to the example of a Mr. Kreibich from Budějovice, who still refused repeated requests to pick up his citizenship papers. "[My] mother would turn in her grave" should I accept German citizenship, the unassuming Kreibich told an Intelligence Service agent. He had applied in the first place only because his son had been sent to a concentration camp. Kreibich was hardly an isolated case. The legal German community was full of "new Germans" and undesirables, as every official in the Protectorate knew. Despite protests from within the Reich Protector's Office that the fault lay with vague criteria laid down by the Ministry of the Interior, the sheer number of applications, and pressure "from influential corners" to increase the number of Germans, Heydrich decided upon a project that one official in the Reich Protector's Office deemed "technically impossible."[76]

In April Heydrich ordered that Race and Settlement Office experts retest all previously successful candidates for German citizenship. Persons "incapable of re-Germanization" were to have their citizenship revoked.[77] Even before then, Race and Settlement Office officials had begun to examine "questionable" citizenship applications in October, and in spring of the next year Heydrich ordered that the agency's racial experts be involved in all cases not yet decided—12,368 as of the end of 1941.[78] Representatives from three agencies—Oberlandräte, the party, and the Race and Resettlement Office—now tested candidates for citizenship and mixed marriages. As in incorporated Poland, however, inconsistency, bureaucratic rivalries, and individual intransigence remained. In Jihlava only 10 percent of the applicants received German citizenship following the SS's intervention; in Plzeň 78 percent passed into Germandom. In Kolín many of the candidates had moved to the Reichsgau Sudetenland or Germany. In Kladno, the newly assigned bureaucrat from the Oberlandrat's office still feuded with the local party Kreisleiter, thus bogging down the whole process. The reorganization of Oberlandräte confused the collection and distribution of important paperwork. Candidates for citizenship sometimes refused to participate in the testing process; German women in mixed marriages continued to avoid registration.[79] Willing crossovers could claim German heritage, and examiners still had few methods of verification. Finally, the subjects could feign political loyalty, as Intelligence Service agents had warned, while remaining "Czech."[80] "A uniform principle has been established," the ever enthusiastic, and now sychophantic, Oberlandrat Molsen of Olomouc wrote to Prague. "Only those capable of re-Germanization are accepted into the German state community and those not capable of being re-Germanized are snipped away." State officials, he claimed, were learning about examination methods, and SS racial experts had been gaining expertise in the practical matters of governance. Soon thereafter Molsen's office was shut down.[81]

Other methods intermingled with Heydrich's short-term goals and Germany's growing dependence upon foreign laborers. By the end of summer army commanders, economic planners, and other top Nazi leaders realized that Soviet defeat would not come quickly. The economy required restructuring—and, most important, more laborers— to allow the German war economy to function at even higher capacity. The German population still had to be cushioned from the type of deprivations suffered during World War I. On the last day of October 1941 Hitler declared that Soviet prisoners of war who had previously been left to die in captivity were "to be extensively exploited" as laborers, in Germany and in Eastern Europe, and a week later Göring issued guidelines for the assignment of Soviet workers, both prisoners of war and civilians, in Germany.[82] Göring's underlings, however, had begun to take economic policy making into their own hands. Other men assumed powers previously claimed by Göring. In December 1941 Albert Speer, the soon-to-be Reich minister for armaments and munitions, obtained from Heydrich a promise to send sixteen thousand Czech construction workers to the Reich.[83] But ideology, Heydrich insisted, could not be abandoned. Just before Speer's visit to Prague, Heydrich presided over a Reich Security Main Office meeting that laid out plans for the segregation and policing of the foreign workers in Germany: "While all agree that the economic aspects are relevant and pressing, we must resist any attempt to defer racial and völkisch-political questions until after the war has ended, since it is uncertain how long the war may continue."[84] In February Heydrich announced to Protectorate officials that seventeen- and eighteen-year-old Czech laborers would be gathered into camps where they would be subjected to "völkisch-racial" tests. No doubt inspired by policies that Himmler implemented in incorporated Poland in 1939 and 1940, he insisted that Czechs "capable of becoming Germans" would be assigned to work in the Reich. The "un-Germanizable" youth, and perhaps their families, would be shipped to Russia, where Heydrich planned to employ them to oversee the other Slavic peoples and Europe's Jews.[85] Outside pressure for Czech laborers only increased. In March Hitler named Fritz Sauckel plenipotentiary-general for the mobilization. The former Gauleiter of Thuringia was empowered to draw foreign laborers from all over Europe to Germany to work as slave laborers. In May, Bertsch, as the head of the Economics Section within the Reich Protector's Office, took control of the newly created Ministry of Industry and Work, which empowered him to enlist nearly anyone to work in war-related industries. Hitler, mindful of the Protectorate industry's own importance to the war, ordered Sauckel—and by extension Bertsch—to limit their requisitioning of Czech laborers to anyone not already employed, but the enlistments continued. In May a Protectorate decree made all able-bodied Protectorate inhabitants subject to labor mobilization and assignment to factories in Germany and elsewhere. In the next four months, forty thousand names were added to the rolls.[86]

Meanwhile, in the Protectorate, the testing and registration process only widened. In April 1940 the Reich Protector's Office had decreed that all mixed Czech-German marriages would require the approval of the local Oberlandrat. (Marriages between party members and Czechs, Poles, and Magyars still fell under the jurisdiction of the local Gauleiter.) Local medical officials, party officials, government bureaucrats, and police submitted their own reports for the Oberlandrat's consideration. By autumn, if not earlier, The Race and Settlement Office became involved as well (Figs. 4.3 and 4.4). As the deportation of the Jews gained momentum, Heydrich's office announced plans to have experts from the Race and Settlement Office examine Czech women who had married Germans before the occupation. Also to be examined were children born out of wedlock to Czech-German partners.[87] School doctors in Kolín, and no doubt elsewhere, filled out cards, replete with photographs, describing each pupil's body type, skin and hair color, "spiritual liveliness," and father's profession.[88] In Jihlava, and again no doubt elsewhere, Race and Settlement Office experts kept a busy schedule of visiting local schools in order to examine these cards.[89] In March the Ministry of the Interior decreed that inhabitants of the Protectorate, Alsace, Lorraine, and Luxembourg obtain new identity cards, *Kennkarten*. By the end of the month Heydrich announced that everyone in his realm between the ages of twenty-five and forty-three, with the exception of soldiers, the SS, German police, mobi-

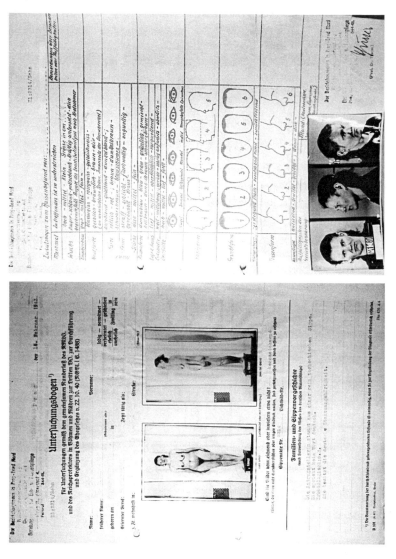

Figure 4.3 Medical examination record from a mixed Czech-German couple's marriage application file. Státní oblastní archiv v Praze, Oberlandrat Kolín, box 20, inventory number 14. (Reproduced by permission of the Státní oblastní archiv v Praze.)

164

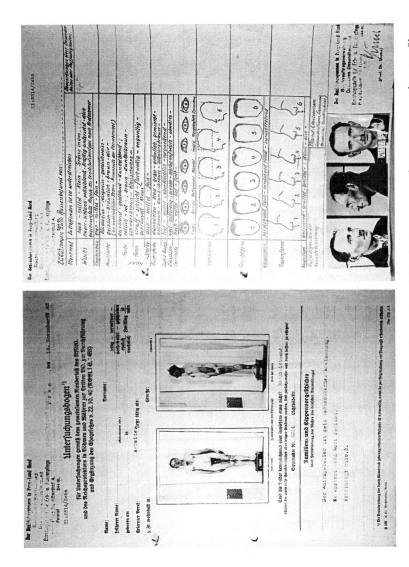

Figure 4.4 Medical examination record from a mixed Czech-German couple's marriage application file. Státní oblastní archiv v Praze, Oberlandrat Kolín, box 20, inventory number 14. (Reproduced by permission of the Státní oblastní archiv v Praze.)

165

lized workers, and Jews, had to register for Kennkarten at the offices of the local Oberlandrat.[90] In May Heydrich reported to Berlin that Race and Settlement Office experts had fanned out across the Protectorate with five X-ray machines. Their aim was to create a racially ordered cross section of society, all done under the cover of a Protectoratewide campaign against tuberculosis.[91]

Although aimed at achieving the distant goal of Germanization, the effects of Heydrich's testing and registration schemes had immediate consequences for Protectorate inhabitants. A "racially unsuitable" Czech man who had had intercourse with a German woman was sent to a concentration camp. If a marriage was approved, the male candidate was identified as a German, both in the eyes of his compatriots and the state. Czech mothers married to Germans were required to raise their children as Germans. Failure to do so meant having their children kidnapped and put up for adoption.[92] The effects of Heydrich's racial policy, however, went beyond the family. It reinforced his goal of ensuring domestic peace and industrial productivity. Tens of thousands of young men were shipped abroad to work in Germany and other parts of German-occupied Europe. As the war dragged on, more and more Czechs—both men and women—were forced to work as slave laborers abroad.[93] Anyone not carrying a new identity card was immediately arrested, allowing police authorities to track down parachutists, partisans, Jews in hiding, and other inhabitants living outside the law.[94] Other, far-reaching consequences threatened. By May of 1942 more than fifteen thousand Protectorate inhabitants were displaced from their homes, mostly to make room for newly constructed army bases. At the same time, the registration process seemed to be gaining a momentum all its own. As early as February 1942 Heydrich announced to leading Nazi officials in Prague his plans to use information gained from his Kennkarte registration to have the Land Office mark, in red ink, properties targeted for Germanization: Nazi officials would expel the owners, making room for German settlers. In that same meeting Heydrich was searching for ways to expel even more Czechs, as he wrote, "in a camouflaged way." Although Heydrich remained wary of wartime demands, he seems to have been suggesting that Czechs might have been just months away from the type of deportations suffered in Alsace, Lorraine, Luxembourg, Slovenia, Poland, and lands farther eastward.[95]

Assassination

Back in London, Beneš worried. The lack of Czech resistance to the Nazis was damaging his diplomatic position and endangering his goals of reestablishing Czechoslovakia along its pre-Munich borders. The "subject of meaningful resistance," Beneš's intelligence chief wrote after the war, "cropped up with humiliating insistence. Hard-pressed on their own battlefields, the British and the Soviets kept pointing out to Beneš the urgent need for maximum effort from every country, including Czechoslovakia."[96] Although wary of more spectacular actions against the Nazi regime, Beneš continued to encourage acts of sabotage and popular defiance. His lifelong project, the Czechoslovak state, appeared to be hanging in the balance.

Czechoslovak plans to drop agents trained in intelligence, communications, and sabotage into the Protectorate had begun before Heydrich's arrival. In October a plan to assassinate Heydrich had begun to emerge, although who exactly gave the order was unclear. Primary documents on the planning are unavailable. Beneš, who kept his ministers isolated from each other, gave his most important orders orally. He later denied any role. Memoirs offer conflicting interpretations and re-creations of the events. Still, there is little doubt that Beneš and his intelligence chief knew about the operation. The Czechoslovak president feared a compromise peace that would leave the Bohemian lands within the German sphere of influence. The British had still not disavowed the Munich agreement. The Soviets were dropping their own parachutists in the Protectorate. Their actions threatened to undermine Beneš's political position to the advantage of the Communists. The democratic underground had been paralyzed. Thus, the assassination of the head of the Nazi Intelligence Service promised to spur resistance within the Protectorate and impress Allied leaders.[97]

After months of training with Britain's Special Operations, Jozef Gabčík, a Slovak, and Jan Kubiš, a Czech, parachuted into a snowy field twenty miles outside Prague, far from the planned drop site. A local gamekeeper soon found them. After seeing their parachutes buried in the snow and an empty can of meat with a British label in a nearby hut, he followed their footprints to an abandoned quarry. He was soon joined by a local miller. Gabčík had seriously injured his foot during the landing.

Luck, however, would be on the parachutists' side that day. The miller, who happened to be a member of an underground Sokol group, promised to put them in touch with comrades in Prague. Shortly after the new year Gabčík and Kubiš took the train to Prague and spent the next five months moving among various safe houses in the capital. Their equipment, which included bomb-making materials and pistols, followed.[98]

Other parachutists were less fortunate. The parachutists who had flown with Gabčík and Kubiš split up shortly after landing. One, group leader Alfred Bartoš, managed to reestablish contact with ÚVOD and to construct a radio transmitter, which soon began beaming information on industrial production and the population's mood back to London. A plan to coordinate with the British the bombing of the Škoda Works in Plzeň faltered, however. Other missions failed after the parachutists fell into the hands of the Gestapo. Surprised by the pervasiveness of the police state, holding poor-quality false documents, and left alone to survive, many had simply panicked. Some committed suicide. In one case a parachutist sent word to his mother that he was alive and fine. The excited mother told an acquaintance, who promptly reported the news to the Gestapo. The parachutist's father and two brothers were held as ransom until the parachutist turned himself in.[99] In May Bartoš demanded that the parachute drops be halted. "[Y]ou are sending us people for whom we have no use," Bartoš told London. "[T]hey are a burden on the organizational network which is undesirable in today's critical times. The Czech and German security authorities have so much information and knowledge about us that to repeat these operations would be a waste of people and equipment."[100]

Bartoš also managed to make contact with Gabčík and Kubiš. Before long, to his horror and the horror of other members of the underground, the men's mission became apparent. Twice in early May ÚVOD remnants broadcast a desperate message to Beneš: "The assassination would not be of least value to the Allies, and for our nation it would have unforeseeable consequences. It would threaten not only hostages and political prisoners, but also thousands of other lives. The nation would be the subject of unheard-of reprisals. At the same time it would wipe out the last remainders of any [resistance] organization. It would then be impossible for resistance to be useful to the Allies. Therefore we beg you to give the order through Silver A for the assassination not to take place.

Danger in delay, give the order at once."[101] On May 15 Beneš sent a message back to the underground. He did not respond directly to ÚVOD's plea. Nor did he cancel the operation: "I expect that in the forthcoming offensive the Germans will push with their forces. They are sure to have some success. . . . In such a case I would expect German proposals for an inconclusive peace. The crisis would be a serious one, and it would shake some people even here among the Allies. . . . In such a situation, an act of violence such as disturbances, direct subversion, sabotage, or demonstrations, might be imperative or even necessary in our country. This would save the nation internationally, and even great sacrifices would be worth it."[102] Gabčík and Kubiš, despite final pleas from their underground protectors to abandon the mission, decided that it was time to act. On the morning of May 27 they positioned themselves near a sharp bend in the road in the Prague suburb of Holešovice. When Heydrich's Mercedes turned the corner, Gabčík leaped out, but his gun jammed. Heydrich ordered the car to stop and stood up with his pistol. From a nearby hiding place Kubiš threw a bomb, which missed its target and exploded against the car's rear wheel. Shrapnel shattered the windows of a passing tram. The assassins escaped in different directions, and Heydrich, after briefly giving chase, fell over in pain, a rib broken, his diaphragm ruptured, and external objects lodged in his spleen. At the hospital he at first refused to let the local German doctor operate, demanding that a surgeon from Berlin perform the needed surgery. By noon a compromise was reached and Heydrich was rolled into the operating room.[103]

Paranoia and rage spread among Nazi leaders and Protectorate Germans. Less than an hour after the assassination attempt Hitler ordered Frank to order the execution of up to ten thousand Czechs, some from among concentration camp inmates and some from among the Protectorate's general population. Anyone who had helped the assassins or had information and failed to report it to the police would be shot, along with their families. Informants providing information leading to the assassins' arrest were promised a reward of one million reichsmarks.[104] Police had to restrain Protectorate Germans from lynching their Czech neighbors. In Jihlava local Germans attacked Czech stores and locales.[105] Nazi authorities imposed martial law throughout the Protectorate, and the Reich Protector's Office announced that Czechs over sixteen years of age had until midnight of Friday, May 29, to obtain their new identification papers. (To accommodate the demand, local Oberlandrat offices remained open from 7:00 A.M. to midnight.) Anyone found without the proper papers on Saturday was to be shot.[106] Summary courts began sentencing hundreds to death again; even people charged with "approval of the assassination attempt" came before the courts. Calling Beneš "Public Enemy Number One," Hácha warned that anyone who "works against the Reich in the slightest way will be destroyed." Moravec reminded Czechs that in France ten hostages had been executed following the assassination of a low-ranking German officer: "Just think a little bit what would await the Czech people if the culprits were not found." For a moment, it seemed that the Czechs had earned a slight reprieve. Frank, the detested Sudeten German chauvinist, had flown to Berlin to convince Hitler to scale back his reprisal measures. The perpetrators were certainly sent from England, he argued. To engage in mass killings and mass executions meant abandoning Heydrich's policies, endangering the armaments industry, and playing into the hands of enemy propaganda. Hitler rescinded his order for mass executions. Then, on June 4, Heydrich died from his wounds.[107]

"Nothing can prevent me from deporting millions of Czechs if they don't wish for peaceful co-existence," Hitler screamed at Hácha after the funeral. Wartime needs no longer concerned him. The assassins must be found.[108] An hour after a June 9 meeting Frank, from Berlin, telephoned the Intelligence Service to say that the Führer had ordered the village of Lidice destroyed. German troops and police shot 173 male inhabitants of the village, sent the women to concentration camps, and razed all its buildings to the ground—after they had registered the population, livestock, and property. Race and Settlement Office officials examined the children for "Germanizability." Seven were sent to the SS home for children at Lebensborn, given new names and identification papers, and assigned to German families. Gestapo officials, registration books in hand, shot twenty-six more inhabitants in the coming days. The Gestapo tracked down eleven men working the night shift in a nearby factory. They found a miner with a broken leg resting in a nearby hospital. Another man was shot after hiding in the woods for three days. Nazi police sent four pregnant women to hospitals in Prague. After the children were born, the mothers were sent to concentration camps, without their children. Why Lidice, a sleepy village near Kladno, was chosen for destruction is unclear. German police had found no evidence of anyone in the village being involved in the assassination.[109]

The massacre radicalized an already intense atmosphere. Nazi propagandists bragged about the killings and warned that more might come. Intelligence Service agents reported that Protectorate Germans hailed the massacre with "great satisfaction and sometimes open joy. Local Germans find their constant warnings against the Czechs confirmed; they even say that officials in high places will now perceive how the Czechs should be treated." Protectorate authorities promised, along with clemency, an increased award sum for anyone who knew of the assassins' location, and they announced drastic measures if the assassins were not handed over by June 18. As the date approached, the tensions came to a crescendo. Rumors spread that the Nazis would execute every tenth Czech. Many Czechs gave serious thought to suicide.[110] Two days before the deadline a Czechoslovak parachutist, Karel Čurda, walked into Gestapo headquarters in Prague. He claimed to fear for his family and to have become disenchanted with the exile government. He did not know Gabčík and Kubiš's location, but he did betray those who had provided the safe houses. A wave of arrests followed. After withstanding hours of brutal interrogation, one of the men slipped that the assassins were hiding in an Orthodox church in Prague along with nine other parachutists. German police and SS agents surrounded the church. After six hours of resistance, the parachutists who had not already died from bullet wounds committed suicide.[111]

Beneš was ecstatic following the assassination attempt. He immediately sent out a radio message to Bartoš: "I see that you and your friends are full of determination. It is proof to me that the entire Czech nation is unshakeable in its position. I assure you that it's bringing results. The events at home have had an incredible effect [here] and have brought great recognition of the Czech nation's resistance."[112] After the massacres at Lidice he transmitted another, chilly message to Bartoš: "What the Germans are doing is horrible, but from the political point of view they gave us one certainty: under no circumstances can anyone doubt Czechoslovakia's national integrity and her right to independence."[113] As the president had intended, Czech and Allied propaganda seized upon recent events. Most credited the home resistance with the assassination, making no mention of parachutists. For their part, British leaders had no intention of admitting their knowledge of a foreign leader's assassination. The Lidice killings, undertaken far from the front lines and broadcast with pride by German propagandists, made the front pages of newspapers around the world. Locations in Illinois, Mexico, Brazil, and Panama were renamed Lidice. Cecil Day Lewis and Edna St. Vincent Millay wrote elegies to the village, and war bonds posters called on Americans to "Remember Pearl Harbor and Lidice." "The Nazis are stupid beasts," Thomas Mann wrote from the United States. "They wanted to consign the name of Lidice to eternal oblivion, and they have engraved it forever into the memory of man by their atrocious deed. . . . [N]ow it is world famous." Long before Auschwitz, Lidice had become the symbol of Nazi evil around the world. In August the British government declared the Munich agreement invalid.[114]

Days after the deaths of Gabčík and Kubiš Gestapo agents moved on Bartoš, who died from wounds suffered during the ensuing gunfight. With the help of informants, Gestapo agents rounded up, one by one, members of ÚVOD, the underground Sokol, and the Communist resistance, including the entire Central Committee. The underground was almost completely wiped out. In Prague Eliáš was shot. More innocents fell victim in the village of Ležáky, where Gestapo agents found Bartoš's transmitter. All its adult inhabitants were shot. The children were handed over to German authorities and the buildings reduced to rubble.[115] Excluding those killed at Lidice and Ležáky, 3,188 Czechs were arrested and 1,357 were sentenced to death. Almost five hundred received the death sentence simply for approving of the assassination. Up to four thousand people with relatives amongst the exiles were rounded up and placed in camps throughout Moravia.[116] In July a decree from the Reich Protector's Office increased the number of offenses that could bring the death penalty: taking part in "anti-Reich" activities, falsifying identity papers, handling false identity papers, or lending out one's own documents. Thousands of Czechs had waited in lines outside local Oberlandrat offices, sometimes throughout the day and night, to register. Later in the year when the Reich Protector's Office demanded that local officials account for every Protectorate inhabitant, bureaucrats from Brno reported that only fifty-eight people were missing. All but one of them were Jews.[117]

The Czech population still seemed in danger of mass deportations. Shortly after Heydrich's assassination Himmler pledged that the Protectorate "will be completely inhabited by Germans . . . from the perspective of blood."[118] That December Professor Meyer estimated that 3,625,000 Czechs could become Germans, and 1,415,500 German settlers would have to be added to the existing German population of 224,500. The remaining, unmentioned 3.5 million Czechs were, no doubt, doomed to deportation to the East. Party officials in Berlin promised to begin expelling the Czechs as soon as the "evacuation" of the Jews was finished. The next spring Frank told a gathering of Nazi Party members that "racially unworthy Czechs" would be deported and replaced with "fresh German blood." About thirty experts from the Race and Settlement Office remained stationed in Prague until the end of the war.[119] Race and Settlement Office agents and party officials continued to rifle through old citizenship applications. The former continued to examine schoolchildren through 1943. They tested candidates for mixed Czech-German marriages almost to the end of the war.[120]

Meanwhile, the murder of the Jews continued. In a pattern followed all over Europe, ten trains brought more than eighteen thousand victims from Terezín to Treblinka in autumn 1942. Over the next two years another twenty-nine trains brought almost thirty thousand more to Auschwitz and Bergen-Belsen.[121] In March 1942 about three-fourths of all the Jews whom the Nazis and their accomplices would murder were still alive. Eleven months later three-fourths of the roughly six million victims of the Holocaust were dead.[122] In the Protectorate, as in Germany, the exclusion and murder of Mischlinge gained momentum as well. Six days before the assassination attempt on Heydrich the Reich Security Main Office ordered that, with the exception of partners in "privileged" mixed marriages, all Mischlinge in the German Reich, which included the Protectorate, were to be shipped to Terezín. Frank oversaw the first transport in autumn 1942, and by the end of the war only those granted exceptions remained outside Terezín. More than 33,400 Mischlinge from various parts of the Reich died there.[123]

In practice, however, Germanization plans faltered at the very moment when the murder of Europe's Jews reached its apex. The two paths toward destruction diverged. Without Heydrich's energy and administrative acumen plans for racial testing faltered. In July officials from the Race and Settlement Office reported that their project of X-raying the population had stalled. Gas initially intended to fuel their trucks had been requisitioned for the destruction of Lidice. The experts, their vehicles, and their X-ray machines remained idle. Their leading officer, whose men had been X-raying Czechs under the cover of an antituberculosis campaign, actually came down with the disease and left Prague.[124] Old political rivalries and Reich-Sudeten German tensions resurfaced. "We will never make a Czech into a German. . . . We must find means of getting rid of the Czechs. That is our goal," a Nazi Party official and Sudeten German told Race and Settlement Office members in a meeting that summer. Although admitting that X-ray examinations of schoolchildren showed more Eastern and East-Baltic characteristics than had been expected, the SS's racial exports maintained that the majority of Czechs, including their best patriots, would be made German: "For the moment we must not show our cards. In two to three years we will employ an even more intense and open brutality in dealing with the Czechs."[125] Frank and Jury wrangled again over Germanization policy and political influence within the Protectorate. In December 1942 the former head of the Prague Gestapo, whom Frank had refused to name head of the Intelligence Service in Prague, wrote a letter to Himmler accusing Frank's son of being recently baptized. Luckily for Frank, Himmler let him off with a word of warning, confident that "your wife alone is guilty here." Representatives from five different agencies—the SS Race and Settlement Office, the Gestapo, the Health Department, the regular police, and the Nazi Party—examined every application for German citizenship.[126]

Nazi leaders also turned to other, more immediate concerns. Plans to examine Czech children whose parents had been executed or had died in concentration camps were abandoned, an SS official wrote, because it would cause an "unbearable" state of affairs within the communities that had taken in the children, endangering "the maintenance of labor peace necessary for the unlimited production of war matériel."[127] In June Sauckel renewed his demand for Czech laborers. By the end of the year more than 135,000 men—almost one of every fifty Protectorate inhabitants—were working in Germany or parts of German-dominated Europe.[128] Although pamphlets published in Prague instructed factory foremen in Germany to encourage Nazi thinking and pro-German feelings among Czechs assigned to them, by the end of 1942 racial selection was no longer directly linked to labor assignments.[129] In February 1943 Meyer presented his last version of the Generalplan Ost, and Himmler abandoned his settlement projects in Lublin and Zhytomyr.[130] After a string of Wehrmacht losses in the Soviet Union and Africa in winter 1942, victory on the battlefield took precedence over transforming nations. Heydrich's short-term goals of maintaining domestic peace and industrial productivity became paramount, not just in the Protectorate but throughout all of Hitler's Europe.

Because of the fragmented evidence, Isabel Heinemann notes, it is difficult to determine the exact number of Czechs subjected to racial examinations. The population tested numbers at least in the tens of thousands. If one counts the tests undertaken by the X-ray commissions and the information provided by doctors working for the Race and Settlement Office, the number might be hundreds of thousands.[131] One can only guess, too, what might have happened if Heydrich had not been killed. On the one hand, the registration process had gained a seemingly unstoppable momentum, and before Heydrich's death the SS was ascendant in the Protectorate. Heydrich was eliminating administrative drag. Unlike in the Zhytomyr region of Ukraine, where disagreements among local officials helped bog down Himmler's resettlement plans, Heydrich could simply remove officials who disagreed with his Germanization plans.[132] Yet, on the very day of his assassination Heydrich was on his way to Berlin to meet with Hitler, who, some documents suggest, intended to assign Heydrich to France, where resistance to Nazi rule had been mushrooming.[133] Furthermore, time might have run out before Heydrich could have implemented any more measures. By spring 1943 German's military misfortunes required that ideologues all over Europe, even Himmler, put their Germanization plans on hold. Most important, Heydrich had to consider the Czechs' contribution to the war effort, both during his rule and, had he lived, in summer 1942. Cowed and coddled, Czech workers were still producing invaluable tanks, artillery, and other armaments for the eastern front. They could not simply be sent to the Arctic.

Similarly, the Protectorate's location, both as part of the inner industrialized circle of Germany's Großraumwirtschaft and its distance from the front lines, mitigated against widescale terror and violence there. For the territories east of Poland planners in spring 1941 envisioned drastically lowering the population's consumption, de-urbanizing and de-industrializing, and harnessing the region's agricultural production for the war effort. A lack of German troops to occupy the territories and a lack of transport needed to remove prisoners of war and shift food resources resulted in mass starvation.[134] Wartime chaos radicalized the SS and other agencies. Killing the Jews and sucking the economy dry took precedence over Lebensraum dreams, but Himmler and others developed plans to create small-scale German colonies in the East. The Ukrainians' spot within the Nazis' imagined hierarchy, and their level of Germanizability, slid down the ladder. "We are a master race," Reichkommissar for Ukraine Koch reminded a conference of Nazi Party members in early 1943, "that must remember that the lowliest German worker is racially and biologically a thousand times more valuable than the population here."[135] Heydrich, in the interest of promoting domestic peace and continued industrial production, terrorized the Protectorate's inhabitants, but the acting Reich protector would have never, as Koch had done, literally hunt inhabitants in a local reserve.[136] Instead, he employed a combination of social benefits and terror to ensure that industrial production continue apace. Faced with demands that he send Czech workers to the Reich, he decided to combine raw labor needs with vague Germanization plans. The Protectorate's economic role could not be ignored, even by the second most powerful man in the SS.

Protectorate Jews were, of course, not spared. Indeed, the timing of their destruction speaks volumes about what differentiated the murder of the Jews from Heydrich's Germanization plans for the Protectorate, and perhaps throughout Hitler's Europe. Just one month before the Wannsee Conference Heydrich agreed to send Czech construction workers to Germany. At the very moment when labor needs became most acute, Nazi officials and their henchmen set in motion forces that would lead to the mass, industrialized murder of every Jew on the continent. After Heydrich's death Protectorate officials dropped most Germanization measures. The trains to Terezín, and then to Auschwitz, continued to roll. Nazi officials ceaselessly debated the usefulness of Jewish labor, yet, beginning in 1941–1942, the drive to extermination appeared to have gained a momentum all its own, a destructive force that required cooperation across a slew of agencies and massive amounts of resources. In the Protectorate, as in Germany, the exclusion and murder of Mischlinge continued until the last days of the war. Germanization garnered neither the sense of urgency nor the consensus that made the murder of the Jews possible.[137]

More comparisons merit attention. Nazi racial policies depended upon the creation of categories; yet the means by which the Nazis categorized peoples, like their ultimate aims, differed greatly.[138] Policies toward the Jews differed from Germanization measures in that the goal of the former was exclusion and then extermination. Czechs with sufficient German blood and immersion in things German could, in the words of Heydrich's favored academic in Prague, "emerge into the Volk" (*umvolken*).[139] Nazi officials disagreed about whether the same could happen to Jews, but the fate of the Mischlinge suggests that Heydrich and others believed that Jewishness could never be entirely subsumed. Moreover, the Nuremberg Laws provided relatively clear definitions about who was a Jew. Nazi leaders could find Jews thanks to birth certificates and Jewish congregation membership papers. While hardly about "race," the destruction of the Jews posed relatively few definitional challenges. A clear definition of what made, or could make, a German never emerged. The identification of potential Germans bears similarity to measures to hunt down the Gypsies, in which racial and sociological judgments intermingled. Yet the Germanization of Czechs, in contrast, forced officials to ask what made a German, a project whose absurdity was only multiplied by polycracy and human diversity. Nazi attitudes toward the Slavs—indeed, toward most non-German Europeans—varied wildly, whereas anti-Jewish measures began and ended with a vague but powerful ideological predisposition.[140] That Nazi leaders could, with fewer difficulties, categorize its Jewish victims made the realization of that policy easier.

When words like "Jew," "Mischlinge," "Gypsy," or "German" were attached to an individual, escaping the label and its attendant fate proved nearly impossible. Nazi leaders sent tens of thousands of Jews and Gypsies to their deaths. Although sparing the population of the Protectorate the horrors of deportation, Heydrich's registration drive made policing that population even easier for Nazi authorities. These various measures of inclusion and exclusion also point to yet another seismic shift in the play of nationality politics in Bohemia and Moravia. Before 1940 "Germanization," like "Czechification," referred to the taking over of a business, obtaining land or property, winning the majority in city elections or a local census, or gaining a school—usually in areas straddling the imaginary borders dividing Czech and German areas. The Czechoslovak government was complicit in small-scale settlement schemes, but, generally speaking, Germanization and Czechification measures were largely aimed *at* economic and political structures. Formerly, individuals could become "German" by participating in German clubs, speaking German in public, or somehow acting "German." Before, nationality had been an individual affair. For many people in mixed areas nationality had been an individual choice. Although Oberlandräte and then party members judged the applications of candidates for German citizenship, most applicants before Heydrich's arrival chose to join Germany's legal community. Later Germanization schemes were aimed at whole territories and whole populations. By 1942 racial experts and other state officials decided who was a Czech, German, Jew, or Gypsy and thus sealed the fates of thousands.

The state-run process of identifying, segregating, and then expelling individuals continued with strikingly similar methods but diametrically opposed goals after the war when the Czechoslovak state embarked upon the "organized transfer" of Germans. The segregation and labeling of Jews provided practical lessons. Yet again state officials faced the same vexing question: "What is a German?" In the meantime, Nazi officials continued to try to make Germans out of Czechs in the schools. In the factories Czechs continued to work for the Reich's war machine. Resistance groups had virtually been wiped out, and the police state seemed to have eyes everywhere. Beneš continued to fret about his standing abroad, and patriots in the Protectorate warned that the very survival of the "nation" was hanging in the balance. When Beneš did return in 1945, he found an economy and society that had been utterly transformed, and he found a "nation" that he barely knew or wanted to understand. What they shared was an overriding desire to expel all the Germans from Czechoslovakia.

5

Surrounded by War,
Living in Peace

In the common narrative of the Protectorate years, Lidice is the climax and the expulsions of the Germans are the dénouement. But the Czechs who lived under Nazi rule after the massacres at Lidice saw a major shift in political power, a new phase of propaganda, and further economic and social transformations. It was this society, not the one existing immediately after Heydrich's assassination, that entered the postwar period. Its members expelled the Germans and watched as the Communists took power. Before liberation, however, most Czechs were intent on survival.

After the massacres at Lidice, Czechs lived through two painful years under a regime that demanded obedience, conformity, and continued industrial productivity. With few exceptions, Czechs avoided tripping over lines that led to certain arrest. Workers continued to be paid hefty salaries, and production figures remained high. "A trip to Prague at the end of 1942 was a trip to tranquility," one Reich German visitor wrote. "Surrounded by war, a truly worldwide conflagration, the Protectorate was the only Central European land living in peace." The Czechs were hardly suffering at all, a Polish correspondent angrily reported to Beneš's government eighteen months later. Armed resistance was nowhere to be found, and patriots satisfied themselves with "make-believe forms of national life." As a result, he concluded, "the Czech has the right to sit next to the German," whereas the Pole, Jew, and Gypsy are forced to suffer and die.[1]

Life under occupation raised a number of uncomfortable questions. How to differentiate between victim and perpetrator? What constitutes "resistance" and "collaboration," "innocence" and "guilt"? How should one act correctly in a world gone mad? By what criteria were people's actions to be judged? For their part, Beneš and other officials in London claimed that "resistance," and thus morally correct behavior, primarily consisted of militarily useful actions and industrial sabotage that contributed to the Allies' war effort. In addition, the Czechoslovak government-in-exile condemned anyone who in any way aided the Nazi regime and kept its military machine running. Patriots countered with their own criteria for judging behavior. "Good Czechs" disobeyed the regime when possible and, most important, acted Czech in the few ways that were still possible. Patriots worried less about the lack of "resistance" than about a nation riven by class and generational divides and a society infected by Gestapo informants. Yet most Czechs acted correctly, they protested; the nation was "healthy." In the last years of the occupation a gap opened between Beneš's government and people at home over what constituted correct and laudable behavior.

Dichotomies

At the beginning of 1943 Nazi Germany's military situation had become desperate. Soviet forces launched a massive counterattack against Axis troops who had entered the city of Stalingrad. After six weeks of vicious fighting the commander of the German Sixth Army defied Hitler's prohibition on any retreat and withdrew from the city. From this point, the slow, inexorable Soviet march toward Berlin began. By the end of 1943 the Red Army had recaptured two-thirds of the Soviet territory taken by the Germans. The United States had entered the war in December 1941, and in November 1942 Allied forces broke through the German-Italian lines near El Alamein in Egypt. In June 1943 Allied troops landed in Sicily. The Anglo-American bombing campaign intensified in the spring of 1943. In June 1944, as Soviet troops were poised to enter the General Government, British and American forces landed at Normandy.[2]

The defeats in the winter of 1942–1943 required a radical rethinking among Nazi leaders in Berlin, and in Prague. In January Goebbels outlined a new propaganda message. Inflated reports of German victories gave way to fearful warnings that defeat was possible. "No matter where individual Germans may stand on National Socialism," he announced at a conference in January 1943, "if we're defeated everyone's throat will be slit." He declared the beginning of a "total war" that required male and female registration for compulsory labor service in Germany and the mobilization of society. Rather than German conquest for Lebensraum, the war became, according to Goebbels, a struggle against Bolshevism on behalf of all Europe.[3] "The Protectorate is a Reich land, and it cannot stand on the sidelines," Frank told an audience of Czechs following Goebbels's declaration of "total war."[4] As the front lines drew closer, Frank and Moravec parroted Goebbels's main points. Grandiose celebrations of German victory were replaced by appeals to somber realism. Czechs, they contended, faced a simple choice between Germany's "New Order" and Bolshevik oppression, and hence between pro- and anti-German sentiments. "We know [the Germans] quite well. They like our Czech music, Czech national costumes, and when one finds oneself in a screwed-up situation, they are kind people," Moravec, apparently without blinking an eye, told an audience in 1944 (Fig. 5.1) The Russians, he continued,

Figure 5.1 Moravec delivering an anti-Bolshevik speech in Pelhřimov, June 2, 1944. (Reproduced by permission of the Česká tisková kancelář.)

were just as foreign to the Czechs as the Chinese. Soviet rule would result in the Czech economy's being harnessed entirely to meet the foreigners' demands. Unlike Moravec's previous speeches, one London informant wrote, this one was "very elegiac. Only rarely did he raise his
voice even a little bit. Gone was the Teutonic blathering. He spoke as if
from the grave."[5]

Nazi Germany's increasingly desperate situation also required mobi-
lizing every ounce of Czech labor for the war effort. A little more than a
year after Heydrich's assassination Frank had nudged aside his rivals to
become the uncontested master of politics in the Protectorate. On orders from his superiors in Berlin, however, Frank largely abjured Germanization plans and anti-Czech rantings in favor of measures to support the German war effort.[6] The Protectorate's industries, already
crucial to Germany's war effort early in the war, became invaluable after
British and American bombers began obliterating German cities and industrial complexes. Economic planners refitted even more factories for
armaments production, relocated German factories to the Protectorate,
and built others from scratch, sometimes underground. The famous
shoe factory in Zlín was refitted to make V1 and V2 rockets as well as
tires for the German army. The Škoda factory in Plzeň that had formerly
made cars now made tanks and airplane engines.[7] Bertsch's Department
of Economics and Labor assigned tens of thousands of men and women
to work in Protectorate industries. His department assumed the right to
dissolve any factory or business not considered essential to the war, thus
freeing up even more labor for heavy industry. The result was a massive
overhaul of the Bohemian lands' economic structure. From 1939 until
the end of 1944 the total number of industrial workers in the Protectorate rose from 730,000 to 880,000. The number of those working in
the textile industry dropped by 43 percent; in the leather industry, by 20
percent. By contrast, the number of those employed in the chemical industry rose by 20 percent.[8] The number of people working in metal or
metal-working factories almost doubled, from 314,000 to 512,000, over
the same period of time.[9] Bertsch's office, with the help of the mostly
Czech-run Office of Work (Úřad práce), continued to deport thousands
more forced laborers from the Protectorate, although in smaller numbers than in 1942 (Fig. 5.2). From early 1943 until April 1944 the Department of Economics and Labor assigned another 75,000 Czech men
and women born between 1918 and 1924 to work in Germany, Austria,

Norway, and elsewhere in Europe. Brass bands bid them farewell as they left for positions in airplane factories, emergency squads (*Technische Nothilfe*), air defense units (*Luftschutz*), and other duties. In the last year of the war teachers and the senior classes were taken from the secondary schools to dig trenches in Austria, erect fortifications in Silesia, or aid in other desperate acts of defense.[10]

The topic of the Czechs' contribution to the war effort also consumed leaders in London, and especially Beneš. And once again, Beneš worried. The political capital gained from Lidice had been spent, and the Allies demanded more proof that the Czechs were doing their part for the war effort. Beginning in autumn 1943 London radio stations broadcasted

Figure 5.2 A transport of female forced laborers about to depart for Germany, January 25, 1944. (Reproduced by permission of the Česká tisková kancelář.)

calls for Czechs to participate in industrial sabotage and other militarily useful acts of resistance. Beneš said that the time would come when the Czechs would be called to rise up against the Germans, but they still had duties to fulfill today: "I don't want to lecture you today on where and how you should fight, where you should resist, where you should sabotage. Every one of us knows [the answer] quite well. . . . It would be a great mistake, it would be a national sin and crime, if it was said of us that we can or should wait while millions in the armies of the Allies bring about the ruin of Germany. . . . And therefore I repeat: To battle! Today, tomorrow, every day! Everyone as he can, purposefully and systematically, carefully, and persistently."[11] Calls from Beneš's colleagues were more dramatic. "A cornered rat is at its most dangerous," Justice Minister-in-exile Jaroslav Stránský told his listeners. Therefore, the choice facing Protectorate inhabitants was not one between safety and danger: "You have no other choice than to be the hammer or the anvil. Death awaits thousands of you and your children. We on the outside know [the situation], believe me, better than you in your prison. The freedom of our country, the future of our nation, the well-being of the republic—these are all great, noble, and things worth dying for."[12] In the first half of 1944 broadcasters again begged the Czechs for acts of sabotage to hamper wartime production and hasten the end of the war. Neither round of pleas had much effect.[13]

In the last two years of the occupation only a tiny proportion of the population remained ready and able to dynamite railroad tracks, relay military information, or attack German troops. Remnants of ÚVOD organized under new leadership, now called the Council of Three (Rada tří), but the domestic resistance was scattered and miniscule. The state of the Communist resistance in the Protectorate was only slightly better. Soviet paratroopers organized small cells in Bohemia and Moravia, but even as late as spring 1945 there were only about thirty partisan groups in the Protectorate. Each had between fifteen and twenty members; the largest had seventy.[14] Within the factories, the picture hardly looked better. Industrial production continued to rise, especially in the armaments industries, and by 1944 Protectorate industries accounted for a greater percentage of the industrial production within the "Greater German" area of Germany, Austria, and the Protectorate than ever before.[15] Productivity per worker, however, did drop. Some informants pointed to individual acts of industrial sabotage, although most reports remained skeptical. "Beware of any reports of sabotage," one London informant reported. "No one would attempt to organize a group action because someone always loses his nerve and the result is arrest and execution, or in the best case [being sent to] a concentration camp." "Outward resistance" in the factories, one member of the underground confessed to London, hardly existed.[16] But slacking and calling in sick were common.[17] In September 1942, 10 percent of the workers at the Vítkovice Ironworks in Moravská Ostrava called in sick on any given day. On an average day in summer 1944 30 percent of the manual laborers at the Plzeň Škoda Works failed to show up for work. Deeply concerned about these tactics, Nazi authorities ordered Gestapo agents across the Protectorate to arrest workers for showing up late to work. At one factory, a worker with tuberculosis was ordered to remain at his place in the assembly line, as were women up to seven months pregnant. Other developments further hampered worker efficiency. High levels of surveillance required more workers, and armaments factory managers, fearful of espionage, were constantly changing their production schedules. Other factory managers complained of a shortage of workers and raw materials. Nor were these problems limited to the Protectorate. Lowered productivity and workers' malaise were common throughout the German Reich.[18]

The reasons for the lack of resistance were clear. Organized and armed underground resistance movements suffered because most of the Czechoslovak army's weapons had been confiscated before the war. Protectorate lands lacked the mountainous terrain enjoyed by Josip Broz Tito's Yugoslav partisans. Few leaders and exemplars remained: "The horrible thing is that people who were in the opposition are gone, shot, silenced," a resistance fighter explained.[19] Surviving outside the Protectorate's tightly controlled economic and social system meant living without ration cards and in constant fear of being identified and jailed. Young men, especially, were subject to intense scrutiny, for police randomly demanded identification cards on the streets, in movie theaters, in stores, and on public transportation. Anyone lacking an identification card was immediately arrested and, in the best case, released with a fine. Beginning in 1944 no one could leave the Protectorate except for war-related reasons. Gestapo agents walked through every train, asking for personal papers.[20] Within tight factory spaces security was especially intense. In the most important positions, each Czech worker had a

German peering over his shoulder. A seemingly omnipresent Gestapo stifled industrial sabotage and other "battle" actions in the factories, mostly thanks to a network of informants that included Czech-speaking Protectorate Germans working within the Intelligence Service and Czech neighbors, workmates, and sometimes even family members. Frank, like Heydrich before him, made the most of terror's "optical effect," carefully targeting transgressors and their families and then advertising these police actions to foster an atmosphere of debilitating fear. Placards announcing arrests and executions were on every corner (Fig. 5.3). Gestapo agents made a point of arresting people in public in order to frighten bystanders. Day and night, Prague inhabitants saw black cars carrying the doomed from Gestapo offices to the infamous Pankrác Prison, where they were subjected to unimaginable torture and the threat of being guillotined.[21]

Fear then mixed with reason as Protectorate inhabitants tried to swim through natural desires for self-preservation and confusing ethical dilemmas. Engaging in "anti-Reich" activities endangered innocents. Frank's regime continued to practice collective punishment, arresting family members and neighbors for the actions of individuals. Bystanders unfortunate enough to live in the vicinity of "anti-Reich" activities also fell victim. Following the destruction of a train line near Tochovic, Frank ordered that twenty males from the village be arrested and sent to Terezín. So small was the village, however, that agents had to spread out into the surrounding areas to meet their quota.[22] After escaping a Polish concentration camp and traversing the Protectorate by foot, Heda Margolius Kovalý arrived in Prague looking for someone to hide her. Some people took her in, but only for a night. Friend after friend refused her, knowing that punishment for hiding anyone without proper documentation meant the death penalty. After mulling it over, one friend, Franta, asked her to leave his apartment:

> I got up and walked to the door. Franta jumped up to stop me.
>   "Please don't leave yet," he said. "I've struggled with these questions endlessly. When and how should one risk one's life? You escaped because you were probably convinced that you'd be killed. But, in my opinion, the chances that you'll lose your life are much greater this way than if you had stayed in the camp. After all, some people will survive even there. You have much less hope in this situation. And am I justified in risking my or anyone else's life for something I consider a

lost cause? What sense does it make anyway to risk one's life for another?"

I stepped back to try and look him in the eye, and Franta threw his cigarette into the ashtray. After another moment of silence, he said, "Okay, It's true. I'm scared."

Again I walked out into the streets. There were pink posters pasted on the walls with long columns listing the names of people who had been executed for "crimes against the Reich." Often, there were three

Figure 5.3 Placard, signed by Frank, listing the names of people sentenced to death for "unfriendly behavior toward the Reich." (Reproduced by permission of the Česká tisková kancelář.)

or four people with the same surname: whole families murdered for trying to help someone like me.[23]

As many Czechs saw it, resistance, as called for by London, meant choosing a worthless death over embarrassing complacency. Minister Stránský's cajoling aside, there indeed was a choice between "safety" and "danger." In Poland's General Government, Nazi violence was unpredictable, and the Polish underground attacked alleged collaborators, thus making cooperation with the regime nonsensical. Nor did the regime do much to seek out Polish collaborators. Terror in the Protectorate, however, carefully targeted transgressors, sparing the rest. In the Protectorate, where cooperation with the regime ensured survival, it made sense to toe the line. By themselves, a report to London argued, Czechs could have little impact on the outcome of the war. The front remained far away. Large European powers had decided the fate of Czechoslovakia in 1938, and the Soviet Union, Great Britain, and the United States would, many said, decide it again: "Therefore everyone thinks: careful, no unnecessary losses, hold out for now and there will come a time, and prepare [for it]." "Our people don't like these calls for sabotage," another informant told London. "They say that they would rather know what they should and could do. One wishes for facts and not 'idle chatter' that would lead to unnecessary risk of life."[24]

In fact, London's calls for resistance and sabotage only made a bad situation worse. "We know better, more than anyone, what we should do," workers muttered; but each time London called for resistance, Gestapo officials countered with more surveillance and arrests. Frank responded directly to Beneš's calls for "resistance" with public announcements of internments and executions.[25] "Calls for sabotage from London do more harm than good," one report to Beneš's government bluntly stated. "They provoke the Germans."[26] Many Czechs quietly complained that their leaders, safely tucked away in London broadcasting booths, had little understanding of their daily travails. In 1944 Jan Masaryk broadcast an announcement that Allied planes would begin bombing Protectorate factories. Czechs at home, he said, must be ready to make sacrifices for victory, and now Protectorate inhabitants will understand what London exiles went through during the Blitz. There were, of course, differences between the two experiences. Masaryk did not live in daily fear of terror. When the bombs dropped in the Protectorate, factory workers were ordered to remain at their posts. Many Czechs listened to Beneš's normally sympathetic foreign minister in disbelief. He must have been drunk at the microphone, they muttered in Moravská Ostrava.[27]

Beneš's calls for resistance were irrational, many voices at home complained. Similarly, home and abroad split when it came to defining "collaboration." For Beneš and others in London "collaboration" meant aiding the enemy. Like Frank, Beneš divided people and actions into two categories—either a person was working for the Reich or against it. As the occupation dragged on, London broadcasters intensified their calls for postwar reckoning with collaborators. "Be careful!" Beneš warned "those on the Czech side" as early as April 1941. "No one will be forgotten; everyone will be subject to retribution." "[E]very crime, every outrage, every murder [will be repaid] a thousand times over," he warned audiences after Heydrich's arrival in Prague, adding vaguely that after the war anyone "aiding in" Nazi crimes would be punished. In the wake of the massacres at Lidice Beneš promised that "we will demand that *every member of the Nazi Party and the Reich government in our land* answer, *individually*, for his actions. We will demand individual answers from *everyone who has helped them, no matter where in our Republic's lands.*"[28] Threats of retribution aimed to discourage collaboration and offered hope for "good Czechs" that moral reckoning, and revenge, would come. At the encouragement of ÚVOD and its successors, Beneš and officials around him came to support retribution as a way of "cleansing" society of corrupting elements and political enemies as part of a postwar political and social revolution. London radio urged Czechs to make lists of "Gestapo scoundrels and quisling helpers." Many resistance fighters and other patriots pledged that known collaborators were "marked."[29]

Behind the scenes, officials in London began preparing legal procedures to carry out retribution trials, and in January 1942, the Czechoslovak government-in-exile signed an agreement with nine other exile governments pledging to try and punish war criminals. The next year, six more countries, including the United States and Great Britain, signed the St. James Declaration, which, among other things, laid the groundwork for the Nuremberg Trials. Czechoslovak ministries began to design their retribution institutions, laws, and procedures, but the process was hampered by confusing legal questions and institutional rivalry.[30] The reality of life under occupation also crashed against the simplistic dichotomies imagined in London. "Beneš understood the term 'collaboration' in its broadest sense," his biographer Zbyněk Zeman writes. "He was unable to make the imaginative effort and understand the difficulties of life in an occupied country, where decisions on collaboration and resistance had to be made by ordinary people on a daily basis."[31] Masaryk described for his audience at home a postwar cleansing process that would be undertaken with "mathematical certainty."[32] But he and his colleagues in London left many questions unanswered. What constituted aid? Where would the lines separating the "dirty" from the "clean" fall? Who was identifying known collaborators, and what controls were in place to distinguish revenge from justice? And yet lines were certain to be drawn.

Although generally supportive of Beneš's and London radio's promises to reckon with Gestapo informants and high-profile Czech traitors, voices from home consistently warned the government-in-exile against painting life in the Protectorate in stark blacks and whites. Local administrators, for example, received mixed reviews. One report praised the mayor of Železný Brod for manipulating the system to improve conditions in his city, adding that "our bureaucrats in the districts often provide help, too, even if they are under control of the Germans." Other bureaucrats were criticized for constantly repeating the same phrase: "But it cannot be otherwise." In one district, Dr. Procházka, a "Czech" who "thinks himself to be totally German," blasted Hitler's speeches through all the town's loudspeakers, causing even German soldiers to retreat to pubs or taverns. Local bureaucrats had to remain at their seats, listening intently, despite the fact that few spoke German.[33] Informants' judgments of Czech police, gendarmes, and government soldiers—who did the dirty work of guarding train tracks against sabotage and locating Czechs attempting to avoid mobilization, trading on the black market, or engaging in other "anti-Reich" activities—varied as well. A propaganda piece from London that condemned government troops as quislings sparked a number of angry responses from voices at home. One government soldier, who was also a member of the underground, warned that such propaganda "cannot lead to unity. Even if we are taking different paths, our goal is the same." "You'd be speaking differently," another government soldier told London, "if you'd been forced to live with five years of Nazi subjugation and had been witness to the shootings and arrests of our brothers and sisters."[34] (The later charge was not entirely fair. When not herded into German death camps, many relatives of émigrés in London and Moscow ended up in camps where Czech gendarmes stood guard.[35])

Even the most consistent target of London radio's most vicious attacks, Hácha, provoked sympathetic responses. Although many reports condemned Hácha as a puppet or worse, few agreed with Beneš that Hácha and his government were "just as answerable for the crimes of Nazism" as Heydrich, Himmler, and Hitler.[36] Protectorate inhabitants still wrote letters to Hácha begging him to help a son or daughter who had been imprisoned or sent to work in Germany. Rather than condemning Hácha as an evil perpetrator of Nazism's crimes, informants at home described him as a weak and tragic figure whose mind was going and who was playing a role forced upon him.[37] Unscrupulous advisers took advantage of Hácha's worsening senility to seize power and advance their own agendas. The advisers, and Moravec was first among them, were regarded as the true and most despicable traitors. Many people, no doubt, also saw in Hácha's compromises and embarrassing helplessness parallels in their own lives. No one could completely avoid "aiding" the regime in some way. Their compromises with the regime, like his, had been subtle and easily rationalized.

The "Health" of the Nation

Patriots at home worried less than did émigrés about Beneš's reputation abroad, the Czechs' contribution to the war effort, or the size and capability of resistance groups. Rather than military resistance or industrial sabotage, they used national frames of reference to judge individuals' actions. They viewed the world within Czech and German dichotomies and contended that resistance, or *odboj,* and moral behavior consisted of opposing a regime that demanded absolute conformity and obedience. Their fight was against a "Germanizing" regime, cleavages that threatened national solidarity, and moral uncertainties in a world where basic values had been turned inside out. To save the "nation," a carefully nurtured creation dating back a century and a half, was a project that obsessed Czech patriots at home. And they, too, had many reasons to worry.

Beneš inquired most about the factories; patriots concerned themselves first of all with the state of the schools—spaces that created good Czechs and national institutions that had provoked intense political, economic, and social tensions between Czechs and Germans before the occupation. After 1939 the schools remained an important battleground for patriots on both sides. Higher education produced the so-called intelligentsia, a disproportionately persecuted group that both Frank and Czech patriots saw as the creators, spokespersons, and conscience of the nation. In addition to arresting large numbers of the so-called intelligentsia, Frank worked to eliminate their emergence in the future. The number of Czechs allowed into college-track high schools dropped precipitously as the occupation dragged on, and university doors in the Protectorate remained closed to Czechs. Only a limited number of medical and engineering students could, subject to approval from racial experts, study in Germany for three years.[38] Of the twenty thousand Czech students who graduated from secondary schools in 1941, only twenty-seven applied to study in Germany—their only opportunity for higher education. In 1943 roughly 3,500 applied to study in Germany, but only 380 were accepted, among whom only half actually made the trip.[39]

Frank also continued to pursue policies first designed by Heydrich that aimed to denationalize Czech youth and eventually make them into Germans. Military losses demanded that other Heydrich-inspired Germanization policies be put on hold. Many believers in the project had given up on making Czech adults into Germans. But some of the acting Reich protector's education policies that did not affect the smooth running of the economy still had life. Nazi leaders hoped—and Czech leaders feared—that teenagers and especially younger children, who did not remember life before the occupation, could still be Germanized, since they were more impressionable than their elders. Here, Nazi officials thought, was a blank slate.[40] Depending on their ages, schoolchildren received instruction of between five and eight hours of German per week. In college-track high schools, subjects like math were taught entirely in German.[41] After the war one teacher remembered how in geography class maps often showed only the Protectorate and the Reich. Teachers, one educator remembered after the war, could use only German-language place names "so that often three-fourths of a Czech sentence in geography class was made up of German words. It was stupid, mangled speech and soon disgusted both pupils and teachers."[42] In history class, František Palacký and Tomáš Masaryk were either disparaged or ignored altogether, replaced by "German greats" like Mozart, Goethe, and Hitler. Teachers were ordered to eschew any mention of the First Republic; and if Czech history was mentioned at all, it was in the context of the medieval "German" Reich. One London informant commented sarcastically, "It seems that before 1933, European history did not exist."[43]

Czech teachers faced immense pressure to conform. Many teachers had to demonstrate proficiency in German in order to keep their jobs, and by 1943 12,500 had undergone "reeducation" training. Pupils and teachers were supposed to greet each other with a "Sieg Heil." German school inspectors regularly made surprise visits to classrooms, and chairpersons of school-exiting exams had to be Germans.[44] When the outsiders were not around, a few Gestapo informants—whether among the students, teachers, or administration—could keep a whole school in line. "The Gestapo even had informants and agents among children," one educator recalled. "Uncertainty and mistrust destroyed any feeling of comradeship among children. The ability of the school to function quickly declined."[45] Despite these pressures, Czech patriots lauded teachers, and especially high school teachers, for being "true heroes," surreptitiously inserting Czech history into their lessons, refusing to offer the "Sieg Heil," and spreading "anti-Reich" ideas. In doing so, they confirmed Frank's and other Germans' worst suspicions.[46] Heydrich had called teachers "the training core for the opposition Czech government [in London]," and Frank accused them of being the most dangerous wing within the intelligentsia. Hitler and other Nazi leaders thought little of teachers in general, whom they considered "effeminate" and representatives of a conservative, static state apparatus, as opposed to the dynamic, transformative Nazi movement.[47] Not surprisingly, then, Frank's regime singled out Czech teachers for persecution. In the first half of 1944 alone one thousand teachers were imprisoned or killed. By the end of the war about five thousand had been sent to concentration camps, where a fifth died. About 40 percent of Czech teachers in the Protectorate, and 60 percent from Prague, had been removed from the classrooms and mobilized for "total war" before liberation.[48]

"One cannot neutralize every single Czech teacher," Heydrich declared to Nazi leaders just months before his death. Thus, he continued, the Nazi regime needed to create its own education system to "bring Czech youth closer to the Reich."[49] Taking a page from the Hitler Youth, Reich Protectorate Office officials created the so-called Kuratorium, whose leaders demanded that youth believe unquestioningly in National Socialist values, act instinctually, and strengthen the body for work, war, and "soul." All 500,000 Czech children between the ages of ten and eighteen became mandatory members and took an oath of allegiance to the Reich. Weekly activities included group exercises and singing. The Kuratorium also established summer camps, took over the administration of sports like hockey, and organized grand festivals.[50] Education measures threatened to make Czech children into Germans and to widen the chasm between generations. Shipping thousands of youth to work in various parts of Europe was bad enough, Czech patriots exclaimed, but now the regime was attempting to Germanize their children. "Czech youth," one bureaucrat in Budějovice worried, "will soon be indistinguishable from German ones."[51] Parents feared that they were losing control over the education of their children, even if some took a confused comfort that children were not learning much because they lacked materials and wasted time jumping up and down on exercise fields. Although wondering if the Kuratorium was effecting any psychological transformations, even the normally pessimistic Intelligence Service gushed about the Kuratorium's successes in leading and coordinating Czech youth.[52]

Other measures inadvertently heightened class and regional differences among Czechs. Patriots worried openly about national unity. Protectorate nationals still employed outside factories resented factory workers' higher wages, accusing them of insularity and selfishness. Other workers took unashamed pleasure at the expense of the persecuted intelligentsia.[53] As Radomír Luža remembers, even sharing a prison cell during the darkest days of Heydrich's rule could not erase class differences: "There was a social ranking in the cell: though we were all friends, each of us knew who in the room was a professional, who was a proletarian. . . . All of us were hungry. But whereas the priest and others would talk of food, family, politics, food, God, the occupation, and food, the workers and poorer fellows talked of food, food, food, and food."[54] The shady world of the black market further accentuated divisions, for higher wages gave workers greater access to scarce goods. In several cases customers attacked local shopkeepers accused of diverting goods for black market sale. Farmers and other village inhabitants with direct access to basic goods enriched themselves at the expense of others. They preferred to exchange clothes, textiles, and other goods rather than accept cash, and they were becoming choosy. "Ach, I already have this [style of] clothing," one correspondent was told. "Come back with something else!" As during World War I, urban inhabitants suffered greater shortages than their fellow patriots in the countryside. And just as some viewed the workers' higher pay as blood money, many watched in anger as villagers did business with Germans, who had more money and goods for trade. No one starved, but resentment bubbled beneath the surface. More people shared the experience of assembly-line work than ever before, and all Czechs subsisted under a strictly controlled ration system. Yet material envy and class antagonisms cut deep gashes across society.[55] Patriots at home feared that Czechs would turn on each other after the war. Thus they united around Beneš, the only person with the authority necessary to hold the country together: "Here at home there is a great danger of bloodletting due to various sides settling old scores. The president must prevent this, step by step."[56]

Patriots at home spoke disapprovingly of political squabbles in London, demanding a postwar system that reduced or eliminated divisive party struggles. What the nation needed above all, they said, was a sense of unity. They also described for London a nation facing increasingly dire deprivations. In both the Protectorate and Germany, work hours lengthened—often to twelve or fourteen hours a day—and working on Saturdays became mandatory. Conditions within the factories deteriorated. After the war the Czechoslovak government estimated that 3,000 Czechs died while in Germany and counted 100,000 physically disabled citizens among its population, many of whom were victims of bombing attacks or tuberculosis.[57] In some places lines for state-distributed food items began to form at five in the morning.[58] In general, Protectorate nationals lacked vitamins, since cabbage was the only vegetable available to most people. Agricultural production, the quality of goods, and average calorie intake plummeted as the war's end approached. The survival of many people depended solely on their ability to obtain goods on the black market. By 1944 it was nearly impossible to get shoes or clothing. "To the question 'Are you satiated?' everyone always answers 'never,' but in the Protectorate no one is hungry," a London informant reported in 1943. In 1944 half of the population of the Bohemian lands suffered from malnourishment. In the last months of the war half were going hungry.[59]

On the interpersonal level, denunciations undid personal relationships and set Czech neighbors, friends, and even family members against each other. German inspectors and Gestapo agents demanded that pupils report on their family activities, including listening to radio broadcasts from London. Many parents legitimately feared that their children would betray them. In a letter written to Moravec one boy asked for guidance in dealing with his parents, whose "intellectual backwardness" and reactionary attitudes made them incapable of "understanding Hitler's New Europe." The same boy denounced a history teacher for speaking ill of Nazism. His classmate stood accused of ripping a picture of Hitler from a magazine.[60] Empowering denouncers brought out the worst aspects of human nature—greed, envy, malice, pettiness, and revenge. Spouses in difficult relationships turned on each other. Others used denunciations to settle property disputes.[61] Some Czechs knocked on Gestapo doors to denounce Communists. *Rudé právo* helped the Gestapo by publishing the names of non-Communist resistance fighters.[62] Motivations varied, but denunciations had several clear and consistent effects. In addition to stifling military resistance and thereby keeping factory assembly lines moving, denunciations threatened to unravel the fabric of society, and even families. Ominous placards reading "Political discussions are forbidden" hung in pubs, restaurants, and other public places. "Everyone fears the person next to him," one informant commented ruefully. The pervading threat of denunciation, as well as other daily travails in the Protectorate, also left people confused and raised a number of questions.[63]

Most Czechs at home felt lost in a world gone mad. Václav Černý, a teacher of Czech literature and member of the underground resistance, fondly recalled how the students he taught during the Protectorate years attempted to come to terms with life under the occupation:

> In my three years of dealing with them I never met a single informant or traitor. This despite the fact that they were boys corrupted by collaborationist families, the pressures of the Kuratorium, the onset of Protectorate slovenliness, and although I even gave bad grades to those who did not know the material, they knew that it was not necessary to know it. It was an earnest generation of students, taking seriously a person's cultivation and character, even when they could not acquire proper cultivation and their character was being undermined. This they understood and took in everything with a certain irony that was part defiance and part smiling sadness. Their internal dispositions [were made up of] a drop of nihilism, a drop of resignation, a drop of hope.[64]

"One does not live now as before," a London informant wrote in 1939. "We cannot say, for example, in fourteen days we'll go there and there. We live without a daily schedule, as, I would say, as if we weren't people."[65] After enduring years of occupation, Czechs felt more confused than ever about basic values. Slacking at work was deemed patriotic by some but as a sign of cowardice and sloth by others.[66] A misstatement by a child could lead to a visit by Gestapo agents looking for parents "guilty" of anti-Reich statements. Misbehavior and disobedience among youth worried some Czechs, but others imaginatively read their transgressions as acts of "resistance." On a tram traveling through Prague, for example, a Czech boy made an obscene gesture in the direction of a disembarking German soldier. "The entire car smiled; only the boy's father was understandably disturbed," the correspondent wrote. The incident, the informant concluded, was proof of the "healthy soul of Czech boys."[67] Many workers who earned pay bonuses by volunteering for Sunday shifts in armaments factories also participated in underground activities. Farmers often fulfilled Nazi quotas but could be generous and courageous in giving food to partisans or refugees. One factory manager was told that unless he retooled his machines to make armaments, the Reich Protector's Office would shut down the factory and transfer its workers to another iron works that had complied. The workers voted and decided to carry out the retooling and stay home with their families.[68] Fathers of students arrested in 1939 joined the Czech Committee for Cooperation with the Germans, hoping that shows of loyalty would win their sons an early release from concentration camps. Once freed, the students had to promise to report on their neighbors to the Gestapo. In such situations, what constituted just and moral behavior?[69]

Patriots offered answers and claimed that, despite immense difficulties, the nation remained united, loyal, and "healthy." Czechs, they maintained, were still acting Czech—and hence correctly—in the few ways still available to them and thus "resisting" the regime. In autumn 1944 one of Beneš's agents interviewed an engineer named Šrajbera, who had just been assigned to work in Sweden. Following a standard set of questions, the Hradec Králové native divided the nation and its "mood" into three categories. He declared that 5 percent of the nation consisted of "downright traitors," while another 20 percent consisted of people who out of "financial, personal, or family reasons" tended to "blow with the wind." The rest were good patriots who formed the "healthy core of the nation." How did the majority distinguish itself? First, Šrajbera explained, they took an active interest in the progress of the war, observed every detail, marked maps, and, most important, passed on the information to others. Second, the "good Czechs" were "instantly identified, thanks to their smiling faces." "Good Czechs"—as many reports from the Protectorate confirmed—were co-nationals who spread rumors and told jokes.[70]

Much fodder for rumors came from London radio reports. German propaganda raged "against Bolshevism, the defense of Europe, and so on," as one London informant put it. Czech news from London, on the other hand, had a reputation for providing trustworthy information, even if the government-in-exile's interpretation of events was not always accurate. Time and again London radio predicted that liberation was just months away, but listeners hardly seemed to mind. Instead, Czechs at home spread their own unrealistically optimistic rumors. Tales spun in 1943 told of Czechoslovak paratroopers who would drop like rain over the Protectorate.[71] As Jan Gross writes of the Poles in the General Government, rumors allowed people to express "deeply felt desires and wishes . . . often out of joint with reality" that helped them to "hang on." As Lydia Flem has noted, rumors, "through the pleasures of expression and understanding[,] . . . bring about a consummation of social relations, a reinforcement of social bonds."[72] Listening to London radio, and sometimes to Moscow radio, Czechs felt a connection not only with the London government but with the thousands of Czechs tuning in at the same moment. Passing on news the next day, they sustained bonds that occupation policies and Gestapo informants threatened to sever. Avoid "propagandistic, empty chatter," one London informant warned. People desire something "dense, real, that they can whisper the next day."[73]

Protectorate jokes, on the other hand, were almost entirely home-made.[74] Like rumors, jokes united Czechs and expressed longed-for hopes, but they dealt in multilayered wordplays and macabre ironies that contrasted to the straightforward, serious, and often Manichaean phrases and sentences coming from propagandists at home and abroad.[75] "We're not afraid, we don't live there," was the Czech response to a propaganda poster calling on them to prevent the Bolsheviks from bombarding the Castle, the historic home of Czech leaders and now seat of the Nazi government. Nazi claims that scientists were developing a secret weapon that would end the war provoked a similar response: "The Germans have a new weapon: A two-meter long pole with a white ribbon." Upon hearing word that German men in their sixties were being mobilized, Czech jokesters remarked that the old men might actually be useful to the war industry. They did, after all, have silver hair, golden teeth, and legs made of lead.[76] Jokes demonstrated to patriots that "resistance" to Nazi rule still existed, as one London informant explained: "In conclusion I offer a rude and unpleasant joke, but I repeat it because it documents our resistance to the Germans: Grandma Hanačka enters the tram in Prague with a heavy sack and a suitcase. While stowing her baggage, she, how do I say it, behaves badly. The Germans in the car hold their noses in opposition. The grandmother gives them a spiteful glance and turns to her Czech fellow-travelers: 'They've shut our mouths tight, but they can't do the same to our a . . .'"[77] Such jokes did worry at least one London informant, however. Pointing to another joke about flatulence, he described a growing trend toward incivility in which "everywhere people are speaking very obscenely."[78]

Jokes were also less detectable than other displays of national loyalty or "anti-Reich" attitudes. After Lidice, Brno patriots clothed themselves in the national colors (red, blue, and white), and in Prague good Czechs wore red carnations. But even such actions could lead to arrest. In December 1943 local patriots called on Czechs to wear red ties. The Gestapo arrested anyone with a red tie, and then those with red umbrellas.[79] As early as September 1, 1939, the Reich Protector's Office decreed that anti-German speech would be punished, and "in particular cases, with death."[80] Overt, easily noticeable acts of national pride could lead to trouble, but jokes were too nebulous, too slippery to get one arrested. Unless overheard and reported, spoken words left no hard evidence behind. Jokes, with their ironic tones and ambiguous messages, flew underneath the radar of Nazi authorities.

Most important, the rumors and jokes were almost always in Czech. As one joke intimated, speaking Czech, and mocking the regime in Czech, was one thing that the Nazi regime could not prevent. Speaking German was one thing they could avoid doing:

One morning Karl Hermann Frank looked out his window toward the Castle wall and saw, in huge letters, the following message, clear and precise: "Hitler is an ass!" Beside himself with rage, the trusted min-

ister of the Reich dashed straight to Hácha's workplace and let loose a
horrible tirade about the Czechs, their loyalty to Europe, [and so on].
The old man [Hácha] took his cigar from his mouth and made accommodating gestures with his lips: "These people, these people," [he
said.] "And I have repeatedly told them: everything in German, everything in German!"[81]

Speaking Czech drew imagined boundaries around the nation and dis-
tanced the speaker from everything "German" in a world in which "Germanness" and Nazism had become conflated. As one woman remembered of her teenage years under the Protectorate: "I never went to
German films, I didn't tolerate German; we had it in school every day,
daily we had to read German publications, we had to know *The History
of the Hitlerjugend* by Horst Wessel. Everything in me demanded resistance, and therefore I loved Latin, which we had every day. . . . Luckily I
didn't have to major in German. I graduated in Czech, Latin, French,
and Biology."[82] Like their predecessors, patriots derided any Czechs who
spoke more German than necessary. And like Palacký and the
nineteenth-century Awakeners, patriots believed that the Czech language pulsed through the very heart and soul of the nation, animating
the imagined national organism. Thus, when Prague intellectuals after
the war wrote of "the Nazis' battle against the values of the Czech soul,"
they were referring not only to measures aimed against the Catholic
Church but the imposition of German language and other symbols into
Czech films, radio, theater, monuments, museums, and libraries.[83] Because of its intimate, precarious, and constructed emphasis on culture
and language, Vladimír Macura observes, Czech nationality has always
involved a choice of sorts to become a conscious member of the nation
and to participate in the creation of Czech culture. Participating in that
culture meant participating in a project of affirming and re-creating
what it means to be Czech.[84] Czechness began as a cultural project, and
so it was again. (Significantly, Václav Černý subtitled his memoirs "Our
Cultural Opposition during the War.") The context was radically
different, but in its emphasis on language and the "soul of the nation"
Czech nationalism was, once again, recalling the nineteenth century.

People work through tough times, Richard Rorty observes, "by
talking to other people—trying to get reconfirmation of our identities by
articulating these in the presence of others. We hope that these others

will say something to help us keep our web of beliefs and desires coherent."[85] By spreading rumors and telling jokes, Czechs were affirming
their identities more and more. They were fashioning a moral universe
in which acting nationally was the highest good. They were excluding
Germans from their moral community, and they comforted themselves
with the thought that they were resisting the German regime. Jokes and
rumors offered medicine to patriots sick with worry that the national
project might come to an end. Jokes allowed patriots to justify people's
activities at home. Jokes provided a measure by which moral behavior
could be judged. They also provided "proof" that "resistance" continued. Yet one searches in vain among reports by London informants
for the names of heroes past—František Palacký, Jan Neruda, Antonín
Dvořák, Bedřich Smetana, Alphons Mucha, Karel Čapek, Tomáš
Masaryk. One rarely finds their words—"humanism," "liberty," and "democracy," for example. While calling for national solidarity, few informants proffered political programs. Acting Czech, as before, meant
speaking Czech. The words, however, lacked clarity.

Ambiguities

Šrajbera's interpretation aside, jokes and rumors were not always acts of
"resistance." In fact, rumors might have played a role in stifling the kind
of resistance called for by Beneš. Drawing on the work of Michel de
Certeau, we might envisage jokes as small, personal, and calculated victories—opportunities seized at a moment in time. Then the victory disappeared. Joke telling might have acted as a "safety valve," a harmless
vent that allowed Czechs to continue working in factories while
soothing a vague sense of patriotism and integrity.[86] Nazi leaders encouraged rumors about the horrors of the concentration camps as part
of their terror campaign against the population.[87] Furthermore, patriots
often assumed an intentionality on the part of joke tellers and rumor
mongers that was not necessarily there. Rumors empowered the individual possessing the precious information, and, like jokes, reconstituted social relations among neighbors—not just co-nationals.[88]
Whether overcoming the mind's "censor," protesting against modern au-
tomation or rigidity, or degrading dominant values and destabilizing existing hierarchies, jokes have always constituted a challenge to authority.[89] Inhabitants of Nazi Germany often used jokes to express

discontent with a particular policy or aspect of Nazi rule without necessarily rejecting the regime as a whole.[90] Rumors gave voice to anxieties, as Alain Corbain noted of a different context. They exposed many Czechs' deepest fears—that inoculation measures were sterilizing or poisoning children, or that every single Czech would be deported to the East if the Germans won the war. Rumors abounded that the regime intended, one execution at a time, to destroy every Czech. Frank did little to make Czechs think otherwise, promising "about one hundred death sentences per month" with the goal of "liquidating" the nation. One joke expressed fears of extermination with frustration with London's failure to understand this danger and an ironic hope for deliverance: "The *last* two Czechs met on Wenceslas Square [in Prague]," it began. "'Did you hear Honza [on the radio broadcast coming] from London? It's better,' one said to the other. Gestapo agents, hearing this, grabbed them. They were sentenced to death by hanging." Circumstances, however, saved the joke's heroes: "Under the gallows the next morning they greeted each other, one of them commenting: 'It's good that they don't have enough ammunition for a firing squad.'"[91]

Rather than an expression of all-pervasive Czech-German or resistance-collaboration dichotomies, the significance of jokes might be in what they say about the uncertainties and juxtaposition of opposites that characterized life in the Protectorate. In an essay composed amid the political uncertainties of the 1960s, the Marxist philosopher Karel Kosík wrote of World War I: "There is an irony in Socrates and there is also a romantic irony but the 'World War' gave birth to yet another irony: the irony of history, the irony of events, the irony of things. Events themselves bring together and drag down into one space and maelstrom things so dissimilar and mutually exclusive as victory and defeat, the comic and tragic, the elevated and lowly."[92] Discovering the irony of history, events, and things in Protectorate jokes is not difficult. Referring to the Iron Cross medals bestowed upon war heroes, one joke went: "What is the difference between the Romans and the Germans? The Romans put hopeless miscreants on the cross. The Germans put crosses on hopeless miscreants." For workers, there was the irony that being employed under the Protectorate was no better materially, because of shortages, than being without work before the occupation: "The youngest member of the family once asked his mother what beef fat was. His mother answered: 'Fat is something that we had before, when your father was unemployed, that we spread on bread.' "[93] Frank, Beneš, and patriots at home used the vocabulary of war to divide people and actions into one of two mutually hostile camps, yet ambiguity and uncertainty constituted the essence of daily life under the Protectorate. Rather than use the simplistic vocabulary of battle and war, many joksters chose to express themselves in ironic, multivalent tones. Jokes made at least partial sense of a confusing situation while providing comic relief and a shared laugh during trying times.[94]

Nor were the jokes and rumors always in Czech. Czechs were not the only ones telling jokes in occupied Europe.[95] In fact, many Czech jokes had crossed over the imagined boundary that separated them from Germandom. In Prague and Vienna one could hear the following: "One day Hitler was meditating in his office in front of his own portrait. [Hitler] spread his legs, folded his arms on his waist and stated: 'So how's it going to turn out, Adolf?' At this the painting stirred and let out a voice: 'I'm being taken down and you're going to be hung up.' "[96] Joke-tellers in Germany played with the same caricatures of top Nazi leaders—Himmler as dolt, Göring as glutton. The punchlines and sometimes the entire body of some jokes relayed to London were often in German, no doubt because the wordplay involved could not have been translated.[97] Germans, too, listened to foreign radio broadcasts and spread rumors about the progress of the war. Czechs even joked about it: "The owner of a beer garden turns on the London radio station after he closes for the evening. As the broadcast comes to an end, he hears a rattling outside his door. 'Who is there?' he asks sheepishly. Behind the door a voice yells out in protest: 'This is the police. Goddammit, when you listen to London, could you turn on the loudspeaker in the garden!!' "[98] When Germans told a joke or spread a rumor, were they "resisting" the regime or affirming their German loyalty? Like Beneš's views on resistance and collaboration, the patriots' perspective ignored many uncomfortable questions and used simplistic dichotomies to brush over a complex reality.

Indeed, Šrajbera and other patriots ignored signs of German opposition to the regime and the growing rifts between Protectorate and Reich Germans. When German disloyalty was described, it was usually cited as proof that the regime was nearing collapse. The human costs of war provoked increasing resentment among the local German population. About 500,000 Germans from the former Czechoslovakia had been drafted into Nazi Germany's armed services. Between 160,000 and 194,000 of them died on the front.[99] In 1943 a group of German-speaking women in Chomutov were arrested for taking to the streets and protesting the unbearable conditions that their sons on the eastern front were forced to endure. Like their Czech counterparts, German workers in the Reichsgau Sudetenland slowed down and called in sick in large numbers.[100] From London, Social Democratic leader Wenzel Jaksch still broadcasted speeches to followers at home. Many of the Czechoslovak Communists, at home and in London, were Sudeten Germans. One German-language report to London claimed that many Sudeten Germans remained loyal to Beneš, and that in Prague "the true Prague Germans are often together in being against the Reich Germans. The Germans from the Reich suppress everyone else—the Czechs, Protectorate Germans, Sudetenlanders—and have laid the groundwork for a united front against . . . the Germans from the Reich."[101] Members of the SS like Frank and Sudeten German patriots who joined the Intelligence Service were directly responsible for many of Nazism's most horrific crimes. Many other Germans, both Reich and Protectorate, no doubt supported the Nazi takeover and many aspects of the regime, especially when it furthered nationalist goals at the expense of Czechs. While ignoring the German perspective, however, reports from the Protectorate not only discounted German "resistance" but also ignored the diversity of feelings, motivations, and actions that existed among their hated rivals. And in doing so, the reports helped make possible the demonization of a whole group.

"German" and "Nazi" were not synonyms. By the same token, "Czech" and "Nazi" were not always antonyms. Many of the journalists working for the Ministry of Propaganda had, like their boss and former Czechoslovak legionnaire Moravec, come to their anti-Beneš, pro-German, and anti-Communist views naturally. Realism also played a role. "If we cannot sing with the angels we shall howl with the wolves," one journalist at Lidové noviny wrote days after the Munich agreement. "If the world is to be governed by force rather than by law, let our place be where there is greater force and greater determination. Let us seek—we have no other choice—accommodation with Germany."[102] By 1944, Jiři Pernes writes, Moravec and his writers "identified their fate with the fate of the regime, and began unconditional collaboration."[103] Regardless, they wrote and broadcast in Czech. Although most reports claimed that their propaganda was largely ignored, others insisted that an audience still existed. "The most obedient nation is the Czech nation; during the day it listens to Hácha, and at night Beneš," one London informant lamented.[104] The Kuratorium presented patriots with another disturbing mix of Nazism and Czech nationalism. "Czech youth are estranged from the nation and with the help of the Kuratorium have turned against their fathers, mothers, brothers, and sisters," *Rudé právo* lamented. But by 1944, as Tara Zahra writes, the Kuratorium "traded its failed visions of Germanizing Czech children for the far less contentious program of Nazifying them as Czechs." Not only did the Kuratorium appropriate the Sokol's practice fields and equipment, but many former sokolovci actually counted among Kuratorium leaders. Kuratorium events involved the wearing of traditional peasant costumes, the singing of Czech national songs, and the playing of marches pulled from the region's past. "If the Germans think that they can educate Czech youth in Reich ways of thinking they're barking up the wrong tree," one Czech commented. "These costumes can only strengthen national feeling." The Intelligence Service agent recording the comment added that the Kuratorium's warrior romanticism was creating young nationalist revolutionaries with whom "the Reich will have to reckon in the future."[105]

That uncertain future was fast approaching. The Allied bombing of Germany continued, and as early as 1943 thousands of refugees began to trickle into the Protectorate from Germany.[106] From their beachhead in France in June 1944, Allied troops began their slow, painful push eastward. Allied troops entered Rome that same month. In southeastern Europe, the Red Army and Tito's partisans entered Belgrade in October 1944. Soviet troops entered the General Government in July 1944 and began their march westward toward Berlin. On August 1, as the Soviets came upon Warsaw, the Polish underground army loyal to the Polish government-in-exile in London launched an uprising. Soviet troops did not enter the city but watched as Nazi stalwarts massacred alike innocents and the poorly armed insurgents. By the time the fighting ended on October 2, 1944, German forces had killed at least 150,000 civilians and insurgents.[107] A second uprising followed in Slovakia, where Communist partisans succeeded in killing several top German military officers and gaining control of several provinces. By the end of October 1944 the German military had crushed the rebellion and occupied the whole of Slovakia. Between fifteen and nineteen thousand Slovaks lay dead.[108]

Civilian deaths in Warsaw and in Slovakia were described in grue-some detail by the Protectorate's official media. Such reports were, one Intelligence Service agent wrote, "a thousand times" more effective than all the anti-Bolshevik propaganda combined.[109] The Oberlandrat in Moravská Ostrava was convinced that most Czechs wanted protection from the partisans. "How are we to behave?" one Czech asked. "If we do not support the partisans we will be shot, and if we do support them then we receive the same fate from the German side. Horrible times are coming and these developments are making fools of all of us. The best would be to sell everything and go somewhere where one can live in peace." Most Czechs, an Italian soldier stationed in the Protectorate wrote his family, simply wanted "to steer clear of danger in order to sur-vive this time."[110] Protectorate society was made up of not just heroes or villains, clearly defined perpetrators or victims, or the wholly innocent or the obviously guilty. Justifiably afraid, many Czechs, as well as Ger-mans, simply wanted to avoid the uncompromising horizontal and ver-tical forces that invaded their daily lives. Czech patriots at home and abroad, however, as the next chapter discusses, saw only opportunities.

The search for "resistance," "collaboration," and moral reckoning con-tinued after the war. Home and abroad finally came together. Beneš's government instituted retribution trials that identified and then pun-ished the guilty. Former officials in London and patriots at home memo-rialized heroic national acts, and "myths of resistance" arose to confirm the population's innocence and bravery. As Tony Judt writes, in coun-tries all over Europe Germans and those who actively worked for Ger-mans and their interests were deemed guilty, whereas whole populations were absolved. "Thus to be innocent," Judt continues, "a nation had to have resisted and to have done so in its overwhelming majority. . . . Where historical record cried out against this distortion . . . national at-tention was consciously diverted, from the very first postwar months, to examples and stories that were repeated and magnified ad nauseam in novels, popular histories, radio, newspapers, and especially cinema."[111] "We didn't have arms," a collector of jokes wrote shortly after liberation. "Our only weapon was the joke, which, like a beetle, gnawed away at the feeble foundations of that monstrous colossus." After 1989 Aleš Dubovský, a local historian and former Protectorate national, repeated a similar mantra: "From the first day when the German fascists occupied our town there arose among our inhabitants a cryptic but open fight. . . . Jokes went from mouth to mouth among us and, for the first time, the fascists capitulated."[112] Communist historians writing after 1948 took little note of smiling Czechs. The heroes of their resistance myth were the partisans, aided and inspired by the great Soviet Union, who functioned as a synecdoche for the whole nation. The effect, however, was the same. The ambiguities of life under occupation were forgotten, and the vast majority of Czechs were allowed to live with a clear conscience. Divisions within the nation, and disagreements between patriots at home and officials in London, were ignored.

In the last years of the war these divisions were very real. Telling jokes and rumors, patriots contended, were expressions of solidarity with the nation. While acting Czech, patriots were animating the nation, "resisting" the regime, and continuing the historical battle against the Germans. Beneš and those around him called for a different form of resistance and castigated their countrymen for their inaction. The retribution trials and "resistance myths" healed some of the rifts between the two sides, but before then London officials and patriots at home, as well as "good Czechs" regardless of age or class, united around other things: anti-German sentiments, a consensus that Germans bore a collective guilt for Nazism's crimes, and plans to expel the Germans. In a world filled with ambiguities, grays, and uncertainties, a hatred of everything, and everyone, German became an unquestioned "good" among Czech patriots. The Czechs' hatred of everything, and everyone, German also had its uses, as Beneš soon discovered. And when the tightly wound order of Nazi occupation collapsed into chaos, many "good Czechs" acted upon that hatred, as jokesters had foreseen and encouraged: "Czechs arise!" one imagined cemetery sign read, "and make room for Germans!"[113] At last, Czechs heeded London's calls to fight the honorable fight, to prove their courage and loyalty. Resistance and Czech patriotism, London and the home front, came together.

6

All the Germans Must Go

Just before Christmas of 1943 Beneš sat down in front of a microphone in a Moscow broadcasting station. His radio address that day had much in common with his earlier pronouncements. He made few references to the actual inhabitants of the former Czechoslovakia, save a plea for resistance and sabotage. References to grand diplomacy, the state, and himself dominated. But this day was different, for the Czechoslovak president-in-exile described for his audience "one of the most beautiful instances of my political work and my political life"—the signing of the Treaty of Friendship and Cooperation between Czechoslovakia and the Soviet Union. As Beneš spelled out, the treaty pledged both states to fight Germany together and foster economic relations after the war, while the Soviet Union promised to respect the sovereignty and independence of Czechoslovakia. For the first time, Beneš spoke of wide-ranging, postwar social and economic transformations, a planned economy, and a national front consisting of a limited number of political parties. Fascists, Nazis, and other traitors faced political exclusion and retribution. As he neared the climax of the speech, Beneš promised, with a flourish, that Nazism and Sudeten German Henleinism would be banished forever. In its place would arise "a nation-state of Czechoslovak Czechs, Slovaks, and people from the Carpathian Rus." The Soviet Union, he added, wished Czechoslovakia to be "strong, consolidated, and, as much as possible, nationally homogeneous." The message was clear: the Germans, and Slovak Hungarians, were to be expelled. Before Beneš's trip to Moscow, Churchill and Roosevelt had given vague support to Czechoslovakia's expulsion plans. Now Beneš had Stalin's blessing.[1]

A year and a half later Stalin, Churchill, and Harry S. Truman gathered in Potsdam, Germany. At the request of the Czechoslovak government the three great powers addressed the "transfer" issue, finally agreeing to an "organized and orderly transfer" of German populations from Czechoslovakia, Poland, and Hungary. By 1948 Eastern Europe had been mostly emptied of its Germans. Czechoslovakia expelled more than three million Germans in 1946 and 1947. Hungary expelled 250,000 Germans. Poland, which now included a swath of German-inhabited "Recovered Lands" extending to the Oder and Neisse rivers, expelled 3,325,00 million Germans. Hundreds of thousands of additional Germans throughout Eastern Europe had already fled their homelands. The majority settled in one of Germany's four zones of occupation, eventually making up 16.5 percent of West Germany's population in 1950. A European age of destruction and forced population movements came to an end. The Bohemian lands, Hungary, and Poland, where civil war and state-sanctioned "population transfers" emptied its eastern territories of Ukranians, became nationally homogeneous political units. The political and demographic map of Europe remained relatively unchanged until after 1989.[2]

Much of the impetus for these upheavals came from Beneš's government and his Polish counterparts in London. Both governments, as Norman Naimark points out, maintained that Germans, as a collective, bore the weight of guilt for crimes committed during the occupations and, as such, deserved to be collectively expelled from their homelands. Both governments used the cover of war to settle old scores and to create homogeneous nations. In both Poland and Czechoslovakia popular violence against the Germans and liberation arrived hand-in-hand. Hundreds of thousands were killed or forced across the border even before the Potsdam Agreement. Yet there are important differences between the two cases. The expulsion of the Germans from Poland was intimately tied to the country's border revisions. (The Allies accepted, but did not legalize, the Oder-Neisse line in part because the Soviets, who occupied the country, now demanded it. Poland's new western border also was meant as compensation for the country's loss of eastern territories to the Soviet Union.) Beneš, unlike his Polish counterparts in London, was a living, disconcerting reminder of Great Britain's betrayal at Munich. His political authority was unquestioned. Most important, Beneš maintained close relations with Stalin, whereas the Soviet Union had broken off relations with the Polish government in London in 1943. Czechoslovak Communists in Moscow, true to the interwar Comintern's support for minority rights and united behind a class—not national—struggle for liberation, avoided supporting any expulsion plans. Following Beneš's visit to Moscow, the Czechoslovak Communists fell in step with Beneš and counted among the expulsion plan's most ardent supporters. After 1943 Beneš was in a unique position to parlay his demands among the three great powers. He forced the issue at every moment, and in the end he did everything in his power to see that the Germans were expelled from Czechoslovakia. Without him, the expulsions would not have happened as they did, if at all.[3]

Nor would they have happened without clamoring from home. The road to the postwar expulsions traveled through London, Washington, D.C., and Moscow, but Czech patriots at home set the destination. In 1940 ÚVOD resistance fighters had called for the expulsion of every German from Czechoslovakia after the war. Beneš had called their demands politically naïve. In summer 1941 he conceded that the "maximum" was desirable but prepared the domestic resistance for a "minimum" solution that entailed loss of territory and the expulsions of "only" one million Germans. Even this "minimum" solution was optimistic. At that time neither Britain nor the Soviet Union had recognized Beneš's government. Yet by the end of 1943 Allied approval of the expulsion of nearly every German from postwar Czechoslovakia had become Beneš's primary, if elusive, foreign goal. Voices from home, now extending far beyond the democratic resistance, ensured that Beneš stayed the course. They rejected, loudly and universally, anything but the "maximum" solution. A first set of questions addresses the period up to 1945: What can account for the Czech patriots' seemingly uncompromising demands that every German be expelled? What made demands from home so forceful and convincing that Beneš, at every turn, pushed the Allies toward more radical positions? And what role, in the end, did Beneš's government play in convincing the Allies to acquiesce to the expulsion of millions of people?

A second set of questions takes us from liberation through the Czechification of the Bohemian lands. With the arrival of Allied troops, Czechs set upon their German neighbors, beating them to death, burning them alive, and handing them over to Soviet soldiers to be raped. Czechs later rounded up Germans into camps, where the inmates were subjected to countless humiliations and deprivations. What can explain the unchecked and unprecedented violence in an occupied land that, in comparison to Poland, had been relatively peaceful? What triggered the violence, what made it possible, and how was it justified? By summer 1945, when preparations for the "humane and orderly transfer" of the Germans from Czechoslovakia began, officials faced an old question: what is a German? Once again, a familiar set of issues surrounding questions of economic necessity, demographic reality, and nationality arose. Again, ambiguity would descend into absurdity, but this time the answers would be definite. Bohemia, Moravia, and Silesia became almost entirely Czech.

Among the Allies

Two events constituted milestones in the development of Beneš's expulsion plans. The first came during the darkest days of Heydrich's rule, when the Czechoslovak president made his first public appeal for the partial expulsion of minorities from postwar Czechoslovakia. In a January 1942 article in *Foreign Affairs* Beneš began by asserting that Germans and quislings all over Europe must answer for atrocities committed in the previous years. "Some" Sudeten Germans and Hungarians needed to be punished for betraying the pre-Munich state. In the interest of "equilibrium" in Europe and "the right of every nation to live peaceably and freely within state frontiers," he continued, a more drastic measure would also be necessary: "to carry out a transfer of populations on a very much larger scale than after the last war. This must be done in as humane a manner as possible, internationally organized and internationally financed." He still, however, backed away from any "maximum" solution. Making states such as Czechoslovakia nationally homogeneous "will still be impossible," he wrote, but German districts "must be united only where really necessary and then on the smallest scale possible." Still, as Beneš made clear, the age of minority rights was over. "Human democratic rights" now stood paramount. Transfer plans had been put on the table.[4]

In dealing with the Allies, Czechoslovak officials relied on the word "transfer" to describe plans to deport, expel, and resettle their non-Slavic minorities—Germans and Magyars. (In Czech, they spoke of an "odsun," a seldom-used word that also carried connotations of "shoving" or "pushing" something away.)[5] The language of guilt, moving from individual guilt to collective guilt, allowed the London government to justify these transfer plans up to Potsdam and beyond. As retribution plans began to take form in 1941, radio broadcasts promised that Czechs *and* Germans would be subject to retribution, even if, as Beneš noted privately, a much larger percentage of Germans bore responsibility for events surrounding Munich and the occupation. The St. James Declaration pledged European governments to try both occupiers and local inhabitants. In October 1942 Masaryk told his listeners that loyal Germans would not be subject to retribution. Only "dastardly" Germans had reason to fear postwar justice. Soon, however, Beneš and London officials began to use the language of guilt to claim that Germans, as a collective, deserved punishment; and as the occupation dragged on, officials in London saddled the German nation, which included the Sudeten Germans, with an ever-growing list of crimes. The treachery, in fact, appeared to be inherent within Germanness. "I know that there are decent Germans," one of Beneš's closest advisers, Prokop Drtina, told his listeners after the Lidice massacres, "but it is not within the power of humans to separate Nazism from the German nation." "Innocents are paying for Munich and the fifteenth of March," Jan Masaryk added later that winter, "but the German nation will pay for these things in the future. Not just the Nazis—the German nation." Retribution and collective guilt now came together in Beneš's mind and in official Czechoslovak policy. "The German nation has committed offenses unlike any other [nation] in the world," he told his listeners. "The German nation therefore deserves punishment and the German nation and state will receive punishment. And with it all of those who helped [the German nation]."[6]

The language of guilt had several uses. It served as a cover for settling old scores with the Czechs' national rival, yet it suggested there would remain a certain number of "innocent" Germans, who would then be assimilated. It mixed, at times uneasily, with Beneš's increasingly bold calls for a postwar revolution that would sweep collaborators from society, introduce socialism, and make Czechoslovakia into a "nation-state" of Slavs. Liberation, he promised Czechoslovak soldiers in London, would complete a vaguely defined "spiritual" revolution only haltingly begun by Czechs after World War I:

> But 70 to 80 percent of our Germans did not go through this revolutionary process and accepted the idea of pan-German counterrevolu-

tion and Nazism. . . . We must not allow our Germans to repeat this. Therefore, I support the view that all the guilty must go, of which there will be hundreds of thousands. Using guilt as a basis, it will be necessary to cleanse the Republic, and this applies to all citizens of the Republic, Germans as well as Czechs and Slovaks. It would be unconscionable to reject the Germans who have always been with us. The fact is, however, that after the war the Republic will be a nation-state.[7]

For Beneš, the language of guilt was also necessary in dealing with the Allies. They seemed destined to decide Czechoslovakia's fate, as they had done during World War I, and would determine the country's place within a newly constructed Europe. On a practical level, Beneš knew that any transfer required Allied support, since they would control the areas of Germany and Austria to which the Germans were to be deported. By labeling the Germans tagged for deportation as "guilty," he hoped to make the transfer "legal," more palatable to democratic regimes, and sanctioned by international laws and agreements. Obtaining approval and aid for any such transfer, as Beneš knew, would also require a healthy dose of Realpolitik.

Not surprisingly, then, Beneš's transfer plans evolved in tandem with his other foreign policy goals—official recognition of his government, the annulment of the Munich agreement, pledges to restore postwar Czechoslovakia along its original borders, and guarantees of postwar security—and gained momentum as his position vis-à-vis the Allies improved. As early as February 1940 the Polish government-in-exile in London declared its intentions to absorb parts of East Prussia and deport the Germans from a reconstituted Poland, but Beneš's priorities, for the moment, lay elsewhere. Not until May 1941—just months before his "maximum"-"minimum" message to ÚVOD and the recognition of his government by Great Britain and the Soviet Union—did Beneš raise the issue of internal and external "transfers" with the British liaison to Czechoslovakia, Bruce Lockart. Three months after Heydrich had arrived in Prague, Beneš publicly addressed the transfer issue in *Foreign Affairs*. After the massacres at Lidice, and the Beneš government's masterful exploitation of the tragedy for propaganda purposes, official and public opinion in the West began to turn his way. "Today the brutal treatment meted out to the Czechs is arousing wide-spread indignation, and from all parts of the world requests are coming for reprisals," Lockart told the

U.S. secretary of state, adding that "the chief agents of this bestiality are the Bohemian Germans."[8] That summer the British War Office agreed to annul the Munich agreement and acquiesced to the general principle of transferring German minorities from Central and Southeast Europe after the war. Almost a year later, Roosevelt offered vague support to Beneš's calls for at least partial transfers, emphasizing that the process must be organized and carried out under the auspices of the international community. In the meantime, Beneš continued to press Soviet officials, telling the Soviet ambassador to the Czechoslovak government-in-exile that any transfer should focus on the German middle classes and intellectual elites, as well as anyone "guilty in 1938 and now, in the war."[9]

A second milestone in Beneš's transfer plans came during his visit to Moscow in December 1943. Indeed, Beneš did much more than pursue his goal of expelling the Germans from Czechoslovakia. In Moscow Beneš shored up Soviet support for one of his last unfulfilled foreign policy goals—a pledge of security for postwar Czechoslovakia. In return, he assured the Czechoslovak Communists a predominant role in the postwar government and his evolving expulsion plans. Beneš had many reasons to cast his lot with Stalin and the Czechoslovak Communists. A longtime supporter of socialism, he was sympathetic to the numerous calls from the Protectorate for socialist-style postwar reform. The Soviet Union, with which Beneš had opened full diplomatic relations in 1934, had not betrayed Czechoslovakia at Munich. At a time when Soviet troops seemed most likely to liberate most of the country, Vojtech Mastny observes, Beneš "believed that he could 'swallow and digest' [the Communist Party of Czechoslovakia] by absorbing their program and 'engaging' them in positions of responsibility. Above all, he was certain that he could retain the upper hand by keeping on intimate terms with their Soviet masters."[10] The Czechoslovak Communists played their role. "The order of the day," their leader Klement Gottwald wrote in a note to himself in April 1944, is "*not* a socialist revolution and dictatorship of the proletariat. *But* a workers' revolution of national liberation, a bloc of workers, peasants, urban middle class, and the intelligentsia." In 1935 Gottwald's party had gained only a little more than 10 percent of the vote. Following the Munich agreement, Gottwald had fled Czechoslovakia along with most Communist leaders. Now the party was poised to become the most powerful political force in a postwar Czechoslovakia dominated by the political left. "If you play it well," Beneš told

Communist leaders, "you will win."[11] Beneš, in turn, also received more concrete assurances of Soviet support for his emerging transfer plans. During their December 1943 meeting, Stalin affirmed Beneš's transfer plans, and the next month Beneš received official confirmation of Stalin's support, and a promise that Czechoslovakia need not cede any territory to Germany.[12]

Upon learning of Stalin's pledge to Beneš, the Czechoslovak Communists became, almost overnight, the most enthusiastic supporters of the London government's transfer plans. In doing so, they remained true to a pattern of subservience to Stalin established during the interwar period. After Gottwald's Bolshevik faction seized the party leadership in 1929, its leaders obediently enacted policies and propaganda messages demanded of Comintern members. The very existence of the organization depended on Soviet finance.[13] In another way, the Communists' support for transfer plans marked a radical break with their past, jettisoning a long-standing platform that emphasized class, not national, difference. Significantly, when it was founded, it was the only party that claimed to represent all the nationalities of Czechoslovakia. None of this changed after Munich. Before Hitler's attack on the Soviet Union, the party's propagandists called on Czechs and Sudeten Germans to fight the "imperialist" powers, which included Great Britain and Beneš's government-in-exile. Soon the war against imperialism became a war against fascist Germany, but officially the party called on Sudeten Germans to join the anti-Hitler coalition, while avoiding any talk of the postwar period. A Communist Party delegation visiting Ripka in 1941 insisted that Sudeten Germans be allowed onto the editorial board of London radio broadcasts. "It is inappropriate," the delegation said curtly, "to attack the Sudeten Germans." Hidden from view, however, there existed among Communists in London and Moscow, and among Czechs and Germans in the party, a variety of opinions surrounding the party's "national" stance and the ultimate fate of the Sudeten Germans. When the time came, anti-German chauvinism proved an easy fit. Just weeks before Beneš's visit to Moscow, Gottwald had been reminding the faithful that the enemy was "swastika fascism," claiming that the German proletariat bore no guilt for the events of 1938. Faced with Stalin's approval of Beneš's transfer plans, Gottwald embraced an issue that could ensure him even greater legitimacy at home. His party, he reasoned, could win over support from the other parties by being the most nationalist, the most xenophobic.[14] Sudeten German members of the party were eased aside. "Pan-Slavism" and "nation-state" became key words. Gottwald's broadcasts from Moscow referred to the "bestiality," "conceit," and "arrogance" of "German fascism," and often just the Germans, as opposed to the "humane" and "humble" yet determined Czechs. *Rudé právo* described the Germans as "animals . . . without morality, without human feelings." For the next few years, no party's anti-German stance was more radical than the Communists'. Like Beneš, however, Gottwald still assumed that a large number of Germans would remain in Czechoslovakia, without minority rights and with the assumption that they would assimilate into the larger nation-state.[15]

After Beneš's trip to Moscow in 1943, however, Allied support for his transfer plans began to waver. In Great Britain and the United States, sections of public opinion questioned the morality of expelling millions from their homes. The upheavals threatened to create mass chaos and hunger, and the Great Powers responsible for occupying and administering Germany would be forced to bear the financial and political burden of dealing with the expellees. Throughout 1944 Czechoslovak officials constructed, debated, and analyzed various plans aimed to convince British and American skeptics. Near the end of the year a memorandum entitled "The Problem of the German Minority in Czechoslovakia" was presented to the three Great Powers, France, and the European Advisory Committee. Germans "guilty of disloyalty or a hostile attitude toward the Czechoslovak Republic," the memorandum stated, would be deported to Germany immediately after the war. The remaining Germans could then apply to remain in the country, but only Germans "who have not proved disloyal towards the Czechoslovak Republic" and those who "actively fought for the liberation of Czechoslovakia," provided that they agreed to the "gradual [political and cultural] merging of their descendants with the Czechoslovak people." These two transfers would "not leave more than 800,000" Germans. After defeat, Germany should be forced to accept the deportees and grant them citizenship. The Allies, the memorandum concluded, should ensure that Germany fulfills these obligations and that they "promote the realization of the [transfer] scheme." The U.S. and British governments refused to commit to any plans, however, telling Beneš that such matters could only be dealt with only by the Great Powers, together, after the war. The Soviets remained conspicuously silent.[16]

At Yalta in February 1945 Stalin, Churchill, and Roosevelt made plans for the occupation of Germany and Austria and laid the groundwork for a divided Europe. Although Stalin and Churchill again spoke vaguely about postwar expulsions, the Big Three made no decisions regarding Czechoslovak and Polish transfer plans. Like the question of Poland's western border, the issue was left to a later peace conference. "Foreign governments which have received our memorandum have made only wishy-washy statements," Stránský told his comrades in Moscow in 1945. "We should not rely on the help of England and America." "The Red army will help us a lot," Gottwald replied. "It will anyway certainly depend on how the military advance plays out." Czechoslovakia, Beneš threatened a British representative just before the Yalta Conference, could expel and transfer the Germans with Soviet backing alone. Further, he warned, if his demands were not met, he might "lose control over his countrymen who, after terrible suffering, will take the law into their own hands." The statement was more than just a diplomatic parry. Indeed, Beneš might have genuinely worried that mass violence was unavoidable. At the same time, he had the power to make his prediction come true.[17]

Hate, Unity, and Utility

Shortly after Allied troops stormed the beaches at Normandy in June 1944, Beneš repeated for his countrymen a list of familiar political aims. The war was coming to a close, he said, and Czechoslovakia must begin preparations for the postwar. The country would be a nation-state, he assured listeners at home, rid of Germans and Hungarians, fascists and Nazis. German antifascists would not face punishment, he said, and the transfer of the rest must be orderly. The response from home was immediate and clear: "Dr Beneš's latest speech was a disappointment in Bohemia because he wants loyal Germans to remain among us. There are no loyal Germans. All are the same, and even in the best cases children of loyal Germans are now Pan-Germanists. They cannot stay, not even if they would go to Czech schools, because they would be instilled with the German spirit in secret."[18] A few months later Drtina radioed ÚVOD's successors in the resistance movement that the Great Powers might only acquiesce to allowing two-thirds of the German population to be expelled. The response from home was the same: "We will not tolerate the return of the Germans, or even Jews."[19] Before Heydrich's rule, London informants often distinguished between "good" and "bad" Germans. During Heydrich's rule, and especially after Lidice, they condemned the whole German nation, and when they did distinguish among Germans they singled out "our Germans," or Sudeten Germans, as special targets for hate. Aside from fascists and members of the Czech puppet government, one London informant wrote early in 1942, "there is not a single Czech today who does not feel the most intense hatred of everything that is German. No one distinguishes among Germans."[20] As the occupation dragged on, the language coming from home—born of fear, resentment, personal grudges, shame, opportunism, historical imagination, and a desire for national unity—became more radical and less compromising. The language of guilt figured less in the reports from the Protectorate. Their words expressed a hatred that was more abstract, chauvinistic, and vengeful. Beneš was listening. He understood that his political legitimacy depended upon heeding those voices. He also understood that the emotions behind them could be utilized.

Although the unquestioned master in London, Beneš continuously fretted about his standing at home. His interviewers questioned émigrés and Czechs assigned to work in Sweden about establishing closer ties with the Soviet Union before and after Beneš's trip to Moscow. In both cases, he received the answers he wanted. Again and again, respondents assured him that the majority of Czechs, the "good Czechs," supported and admired Beneš as the unquestioned leader of Czechoslovakia. Even London informants and interview respondents wary of Communism approved of his treaty with the Soviet Union. Among the general population, Czechs supported the alliance for the same reasons that attracted Beneš. The Soviet Union had not betrayed Czechoslovakia at Munich. Pan-Slavism, despite the best efforts of Nazi propagandists, had been experiencing a rebirth. Many in the Protectorate, especially the young, shared with Beneš a "revolutionary élan" that emanated from a desire to break with a corrupted past. There were also practical matters to consider. When, in 1943, it appeared that British and American forces would liberate the Protectorate, Czechs rushed to learn English. As the Red Army approached, Russian became the most popular language to learn.[21] Still, the Czechoslovak president-in-exile had reasons to worry about his standing at home. Legal acrobatics aside, Beneš, like the members of his government, did not obtain his position through popular elections. Many Czechs complained of the ongoing political squabbles among those in the London government. What they desperately desired was political unity.[22] Radio listeners resented London's calls for armed, organized violence against the regime and had their own ideas about what constituted "resistance." Resistance fighters assured Beneš that Czechs wanted transgressors to be punished. (Many, in fact, promised that they would deliver the punishment themselves.) But many Czechs remained wary of Beneš's broad definition of "guilt" and "collaboration." London informants warned that Beneš did not understand life in the Protectorate. Seen in this light, hating the Germans and promising expulsions had many political uses.

An intense hatred of the Germans as a collective provided London officials and Protectorate inhabitants, as well as Czechoslovak Communists, with a common vocabulary. Hating the Germans fit easily into the Czech historical imagination. The words to express that hatred had become common currency early in the nineteenth century, when Palacký and other Awakeners made the Czechs' rivalry with the Germans the main theme of the nation's history and central to national self-identity. Later in the century, patriots imagined that same history as a Darwinian battle for survival between two national organisms. Interwar nationalisms and, paradoxically, minority rights encouraged Czechs, Germans, and European leaders to think in collective terms, allowing patriots to speak generally about the enemy group without distinguishing among individuals and groups within the rival nation.[23]

The occupation, then, became the logical culmination of this battle among collectives, and at the top of the Protectorate regime sat Karl Hermann Frank, who embodied in one person all the essential characteristics of the Czech's imagined enemy—intolerance, chauvinism, and a hatred of all things "Czech." "For more than a thousand years we suffered through compromises with the Germans," one informant to London wrote. "The result is insidious, treacherous people à la Frank."[24] Patriots at home and abroad neatly fit the establishment and practice of Nazi rule within the long flow of Czech-German rivalries in the Bohemian lands. They interpreted the Sudeten Germans' overwhelming vote for a party promising to "return [them] to the Reich" as a decisive rejection of cohabitation and saddled the Sudeten Germans with responsibility for everything that followed. Patriots at home hardly distinguished between the closing of schools and the arrests of leading intellectuals, between language laws and plans to expel millions of their countrymen.

Hating the Germans, thinking in terms of collective attributes, and placing Nazi practices within the long flow of history provided London officials with an opportunity to connect, as Czechs, with their constituencies at home. Hating Germans served another purpose: it promised to unite a nation atomized by Gestapo informants and divided by economic disparities, the black market, mobilization, and political beliefs. Despite differences in class, age, geography, or political stance, most patriotic Czechs now shared one commonality: an intense hatred of anything, or anybody, "German." "Everyone is united in hatred of the Germans," one resistance fighter said. "The solidarity is tremendous," bringing together city-dwellers and those in the countryside, workers and intellectuals. Or, as another resistance fighter proclaimed in 1944, a "hatred of all things German" had become the "common, uniting national idea."[25] Hating Germans, along with spreading rumors, telling jokes, and speaking Czech, became a way in which people could act Czech and prove their loyalty to the nation. Most of the informants to London discounted as opportunists or traitors anyone who did not share their views on the Germans. They ignored the thousands of mixed German-Czech marriages, and only rarely did they make mention of another disturbing product of the Protectorate years: Czechs who had accepted German citizenship. Creating an abstract, wholly uniform enemy reconstructed a simple moral universe that distinguished among "good" and "bad" people. Hating the Germans became the only clear, unambiguous aspect of Czech national identity that survived the occupation. It was the last remnant of a world of nationality politics undone by Nazi repression, contradictions, and compromises.

All "good" Czechs, both at home and abroad, could also agree that after the war Czechoslovakia should be a "nation-state" of Slavs.[26] Both sides could envisage achieving that goal through postwar transfers. Beneš and those around him came of age in a world where "population transfers" and "resettlements" promised to solve political problems associated with minority populations. Both Beneš and the domestic resistance even appropriated the word "Lebensraum" as early as 1940. "The Czech nation also needs its Lebensraum (as Nazi terminology would have it). The Munich borders will not provide it," Beneš told ÚVOD.

ÚVOD agreed: "The [Czech] people know their Lebensraum to be the historical borders [of the Bohemian lands], and it considers the Germans as wholly alien, something that must be removed."[27] Indeed, for Czechs at home the expulsions were especially easy to imagine. Rumors of the Nazis' expulsion and sterilization plans had spread throughout the population as early as 1940.[28] In 1941 a Nazi Party member in Jihlava boasted that Himmler was going to ship all the Czechs beyond the Urals. A low-level official confided to a Czech politician that "the problem of the Czech Volk is the problem of seven million coffins."[29] Czechs learned, by means of underground literature, through foreign radio broadcasts, and even from Nazi leaders about the massive population upheavals in Poland and elsewhere. In the Protectorate, houses and, in some cases, whole villages were cleared out to make room for German settlers from Eastern Europe, army bases, and, later on, families evacuated from bombed-out cities in Germany. Czechs watched as Jews were identified, rounded up in town squares, and then herded into trains. Naturally, many Czechs wondered if they were next. They also promised to learn from the Nazi experience. "We will do it all in the same manner, and even following a Nazi blueprint," and with more cruelty, one correspondent in 1944 said in reference to the postwar expulsion of the Germans.[30]

The Czechs' intense hatred of the Germans, six long years of occupation, and firsthand experience with population transfers produced political demands and political possibilities for Beneš. By 1945 expelling the enemy—every single German—had become an unquestioned "good" among Czech patriots at home. At every step London informants, and especially resistance fighters, pulled Beneš toward the expulsion of all Germans and away from compromise positions struck with the Allies. At the same time, emotions, or what Roger Petersen calls "mechanisms—recognizable, individual-level causal forces—that work to change the level of salience of desires," readied Czechs to beat, kill, and humiliate their neighbors. Intensified emotions flattened out individual complexities and essentialized identities, seeing victims simply as members of a group targeted for violence.[31] Czechs from across the Protectorate promised that after the war "not one German among us will be left alive." "The hatred of the Germans is enormous and for us abroad a bit hard to imagine," observed an American woman who had lived in Prague until Heydrich's assassination. "[Czechs at home] send the message that we should not concern ourselves with the Germans. All have been taken note of."[32]

Many of the emotions stemmed from an array of humiliations, leading Czechs to dream of a world turned upside-down. The regime's victims who survived torture and humiliations were particularly eager to turn the tables. Loss of political status and daily insults to national pride were situated within the long story of Czech-German nationality battles, as seen in one London informant's report: "[The Germans] forbade us from speaking Czech even on buses to the airport in Budějovice for work. The Nazi Party pressured Czech children to go to German schools. Pub owners feared that if they didn't give allegiance to the Germans that German troops and other guests would boycott their establishments. . . . Therefore the sentiment: all Germans must go."[33] Materially, too, Germans benefited most from the occupation. German civil servants received higher pay, and German farmers received special state subsidies. Only German citizens received fruit, and at Christmastime Czechs watched helplessly as Nazi Party members passed out extra flour, sardines, and sugar to their German comrades. Nor did all Germans suffer through long lines for food: "Now and then a German woman insists on going to the front [of the line] and Czechs, out of fear, step aside. Our police, who are guarding the lines, are helpless."[34] Jokes, whose humor often depends on turning worlds upside-down, expressed a desire to take revenge on the Germans while reveling in a violent *Schadenfreude* (in Czech *škodolibost*), the pleasure one draws from seeing another suffer. Often the punch line, and the act of revenge, was given to the joke's Jewish character—the most improbable and delicious inversion possible. Schadenfreude also mixed with desires to enrich oneself at the Germans' expense, as another joke suggests: "A son was walking with his father across the square. From several houses he could see German banners. Jeníček asks his father what the meaning of those banners with crosses is. 'That, Jeníček, is for us to know where the available apartments will be after the war,' the father explained."[35] Acting on their resentment, Czechs would restore the pre-1938 order of things and enrich themselves in the process.

Doing violence to Germans also promised a measure of redemption, allowing "good" Czechs, finally, the opportunity to prove their courage and patriotism. With each arrest, resistance fighters claimed, Czech national feeling and the hatred of all things German went up a notch, yet those left behind could do nothing to rectify these injustices.[36] Helplessness and frustration in the face of the daily insults weighed heavily on many Czechs who muddled along. Calls for action from London added a layer of shame and embarrassment. "We worry that our efforts at active military aid in the liberation of our people will be small, remaining forever a stain on the reputation of our nation and generation," a small group loyal to the Beneš government lamented.[37] After the war the novelist Bohumil Hrabal subtly explored issues of embarrassment, shame, and impotence in *I Served the King of England.* In one scene the protagonist, Jan Dítě, has to undergo a racial screening before being allowed to marry his German lover. The examination prompts a disturbing moment of introspection:

> And so while execution squads in Prague and Brno and other jurisdictions were carrying out the death sentence, I had to stand naked in front of a doctor who lifted my penis with a cane, then made me turn around while he used the cane to look into my anus, and then he hefted my scrotum and dictated in a loud voice. Next he asked me to masturbate and bring him a little semen so they could examine it scientifically. . . . He added that the gob of phlegm that a German woman would spit between my eyes would be as much a disgrace to her as an honor to me. And I knew from reading the papers that on the very same day that I was standing here with my penis in my hand to prove myself worthy to marry a German, Germans were executing Czechs, and so I couldn't get an erection and offer the doctor a few drops of my sperm.[38]

In the tightly controlled world of the Protectorate, there existed few outlets to express national loyalty, to feel any sense of power, so the desires, cloaked beneath the surface, only became more radical as the occupation dragged on. Especially among resistance fighters, the coming liberation offered an opportunity to fight, participate in a revolution, and act nationally. Taking aim at Germans, whether civilian or military, they could prove their mettle.

In fact, a particular mixture of resentment, greed, fear, shame, and frustration born of the occupation experience, combined with a hatred justified by history, explains a remarkable fact: Czech patriots, when they did distinguish among Germans, hated Sudeten Germans most of all. The few ethnic Germans from Bessarabia and Bukovina who trickled into the Protectorate in 1940 might have taken over valuable land and, indirectly, forced people from their homes, but Czechs mocked them as yokels who make bonfires in their new kitchens and cleaned themselves with water from their new toilets. Regular soldiers from Germany and Austria occasionally received sympathetic portrayals and kudos for correct behavior. The judgment of Reich German civilians was mixed. The best, one correspondent wrote, were the Austrians, who were polite and willing to deal on the black market. The worst were Saxons, who terrorized local women.[39] Protectorate Germans were all the same, however: "Every one of our Germans is a worthless piece of human material. We do not want to see a repeat of Munich. We must be certain that our children will be free of Germans. You cannot imagine what they are doing to us, how they humiliate us. Frank must hang. You don't know what fanatics they are, especially their women and children."[40] Protectorate Germans filled the ranks of the Gestapo and the Intelligence Service, and they served as wardens in the Protectorate's most notorious prisons. They were the guards and factory managers who watched over workers at the assembly line. When a Czech living in a mixed community came into contact with the state administration, he was most likely to encounter a Protectorate German. About three thousand Protectorate Germans worked in mostly low- to mid-level bureaucratic posts. Reich Germans generally held the highest posts, out of sight. Protectorate Germans belonged to a singular, historical entity upon which weighed the responsibility for past and present transgressions, and they were the face of the regime.[41]

Sadly, these same emotions and historical arguments contributed to another remarkable development: the rise of virulent Czech anti-Semitism in the last years of the occupation. Quisling newspapers polluted the media with vicious anti-Semitic rhetoric. They encouraged Czechs to denounce Jews who transgressed the many regulations that ruled their lives and worked to destroy personal relations between Czechs and Jews.[42] Czechs who coveted Jewish jewelry, clothing, and other valuables were full of resentment when, after their Jewish neighbors were deported to their deaths, the Czechs were often left empty-handed.[43] Czech anti-Semitism has it own sad history, which includes a long pedigree of patriots accusing Jews of being too rich, successful, and "German." Jews, a London informant explained, still deigned to speak German under the occupation: "Czechs took this as a provocation and therefore it's not surprising that the mood is and will be strongly anti-

Jewish." "Anti-Semitism is stronger than before," another informant reported. "People maintain that Jews had spoken German and identified with Germans. Why didn't they go with us? Now they're in concentration camps or executed."[44] Czech anti-Semites convinced themselves that the Jews' fate was determined by their choices, not by the unfortunate fact that they did not have a Christian birth certificate. The more gracious among Czech informants to London held out to Jews the possibility of a second chance: after the war any Jews who remained would have to speak Czech.[45] Twice in the post-Heydrich era Jan Masaryk was moved to condemn Czech anti-Semitism. While conceding that "some Jews did not behave well" before the occupation—speaking German in Prague cafes, for example—he forcefully argued that many Jews had been good Czech patriots. Further, he described anti-Semitism as a peculiarly German "barbarity" and "disgrace": "And we Czechoslovaks, from all of the experiences of this horrible war, must realize that for us, a small nation neighboring Germany, anti-Semitism is a first step toward Pan-Germanism, which would subsequently thrust a knife in our back."[46]

Masaryk was, no doubt, deliberately playing with irony. "Stab in the back" had been a common turn of phrase among anti-Semites in post–World War I Germany. Heydrich's speeches had been littered with the phrase. There was, however, another, larger and tragic irony that ran through the last years of the occupation: in their all-encompassing hatred of everything "German," Czech patriots had already become everything they imagined their rivals to be—petty, intolerant, chauvinistic, and fanatical. And now they were ready to act. A whole array of emotions, London informants instinctively recognized, threatened to trigger widescale violence aimed at all Germans, even Jews, after the war. These emotions also justified London informants' uncompromising demands that every German be expelled from Czechoslovakia after the war. These emotions, as Beneš and patriots at home realized, had their uses.

Collapse

A perfect storm was gathering in the months leading up to 1945. Following Heydrich's assassination, Frank and other Nazi authorities lived in constant fear that more assassins would drop from the sky. Fear and panic among Germans, amphibians, and Czechs identified as collaborators escalated following the Wehrmacht's defeat at Stalingrad. "Ever since Stalingrad the mood among the Germans has been very bad," one German-speaking London informant wrote. Any sort of "hurrah-patriotism" has disappeared, he added, and has been replaced by a "pronounced panic among Germans in the Protectorate."[47] Germans begged local officials to strip Czech police and Protectorate troops of their weapons, fearing violent reprisals after the war. Some Germans still hoped behavior, and not citizenship or nationality, might allow them to avoid punishment. Many sought out Czech friends. Others began speaking Czech instead of German. Party members removed swastikas from their coats hoping to avoid being put on a Czech "black list." Many people with "German" or "partially German heritage" approached local administrators, begging that their Reich citizenship be annulled. Czech parents, and parents in mixed marriages, began removing their children from German schools. One Kuratorium instructor in Hradec Králové joked that he should start looking for trees from which his teenagers could hang him after the war.[48]

An emerging partisan movement and desperate last acts by Frank further heightened the sense of doom, fear, and panic—and not just among Germans, amphibians, and collaborators. By autumn 1944, partisan activity was on the rise, especially in Moravia. In addition to sabotaging railway lines, partisans also attacked Nazi officials, local Germans, and Czech collaborators. Sometimes they emerged from the woods at night, shooting out windows and doors.[49] The partisans also shot people dead. Often the killings seemed random, unjust. Near Zlín partisans shot a German forest ranger and a local German administrator, hardly the worst of Nazism's criminals. Other partisans killed a German immigrant when he failed to offer them food.[50] By 1944, Frank and officials around him had become obsessed with the growing partisan movement, creating a dialectic that heightened fears among the population. In his increasingly shrill radio announcements, Frank promised to fight to the bitter end. Czechs and Germans were dispatched to build fortifications along the Protectorate's borders. As the Allied armies closed in, he formed two companies of loyal Sudeten Germans to fight to the last person.[51] It was rumored that Protectorate Germans, including women, were being armed and given shooting practice. Other rumors claimed that Frank was organizing guerrilla organizations to continue fighting should the Protectorate fall. "It has now become clear," one London informant wrote in autumn 1944, "that [the end] will not take place without bloodshed."[52]

All over Europe, as well as in the Protectorate, Nazi rule was collapsing. In the first two months of 1945 liberation armies entered Paris and Budapest. Red Army divisions drove through Poland before stopping just forty miles east of Berlin, where they regrouped for a last attack on the German capital. Hundreds of thousands of Germans seized the moment to flee.[53] Former concentration camp prisoners streamed into the Protectorate from the northeast, while tens of thousands of workers assigned to work abroad slowly began to trickle home. The Allied bombing of Moravská Ostrava, Zlín, Brno, Plzeň, and other industrial centers, which had begun in late summer 1944, intensified over the winter months. In Brno, one of the hardest-hit cities, more than thirty thousand apartments were destroyed (Fig. 6.1). Czech and German parents refused to send their children to schools. In Moravská Ostrava, huge numbers of frightened residents fled the city in the early morning hours, just before the bombers usually arrived overhead.[54] Retreating

Figure 6.1 A street in Brno after an Allied bombing raid in August 1944. (Reproduced by permission of the Archiv města Brna.)

Wehrmacht divisions added to the chaos. When Army Group South briefly crossed over into southeastern Moravia, it brought tens of thousands of prisoners of war, slave laborers, and East European SS divisions in tow. Soldiers from the Royal Hungarian First Army, between ninety thousand and one hundred thousand strong, dropped their guns along the side of the road or traded them to Czechs.[55] In Prague, a local doctor wrote in his diary, someone killed a baker and his wife for bread and flour. The electricity went out. A university professor went begging to friends for cigarette butts.[56]

As collapse seemed imminent, more Germans than ever—between 3.4 and 3.5 million *civilians*—found themselves within the borders of the Bohemian lands.[57] Tens of thousands of additional Germans fled into the Bohemian lands from Silesia and other recently liberated territories, telling tales of suffering to fearful Czechs and Germans. Between October 1944 and March 1945 about 100,000 of Slovakia's estimated 130,000–140,000 Germans had been evacuated westward, many of them into the Protectorate.[58] Yet, unlike many Germans from Poland and the eastern territories, the vast majority of Germans in the Protectorate and Reichsgau Sudetenland remained at home as the Allied troops approached. (Beginning in 1943, Reich Germans in the Protectorate had begun putting on pleasant faces in public, but privately, they were selling their property and preparing to leave.)[59] Frank's regime announced evacuation plans only in March 1945, yet instructions on how to prepare for evacuation did not filter down to the local level until April. Most evacuees from Brno made it only as far as western Moravia and eastern Bohemia before finding themselves behind Soviet lines. In the Reichsgau Sudetenland, officials managed an organized evacuation only in the easternmost region. In addition to having little time to prepare, people had other reasons to remain at home, one German native of Jihlava remembered. An escape to Austria—the closest border for many—still meant falling under Soviet control, and many Germans convinced themselves that Beneš's new government would ensure a minimum of order and lawfulness. "If one was to fall into the hands of the Russians, then better [let it happen] in the homeland. That the Czechs would behave as they did, as they did behave, almost no one would have considered possible," he concluded.[60]

Other actors, radicalized by war and occupation, then entered the stage. From the east, the Czechoslovak and Red Armies were approaching. Before being assigned to the eastern front after Beneš's Moscow visit, Czechoslovak soldiers had fought bravely over the skies of Britain and in North Africa. In many cases Nazi officials had arrested their relatives at home. Heavy doses of propaganda and, in many ways, their isolation from society, fanned their nationalism. A British memorandum described the radicalism that gripped the Czechoslovak troops: "Their hero is Žižka, the Czech Cromwell, and their hatred of Germany and everything German is fanatical. Even if it be considered desirable to do so, it is difficult to see how British influence can restrain the violence of these sentiments." Coming face to face with violence on the eastern front radicalized them even further. "Now begins the great cleansing of the Republic of Germans, Magyars, and traitors!" the newspaper for the First Czechoslovak Army Corps announced as it crossed into Czechoslovak territory in October 1944.[61] While in Slovakia, many of the Soviet troops freely robbed and terrorized the local Slovak population; one Bratislava clinic alone reported four thousand two hundred cases of rape. In the Protectorate, partisans (later called revolutionary guards) grew in numbers and stepped up their attacks. In addition to civilian Germans, tens of thousands of regular soldiers and SS also remained in the Bohemian lands. The SS troops radicalized an already intense atmosphere, burning down whole villages and executing their inhabitants. Then Allied and German troops clashed.[62]

All over Europe violence followed on the heels of collapse and liberation. Between 1943 and 1946, ten thousand to fifteen thousand Italians died as a result of popular violence. During the liberation of France, nine thousand to ten thousand people were killed. In Yugoslavia, civil war continued after liberation as Tito's partisans consolidated their power, eliminated political enemies, and took revenge on wartime collaborators. Roughly thirty thousand members of the Croatian Home Army and Slovenian Village Guard alone were executed in forests near the Austrian border.[63] In a 1943 radio address Beneš predicted that the end of the war would be "written in blood."[64] Emotions at home, the collapse of institutions, the dialectic of violence at the local level, and the presence of an increasing number of German civilians, SS, retreating Wehrmacht troops, partisans, Czechoslovak troops, and Red Army liberators set all the conditions for widescale violence. Perhaps Beneš's prediction was destined to come true. Certainly the deck was stacked.

Beneš and his government, faced with calls for the total expulsion of the Germans that could not be realized given the positions taken by Great Britain and the United States, deliberately encouraged popular violence as part of his diplomatic strategy with the Western Allies. "We shall negotiate this in Moscow and will *carry out the whole thing ourselves,*" Beneš, preparing to leave for Moscow in 1945, told Nichols, who had just warned the Czechoslovak government-in-exile to wait for an agreement from the Big Three before enacting transfer plans. "When the day comes, our nation will take up the old battle cry again: Cut them! Beat them! Save nobody! Everyone has to find a useful weapon to hit the nearest German!" a military officer screamed over the BBC airwaves near the end of 1944.[65] It is crucial to the success of the transfer, Drtina told members of the underground, to take immediate measures to frighten "guilty Nazis" into fleeing the country and to strike at those who remain. "The Allied world," he concluded, "will have the greatest understanding for our need to protect our national existence." Resistance fighters at home responded by promising Drtina that the "collective instinct for an explosion of revenge" can be heightened and manipulated.[66]

Beneš and those around him also encouraged violence in the hope that the "revolution" would be pursued at home, that the guilty would be punished. "People have *national and individual responsibilities.* Unlike the last war, after *this* war all decent people have the responsibility to inflict on all guilty persons, without mercy, proper retribution," Beneš declared in his speech after D-Day, although he did remind Czechs that antifascists would be spared transfer.[67] Partisans, revolutionary guards, and others had the green light to act without impunity, and indeed with a legitimacy provided by Czechoslovak officials. They could, finally, respond to Beneš's calls for action while satisfying their own, deeply held grievances. The Czechs, Masaryk told his audience in January 1945, had to join the fight against the (almost defeated) enemy and demonstrate their courage to the world: "Your and our duty, the greatest duty, is to quickly prepare yourselves for the approaching liberation. From Moravská Ostrava, from Těšín, to Litomyšl, to Prague, to Slavic Prague. You know how—you do not have a lot of time."[68]

"Wild Transfer"

The end of the occupation was approaching. Beneš and an entourage of London officials traveled to Moscow. In April Beneš traveled with the

Czechoslovak Communists to the recently liberated Slovak town of Košice, where the political parties hammered out a blueprint for state rule after liberation. Who was setting the agenda was clear from the first paragraph of the ensuing Košice program: "After more than six years of foreign subjugation the time has arrived when our humble country has seen the light of freedom's sun. . . . Thus it is thanks to our great ally the Soviet Union . . . [that] a new Czechoslovak government can be created." Beneš had already agreed to cede much of the Carpathian Rus in easternmost Slovakia to the Soviet Union. He agreed, to his disgust, to allow his longtime rival Zdeněk Fierlinger, the Social Democratic ambassador to Moscow and Communist sympathizer, to be named premier of postwar Czechoslovakia. Right-wing parties, including prewar Czechoslovakia's most popular party, the Agrarians, were banned from the government. The newly formed government, whose ministerial posts were split among four Czech and two Slovak parties, was dominated by the Communists, who reigned over the Agricultural, Information, and Interior ministries. Heading the Ministry of Education was the allegedly nonpartisan Zdeněk Nejedlý, whose Communist sympathies were well known. Similarly, the appointed head of the Ministry of Defense and commander of the First Czechoslovak Army Corps, Ludvík Svoboda, had a very close relationship with Gottwald. The Czechoslovak army was to be modeled after the Red Army. The national front pledged to maintain price controls on basic goods. Major industries, banks, insurance companies, and power plants were to be nationalized. Finally, Communists played a key role in the creation of extremely powerful national committees at the local level. Local governance was to work on three levels, the most powerful being the middle level of 156 district committees and 6 central committees for the major cities. These committees, while charged with the task of enforcing decrees and executing policies handed down from Prague, had sweeping powers over local administration and politics and security matters.[69]

No doubt owing to the Allies' wavering position on the transfer issue, the Košice program balked from any pledge for the near complete expulsion of the Germans.[70] Again, revolution, retribution, transfer, and guilt mixed. The program promised that confiscated agricultural land would be distributed to "those who have proved their worth in the national struggle for liberation—partisans, soldiers, workers in the underground movement, victims of foreign terrorism, etc."[71] The program pledged the government to punish traitors to the Czech and Slovak nations—a list of accused that included Hácha; all the members of his government as of March 16, 1939; Kuratorium functionaries; Gestapo informants; and "traitors among banking, industrial, and agrarian magnates who provided aid to German hegemony." Germans and Magyars proven guilty of "crimes against the Republic" were to be "banished from the Republic forever." The remaining Germans and Magyars would be stripped of their citizenship, but they could then apply for reinstatement of their citizenship. Exceptions were to be made for German and Magyar "antifascists." Individuals who had actively resisted the occupation regime could, after approval from the government, regain their citizenship status.[72] "Here, the question of transfer has been decided," Czechoslovak Communist Václav Kopecký told Beneš's entourage just before they departed Moscow for Košice.[73] Unresolved, however, was how many Germans were to be expelled; nor had the details concerning the return of citizenship to those who opted to remain in Czechoslovakia been decided. The categories "German," "Magyar," and "antifascist" had yet to be properly defined. Remaining, too, was the question of British, American, and possibly Soviet support for the transfer.

As April turned to May, the situation was becoming dire for Frank and others whose fates were tied to the regime. To the north, the Soviet Army was approaching Berlin. To the west American troops entered the Reichsgau Sudetenland, and hence into the lands of former Czechoslovakia. German Army Group South had been cut off south of the Danube. Field Marshal Ferdinand Schörner's Army Group Middle had retreated into Moravia, and as Allied troops approached from the east and the west, Schörner's options began to dwindle. Frank, desperate, sent a former Czechoslovak legionnaire, General Vojtěch Vladimír Klecanda, to the archbishop of Milan and then to the Allied representative in Switzerland to plead for a separate peace. Klecanda returned on May 1 empty-handed. A day later, on Frank's orders, guards at Terezín stood fifty-one prisoners against a wall and shot them.[74] That same day Wehrmacht and SS units crushed an armed uprising near Olomouc, killing thirty-one Czechs and arresting twenty-one more. Czechs also took up arms in Přerov, Nymburk, Jičín, and Rakovník. Reich SS units took up positions just outside Prague. Residents in Prague began tearing down German signs and hanging the Czech colors from apartments, police stations, and radio stations throughout the city. On May 5 General George S. Patton's troops moved deeper into Bohemia. The Red Army was nearing Olomouc. Inside Prague, General Rudolf Toussaint readied his garrison of Wehrmacht troops to defend the capital. That morning two announcers in the city's official radio station decided to speak only in Czech and played Czech songs forbidden by Nazi censors. Fighting between the SS and Czech police and civilians broke out near the radio station around noon, prompting the following from the broadcasters at 12:33 P.M.: "Everyone to the Czech radio station! They're firing at Czech people! Come here immediately! Come help us!" Underground leaders responded with their own calls to arms (Figs. 6.2 and 6.3). Then Prague exploded.[75]

On May 5, five days after Hitler committed suicide and two days before German representatives announced their unconditional surrender, war finally came to Prague. German planes bombed the city; barricades were erected; street-by-street battles raged in various corners of the city. Czech police, gendarmes, and government troops—some of whom ar-

Figure 6.2 Czechs preparing to defend the Prague radio station. (Reproduced by permission of the Vojenský ústřední archiv Fotoarchiv.)

rived by the busloads from Plzeň and Hradec Králové—joined partisans and other armed Czechs in the fighting. Joining them, too, were approximately twenty thousand soldiers under the leadership of the Russian General Andrej Andrejovič Vlasov, of whom three hundred were killed or wounded during the liberation of Prague. Following his capture by the Wehrmacht, Vlasov had switched sides and organized recruits to fight against Stalin. Vlasov's troops had been hunting down partisans and Jews in Moravia only months before the uprising in Prague. Now, as one witness recalled, his "whole street [was] a military encampment for Vlasov's troops. . . . The Czechs [were] standing in front of house doors, bringing the 'vlasovci' beer, bread, and schnapps."[76] While many Germans willingly surrendered their arms, the SS and others loyal to the Reich seemed to have lost their minds. One German witness remembered seeing how "an SS car flew through the streets [of Prague], a young SS-man shooting warning shots to the left and right from a machine gun. . . . On Charles Square a squad of German soldiers arrived,

Figure 6.3 The first victims of the fighting near the radio station. (Reproduced by permission of the Česká tisková kancelář.)

and, full of smiles, handed over their guns to the Czechs. Everyone slapped them on the shoulders and let them go on their way."[77] In various quarters of the city the SS shot captured Czech fighters and used Czech civilians as human shields in front of their Panzer tanks. Armed Czechs rounded up Germans into schools, theaters, and prisons. Many SS-men and other Germans were killed on the spot.[78]

The violence intensified further after the retreat of Wehrmacht troops on May 8 and the entry of Soviet troops the next day. Armed Czechs literally hunted down Germans and Czech collaborators on the streets. Other Germans were gathered into Strahov Stadium, where more were shot. Sick and wounded Germans were shot in hospitals. Armed insurgents and even nurses led Soviet troops to captured German women. Zdeněk David recently recalled the experience of walking through Prague with a friend shortly after the liberation had begun:

> We had followed one crowd to a spot in the middle of Wenceslas Square around an arch (normally, I believe, used for advertising) at the entry point of Vodičkova street. There, several Soviet tankists were standing on their tanks and manipulating containers of the gasoline they normally used for fuel. . . . Today, after almost fifty years, I cannot recall precisely whether it was the Red Army soldiers atop the tanks, or some of our Czech civilians standing beside them, who poured combustible liquid onto two squirming victims in German uniform suspended heads-down from the arch and then set them on fire. Fortunately, we had several rows of people in front of us and could not discern the details of the conflagration, though Milan observed that some degenerates were lighting their cigarettes off the flaming bodies.[79]

Before the fighting came to an end roughly 3,700 Czechs had died and almost 3,000 had been wounded in the week following the Prague uprising. Germans had murdered outright more than 230 Czechs, some of whom were children. In other regions of the Bohemian lands 2,000 armed and unarmed Czechs died as a result of small-scale fighting between May 1 and May 10. Tabulating the number of German dead is more difficult. Many corpses, for example, were taken by car outside the city and buried in mass graves.[80]

On May 11, just east of Prague, Soviet troops cut off the Army Group Middle's escape route to the west and took more than 800,000 German troops prisoner—the last military operation of Europe's war (Fig. 6.4).[81] Yet many Czechs continued to "fight," and the euphemistically termed "wild transfer" continued until August as a whole array of individuals set upon Germans and alleged Czech collaborators. Czechs and Soviet troops raped and humiliated helpless German women. Jailors and prisoners reversed roles. The latter often tortured and executed SS-men, German soldiers, and others in the manner they had witnessed or experienced. "The German has remained our irreconcilable enemy. Don't stop hating the Germans," one Czechoslovak army commander reminded his soldiers in June. "Be tough in dealing with the Germans. . . . The German women and the Hitler Youth are also complicit in the crimes of the Germans. Be uncompromising in your dealings with them."[82]

The violence varied in form and intensity, rippling out from Prague, through the former Protectorate territories, and finally into the former lands of the Reichsgau Sudetenland, where the violence was the most intense. In the Czech-dominated interior, national committees had a better

Figure 6.4 Captured German soldiers outside Prague Castle. (Reproduced by permission of the Česká tisková kancelář.)

chance of establishing order. Some local authorities even arrested and tried vigilantes, although most were eventually released.[83] Many of the worst atrocities took place in or around areas where SS, Wehrmacht, and Vlasov's troops had committed similar acts of violence before and during the liberation.[84] In the U.S. zone, which stretched from Karlovy Vary to Plzeň to Budějovice, the army restricted the power of local national committees and blocked most attempts at expulsions. Local Germans still suffered from overcrowding, hunger, and occasional outbreaks of popular violence. In the rest of the country, Eagle Glassheim writes, Soviet troops sometimes intervened to halt the violence; but, in general, they "provided only arbitrary and sometimes chaotic oversight. Reports of looting and rape by Soviet soldiers were widespread. Often they worked in tandem with Czechoslovak troops, locally appointed police, or Communist partisans, who did their dirty work."[85]

Naturally, violence occurred often and frequently in areas where Germans were concentrated. It is little wonder, then, that the May 5 uprising began in Prague. In addition to being the symbolic center of Czechoslovakia, the city and its surroundings housed roughly 200,000 German soldiers, civilians, and refugees when the calls to arms were made.[86] In the area around Jihlava, commanders of the Fourth Czechoslovak Brigade, composed mainly of Slovaks radicalized by war and the loss of loved ones during the occupation, gave their soldiers free reign to terrorize the local German population. In preparation for a visit by President Beneš on May 12, local authorities rounded up the entire German population into the city's main stadium. A partisan killed one German. When the victim's father asked what had happened, another partisan beat him with the butt of his gun. The remaining men were forced, by whip, to jump up and down until three more dead lay on the field.[87] Just before his arrival in Jihlava in May, Beneš told a crowd gathered in Brno that "the German question in the Republic must be liquidated," a task that that would require "the combined strength of everyone." Shortly thereafter, Czechs in Brno rounded up local Germans into schools and other public spaces.[88] Brno inhabitants pressured local officials to remove the Germans from the city, not least to help ease housing crisis had resulted from the Allied bombing of the city. "The delegations from the factories came to see the national committee, and I was often stopped by people on the street and asked for our decision on the expulsion," Brno's deputy major remembered. "Many pointed out that

Germans lived in fine homes, while many Czechs were still living in houses destroyed by war. The requests for expulsion constantly grew for these reasons as well."[89] Following an institutional back-and-forth among various local elites and the Ministry of the Interior in Prague, Brno officials selected twenty thousand men, women, and children. Workers from the Brno armaments factory, partisans, members of the Czechoslovak army, and other Czechs marched them toward Austria. By the time they reached the border, eight thousand Germans had been added from villages along the route. The acting Austrian government required the march to be halted at the border. Thus, thousands remained in internment camps while the rest were returned to Brno. In the end, however, approximately 1,700 people died from starvation, exhaustion, or outright murder during the march.[90]

In the mostly German-inhabited borderlands partisans, revolutionary guards, and various opportunists from the interior freely appropriated property. They inflicted violence upon local Germans and sometimes even assumed local positions of power. A "wild west" environment lasted for months. Arguments among Czechs, drunk and armed, sometimes ended in murder. When one local German asked for legal papers proving that she had to cede her home, the Czech demanding her departure simply pointed to his gun and said, "This is my authorization."[91] Germans in the borderlands, too, were more likely to be forcibly marched to occupied Germany or Austria. In 1947 a local official in Germany took the testimony of three elderly residents of Litoměřice who were arrested and then interned in a local barracks on June 16: "[Whoever] had something that was disallowed was beaten, and the money [we had] was almost completely taken. We remained there for two nights in bug-ridden spaces without food and lay on wooden floors. At night there were shots, doors were smashed down, girls and women raped, men beaten until bloodied." On the third day they were forced onto a coal car and taken to Teplice and then marched to the border. Young men whipped or shot anyone who could go no farther. Once in Germany, they wandered until August 3 before settling in a locality that could offer them food ration cards. "We were left without a single piece of jewelry, no money, and no memento [from our life in Litoměřice], and in the barracks even our wedding rings were taken from us. We are without bedclothes, clothes, underwear, shoes; to sum up, we have been made into complete beggars."[92]

Beneš and other members of the Czechoslovak government took little direct action to halt the violence, and their few demands for the atrocities to end were half-hearted. Administrative chaos combined with contradictory messages from Prague gave national committees, military contingents, and armed vigilantes freer rein than they might have had otherwise.[93] In fact, Beneš, like many politicians and members of his government, set a tone that justified the violence. Just after the liberation of Prague Beneš encouraged his countrymen to "liquidate" Czechoslovakia's Germans and Magyars "in the interest of a united national state of Czechs and Slovaks." Not coincidentally, an upsurge in violence followed immediately after similar speeches in Brno and Jihlava. "Today the time [for de-Germanization] has arrived," he told a crowd in Tábor in June. "Remember what has happened to us due to Germanization in the hundreds of years since the Hussite era. And so we announce our solution: to de-Germanize everywhere and in all parts of the Republic."[94] "Only the occupiers have been defeated and expelled," Communist leaders announced shortly after the Prague uprising had ended. "But their flunkies are still here among the ranks of our nation. . . . Away with them, uncover and seize them!"[95] The few vigilantes arrested for violent crimes were eventually released. A year after the wild transfer had begun, a Czechoslovak law absolved anyone who had, from the time of the Munich agreement until the end of October 1945, fought for Czech or Slovak liberation or whose actions "constituted just repayment for the behavior of the occupants or their accomplices." Even before the absolution, most of the perpetrators had been free for some time. Many had already moved into apartments and houses forcibly vacated by Germans and had started a new life.[96]

A recent Czech-German historical commission estimated that during the "wild transfer" between 19,000 and 30,00 Germans died, 6,000 as the direct result of Czech violence or of starvation and disease while herded into camps. Roughly 5,000 committed suicide. Somewhere between 600,000 and 900,000 people were driven from Czechoslovakia before August; military authorities alone loaded onto trains almost 450,000 Germans—without differentiating between Reich Germans, Sudeten Germans, and other Germans—before the end of July.[97] In fact, as Tomáš Staněk writes, the deportations intensified over time. In July roughly 5,000 people were being expelled from Czechoslovakia every day.

Among Western leaders concern was growing. Reports detailing the atrocities began to appear in the press.[98] Churchill and Truman, in addition to worrying about public opinion, also fretted about the necessity of feeding and housing the tens of thousands of refugees who crossed into occupied Germany daily from Czechoslovakia and Poland. Like their Polish counterparts, Czechoslovak officials stepped up diplomatic pressure as the Allies prepared to meet for a third major peace conference in July. Premier Fierlinger told the Allies that a decision on some form of transfer was the "most burning question" to date in Czechoslovakia. The U.S. embassy in Prague was warned that without Allied action, more radical elements could seize power from Beneš. British embassy counterparts reported that no end to the expulsions was in sight.[99] Not coincidentally, reports of "werewolves"—German guerrillas allegedly still fighting the Czechoslovak regime—rose as the conference date approached. In July, following an explosion at an arms depot in Ústí nad Labem, local Czechs immediately seized Germans and threw them into the Labe River, where the victims were shot at by revolutionary guards. Another mob set upon Germans in the town square, drowning them in water tanks used to put out the fire. An hour later, between fifty and one hundred Germans were dead. Witnesses later claimed that heightened fears about "werewolves" had driven them to mob violence. (Historians have yet to uncover any evidence of "werewolf" organizations operating in Czechoslovakia.)[100] There were also hints that Czechoslovakia, with Soviet backing, would continue the expulsions even without a firm commitment from Great Britain and the United States. As the Big Three met, General Svoboda began preparing an operation designed to present the Allies with a fait accompli should the talks not produce an acceptable agreement. He calculated that the military could immediately begin expelling 10,000 people daily, thus ridding Czechoslovakia of 2.1 million people by the end of the year.[101]

"Organized Transfer"

Stalin, Truman, and Churchill met at Potsdam for two weeks beginning on July 17. Churchill, whose party lost the elections in Britain before the conference ended, seemed spent. A blunter and more confident Truman learned midway through the conference that scientists had successfully tested the atom bomb, and thus he had an incentive to postpone concrete decisions until his bargaining position improved further. The Allies did manage to establish an international military tribunal at Nuremberg, and they set in motion talks that led to the peace treaties with Bulgaria, Romania, Hungary, and Italy. Boundaries across Europe were revised, and Stalin pledged to join the United States in its war with Japan. The Big Three agreed to treat Germany, divided into four zones under the control of the three Allies and France, respectively, as a "single economic unit" but to leave the zones subject to "varying local conditions," thus laying the groundwork for a divided Germany.[102] An Allied Control Council was assigned to oversee all questions regarding Germany. The Soviet Union obtained the right to exact war reparations from the Soviet zone and to receive a percentage of industrial equipment from the Western zones in return for agricultural products. Moreover, the Allies agreed to postpone the question of Poland's western border for a later peace conference, effectively accepting that the "Recovered Lands" now fell within Poland's border.

Issues surrounding Poland's border, the administration and cost of accommodating millions of refugees, and the prospect of "channeling" the wild and uncontrolled expulsions informed discussions of postwar transfers.[103] On the sixth day of the conference, Churchill, who at Yalta had told Stalin that he was "not at all shocked at the idea of transferring millions of people by force," made a remarkable statement: "The British had grave moral scruples about vast movements of population." Truman, too, wondered where "nine million" Germans would go. Stalin retorted that the Poles and Czechs had initiated the expulsions, at which point Anthony Eden, Britain's foreign minister, interjected that it was Beneš who had demanded that the transfer issue be addressed at Potsdam. It was not too late to take control of the process, Stalin then suggested. In time, a compromise between the seemingly inevitable expulsions and the need for security in occupied Germany was struck. Czechoslovakia, Poland, and Hungary would undertake the "transfer to Germany of German populations . . . in an orderly and humane manner," and in consultation with the Allied Control Council. For the moment, however, the expulsions were to cease. "We made it clear that we did not like the idea of mass transfers anyhow," a member of the British delegation wrote to a Foreign Ministry official on August 1. "As, however, we could not prevent them, we wished to ensure that they were carried out in as orderly and humane a manner as possible and in a way which would not throw an intolerable burden on the occupying authorities in Germany."[104]

The Czechoslovak government pledged to halt the expulsions, but the marches across the border, the beatings, the rapes, and the murders continued. Order did come, however, although in disturbingly familiar forms. By November 1945 about 150,000 people had been interned in the former Terezín concentration camp, labor camps, camps for Gypsies, and army barracks, as well as movie houses, hotels, and schools throughout Bohemia and Moravia.[105] A presidential decree that September mandated that all German men between the ages of fourteen and sixty could be mobilized for labor duty.[106] A second decree, issued a month later, closed the German university in Prague, undid German organizations, and censored the use of German in public.[107] The state confiscated all movable and immovable property belonging to Germans, Magyars, political enemies of the state, and anyone who had aided in Germanization measures during the occupation, placing the property into newly established "National Renewal Funds" (*Fondy národní obnovy*).[108] Germans were forced to register with the local police and to place white patches, fifteen centimeters in diameter with a large N for German (*němec*), on their chests (Fig 6.5). Former members of any Nazi organization had to wear a special armband, as did any German determined to be an "antifascist." Germans were limited in what hours they could venture out of doors and how far from their residence they could wander. Czech authorities distributed to Germans rations equal to those received by Jews during the war.[109] Politicians from Beneš on down to local elites spoke of a Czech "Lebensraum," "liquidation," "cleansing," and their determination to find a "radical solution to the German question."[110] Although the scale, form, and ideological underpinning behind these measures differed radically from the justifications cited by their Nazi predecessors, the Czech leaders, as they had throughout their history, were copycatting their German rivals.

The establishment of order and preparations for the transfer also raised a familiar question: what is a German? During the exile and the wild transfer, members of the Czechoslovak government haggled over various definitions and categories until the issue was resolved—or so it seemed—by Presidential Decree Number 5, issued on May 19, 1945, which dealt with the seizure of German, Magyar, and collaborationist property. Any individuals who had declared themselves to be German in any census after 1929 or had belonged to an association or political party deemed to be German were decreed German. The same definition applied to Magyars.[111] This definition, it can be assumed, also included Reich citizenship—a seemingly simpler identifier of German nationality. But numerous problems arose. On Frank's orders, Nazi officials destroyed thousand of documents as Allied troops approached. Plundering Soviet troops destroyed more documentation.[112] And disturbing questions hung in the air. What about the nearly 300,000 "Czechs" who had become

Figure 6.5 Germans in Prague awaiting their transport from the city, May or June 1945. (Reproduced by permission of the Česká tisková kancelář.)

Reich citizens during the occupation? What about Czech women married to Germans, and vice versa?

Before the end of the war, one informant told London, "Our people call out clearly: 'All Germans out.' Even socialists. Even those who just became Germans."[113] After the war, public voices repeated the same demands. As one contributor to the intellectual weekly *Dnešek* wrote: "Whoever betrayed the nation and declared himself to be a German has disavowed himself of other nationalities. This avowal constitutes a declaration that he identified with Germandom, that he agreed with the advancement of the German nation, that he agreed with Nazism, and even that he agreed with its crimes. . . . Whoever claimed to be a German belongs with Germans across the border."[114] Yet, despite the protests, the Czechoslovak government soon allowed many amphibians the chance to cross over again. Presidential Decree Number 33, issued the day that the Potsdam Conference ended, stripped "Germans," excluding those deemed to have actively fought against the Nazi regime, of their citizenship. Yet the decree also announced that "Czechs, Slovaks, and other members of Slavic nations" who had obtained Reich citizenship "under threat of denunciation or particular circumstances deemed exceptional" were not to be regarded as Germans.[115] More than 140,000 "Czechs" with Reich citizenship applied for reinstatement of their Czechoslovak citizenship after the war, and many had their wishes granted. In June 1945 local officials in České Budějovice accepted only thirty-four of at least four thousand petitions for the reinstatement of citizenship. Almost a year later, in March 1946, the same commission restored citizenship to nearly one thousand people. That same month, two out of every five applicants in Brno had their Czechoslovak citizenship returned to them. Then, in July 1946, a Ministry of the Interior ordinance announced that anyone whose mother tongue was Czech, had attended a Czech school, or had marked "Czechoslovak" in the 1930 census was not to be expelled, even if his or her citizenship had not been reinstated. As Jeremy King writes, a simple principle now guided the reinstatement of citizenship: "Once a Czech, always a Czech."[116]

Why the softening? One reason for the reversal might have been politics within the Communist-controlled Ministry of the Interior, which dealt with matters concerning citizenship. Many "Czechs" who had registered as Reich citizens during the war joined the party shortly after liberation, hoping for a safe haven from popular revenge and retribution trials.[117] But the main impetus behind the change seems to be a concern that Nazi rulers also shared—the need to have enough bodies to keep the economy running. Back in London, officials had, as early as 1944, begun to worry about labor shortages, and some suggested that amphibians could be made into Czechs. As plans for the "organized transfer" took form, officials at various levels proposed deporting known Nazis first and workers last. Officials in the borderlands begged Prague to allow Germans to remain through the 1946 harvest, albeit to little avail.[118] Public voices, too, began to worry about the "health" of their national organism if stripped of co-nationals. As *Lidová demokracie* wrote in April 1946:

> The expulsion of Germans from Yugoslavia, Hungary, and Romania, as well as from Poland and Czechoslovakia, will increase the density of population in rump Germany while considerably decreasing it in our land. . . . This gain has great political value for our future—on one condition, however: that our numerical strength does not stop growing but on the contrary continues to increase. It is undoubtedly a life and death question for us Czechs; to ensure social, economic, and moral preconditions for biological increase is one of the main tasks of our state policy.[119]

Editorial writers worried that Czech "blood" might be lost. "We want to and must save for our nation every drop of honorable Czech blood," Premier Fierlinger stated. "We are not a nation large enough to waste our own blood," a Ministry of the Interior official wrote. "[E]ven large nations do no indulge in such a luxury."[120]

The "health" of the nation also depended upon the reproductive capacity of its women. Thus, there arose among Czechoslovak leaders a special concern for women in mixed marriages, a concern shared by many Czechs who also saw the women as innocent victims of circumstance. As one statistician wrote in June 1946: "Demographically speaking, the Czech nation faces a serious problem for the future. Every marriage that breaks apart without fulfilling its reproductive mission will be a loss."[121] And like their Nazi predecessors, Czechoslovak leaders undid a previously existing citizenship law that made the wife's citizenship that of her husband. Czech women married to Germans, along with their children, would be judged not only independently but "benevolently" as well. German husbands, however, were not given the same consideration. Thus many Czech wives—their husbands in camps or awaiting deportation, their husbands' property confiscated, and they themselves unable to find work—began leaving the country voluntarily. Finally, in January 1947 the Ministry of the Interior allowed intermarried German husbands to apply for reinstatement of their Czechoslovak citizenship, provided that they had married before March 16, 1939, and that their wives were Czechoslovak citizens.[122]

As well as dealing with questions of nationality, officials were forced to face questions swirling around the terms "guilt" and "innocence," which had been so central to Beneš's rhetoric while in exile. The Košice Program, similar to the London government's memorandum to the European Advisory Committee, promised to divide Germans into three groups. Germans guilty of crimes against the republic would be immediately expelled. "Loyal citizens of German nationality" would be offered the option of remaining in Czechoslovakia, as would the most "innocent" of all, "antifascists." As the transfers unfolded, it soon became clear that, among the groups mentioned here, only the "antifascists" would actually have their citizenship reinstated. The definition of what made an "antifascist" also narrowed. According to the Košice program, an "antifascist" was anyone who had actively struggled against the Sudeten German Party before 1938 while supporting Czechoslovakia, anyone who had suffered arrest or punishment at home after Munich because of loyalty to Czechoslovakia, *or* anyone who had been forced to flee abroad, where he or she actively fought for the liberation of Czechoslovakia. Presidential Decree Number 5, however, reduced the definition to three necessarily bundled requirements: an antifascist was someone who "remained true to the Czechoslovak Republic, never committed an offense against the Czech and Slovak people, *and* either actively participated in the liberation of Czechoslovakia or had suffered Nazi terror." Powerful bureaucracies and political maneuverings then conspired to further reduce the number of antifascists. The Ministry of the Interior instructed committees charged with reviewing applications for reinstatement of citizenship that they should consider the individual's behavior before, during, and after Nazi rule when granting antifascist status. It warned against looking kindly on anyone who had resisted the regime for "opportunistic reasons." Even if individuals managed to regain Czechoslovak citizenship, their property might already have been confiscated by the Ministry of Agriculture, which had its own, even tighter criteria for determining who was an antifascist. Communist leaders narrowed the field even further, manipulating the decision-making process to guarantee that only Communists and Social Democrats obtained the label. In November 1946 only 13,045 Germans with antifascist credentials remained in Czechoslovakia.[123]

Another set of issues swirled around questions of guilt. People's Courts, which tried the most serious crimes, prosecuted more than thirty thousand collaborators and war criminals, while local courts heard almost 135,000 cases dealing with "offenses against national honor." In the end, 700 defendants were executed, more than three times the number of people killed by Communist authorities from 1948 to 1968.[124] The courts' sweep was broad. People accused of attending German theaters, hunting with Germans, or having applied for German citizenship could be prosecuted for "offenses against national honor." Retribution courts, especially at the highest levels, also prosecuted and sentenced Germans. Germans received 60 percent of the death sentences and 70 percent of the prison sentences handed out by People's Courts. (Not surprisingly, many of these so-called Germans had been Czechs before the occupation.) A presidential decree from summer 1945 declared that people could be punished for having been members of the SS, SA, Nazi Party, and prewar Sudeten German Party. The leading members of these organizations were locked away in Prague's Pankác Prison—once used by the Gestapo—along with Frank, members of the occupation-era Czech government, collaborationist journalists, Lida Baarová, the Czech leader of the League against Bolshevism, and other Czech notables. At the government's encouragement, each trial attracted the attention of an increasingly sensationalist press.[125]

As Benjamin Frommer argues, not only were Czechs and Germans tried under the same laws and interned together, but they often were subjected to the same experience of disenfranchisement and dispossession. Yet, he continues, the need to establish collective German guilt, and to expel the Germans, complicated and eventually undermined the retribution process. Frank's highly publicized trial included long sessions that relived the horrors of Lidice. As in many other trials, his crimes were portrayed as collective German crimes. In autumn 1947 some of the last German war criminals faced trial. The prosecution drew upon a long history of German treachery leading up to Munich and the occupation to gain a conviction of fifteen Sudeten German Party members. "This just punishment," a Czech newspaper concluded following the verdicts, "is the symbolic conclusion to the final parting of the democratic Czech population from the German parasites. . . . The day has come when once and for all the 'Sudeten fifth column' has ceased its activities." Many Ministry of the Interior officials worried that retribution trials would slow the transfer, and this while internment camps were overflowing. The American authorities said they would accept only whole families. Membership in some organizations was decriminalized, and by spring 1947 almost fifteen thousand Germans were released from custody in order to be expelled. The so-called transfer remained paramount.[126]

Prague officials attempted to draw lines between Czechs and Germans, "innocent" and "guilty," yet it was at the local level where elites attached labels that would decide the fate of thousands. And, as during the war, forces from below worked to pull Czechoslovakia toward even more radical stances vis-à-vis the German population. Throughout the wild transfer, powerful local national committees punished and sometimes executed Czech collaborators as well as Germans. They seized property and then redistributed it as they wished—with little or no oversight from above. National committees also had the last say on matters of nationality. They fashioned their own criteria as to what constituted a German and which Germans would be expelled.[127] Local elites even ignored exemptions made for German antifascists, confiscated their property and radios, forced them to wear white "German" armbands, assigned them to labor details, and even expelled them. National committees even ignored directives from the Ministry of the Interior in order to pursue more radical expulsion plans. On numerous occasions Czech women married to Germans were treated as German nationals, given German rations, and prepared for deportation. In České Budějovice, Ministry of the Interior officials pulled "Czech" women off the trains just before their departure to Germany. Courts appointed by national committees determined the fates of thousands who applied for reinstatement of their German citizenship. Sometimes national committees expelled the "Germans" before their own courts had reached a decision.[128]

Despite Ministry of the Interior decrees to the contrary, many national committees also treated Czechoslovakia's surviving Jews as Germans. Roughly ten thousand of the Bohemian lands' Jews survived the war, between fifteen hundred and two thousand of whom had claimed German nationality during the 1930 census. Many national committees forced these Jews to wear the white *N* armband, gave them German rations, and in some cases even expelled them from Czechoslovakia. "All the Germans must go," an article in *Dnešek* argued. "I don't know why anything should be held up due to investigations as to whether these Germans had Aryan or non-Aryan grandmothers. Transfer [odsun]."[129] Powerful national committees, greed, anti-Semitism, and vague decrees from Prague combined to prevent Jews from having Aryanized property returned to them. Upon returning home from concentration camps, many Jews found local Czechs living in their apartments, unwilling to vacate. A presidential decree issued in May 1945 stated that "state unreliable" persons, which included Germans, Hungarians, and members of various Nazi and collaborationist organizations, would have their property confiscated. Exceptions were made, however, for anyone who had suffered "national, racial, or political persecution," and a month later another decree made exceptions for anyone who had actively fought for the liberation of Czechoslovakia. Another decree the following October, however, declared that the state would confiscate property from anyone who had participated in Germanization projects within the Czechoslovak lands or who had become an enemy of Czechoslovakia. In Prague, local officials gathered lists of German theater subscribers and accused the Jewish members of participating in a Germanization project. In addition to blocking the return of their property, the Prague national committee concluded that their "German" Jews were subject to *"Sonderbehandlung"* (a Nazi euphemism translated literally as "special treatment") and would be "repatriated" to Germany. Not until September 1946 did the Ministry of the Interior declare that "persons of Jewish descent" were exempted from the property confiscation decrees. Even then, national committees often ignored the new directive. Czechs still refused to vacate apartments and houses once inhabited by Jews.[130]

Anti-Semitism and petty materialism had survived the occupation, as had a popular hatred of anything or anyone German. Postwar nationalism, Karel Kaplan writes, took on a disturbing "anti-social" element after the war, characterized above all by a virulent anti-Germanism.[131] Political leaders kept the temperature high, trying to top their opponent's anti-German credentials and promising to be "toughest" with the Germans. Politicians still drew their legitimacy from the "nation," and the nation was, at least according to correspondents in London during the war, filled with rage toward the Germans. It demanded their expulsion, and even sometimes their lives. In a world where the sole dividing lines had become "Czech" and "German," or "innocent" and "guilty," to be in the former camp meant to support the expulsions. In fact, one wonders how any "good Czech" could have questioned notions of collective German guilt, the justifiability of hating a whole group, and the transfer. Maintaining "social relations" with Germans could lead to being charged with "offenses against national honor." Some individuals did, however, show immense courage in this time of heated nationalist rhetoric. After seeing the suffering endured by Germans in the internment camps, the well-known pacifist Přemysl Pitter defied both public opinion and warnings by the state and erected homes for German children. A small number of Catholic writers dared to question the notion of collective guilt. Along marginal issues such as mixed marriages Czech writers found enough moral space to question the expulsions. Yet these actions were the exception, and far from the rule.[132]

In January 1946 the transports restarted, and by the end of October 6,580 locomotives had pulled 67,748 train cars filled with Germans into American- and Soviet-occupied Germany. The 1950 Czechoslovak census counted only 165,117 Germans, the majority of whom were miners, industrial workers and their families, and Germans in mixed marriages.[133] Německý (German) Brod became Havlíčkův Brod, named in honor of the great nineteenth-century Czech poet. Monuments and graveyards were destroyed. No German-language schools were allowed. "We are finished with the Germans in Czechoslovakia," Jan Masaryk said. "There is no possible way to get us to live under the same umbrella again."[134] Bohemia, Moravia, and Silesia had truly become the "Czech lands."

The impetus and justifications for the transfers began with an all-encompassing hatred of anything and anyone German. For Czechs at home, anti-German sentiments provided an outlet for the fears, frustrations, and embarrassments that had characterized life under the Protectorate. It united Czechs divided by age, geography, and class in a society atomized by Gestapo informants. "Good" Czechs at home and their leaders abroad, despite passionate disagreements about the issues swirling around "resistance" and "collaboration," could agree that hating, and expelling, the Germans was historically, morally, and politically justified. The concept of collective guilt, like the retribution trials and the "myth of resistance," allowed the rest of the population, the "innocent" ones, to live with a clear conscience. For Beneš and others, "cleansing" society of the guilty and creating a nation-state promised to complete a "revolution" only haltingly begun after World War I. "Revolution," "nation-state," "guilt," historical imagination, and the hard experience of life under Nazi occupation all came together in plans to expel the Germans.

Hatred made the expulsions imaginable and justifiable, but the collapse of Nazi institutions, the appearance of radicalized actors on the scene, and choices made by powerful leaders ensured that the expulsions unfolded the way that they did. As the war came to an end, Frank's blustering, SS atrocities, and partisan violence radicalized an already intense atmosphere. Nazi rule then collapsed. The Czechoslovak and Red Armies entered the scene, and violence on a wholly new scale broke out in Prague.[135] Amid the ensuing chaos, passions and opportunism could run relatively unchecked. The violence had Stalin's blessing, and sometimes direct aid from his army. Churchill and Roosevelt offered vague support to Polish and Czechoslovak transfer demands, but, as Klaus-Dietmar Henke writes, their indecision left the door open for a whole array of participants, both Communist and non-Communist, to take matters into their own hands.[136] Beneš and members of his government did just that. Claims that *all* Germans were responsible for Nazism's crimes and demands that all Germans must be expelled came first and most forcefully from home, but Beneš and members of the Czechoslovak government-in-exile set the context for violence. Radio broadcasts and then public speeches encouraged Czechs to join the "fight" against the now-defeated enemy. Once in power, the Czechoslovak government took few measures to halt the violence. Later, it pardoned vigilantes and robbers.[137]

The violence continued after the Allies, at Potsdam, approved the "orderly and humane" transfer. Hatred of the Germans and demands to expel every German from the country contoured the execution of the "organized" transfer. Powerful notions of collective German guilt narrowed the number of "innocent" Germans, or "antifascists." Transfer demands undermined attempts to adjudicate and punish individual German guilt. Yet serious concerns about the nation's economy and "health" caused officials in Prague to ensure that "Czechs" would not be deported, and the actual assignment of German nationality was an uneven and confused process. In the end, the final answer to the question "What is a German?"

was not found among officials, academics, and leading nationalists but determined at the local level on a person-to-person basis. Most significant, the assigning of nationality was definitive. Nationality, something once acted out in civil and political society before the occupation, was now something that the state affixed to individuals.

Gone, too, were many of the best words and highest ideals of the pre-occupation period. In a radio address to the Protectorate in 1940 Beneš had recalled for his countrymen the elegy he had given at former Czechoslovak president Tomáš Masaryk's funeral three years earlier: "I emphasized that his whole life had been a struggle for individual dignity, for political, social, and national freedom and justice, a struggle against everything absolutist, religious and cultural hatred, state and national violations in the name of the larger nation or state, a struggle also against war and against the force of the weak against the strong; in short, a struggle for the principles of humanitarian democracy. . . . Everything that I call out to you [at home] is in the spirit and in the memory of our first president and to the fulfillment of his goals and to the completion of his life's works."[138] Then, too, Beneš spoke vaguely of revolution. But over time the goals and nature of the revolution changed, and the Czechoslovak president called up and drew from the basest of emotions to realize it. In 1945 the nation was united perhaps as never before behind a project that promised to end the Czech-German rivalry. Many Czechs seized the opportunity to make amends with past wrongs and to transform the Bohemian lands into a nationally homogenious political unit. Anti-German rhetoric, always important to the patriots' verbal repertoire, had become the deformed, albeit powerful, focal point of a Czech national identity stripped of many of its positive values. After six long years of Nazi rule, followed by "wild" and "organized" transfers, the world that had created Tomáš Masaryk had been swept away. Now Czechoslovak leaders, led by the Communists, were ready to continue the revolution.

Conclusion

A number of stories came to an end in the years from 1945 to 1948. Hugo Jury, Konrad Henlein, and Emanuel Moravec committed suicide. The Allies brought Konstantin von Neurath before the International Military Tribunal in Nuremberg, where he was found guilty on four counts, including crimes against humanity, but was only sentenced to fifteen years in prison. On May 9, in the middle of the Prague uprising, Karl Hermann Frank and his family escaped the city by car. They made it as far as a small village in the U.S.-controlled zone of Western Bohemia before a Czech police sergeant recognized Frank. After several months in American custody, Frank was returned to Prague, where he was tried by a Czechoslovak court and finally executed in 1946. Millions of his fellow Sudeten Germans, like ethnic Germans from all over Eastern Europe, began new lives in the various occupied zones of Germany and elsewhere. In 1950, one in every five West German inhabitants, or about eight million people, had arrived after World War II.[1] Emil Hácha, overtaken by senility, died in his cell awaiting trial. Ferdinand Peroutka, who survived two concentration camps and twenty-seven months of solitary confinement, returned to Prague and his life as a writer and political essayist. Jan Masaryk retained his post as minister of foreign affairs. President Edvard Beneš remained a powerful, unifying figure in Czechoslovak politics. These stories, too, soon came to an end. In February 1948 Klement Gottwald's Communist Party staged a coup and soon gained control over the whole government. In a Europe increasingly divided into two camps, Czechoslovakia was now firmly within the Soviet half. Peroutka fled abroad, eventually being named head of Radio Free Europe's Czech section. In an event still full of mystery, Masaryk fell to his death from a Ministry of Foreign Affairs window shortly after the coup. Beneš abdicated in June 1948. Two months later he suffered a stroke, fell into a deep coma, and died shortly thereafter.

With Beneš's death and the Communists' rise to power, the Bohemian lands and Czechoslovakia entered a new historical era. Soviet rulers imposed—not always successfully—common political frameworks, common economic models, common slogans, and common forms of repression upon the countries of Eastern Europe. (Yugoslavia remained an important exception.) Nazi occupation by no means predetermined the rise of Communism and the success of Stalinist rule in Czechoslovakia. There was much to distinguish the Protectorate experience from that of other Eastern European lands, and much that distinguished Communist Czechoslovakia from its counterparts in the Soviet bloc. Many wartime and postwar developments in the Protectorate find parallels in Western European countries. "In contradistinction to Stalinism," Norman Naimark writes, "revolution is not a homogenizing experience."[2] The Nazi occupation and its aftershocks did, however, prepare the way for the imposition of Soviet rule in Czechoslovakia, as elsewhere in Eastern Europe, by destroying and radically transforming the pre-1938 world.

Quite ill, Beneš arrived in Prague on May 16, 1945, to cheering crowds. He also arrived with a political program, designed months before in Košice. As planned, various levels of national committees took control at the local and regional levels of the country. In Prague, the government consisted of a National Front of six parties, dominated by the Communists and Social Democrats, and diverse groups of trade unions, cooperatives, and associations. Foreign policy, despite silent protests by Jan Masaryk, sought to maintain close ties to the Soviet Union while positioning Czechoslovakia as a "bridge" between an increasingly divided East and West. At home, in addition to expelling the Germans, the government initiated retribution trials that promised to "cleanse" the country of collaborators and traitors. Beneš and his government also pursued a radical social and economic revolution that was both inspired and made possible by six long years of occupation.

In the economy, the state remained everywhere. Price controls were set on basic goods. Iron and steel, mining, chemical, pharmaceutical, and other industries, in addition to banks and insurance companies, came under state management. Only enterprises with fewer than five hundred employees that belonged to certain industrial sectors were excluded from nationalization. A year and a half later, four out of every five Czechoslovak workers were employed in industries and companies absorbed by the state.[3] National administrators took over enterprises confiscated from Germans and others. In the borderlands, state officials experimented with various forms of ownership, management, and distribution of commercial licenses.[4] In 1946 the Czechoslovak government announced a Two-Year Plan, making it, as Alice Teichová points out, "the second country after the Soviet Union to take the path of a planned economy."[5] Trade, production, and wage levels were often controlled from Prague. The program also included a vaguely familiar "national mobilization of labor"—a propaganda campaign aimed at increasing production levels and obtaining full employment, including the employment of women. Women, first mobilized in the last years of the occupation, now entered the workforce in growing numbers.[6]

Working-class prestige and incomes continued to rise while the middle classes were fast disappearing. The destruction of the Jews depleted the Bohemian lands of a once vibrant entrepreneurial class.[7] The wild and organized transfers further depleted the middle class of its Germans, and Communist-run national committees were keen to prosecute Czechs who had profited from the war. The Czechoslovak government then further leveled the playing field. As part of an effort to dampen rising inflation and stabilize the crown's exchange rate, 85 percent of the money in circulation was withdrawn. All bank accounts, life insurances, and government securities were frozen; they could be released only with the blessing of a state agency. In 1947, after intense prodding from the Communist Party, the government hit the wealthiest sector of society with a one-time property tax that took in 1.1 billion crowns. At the same time, the gap between industrial and white-collar workers continued to shrink. The average white-collar worker's salary was only 24.5 percent higher than that of his counterpart among industrial workers by 1948.[8] Members of the working class, coddled under the occupation, gained confidence. After the liberation, elected workers' councils held sway in factories and sometimes obtained ownership of them. Workers also gained the sympathy of large swaths of the population that had been forced into assembly-line work under the occupation. The Nazi regime had, in effect, established Bohemia and Moravia's first welfare state. The regime had guaranteed workers employment, food, insurance, and other benefits like tickets to sporting events. In some ways, workers had become a privileged class years before the Communists took power.[9]

Familiar institutions from the interwar period reappeared, but after the occupation their content and form changed. Associational life was centralized and tied to political party organizations as never before. Civil and political society, although slowly recovering, remained deformed. Many smaller clubs and associations failed to reorganize after the war. Associations like the Ústřední matice školská (Central School Foundation), the largest of its kind dedicated to the building of Czech schools before the war, reconstituted but now had little influence. Trade unions, which counted two million members, merged. Their leadership often took direct orders from Social Democratic and Communist leaders. Other political parties took control of peasant associations and gymnastics clubs. Even resistance fighters, whose voices had counted for so much during the occupation, were excluded from power by Beneš and other professional politicians who had spent the occupation years in exile.[10] As before the occupation, a small number of party leaders in Prague made the bulk of the government's political decisions.

Yet participation in civil and political society was perhaps more important to daily existence than ever. Party leaders, as before, filled their appointed ministries with their own. The composition of national committees was also based on party membership. Party politicians made economic decisions that had once been left to private individuals and market forces.[11] No wonder, then, that by mid-1946 more than 1.5 million people had become members of the Czech Communist, National Socialist, and Social Democratic parties. (Records created by the People's Party do not allow for a reliable calculation of its membership figures.)[12] "It is everywhere taken for granted that postwar life will not be so politicized, and I mean this in every respect. . . . *Everyone says this*," a correspondent to the Czechoslovak government-in-exile reported in 1944. The warning seemed to go unheeded. Party politics, indeed politics in general, mattered more than ever before to people's lives.[13]

The expulsion of three million Germans had immense repercussions for both the economy of the Bohemian lands and their reemerging civil and political societies. The state worked aggressively to transplant Czechs to the borderlands in an effort to prevent economic collapse in the region. In fact, as Adrian von Arburg has shown, the Settlement

Office in Prague, which also oversaw many aspects of the "organized transfer," had seriously considered forcibly resettling Czechs in the borderlands. The office also oversaw what Arburg calls the "internal transfer" (*vnitři odsun*) of tens of thousands of ethnic Magyars and Roma from Slovakia to the borderlands. Eventually, almost two million Czechs from the interior and from abroad made an attempt at a new life along the peripheries of the Bohemian lands.[14] But many buildings remained abandoned. Nature enveloped once productive fields. Villages became ghost towns. Political and cultural differences divided newcomers and natives, the latter often accusing the former of being gold diggers. Czechs raised in the countryside "ruralized" Brno, once home to a thriving German and German-Jewish urban, middle-class cultural milieu. Glassworks and other light industries were especially hard-hit by the departure of skilled German craftsmen and workers. State officials in the borderlands played an even more dominant role in distributing land seized from Germans and running local industries.[15]

With the Germans gone, a driving force behind associational and political life disappeared. The very reason for the existence of many clubs vanished. Yet in other ways the Germans never went away. Anti-German hatred and a Social Darwinist language radicalized by six long years of occupation continued to poison public discourse even as the Germans were registered, segregated, and then deported. Mythmakers, often with the help of graphic images, fixed the massacres at Lidice and other forms of Nazi terror into popular memory. The "fight" continued to be fought, the horrors remembered, albeit selectively. The following 1946 depiction of the Prague uprising was typical: "The Germans go to extremes of violence—they shoot firemen who try to isolate the conflagration of whole blocks; they shoot rescue squads who try to save women and children from these houses. They bombard hospitals. With ruthless brutality, they drive the population before their tanks, they pull Czech women and children out of raid shelters and tie them to the tanks going to attack the barricades. They cut the throats of children or strangle them; they pull out their eyes with specially designed instruments; they pollute corpses."[16] Every major Czech political party made hating the Germans, and supporting the expulsions, central to its platform. The 1946 elections provoked an orgy of anti-German rhetoric in which each party tried to prove its patriotic credentials. Not surprisingly, politicians soon drew upon anti-German rhetoric to bludgeon each other. Communist propagandists, for example, reveled in beating down Ladislav Feierabend, a leader of the Agrarian Party before the occupation and a member of the Czechoslovak National Socialists after the liberation who had served in the Czech puppet government before escaping to London in 1940. "Feierabend exported wheat [to Germany], we export Germans," one Communist slogan proclaimed, warning voters of "reactionary" elements within the rival party.[17]

Other beliefs took new forms, recast with rhetoric full of hate. The expulsions crowned Social Darwinist views of history with new legitimacy, even among writers who had previously called for decency and national introspection. "Czech aggression toward the Germans which played itself out in the days of May," Peroutka wrote in 1947, "did not depend upon the principles of formal justice. It was a battle of nation against nation; it was war; it was a long-prepared playing out of unexpressed feelings of cruelty and cunning towards each other."[18] Professional scholars, publicists, and politicians reworked old themes and introduced a conclusion to the story of Czech-German struggles. The expulsions, for example, promised to redress crimes that stretched back to the Habsburg defeat of supposedly Czech nobles at White Mountain in 1620. In Czech historical memory, this event initiated three hundred years of Habsburg dominance and Czech cultural darkness.[19] At the Second Congress of Czechoslovak historians in 1947, only one participant raised the issue of Czech atrocities committed against Germans immediately after liberation. Most participants contented themselves with accepting history's "lessons" and the laudable conclusion to Czech-German history in the region.[20]

Other, less noticeable transformations constituted a radical break from the past. Six years of occupation and then the postwar expulsions discredited old beliefs. Czechs quickly discarded values once held dear. Many people seemed at a loss philosophically and psychologically. As Jan Gross, speaking of a common Eastern European phenomenon, writes: "One could not hope to understand the period without the realization that the wartime experience of spiritual crisis, crisis of values, and normative disorganization profoundly affected notions of commonweal, collective good, and group interests in the societies of the region. The old operative definitions of legality, justice, legitimacy, common purpose, national interest, or raison d'état were put in doubt, shattered."[21] Although collaborators were brought to trial and the Germans, as a whole, had been punished with expulsion, Nazi rule had taught an important lesson: raw power and violence won out over fundamentally democratic values of negotiation and compromise. The "wild" and then "organized" transfers drove home the idea that violence could best achieve political aims. The government's amnesty of Czechs who had robbed, beaten, and murdered Germans during the wild transfer undermined the idea of human rights. Chauvinism and opportunism, once again, seemed to trump decency and law.[22] Property rights, already undermined by Aryanization and nationalization measures, were dealt another blow after the war. Czechs from the interior simply appropriated apartments or took over businesses from Germans. As part of a first wave of land reform, the Czechoslovak government redistributed 1.8 million hectares of arable land to Czech and Slovak settlers. Most of that land had once belonged to Germans.[23] The Second Republic and Nazi rule had discredited right-wing politics, swinging much of the population to the political left while making conservative political positions less tenable. Whereas Czech nationalists had historically, since the nineteenth century, alternately looked East and West, now they turned definitively toward the East. Postwar nationalists hated the fact that the Western powers had betrayed Czechoslovakia at Munich. Unlike before the war, leading Czech patriots hated Western culture and Western socioeconomic systems, which had appeared to collapse in the face of Nazi rule. Indeed, few things seemed certain, other than hating the Germans and accepting the legitimacy of the expulsions.[24]

Into this vacuum stepped the Communist Party, which won 38 percent of the vote in the 1946 election.[25] Communist ideology provided a rational interpretation of the occupation years that made sense. The Communist Party promised new beginnings and a radical break with the dead weight of the past, represented by the Western governments and the older generation of Czech politicians now returning to power. As Milan Kundera, whose first publications included sugary odes to Stalin, later remembered: "Yes, say what you will—the Communists were more intelligent. They had a grandiose program, a plan for a brand-new world in which everyone would find his place. The Communists' opponents had no great dream; all they had were a few moral principles, stale and lifeless, to patch up the tattered trousers of the established order. So of course the grandiose enthusiasts won out over the cautious compromisers."[26] Behind these grandiose enthusiasts stood the Soviet Union, which had defeated the Germans and now stood as protector of fellow Slavs. Socialism also enjoyed wide support. During the war the democratic resistance loyal to London had vociferously called for a sweeping socialist revolution after the war. Beneš, while wary of upsetting his British allies, shared their desire for postwar change. After 1945 Communist and non-Communist intellectuals, with the exception of their Roman Catholic counterparts, often shared a desire to break with the past and to reorient Czech politics toward the Soviet east. They enthused about plans to create a vaguely defined socialism. In doing so, Bradley Abrams argues, they unwittingly created a political context that encouraged popular support for the Communists.[27]

An energized youth, a culture of denunciations, and control over vital political institutions further aided the Communists. In 1947, one-quarter of Czechoslovakia's population was between fifteen and thirty years of age. Many, like Kundera, had only vague memories of interwar, democratic Czechoslovakia. Almost a quarter of all partisans operating in the Protectorate in late August 1944 were twenty-four years of age or younger.[28] For them and others their age, the young radical Zdeněk Mylnář later remembered, war fostered a "Manichean view of the world" and a "primitive radicalism" that aimed at their careful, prudent parents. "We were the children of war," he continued, "who, not having actually fought against anyone, brought our wartime mentality with us into those first postwar years, when the opportunity to fight for something presented itself at last."[29] National Socialists complained that the Communists' incessant demands for retribution created a pervading sense of fear among the population that, combined with police "gestapoism," was dividing the nation.[30] Newspapers and party leaders of all political hues solicited denunciations as part of the retribution process. The Communists, however, were particularly aggressive in this respect. The effects on society, as a writer for the National Socialist *Masarkův lid* (Masaryk's People) observed, were uncomfortably familiar: "Before, someone hurled words at you: 'praises the assassination,' 'listens to foreign radio,' 'insults the Leader [Führer]'—and off you went. To a concentration camp or to death. Today, someone else hurls words at you: 'asocial,' 'Germanophile'; in some places a simple determination suffices: 'not a member of the party.' You'll lose your job; they'll hand you over to the appropriate authorities; you'll sit eighteen months in jail, and in the end it will be discovered that it's not true."[31] The Communists also benefited from an increasingly powerful state and state patronage. The Communist-controlled Ministry of Agriculture doled out land taken from the Germans and hence won wide support among peasants and inhabitants of the borderlands. The Ministry of the Interior lorded over economic measures like the nationalization of industries. Following the 1946 election, the Communist Party further strengthened its influence at the local level when Communists gained control of 78 percent of district national committee chairs in the Bohemian lands.[32]

Of course, the argument should not be overstated. The establishment of Communist rule in Czechoslovakia, and the type of Communist rule that its inhabitants got, was made possible, but not predetermined, by domestic forces unleashed during the occupation years. In Slovakia, more than 60 percent of voters cast ballots for the anti-Communist and anti-Czech Catholic Democratic Party.[33] Moreover, 60 percent of Czech voters did not choose the Communists. Although Communist-led student action committees sprouted up at universities, few professors were members of the Communist Party. Centrist parties gained more votes than Communists in the university student union elections of 1946 and 1947.[34] Even those who voted for the Communist Party were not necessarily voting to end democracy. Gottwald promised voters that his party would lead the country down a "Czechoslovak" path to socialism; Beneš, like his counterparts in Hungary, was determined to chart out a "third way" between increasingly hostile Western and Soviet powers.[35]

In fact, events in Czechoslovakia have many parallels with those in Western Europe. Virulent anti-German sentiment was common across Europe, as was the nationalization of major industries. Like their counterparts in Eastern Europe, Western European governments arrested, tried, and punished wartime collaborators. Belgian authorities prosecuted more than fifty-seven thousand people and sentenced almost three thousand to death. In France, roughly 130,000 collaborators received some form of punishment. In the Netherlands that number was 113,000, or almost one in every one hundred citizens.[36] Western European politics, too, swung to the left. Just months after the end of war in Europe, the Labour Party won the elections in Britain, unseating Winston Churchill with slogans like "The Labour Party is a socialist party and is proud of it." In France, the Communist Party received almost 27 percent of the vote in 1946, more than any other party. That same year the Italian Communist Party won 19 percent of the vote, forming a "tri-partite" coalition with Socialists and Christian Democrats.[37]

Further, while Czechoslovakia's politics might have been more prone to left-wing politics, and Communist rule, than its East-Central European neighbors, until 1947 it seemed in less danger of Soviet domination. The countries of East-Central Europe may have shared certain wartime and postwar experiences in varying degrees: accelerated industrialization, state-coordinated economies, the destruction and removal of whole populations, the weakening of the middle classes, a discredited political right wing, a shared desire among many to break from failed interwar governments, a radicalized youth, and a crisis of values born of massive violence and upheavals.[38] But in Poland anti-Russian sentiment had long historical roots, and more recently, in 1939, the Soviets had participated in the destruction of Poland. Stalin had prevented the return of Poland's London government-in-exile. Bands of anti-Communist resistance fighters roamed the eastern territories. In Hungary, the conservative Smallholder's Party won 57 percent of the vote. The Communists received a disappointing 17 percent.[39] Yet both countries, sooner or later, came under Soviet domination, thanks to raw power. Soviet authorities dominated Allied Control Commissions in the former puppet states of Hungary, Romania, and Bulgaria, where they could reject any government decision, candidacy, or publication. The Soviet secret police arrested and deported thousands from these countries. In Czechoslovakia, Soviet advisers played a murkier role. Perhaps most important of all, whereas Soviet (and American) armies withdrew from Czechoslovakia in winter 1945, the Red Army, although reduced, remained in Poland, Romania, Hungary, and Romania. Military tribunals in these countries targeted political opponents and influenced local courts. At any moment, the Soviet armies could have taken power.[40]

By the end of 1945 only Tito's Yugoslav Partisans had taken complete control of their government, eliminated their rivals, and embarked on a revolutionary path to socialism. Coalition governments ruled elsewhere because Stalin had counseled gradualism to European Communists. Then, in 1947, larger geopolitical forces came into play. In March the U.S. administration announced the Truman Doctrine, which granted Greece and Turkey aid to fight Communist insurgents, thus initiating a foreign policy strategy that would reign until 1989—the "containment" of Communist rule around the world. The Truman administration forced coalition governments in France and Italy to abandon the Communists and announced the creation of the Marshall Plan for Economic Recovery. At the behest of Stalin, the Czechoslovak and other Eastern European governments politely refused the offer of help. Later that autumn, at the first meeting of the Cominform, the Yugoslavs and Soviets condemned coalition governments, gradualism, and national paths to socialism. One by one, the Communists in East Germany, Poland, Hungary, Romania, and Bulgaria eliminated their political rivals. They established the supremacy of the Communist Party. They embarked on Soviet-style industrialization plans and reorientated their trade eastward. "Little Stalins" stood atop each government, and ideological conformity was imposed upon a diverse region. The Iron Curtain had come down.

At the Cominform meeting the Czechoslovak Communists had been singled out for having failed to "resolve the question of power."[41] Months later, power was handed to them. Someone had been mailing bombs to non-Communist ministers, but the Communist-controlled Ministry of the Interior refused to investigate the crimes. Moreover, the Ministry of the Interior proceeded to purge the police organs of the few remaining non-Communists. In February 1948, ministers of the National Socialist, Czech Populist, and Slovak Democratic parties resigned in protest. Still, the majority of cabinet posts, including those held by the Social Democrats and the nonpartisan foreign minister Jan Masaryk, remained filled, meaning the government did not fall. "At first, I couldn't believe it would be so easy," Gottwald remarked later. "But then it turned out that this is just what happened—they handed in their resignations. . . . I prayed that this stupidity over resignations would continue and that they would not change their minds."[42] Having not thought out the possible endgames, the protesters' only hope was that Beneš would refuse their resignations.

But Beneš decided to accept the resignations, allowing the Communists to form their own cabinet with Communists and supporters from other parties. As before, he might have considered geopolitical forces from the outside to have been overwhelming. But, at home, something was different this time—a difference that no doubt influenced his decision as well. In 1938 Czechs, as well as a number of Germans, had enthusiastically mobilized in the face of Nazi aggression, determined to defend the Czechoslovak project. In 1948 the Communists' blustering threatened to tear the now homogeneous nation apart. Encouraged by the Communist Party, hundred of thousands of protesters filled city and town squares across the country, and millions of workers took part in a one-day general strike on February 24. "Action committees" organized in factories. Armed militias roamed Prague and stationed themselves outside public buildings. The Ministry of the Interior's security police, with the help of well-placed Communist sympathizers, began harassing non-Communist political officials.[43] Few protested the Communists' aggressions. After liberation, non-Communist intellectuals had haughtily berated their countrymen for not shedding their "Protectorate mentality," which they characterized as "indifference," "defeatism," "chicken-heartedness," and a willingness "to sell [one's] convictions for selfish reasons."[44] "We have to realize," one young Czech woman told an English friend, "that the occupation produced cowards as well as heroes. During the years when young people were growing up, morals were inverted; evil was often shown to be more profitable than the truth. Those who grew used to whispering cannot speak out naturally now; they either shout or whisper."[45]

Twice in ten years Beneš had lost his state. Soon after the Communists seized power in 1948, an attempt to transform society according to ideological principles began anew. The regime nationalized all enterprises with more than fifty employees and all enterprises engaging in foreign or wholesale trade. Land collectivization moved ahead slowly, but steadily, so that by 1960, 90 percent of Czechoslovakia's arable land belonged to collectives.[46] Six years after the coup, four-fifths of Czechoslovakia's foreign trade was with the Soviet Union and Eastern European countries. Non-Communist political parties were either purged or folded into the Communist Party. Authorities shut down newspapers and periodicals. They absorbed into the state apparatus clubs and associations like the Sokol and dissolved those not tied directly to the state. University administrators modeled their institutions and pedagogical methods after the Soviets. The Ministry of the Interior demanded that every inhabitant claim a permanent residence, which was noted on a personal identification card. Using this information, authorities could locate and track every individual in the country. Camps and prisons filled with people labeled "class enemies," "saboteurs," and "asocial elements," including members of the democratic resistance and the London-based Czechoslovak army. Many new prisoners shared cells with Nazi war criminals and Czech collaborators.[47] In many ways Nazi rule had made the Communists' task easier. Nazi rule had created an economy largely coordinated by the state and empowered the working class. It had destroyed civil and political society, which emerged weak and deformed after 1945. It had created citizens practiced in the art of denunciation. The occupation years had fostered public enthusiasm for socialism and the Soviet Union. The occupation experience had discredited the past, left a value system in disarray, and encouraged hateful political rhetoric. Nazi rule in the Bohemian lands had not necessarily led to the establishment of Communist rule, but it certainly gave it a good start.

The traveler who visited Czechoslovakia shortly after 1989 could have observed something remarkable: so much in the Bohemian lands was uniformly "Czech." The beer was Czech, the cars were Czech, and most of the businesses, even after economic reforms, remained in Czech hands. Despite a long political marriage to the Slovaks, Czech culture seemed incredibly uniform as well. One still heard regional dialects, but Czechs knew all the same folk songs, the same authors, and the same clichés. Czechs related their history as if reading from the same script— no wonder, since under Communism history books were all the same, and after 1989 changes in content and themes were slow in coming.[48] The Czech Republic, created after the disintegration of Czechoslovakia in 1993, was an ethnically homogeneous nation-state. According to the 1991 and 2001 censuses, Roma, Germans, and Poles made up about 1 percent of the Bohemian lands' roughly ten million inhabitants. In 2001, Slovaks were the Czech Republic's largest minority with 193,000 people.[49]

Today, however, the visitor can see difference. The year 1989 marked the return of confrontations with diversity, the return of debates over what it means to be Czech, and the return of questions as to who has authority over the construction of identity. Many Czechs, especially younger ones, have absorbed foreign ideas through travel and communication with other countries. Integration into the European Union promises the arrival of more foreign investors, and the Czech Republic will soon join an aging Europe whose economy and social services, demographers predict, will become even more dependent on immigrant workers.[50] A new generation of Czech historians has begun to question the established approach to history, calling for a diversity of views and approaches to the study of the past. In doing so, they are also asking what it means to be Czech.[51] The homogeneous and unified Czech nation is disintegrating. Social critics and philosophers have blamed the usual suspects—globalization, Americanization, postmodernism—but there is nothing new about such fearful developments. From the national awakening in the early nineteenth century until the end of the First Republic, controversies over the nature of Czechness pervaded public discourse. Even complaints that ethnic mixing and foreign infiltration are a danger to the "nation" are old. In fact, the historian is briefly overcome by a sense of déjà vu.

Still, these are only weak echoes from a world of yesterday. Not only are most of the Germans and Jews gone, but so is a whole world distinguished by a peculiar form of nationality politics. Before the war, inhabitants of the Bohemian lands acted nationally in myriad ways: by belonging to clubs, marching in the streets, buying newspapers, voting for a political party, participating in the census, shopping at certain stores, watching certain movies, and speaking a particular language—to name just a few. The pre-1939 world was not a multicultural paradise. Patriotic rhetoric, especially after the rise of Social Darwinism in the late nineteenth century, was often vicious and myopic. Political anti-Semitism flourished along with the rise of mass politics before World War I. The First Czechoslovak Republic too often acted solely as a government by and for the Czechs. Yet oft-forgotten is that before 1939, and even during the first months of Nazi rule, nationality politics in the Bohemian lands inspired and shaped a thriving civil and political society. Often forgotten, too, is that for many people nationality was an individual choice. Only in a limited number of cases did the Czechoslovak government decree a person's nationality. Not that long ago many people in the Bohemian lands were bilingual. Some switched national identities according to various situations. Others were unsure of their national group. Regional, class, or religious identities often seemed more important than national ones.

One of the most striking legacies of the Nazi occupation and its immediate aftermath is the destruction of this pre-1939 world of nationality politics. Nazi leaders not only destroyed a once vibrant civil and political society. They assumed, over time, the right to determine national identity. In 1930 any male could have declared himself to be a

German. In 1940 any male could have applied for Reich citizenship. Given the open-ended criteria of the citizenship law and political pressures to increase the number of Germans in the Protectorate, that male's chances of being accepted were good. To remain a Protectorate national and thus passively count oneself among Czechs was even simpler. Still, the gap between nationalities widened as officials constructed a legal, enforceable line between Protectorate nationals (Czechs) and Reich citizens (Germans). The regime segregated and then labeled Jews as such before deporting them to their deaths. Racial experts and other state officials began identifying Germanizable Czechs, a process that was fast gaining momentum before Heydrich's death in 1942. Before 1940, Germanization, like Czechification, referred to the taking over of a business, obtaining land or property, winning the majority in city elections or a local census, or gaining a school—usually in areas straddling the imaginary lines dividing Czech and German border areas. The Czechoslovak government was complicit in small-scale settlement schemes, but its measures aimed at transforming society along national lines paled in comparison to Nazi plans. The Nazi regime, rather than refereeing nationality politics, was determined to dictate play. Its total Germanization schemes targeted whole territories and whole populations. The Nazi regime, not the individual, decided who was a Czech, German, Jew, or Gypsy.

The disappearance of this world also transformed what it meant to be Czech and to be German. To be Czech, patriots at home claimed in 1939, simply meant to act Czech in ways borrowed from the past—gathering for public demonstrations, buying from certain stores, and even participating in a bizarre registration drive by the National Solidarity Movement. The regime, however, eventually succeeded in closing off most of the avenues by which one could act Czech. By 1943 being a good Czech meant little more than speaking Czech, even if in a whisper. It also meant, above all, hating anything or anybody German. Correspondents to London rarely spoke of politics or heroes past. They rarely used words like "humanism," "freedom," and "democracy" that had so often been intertwined with Czech nationalist rhetoric. The occupation experience discredited old values, split society, and created gaping differences between Beneš's government in London, patriots at home, and other Czechs. Yet all "good Czechs" could agree on hating Germans. Stripped of its former values, anti-Germanism was the only, albeit powerful, centerpoint of Czech national identity. Protectorate and Reich Germans, on the other hand, disputed what it meant to be German. Racial and legal experts struggled to find a workable definition of what made, or could make, a German. Some Reich Germans even contended that Czechs seemed more German than the Sudeten Germans. Ironically, while the occupation experience splintered and frustrated German patriots, the Czech national movement crystallized as perhaps never before.

The Nazi regime undid civil and political society. Its leaders assumed the right to decide nationality and introduced techniques that placed individuals into separate national or racial categories. Six years of occupation united most Czechs in a vicious hatred of anybody and anything German. These three developments came together after 1945 when the Bohemian lands became the Czech lands. Once Beneš had decided to expel every German from Czechoslovakia, his government deliberately provided the context for popular hatred to be fomented among a defeated population. The Nazi regime's attempts at sculpting society provided Czech expulsion plans with further inspiration and legitimization. Czechoslovak officials even copied Nazi measures previously used to segregate and label Jews. Once the Allied powers approved the "organized" transfer at Potsdam, the Czechoslovak government provided vague criteria for determining nationality; but the final, and sole, decision was left in the hands of local elites. Choice among nationalities no longer existed. A rivalry that had infused energy into a dynamic political and civil society ended. Nationality was no longer something expressed in public but a label that the state affixed to the individual, imposed at the cost of individual liberty and freedom of expression.

Looking back, one might ask to what extent *Prague in Black* has been about nationality and nationalism. It is not a story of nation versus nation. Nor is it a story of injustices suffered on both sides. Instead, it is a story of people living at a time when nationality mattered more than ever before, when it could determine food rations, work relationships, marriage, the schooling of one's children, and eventually one's domicile or whether one lived or died. Nationality issues, the creation of a German Lebensraum, and the "health" of the German Volk obsessed Nazi rulers in the Protectorate and elsewhere in Europe. Anti-Semitism was one of their few focal points in an ideology riddled by vagueness. Among Czechs, despair over a lost loved one or frustration with a haughty bureaucrat was channeled into a hatred of a whole group of people—a hatred justified by history and fueled by nationalist rhetoric. The legitimacy of Beneš's government rested on promises to fight and defeat the Germans. In short, this is a story of people living at a time when the forces of history seemed hopelessly overpowering, and when collective rights, collective punishment, and collective struggles trumped any concern about individual rights. The question facing historians now is how nationality became the sole, if imprecise, indicator of one's fate. The challenge is to remember that the participants—victims, perpetrators, and bystanders alike—were more than just Jews, Germans, and Czechs.

"In our age," George Orwell wrote in 1946, "there is no such thing as 'keeping out of politics.' All issues are political issues, and politics itself is a mass of lies, evasions, folly, hatred, and schizophrenia."[52] In the Bohemian lands from 1939 to 1947 everything was political, and nationalism tinged every aspect of politics. "How can you say that I have not done enough against Nazism?" a Protectorate German in Prague pleaded to a member of the democratic resistance as the war drew to a close. "I have correct relations with the Czech people, suffer sabotage, I helped Jews . . . and now I'm speaking to you and am telling you everything that I know. I am a technician who doesn't care about politics, about the army, but I'm telling you everything that I know."[53] The last words, however, must be left to Milena Roštiková. In 1944, Communist partisans approached Roštiková's husband demanding that he act as a loyal Czech, while Nazi leaders demanded conformity with the regime. He sided, for a moment, with the former. He was then arrested and sentenced to death by a Nazi court for sabotage and aiding the Communist resistance. "From a German standpoint this may seem like the correct remedy," Roštiková wrote to Frank in a letter pleading for clemency. "My husband, however, is a Protectorate national. He lives under other conditions, for there are powers in the Protectorate that are always in the position to pressure a Czech politically. . . . Politics is everything, every conversation, every answer, every gesture. Extremely numerous are the possible ways one can fall upon bad luck."[54] Her despair recalls a sadly familiar dilemma. Her words speak to a defining aspect of Europe's twentieth century.

Place-Names in Czech and German

Brno Brünn
Budějovice (České Budějovice from 1920 to 1941, and after 1945) Budweis
Domažlice Taus
Hodonín Göding
Hradec Králové Königgrätz
Jičín Jitschin
Jihlava Iglau
Karlovy Vary Karlsbad
Kladno Kladno
Klatovy Klattau
Kolín Kolin
Kroměříž Kremsier
Lety Lety
Liberec Reichenberg
Litoměřice Leitmeritz
Litomyšl Leitomischl
Mělník Melnik
Moravská Ostrava (Ostrava after 1945) Mährisch-Ostrau
Německý Brod (Havlíčkův Brod after 1950) Deutschbrod
Nymburk Nimburg
Olomouc Olmütz
Opava Troppau
Pardubice Pardubitz
Plzeň Pilsen
Praha (referred to as Prague in the text) Prag
Přerov Prerau
Prostějov Proßnitz
Rakovník Rakonitz
Tábor Tabor
Teplice Teplitz
Terezín Theresienstadt
Těšín Teschen
Vyškov Wischau
Železný Brod Eisenbrod
Zlín (Gottwaldov from 1949 until 1990) Zlin

Abbreviations

AHY	*Austrian History Yearbook*
AOP	Miroslav Kárný and Jaroslava Milotová, eds., *Anatomie okupační politiky hitlerovského Německa v "Protektorátu Čechy a Morava": Dokumenty z období říšského protektora Konstantina von Neuratha* (Prague: Ústav československých a světových dějin ČSAV, 1987).
AV ČR	Archiv Akademie věd České Republiky
BB	Bundesarchiv Bayreuth
Boh	*Bohemia. Zeitschrift für Geschichte und Kultur der böhmischen Länder*
ČČH	*Český časopis historický*
CEH	*Central European History*
ČTK	Česká tisková kancelár
DHČSP	Libuše Otáhalová and Milada Červinková, eds., *Dokumenty z historie československé politiky, 1939–1943*, 2 vols. (Prague: Academia, 1966).
EEPS	*East European Politics and Societies*
GPO	United States Government Printing Office
HIWRP	Hoover Institution on War, Revolution, and Peace, Stanford University
HV	*Historie a vojenství*
IMT	*Trial of the Major War Criminals before the International Military Tribunal: Proceedings and Documents* (blue set)
JMH	*Journal of Modern History*
JS	Jaromír Smutný collection, Rare Book and Manuscript Library, Columbia University
K.	Karton (box)
MZAB	Moravský zemský archiv v Brně
NARA	National Archives and Records Administration, College Park, Maryland
OLR	Oberlandrat
ONH	Jaroslava Milotová and Miroslav Kárný, eds., "Od Neu-

	ratha k Heydrichovi: Na rozhraní politiky hitlerovského Německa v 'Protektorátu Čechy a Morava,' " *SAP* 39, no. 2 (1989): 281–394.
Ost-Dok 20	Ost-Dokumentation 20
Ost-Dok 21	Ost-Dokumentation 21
PPRH	Miroslav Kárný and Jaroslava Milotová, eds., *Protektorátní politika Reinharda Heydricha* (Prague: Archivní správa MV ČR, 1991).
RG	Record Group
RGBl	*Reichs-gesetzblatt*
SA	Sturmabteilung
SAP	*Sborník archivních prací*
SD	Sicherheitsdienst
SDNU	Sbírka dokumentů nacistických úřadů a institucí na území okupovaných českých zemí
SD-PE-15-March-1940	"Die politische Entwicklung im Protektorat Böhmen und Mähren seit dem 15. März 1939," SD report, 15 March 1940, VHA, SDNU, k. 7, sbírka č. 74, jednotka 46.
SD-PE-1940	"Die politische Entwicklung im Protektorat Böhmen und Mähren im Jahre 1940," SD report [no date], VHA, SDNU, k. 8, sign. 50, sbírka č. 74, jednotka 43.
SDUNO	Sbírka dokumentů ústředních nacistických orgánů politické policie
Sign.	signatura (folder)
SOAP	Státní oblastní archiv v Praze
TWC	*Trials of the War Criminals before the Nuremberg Military Tribunals under Control of Council Law N-10* (green set)
ÚŘP	Úřad říšského Protektora
USHMM	United States Holocaust Memorial Museum archives
ÚVOD	Ústřední vedení odboje domácího
VHA	Vojenský historický archiv
VRBM	*Verordnungsblatt des Reichsprotkors Böhmen und Mähren*

Notes

Introduction

1. Emil Vanday, "Czech Area Seized," *New York Times,* March 16, 1939, A1, A17. George Kennan, *From Prague after Munich: Diplomatic Papers* (Princeton, N.J.: Princeton University Press, 1968), 87.
2. Detlef Brandes, *Die Tschechen unter deutschem Protektorat,* vol. 1 (Munich: R. Oldenbourg, 1969), 169.
3. In 1939 the *New York Times* reported that the area of the Protectorate equaled 18,158 square miles. Vanday, "Czech Area Seized," A17. According to the U.S. Census Bureau, Vermont's total area is 9,249.3 square miles. New Hampshire's total area is 8,969.4 square miles. "Table 1. Land Area, Population, and Density for States and Counties: 1990," *www.census.gov* (accessed 12/16/05).
4. During the March 2001 census 94 percent of the Czech Republic's more than ten million citizens declared themselves to be "*český*" (which doubles as both "Czech" and "Bohemian" in the Czech language), Moravian, or Silesian. The next largest nationality group consisted of Slovaks, with 193,190 people. Less than 40,000 citizens counted themselves as Germans. See the Czech Statistical Office tables on nationality counts in "Obyvatelstvo podle věku, národnosti a podle pohlaví k 1. 3. 2001," *www.czso.cz* (accessed 12/16/05). For a description of the preliminary 2001 census results, which differed only slightly from those published on the Statistical Office's Web site, see Radio Prague's project report "Minorities in the Czech Republic," *www.radio.cz* (accessed 12/16/05).
5. Ernest Gellner, *Nations and Nationalism* (Ithaca, N.Y.: Cornell University Press, 1983), 139–140.
6. Nazi officials counted 118,310 Jews in spring 1939. More than 26,111 managed to emigrate before the deportations had begun. Livia Rothkirchen, "The Jews of Bohemia and Moravia, 1938–1945," in Avigdor Dagan, Gertrude Hirschler, and Lewis Weiner, eds., *The Jews of Czechoslovakia,* vol. 3 (Philadelphia: Jewish Publication Society of America, 1984), 60. Ctibor Nečas, *Holocaust českých Romů* (Prague: Prostor, 1999), 175.

7. *Statistická ročenka republiky Československé* (Prague: Orbis, 1957), 42.
8. Hans Joachim Beyer, *Umvolkung: Studien zur Frage der Assimilation und Amalgamation in Ostmitteleuropa und Übersee* (Brno: Rudolf M. Rohrer, 1945), 9–11. See also James Edward Bjork, "Neither German nor Pole: Catholicism and National Ambivalence in Upper Silesia, 1890–1914" (Ph.D. diss., University of Chicago, 1999); and Richard Blanke, *Polish-Speaking Germans? Language and National Identity among the Masurians since 1871* (Vienna: Böhlau, 2001).
9. Benjamin Frommer, *National Cleansing: Retribution against Nazi Collaborators in Postwar Czechoslovakia* (Cambridge: Cambridge University Press, 2005), 18. As Frommer writes, the estimate could have been a conservative one. Minister of the Interior Václav Nosek had been referring only to Czechs who had become Reich citizens under compulsion—pressures that existed to a much larger degree in the Těšín region, a mixed region absorbed by Poland in 1938 and then incorporated into the Reich in 1939. See also Maria Rhode, "Der Wechsel des nationalen Bekenntnisses in der Tschechoslowakei 1930–1950 und seine Bedeutung für die Zahl der sudetendeutschen Vertreibungsopfer," in Detlef Brandes, Edita Ivaničková, and Jiří Pešek, eds., *Erzwungene Trennung: Vertreibung und Aussiedlung in und aus der Tschechoslowakei 1938–1947 im Vergleich mit Polen, Ungarn und Jugoslawien* (Essen: Klartext, 1999), 179–196; and Jeremy King, *Budweisers into Czechs and Germans: A Local History of Bohemian Politics, 1848–1948* (Princeton, N.J.: Princeton University Press, 2003), 185.
10. On the number identified by the Nuremberg Laws, see Rothkirchen, "The Jews," 37. According to Pavel Škopil, 330,000 former Czechoslovak citizens, 265,000 of whom were marked as Jews, perished at the hands of the Nazi regime. "Probleme bei der Berechnung der Zahl der tschechoslowakischen Todesopfer des nationalsozialistischen Deutschlands," in Detlef Brandes and Václav Kural, eds., *Der Weg in die Katastrophe. Deutsch-tschechoslowakische Beziehungen 1938–1947* (Essen: Klartext, 1994), 161–164, esp. 164.
11. The term "acting nationally" and the paragraph that discusses the state's marking of nationality on the individual owe an intellectual debt to the work of Rogers Brubaker and Fredrick Cooper, who prefer the term "identification" to "identity" because the former "invites us to specify the agents" doing the identifying. "Identification" also points toward processes, they continue, whereas "identity," in addition to being too vague to be useful, suggests a static condition. "Beyond 'Identity,'" in Rogers Brubaker, *Ethnicity without Groups* (Cambridge, Mass.: Harvard University Press, 2004), 28–64, esp. 41–44.

12. "Civil society," borrowing from Valerie Bunce, is taken here to refer to "associational life, with associations understood to be independent of the state and to exist in the space between the family and state." "Political society" consists of "organized activity of citizens in common pursuit of selecting who rules and influencing the agenda and decision of the rulers." Valerie Bunce, "The Historical Origins of the East-West Divide: Civil Society, Political Society, and Democracy in Europe," in Nancy Bermeo and Philip Nord, eds., *Civil Society before Democracy: Lessons from Nineteenth-Century Europe* (Lanham, Md.: Rowman & Littlefield, 2000), 214.

13. Eva Hahnová, *Sudetoněmecký problém: Obtížné loučení s minulostí* (Prague: Prago Media, 1996), 51; Hahnová (writing under the name Eva Hahn), "Die deutsche Bohemistik—von außen gesehen," *Osteuropa* 4 (1999): 387–396; Volker Zimmermann, "Složitý vztah k minulosti—sudetští Němci a národní socialismus," *Mezinárodní vztahy* 4 (1996): 29–38; Zimmermann, "Sudetendeutsche Perspektiven auf den Nationalsozialismus: Einstellungen und Wertungen von der NS-Zeit bis heute," in Monika Glettler, Ľubomír Lipták, and Alena Míšková, eds., *Geteilt, besetzt, beherrscht: Die Tschechoslowakei 1938–1945: Reichsgau Sudetenland, Protektorat Bohmen und Mahren, Slowakei* (Essen: Klartext, 2004), 229–248; Michael Kopeček and Miroslav Kunštát, "'Sudetoněmecká otázká' v české akademické debaté po roce 1989," *Soudobé dějiny* 10, no. 3 (2003): 293–318; Chad Bryant, "The Thick Line at 1945: Czech and German Histories of the Nazi Occupation and the Postwar Expulsion/Transfer," *National Council for Eurasian and East European Research Working Papers* (February 13, 2006).

14. Jan Křen, *Bílá místa v našich dějinách?* (Prague: Lidové noviny, 1990); Hahn, "Die deutsche Bohemistik," 388.

15. Vojtech Mastny, *The Czechs under Nazi Rule: The Failure of National Resistance, 1939–1942* (New York: Columbia University Press, 1971); Detlef Brandes, *Die Tschechen unter deutschem Protektorat*, 2 vols. (Munich: R. Oldenbourg, 1969, 1975). See also Shiela Grant Duff, *A German Protectorate: The Czechs under Nazi Rule* (London: Frank Cass, 1970); and Gotthold Rhode, "The Protectorate of Bohemia and Moravia, 1939–1945," in Victor S. Mamatey and Radomír Luža, eds., *The History of the Czechoslovak Republic, 1918–1948* (Princeton, N.J.: Princeton University Press, 1973), 331–372.

16. Typical, although not without merit, are Vladimír Konopka, *Lidice* (Prague: Naše vojsko, 1958); Václav Král, ed., *Lesson from History: Documents concerning Nazi Policies for Germanization and Extermination in Czechoslovakia* (Prague: Orbis, 1960); Václav Král and Karel Fremund,

eds., *Chtěli nás vyhubit* (Prague: Naše vojsko, 1961). Král went on to become one of post-1968's most notorious "normalizers" in the Czechoslovak Academy of Sciences.

17. Jan Křen, *Do emigrace: Buržoazní zahraniční odboj 1938–1939* (Prague: Naše vojsko, 1963); Jiří Doležal and Jan Křen, eds., *Czechoslovakia's Fight: Documents on the Resistance Movement of the Czechoslovak People, 1938–1945* (Prague: Czechoslovak Academy of Sciences, 1964); Libuše Otáhalová and Milada Červinková, eds., *Dokumenty z historie československé politiky, 1939–1943,* 2 vols. (Prague: Academia, 1966). Local historians took the lead in writing about life under Nazi rule. See, for example, Josef Kmoníček, "K problematice nacistické okupace Náchodska v letech 1939–1940," *Východní Čechy 1964: Vlastivědný sborník prací o přírodě, dějinách a hospodářství východních Čech* (Havlíčkův Brod: Východočeské nakladatelství, 1964), 5–19; Antonín Ševčík, "Příspěvek k dějinám okupační správy v Brně v letech 1939–1945," *Brno v minulosti a dnes. Sborník příspěvků k dějinám a výstavbě Brna,* vol. 6 (Brno: Krajské Nakladatelství v Brně, 1964), 127–137; Václav Zima, "Kulturní život středních Čech v době okupace," *Středočeské kapitoly z dějin okupace* (Prague: Krajské osvětové středisko SKNV, 1964), 120–146.

18. Jaroslav Kokoška and Stanislav Kokoška, *Spor o Agenta A-54: Kapitoly z dějin československé zpravodajské služby* (Prague: Naše vojsko, 1994); Václav Kural, *Vlastenci proti okupaci: Ústřední vedení odboje domácího 1940–1943* (Prague: Ústav mezinárodních vztahů, 1997); Dušan Tomášek and Robert Kvaček, *Causa Emil Hácha* (Prague: Themis, 1995); Tomáš Pasák, *JUDr. Emil Hácha* (Prague: Horizont, 1997); Jiří Pernes, *Až na dno zrady: Emanuel Moravec* (Prague: Themis, 1997); Tomáš Pasák, *Český fašismus, 1922–1945, a kolaborace, 1939–1945* (Prague: Práh, 1999); Dušan Tomášek and Robert Kvaček, *Obžalována je vláda* (Prague: Themis, 1999).

19. Jiří Doležal, *Česká kultura za Protektorátu: Školství, písemnictví, kinematografie* (Prague: Národní filmový archiv, 1996); Alena Mišková, *Německá (Karlova) univerzita od Mnichova k. 9. květnu 1945* (Prague: Karolinum, 2002); Miroslav Kárný, *"Konecné řešení": Genocida českých židů v německé protektoratní politice* (Prague: Academia, 1991); Helena Krejcová, Jana Svobodová, and Anna Hyndráková, eds., *Židé v Protektorátu: Hlášení židovské náboženské obce v roce 1942* (Prague: Ústav pro soudobé dějiny, 1997); Livia Rothkirchen, *The Jews of Bohemia and Moravia: Facing the Holocaust* (Lincoln: University of Nebraska Press and Yad Vashem, 2005); Nečas, *Holocaust.*

20. Pavel Maršálek, *Protektorát Čechy a Morava* (Prague: Karolinum, 2002); Tomáš Pasák, *Pod ochranou říše* (Prague: Práh, 1998).

21. As historian Jan Gebhart writes, "[T]he most keenly felt lack [in Czech historiography] . . . is due to the absence of an overall treatment of the years of war and occupation, which has not been forthcoming even with the radical change in the regime, the removal of ideological pressures, and the opening up of archival sources." The article provides an excellent overview of recent scholarship on the Protectorate. "Historiography of the Period 1938–1945," *Historica* 7–8 (2001–2002): 145–163, quotation from 163. On Slovakia, see Tatjana Tönsmeyer, *Das Dritte Reich und die Slowakei 1939–1945: Politischer Alltag zwischen Kooperation and Eigensinn* (Paderborn: F. Schöningh, 2003). For an overview of Czech-Slovak relations, see Jan Rychlík, *Češi a Slováci ve 20 století: Česko-slovenské vztahy 1914–1945* (Bratislava: Academic Electronic Press, 1997). On the Reichsgau Sudetenland, see Volker Zimmermann, *Die Sudetendeutschen im NS-Staat: Politik und Stimmung der Bevölkerung im Reichsgau Sudetenland (1938–1945)* (Essen: Klartext, 1999); Ralf Gebel, *"Heim ins Reich": Konrad Henlein und der Reichsgau Sudetenland (1938–1945)* (Munich: R. Oldenbourg, 1999); Zdeněk Radvanovský, ed., *Historie okupovaného pohraničí, 1938–1945,* 8 vols. (Ústí nad Labem: Univerzita Jana Evangelisty Purkyně, 1998–2004): Jan Kouřil, Josef Bartoš, and Jaroslava Čajová, eds., *Zapomenuté pohraničí. Šumvald u Uničova 1938–1945: Svědectví, vzpomínky, dokumenty* (Prague: JANUA, 1999).
22. King, *Budweisers;* Frommer, *National Cleansing;* Eagle Glassheim, *Noble Nationalists: The Transformation of the Bohemian Aristocracy* (Cambridge, Mass.: Harvard University Press, 2005); Melissa Feinberg, *Elusive Equality: Gender, Citizenship, and the Limits of Democracy in Czechoslovakia, 1918–1950* (Pittsburgh: University of Pittsburgh Press, 2006).
23. For studies on nationality and nationalism before 1938, see the notes to the historical background section of this introduction. The most comprehensive work on the second half of the Protectorate years is Brandes, *Die Tschechen,*vol. 2. Works that do stretch beyond 1942 have tended to focus on Czech collaborators and the Protectorate's most powerful German leader, Karl Hermann Frank. Tomášek and Kvaček, *Causa Emil Hácha;* Pasák, *JUDr. Emil Hácha;* Tomášek and Kvaček, *Obžalována je vláda;* René Küpper, "Karl Hermann Frank als deutscher Staatsminister für Böhmen und Mähren," in Glettler, Lipták, and Mišková, *Geteilt,* 31–52. The state of armed, organized resistance movements in the Protectorate before liberation is explored in Stanislav Kokoška, *Praha v květnu 1945: Historie jednoho povstání* (Prague: Lidové noviny, 2005).
24. Václav Kural, *Místo společenství-konflikt! Češi a Němci ve velkoněmecké Říši a cesta k odsunu, 1938–1945* (Prague: Ústav mezinárodních vztahů, 1994);

Emilia Hrabovec, *Vertreibung und Abschub: Deutsche in Mähren 1945–1947* (Frankfurt: P. Lang, 1995); Jitka Vondrová, ed., *Češi a sudetoněmecká otázka, 1939–1945: Dokumenty* (Prague: Ústav mezinárodních vztahů, 1994); Detlef Brandes, *Der Weg zur Vertreibung, 1938–1945: Pläne und Entscheidungen zum "Transfer" der Deutschen aus der Tschechoslowakei und aus Polen* (Munich: R. Oldenbourg, 2001); Francis Dostál Raška, *The Czechoslovak Exile Government in London and the Sudeten German Issue* (Prague: Karolinum, 2002). See also Brandes, Ivaničková, and Pešek, *Erzwungene Trennung*. For an excellent review of recent literature on the postwar expulsion of the Germans from Czechoslovakia, see Adrian von Arburg, "Tak či onak: Nucené přesídlení v komplexním pojetí poválecné sídelní politiky v českých zemích," *Soudobé dějiny* 10, no. 3 (2003): 253–271.

25. Dieter Schenk, *Hitlers Mann in Danzig: Albert Forster und die NS-Verbrechen in Danzig-Westpreußen* (Bonn: Dietz, 2000); Phillip Terrell Rutherford, "Race, Space, and the 'Polish Question': Nazi Deportation Policy in Reichsgau Wartheland, 1939–1941" (Ph.D. diss., Pennsylvania State University, 2001); Rolf Dieter-Müller, *Hitlers Ostkrieg und die deutsche Siedlungspolitik* (Frankfurt: Fischer, 1991); Mechtild Rössler and Sabine Schleiermacher, eds., *Der "Generalplan Ost": Hauptlinien der nationalsozialistischen Planungs- und Vernichtungspolitik* (Berlin: Akademie Verlag, 1993); Bruno Wasser, *Himmlers Raumplanung im Osten: Der Generalplan Ost in Polen, 1940–1944* (Basel: Birkhäuser, 1993); Czesław Madajczyk, ed., *Vom Generalplan Ost zum Generalsiedlungsplan* (Munich: Saur, 1994); Madajczyk, *Die Okkupationspolitik Nazideutschlands in Polen 1939–1945* (Berlin: AkademieVerlag, 1987); Doris Bergen, "The Nazi Concept of 'Volksdeutsche' and the Exacerbation of Anti-Semitism in Eastern Europe, 1939–1945," *Journal of Contemporary History* 29, no. 4 (1994): 569–582; Isabel Heinemann, *"Rasse, Siedlung, Blut": Das Rasse- & Siedlungshauptamt der SS und die rassenpolitische Neuordnung Europas* (Göttingen: Wallstein, 2003).

26. The burgeoning literature on Germanization plans and the Holocaust in Nazi-occupied Europe, much of which has profited from newly accessible archival materials in Eastern Europe, is too vast to list here. A pioneering contribution to the field was Götz Aly, *"Final Solution": Nazi Population Policy and the Murder of the European Jews*, trans. Belinda Cooper and Allison Brown (London: Oxford University Press, 1999), originally published in German in 1995. See also Thomas Sandkühler, *"Endlösung" in Galizien: Der Judenmord in Ostpolen und die Rettungsinitiativen von Berthold Beitz 1941–1944* (Bonn: J. H. W. Dietz Nachfolger, 1996); Dieter Pohl, *Nationalsozialistische Judenverfolgung in Ostgalizien 1941–1944*

(Munich: R. Oldenbourg, 1997); Christian Gerlach, *Kalkulierte Morde: Die deutsche Wirtschafts- und Vernichtungspolitik in Weissrussland 1941 bis 1944* (Hamburg: Hamburger Edition, 2000); Wendy Lower, *Nazi Empire-Building and the Holocaust in Ukraine* (Chapel Hill: University of North Carolina Press in association with the U.S. Holocaust Memorial Museum, 2005). For a synthesis that also draws on new documentation, see Christopher Browning with Jürgen Matthäus, *The Origins of the Final Solution: The Evolution of Nazi Jewish Policy, September 1939-March 1942* (Lincoln, Neb., and Jerusalem: University of Nebraska Press and Yad Vashem, 2004). For an insightful overview of this literature, see John Connelly, "Rule by Inspiration," *London Review of Books*, July 7, 2005, 27–28. On Nazi attempts to define and label Jews as such, see Omer Bartov, "Defining Enemies, Making Victims: Germans, Jews, and the Holocaust," in Amir Weiner, ed., *Landscaping the Human Garden: Twentieth-Century Population Management in a Comparative Framework* (Stanford, Calif.: Stanford University Press, 2003), 135–136; and Thomas Pegelow, "Linguistic Violence: Language, Power and Separation in the Fate of Germans of Jewish Ancestry, 1928–1948" (Ph.D. diss., University of North Carolina at Chapel Hill, 2004).

27. Jan Gross, "Social Consequences of War: Preliminaries to the Study of Imposition of Communist Regimes in East Central Europe," *EEPS* 3, no. 2 (Spring 1989): 198–214. Since 1989 Gross has published several revised versions of this article. See Gross, "War as Revolution," in Norman Naimark and Leonid Gibianskii, eds., *The Establishment of Communist Regimes in Eastern Europe* (Boulder, Colo.: Westview Press, 1997), 17–40; and Gross, "Themes for a Social History of War Experience and Collaboration," in István Deák, Jan T. Gross, and Tony Judt, eds., *The Politics of Retribution in Europe: World War II and Its Aftermath* (Princeton, N.J.: Princeton University Press, 2000), 15–36. On page 22, Gross calculates the number of displaced Europeans. See also Norman M. Naimark, "Revolution and Counterrevolution in Eastern Europe," in Christiane Lemke and Gary Marks, eds., *The Crisis of Socialism in Europe* (Durham, N.C.: Duke University Press, 1992), 61–83; and Bradley Abrams, *The Struggle for the Soul of the Nation: Czech Culture and the Rise of Communism* (Lanham, Md.: Rowman & Littlefield, 2004), 9–38. On the Czechoslovak case in particular, see Nina Pavelčíková, "Změny v rozmístění a sociální skladbě obyvatel českých zemí za okupace, jejich souvislosti s poválečným vývojem," *Slezský sborník* 90, no. 1 (1992): 1–10; Zdeněk Sládek, "Vliv nacistické nadvlády na politický vývoj v Čechách a na Moravě," *Soudobé dějiny* 1, nos. 4–5 (1995): 532–536; Hans Lemberg, "1938–1948—Die Katastrophe Mitteleuropas und die Nachkriegszeit," *Das künftige Mitteleu-*

ropa: Tradition und Perspektiven (Prague: Karolinum, 1998), 13–42; and Abrams, *Struggle*.

28. Eric Weitz, *A Century of Genocide: Utopias of Race and Nation* (Princeton, N.J.: Princeton University Press, 2003); Jiří Pešek, "20. století—doba nucených migrací, vyhnání a transferů," *Dějiny a současnost* 24 (2002): 42–47. On Soviet nation-making, see Yuri Slezkine, "The USSR as a Communal Apartment, or How a Socialist State Promoted Ethnic Particularism," *Slavic Review* 53, no. 2 (Summer 1994): 414–452; Terry Martin, *The Affirmative Action Empire: Nations and Nationalism in the Soviet Union, 1923–1939* (Ithaca, N.Y.: Cornell University Press, 2001); Amir Weiner, "Nature, Nurture, and Memory in a Socialist Utopia: Delineating the Socio-Ethnic Body in the Age of Socialism," *American Historical Review* 104, no. 4 (Oct. 1999): 1114–1155; Peter Holquist, "To Count, to Extract, and to Exterminate: Population Statistics and Population Politics in Late Imperial and Soviet Russia," in Ronald Grigor Suny and Terry Martin, eds., *A State of Nations: Empire and Nation-Making in the Age of Lenin and Stalin* (Oxford: Oxford University Press, 2001): 111–144; Francine Hirsch, *Empire of Nations: Ethnographic Knowledge and the Making of the Soviet Union* (Ithaca, N.Y.: Cornell University Press, 2005). See also Eric Lohr, *Nationalizing the Russian Empire: The Campaign against Enemy Aliens during World War I* (Cambridge, Mass.: Harvard University Press, 2003); Timothy Snyder, *The Reconstruction of Nations: Poland, Ukraine, Lithuania, Belarus, 1569–1999* (New Haven, Conn.: Yale University Press, 2003), esp. 154–201; and Kate Brown, *A Biography of No Place: From Ethnic Borderland to Soviet Heartland* (Cambridge, Mass.: Harvard University Press, 2004).

29. Norman Naimark, *Fires of Hatred: Ethnic Cleansing in Twentieth-Century Europe* (Cambridge, Mass.: Harvard University Press, 2001); Philipp Ther, "A Century of Forced Migration: The Origins and Consequences of 'Ethnic Cleansing,'" in Philipp Ther and Ana Siljak, eds., *Redrawing Nations: Ethnic Cleansing in East-Central Europe, 1944–1948* (Lanham, Md.: Rowman & Littlefield, 2001), 43–74; Mathias Beer, ed., *Auf dem Weg zum ethnisch reinen Nationalstaat? Europa in Geschichte und Gegenwart* (Tübingen: Attempto, 2004). The wars in Yugoslavia no doubt served as an impetus for such studies, whose authors suggested that "ethnic cleansing" in the Balkans was not the product of "ancient hatreds" but the culmination of modern European forces. The studies owe a great intellectual debt to Ernest Gellner, Zygmunt Baumann, and James Scott, who analyzed the many ways that states have made nations through assimilation and violence. Gellner, *Nations*; Zygmunt Baumann, *Modernity and the Holocaust* (Ithaca, N.Y.: Cornell University Press, 1991); James C. Scott, *Seeing like a State: How Certain Schemes to Improve the Human Condition*

Have Failed (New Haven, Conn.: Yale University Press, 1998). For a thoughtful critique of this literature, see Mark Mazower, "Violence and the State in the Twentieth Century," *American Historical Review* 107, no. 4 (Oct. 2002): 1158–1178.

30. "Although the modern state and integral nationalism have been critical to ethnic cleansing in this century, political elites nevertheless bear the major responsibility for its manifestations. . . . Political elites . . . are backed up by state and party apparatuses, police forces, militaries, and paramilitaries. They are also supported by professionals—lawyers, doctors, professors, engineers—who more often than not are both the architects and the beneficiaries of the modern state." Naimark, *Fires*, 10.

31. Gross, "Themes," 22; Gerhard L. Weinberg, *A World at Arms: A Global History of World War II* (New York: Cambridge University Press, 1994), 894.

32. For an excellent discussion of Herder's influence on Czech nationalism, see Emanuel Rádl, *Válka Čechů s Němci* (Prague: Melantrich, 1993 [1928]), 170–173. On the crucial importance that early patriots placed on language and culture, see Vladimír Macura, "Problems and Paradoxes of the National Revival," in Mikuláš Teich, ed., *Bohemia in History* (Cambridge: Cambridge University Press, 1998), 144. See also Macura, *Znamení zrodu: České národní obrození jako kulturní typ* (Jihočany: H&H, 1995); and Hugh LeCaine Agnew, *Origins of the Czech National Renascence* (Pittsburgh: University of Pittsburgh Press, 1993).

33. In 1863 there were just ten political papers published in Czech. From 1863 to 1893 the number of specialized Czech language periodicals rose from 17 to 120. Bruce Garver, *The Young Czech Party, 1874–1901, and the Emergence of a Multi-party System* (New Haven, Conn.: Yale University Press, 1978), 102. Results from the 1900 census show that only 6 percent of those who claimed Czech as their language of daily use were illiterate; 8 percent of declared German-speakers could not read. Hillel J. Kieval, *Languages of Community: The Jewish Experience in the Czech Lands* (Berkeley: University of California Press, 2000), 13. See also Otto Urban, *České a slovenské dějiny do roku 1918* (Prague: Aleš Skřivan, 2000), 257.

34. Jiří Rak, "Obraz Němce v české historiografii 19. století," *Obraz Němců, Rakouska a Německa v české spolecnosti 19. a 20. století* (Prague: Karolinum, 1998), 49–75; Derek Sayer, "The Language of Nationality and the Nationality of Language: Prague 1780–1920," *Past and Present,* no. 153 (Nov. 1996): 164–210; Elizabeth Wiskemann, *Czechs and Germans: A Study of the Struggle in the Historic Provinces of Bohemia and Moravia* (London: Oxford University Press, 1938), 118.

35. Jiří Kořalka, *Tschechen im Habsburgerreich und in Europa 1815–1914* (Munich: R. Oldenbourg, 1991), 23–75; Jan Křen, *Die Konfliktgemeinschaft:*

Tschechen und Deutsche 1780–1918 (Munich: R. Oldenbourg, 1996), 27–43.

36. All associations had to register with local authorities, abstain from unlawful or antistate activities, publish their statutes, and be subject to occasional inspection by the state. Political groups and political parties could not accept women, foreigners, and those under a certain age, a rule that remained in force during the interwar period. After 1867, although government spies continued to infiltrate various clubs, police representatives no longer attended club meetings and membership restrictions were loosened. Peter Burian, "Das Vereinswesen in den böhmischen Ländern," in Ferdinand Seibt, ed., *Vereinswesen und Geschichtspflege in den böhmischen Ländern: Vorträge der Tagung des Collegium Carolinum in Bad Wiessee vom 25. bis 27. November 1983 und vom 23. bis 25 November 1984* (Munich: R. Oldenbourg, 1986), 42; Claire E. Nolte, *The Sokol in the Czech Lands to 1914: Training for the Nation* (New York: Palgrave, 2002), 79. On the importance of civil society to the development of national movements elsewhere in the Habsburg monarchy, see, for example, John-Paul Himka, *Galician Villagers and the Ukrainian National Movement in the Nineteenth Century* (New York: St. Martin's Press, 1988); and Keely Stauter-Halsted, *The Nation in the Village: The Genesis of Peasant National Identity in Austrian Poland, 1848–1914* (Ithaca, N.Y.: Cornell University Press, 2001).

37. Nolte, *The Sokol*, 31, 185; Andreas Luh, *Der deutsche Turnverband in der ersten Tschechoslowakischen Republik: Vom völkischen Vereinsbetrieb zur volkspolitischen Bewegung* (Munich: R. Oldenbourg, 1988), 27.

38. Garver, *The Young Czech Party*, 357–358.

39. By the turn of the century, the Bohemian lands accounted for over half of Austria's industrial plants and by 1913 for 57 percent of its industrial workers. Jana Geršlová, "Die wirtschaftliche Vergangenheit der böhmischen Länder (1870–1914): Industrie, Handel, und Banken," *Vierteljahrschrift für Sozial- und Wirtschaftsgeschichte* 87, no. 3 (2000): 320; Derek Sayer, *The Coasts of Bohemia: A Czech History* (Princeton, N.J.: Princeton: University Press, 1998), 84. In 1921 half the region's population lived in towns with more than two thousand inhabitants. Daniel Miller, *Forging Political Compromise: Antonín Švehla and the Czechoslovak Republican Party, 1918–1933* (Pittsburgh: Pittsburgh University Press, 1999), 3.

40. On the rise of mass politics, see Garver, *The Young Czech Party*; and Jiří Malíř, *Od spolků k moderním politickým stranám: Vývoj politických stran na Moravě v letech 1848–1914* (Brno: Filosofická fakulta Masarykovy university v Brně, 1996). On political battles at the local levels of government, see Peter Bugge, "Czech Nation-Building, National Self-Perception, and

Politics, 1780–1914" (Ph.D. diss., Aarhus, 1994), 319; Gary Cohen, "Neither Absolutism nor Anarchy: New Narratives on Society and Government in Late Imperial Austria," *AHY* 29, pt. 1 (1998): 44–45; and King, *Budweisers*. On censuses, see Emil Brix, *Die Umgangssprachen in Altösterreich zwischen Agitation und Assimilation: Die Sprachenstatistik in den zisleithanischen Volkszählungen 1880 bis 1910* (Vienna: Böhlau, 1982); Zbyněk A. B. Zeman, "The Four Austrian Censuses and Their Political Consequences," in Mark Cornwall, ed., *The Last Years of Austria-Hungary: Essays in Political and Military History, 1908–1918* (Exeter, UK: University of Exeter Press, 1990), 31–39.

41. The 1880 census counted 4,977,580 people in Bohemia and Moravia who claimed Czech as their language of daily use. By 1910 the number had risen to 6,110,889. During that same period, the number of German-speakers rose from 2,683,081 to 3,187,159. Urban, *České a slovenské dějiny*, 256. See also Bruce M. Garver, "A Comparison of Czech Politics in Bohemia with Czech Politics in Moravia, 1860–1914," in M. B. B. Biskupski, ed., *Ideology, Politics, and Diplomacy in East Central Europe* (Rochester, N.Y.: University of Rochester Press, 2003), 11. On Vienna, see Brigitte Hamann, *Hitler's Vienna: A Dictator's Apprenticeship*, trans. Thomas Thorton (New York: Oxford University Press, 1999), 305.

42. Catherine Albrecht, "Chambers of Commerce and Czech-German Relations in the Late Nineteenth Century," *Boh* 38, no. 2 (1997): 299.

43. On Budějovice and Olomouc, see King, *Budweisers*, 132; and Garver, "A Comparison," 12. On Prague, see Gary Cohen, *The Politics of Ethnic Survival: Germans in Prague, 1861–1914* (Princeton, N.J.: Princeton University Press, 1981), 145–148; and Sayer, *The Coasts*, 102.

44. The term "professional nationalists" is from Křen, *Die Konfliktgemeinschaft*, 219.

45. Catherine Albrecht, "The Rhetoric of Economic Nationalism in the Boycott Campaigns of the Late Habsburg Monarchy," *AHY* 23 (2001): 58–60.

46. Burian, "Das Vereinswesen," 49; Kieval, *Languages*, 41. See also Tara Zahra, "Reclaiming Children for the Nation: Germanization, National Ascription, and Democracy in the Bohemian Lands, 1900–1945," *CEH* 37, no. 4 (Winter 2004): 503–509.

47. Pieter Judson, " 'Not Another Square Foot!' German Liberalism and the Rhetoric of Ownership in Nineteenth-Century Austria," *AHY* 26 (1995): 93. For nationality politics on the borderlands, see also Mark Cornwall, "The Struggle on the Czech-German Language Border, 1880–1940," *English Historical Review* 59, no. 433 (Sep. 1994): 914–951.

48. Silesia, for example, had only a minority of Czech-speakers, most of them workers who supported the Social Democratic Party, and a large Polish-

speaking contingent of 235,224 inhabitants, a little less than 32 percent of the region's population. Moravia remained more politically conservative, more supportive of the Catholic Church, and more agrarian than Bohemia. In the absence of a strong Czech middle class and rapid urbanization, German political parties remained powerful, more confident in their position than their Bohemian counterparts, and more willing to compromise with their Czech rivals. Czech voters in Moravia shied away from radical nationalist parties. Urban, *České a slovenské dějiny,* 256. Garver, "A Comparison," 1–30.

49. According to the 1910 census between 80 and 95 percent of the inhabitants of Bohemia, Moravia, and Silesia chose Catholicism as their religion. Elisabeth Kovács, "Die Katholische Kirche im Spannungsfeld von Nationalismus und Patriotismus zwischen 1848 und 1918," in Ferdinand Seibt, ed., *Die Chance der Verständigung: Absichten und Ansätze zu übernationaler Zusammenarbeit in den böhmischen Ländern 1848–1918: Vorträge der Tagung des Collegium Carolinum in Bad Wiessee vom 22. bis 24. November 1985* (Munich: R. Oldenbourg, 1987), 49. On Catholic gymnastics organizations, see Nolte, *The Sokol,* 142–144, 153–154.

50. István Deák, *Beyond Nationalism: A Social and Political History of the Habsburg Officer Corps, 1848–1918* (New York: Oxford University Press, 1990), 56; Veronika Sušová, "Integrační role rakouského císaře v rakouské státní propagandě 19. století," *Kuděj* 1 (2004): 32–46; Sušová, "Vzbudit věrnost a oddanost: Dějepis jako nástroj politické socializace v Rakousko-Uhersku a Rusku druhé poloviny 19. století," *Dějiny a současnost* 5 (2004): 15–19; Glassheim, *Noble Nationalists,* 10–49.

51. Gary B. Cohen, *Education and Middle-Class Society in Imperial Austria, 1848–1918* (West Lafayette, Ind.: Purdue University Press, 1996), 184.

52. Sayer, *The Coasts,* 84.

53. Kořalka, *Tschechen,* 93–95. In Bohemia, German-speakers made up 43 percent of the civil servants at the two highest grades, the third and fourth class, and dominated the very highest positions within the state administration. Miloslav Martínek, "K problému struktury státního úřednictva v Čechách na počatku 20. století," *Sborník historický* 21 (1974): 75–117.

54. Robert Luft, "Nationale Ultraquisten in Böhmen: Zur Problematik 'nationaler Zwischenstellungen' am Ende des 19. Jahrhunderts," in Maurice Godé, Jacques Le Rider, and Françoise Mayer, eds., *Allemands, Juifs et Tchèques à Prague de 1890 à 1924* (Montpellier: Bibliothèque d'études germaniques et centre-européennes, 1996), 43; Zahra, "Reclaiming Children," 505.

55. For a fascinating discussion of the choices faced by one working-class family, see Karl. F. Bahm, "Beyond the Bourgeoisie: Rethinking Nation,

Culture, and Modernity in Nineteenth-Century Central Europe," *AHY* 29, no. 1 (1998): 19–35.

56. On the Moravian Compromise, see T. Mills Kelly, "Last Best Chance or Last Gasp? The Compromise of 1905 and Czech Politics in Moravia," *AHY* 34 (2003): 279–301; King, *Budweisers*, 140–147, 152; Jiří Kořalka, "Nationality Representation in Bohemia, Moravia, and Austrian Silesia, 1848–1914," in Geoffrey Alderman et al., eds., *Comparative Studies in Governments and Non-dominant Ethnic Groups in Europe, 1850–1940*, vol. 4, *Governments, Ethnic Groups, and Political Representation* (New York: New York University Press, 1991), 108–109; Jiří Malíř, "Der Mährische Ausgleich als Vorbild für die Lösung der Nationalitätenfragen?" in Thomas Winkelbauer, ed., *Kontakte und Konflikte: Böhmen, Mähren und Österreich: Aspekte eines Jahrtausends gemeinsamer Geschichte* (Horn-Waidhofen an der Thaya: Waldviertler Heimatbund, 1993), 337–346; and Zahra, "Reclaiming Children," 510–115. On pressure by German employers, see Cohen, *The Politics*, 90. On women's participation in civil and political society, see Katherine David, "Czech Feminists and Nationalism in the Late Habsburg Monarchy: 'The First in Austria,'" *Journal of Women's History* 3, no. 2 (Fall 1991). 27, 36–38.

57. Gustav Fleischmann, "The Religious Congregation," in *The Jews of Czechoslovakia*, vol. 1 (Philadelphia: Jewish Publication Society of America and Society for the History of Czechoslovak Jews, 1968), 276–278. Ruth Kestenberg-Gladstein, "The Jews between Czechs and Germans in the Historic Lands, 1848–1918," in *The Jews*, 1: 46.

58. Luft, "Nationale Ultraquisten," 47–48; Marek Nekula, "Česko-německý bilingvismus," in Walter Koschmal, Marek Nekula, and Joachim Rogall, eds., *Češi a Němci. Dějiny-kultura-politika* (Prague: Paseka, 2001), 152–158.

59. On the Jews' adherence to German liberalism and the rise of Czech-Jewish and Zionist movements, see Hillel J. Kieval, *The Making of Czech Jewry: National Conflict and Jewish Society in Bohemia, 1870–1918* (New York: Oxford University Press, 1988).

60. Kořalka, "Nationality Representation," 86; King, *Budweisers*, 7.

61. Kieval, *Languages*, esp. 33; Kieval, *The Making of Czech Jewry*, 66.

62. Nolte, *The Sokol*, 146.

63. Kieval, *The Making of Czech Jewry*, 13.

64. Wilma Iggers, "The Flexible National Identities of Bohemian Jewry," *East Central Europe* 7, no. 1 (1980): 39–48; Scott Spector, *Prague Territories: National Conflict and Cultural Innovation in Kafka's Fin de Siècle* (Berkeley: University of California Press, 2000).

65. Joseph Rothschild, *East Central Europe between the Two World Wars* (Seattle: University of Washington Press, 1974), 89.

66. On the Slovaks within Czechoslovkia, see Jan Rychlík, *Češi a Slováci ve 20 století: Česko-slovenské vztahy 1914–1945* (Bratislava: Academic Electronic Press, 1997).

67. Pavel Váša and František Trávníček, *Slovník jazyka českého* (Prague: Fr. Borový, 1937), 1054.

68. On Czech civil servants in Slovakia, see Valerián Bystrický, "Der Abschub der tschechischen Staatsangestellten aus der Slowakei 1938–1939," in Peter Heumos, ed., *Heimat und Exil: Emigration und Rückwanderung, Vertreibung und Integration in der Geschichte der Tschechoslowakei: Vorträge der Tagungen des Collegium Carolinum in Bad Wiessee vom 20. bis 22. November 1992 und 19. bis 21.November 1993* (Munich: R. Oldenbourg, 2001), 111–132, esp. 111–113. On nostrification, see Victor S. Mamatey, "The Establishment of the Republic," in Victor S. Mamatey and Radomír Luža, eds., *The History of the Czechoslovak Republic, 1918–1948* (Princeton, N.J.: Princeton University Press, 1973), 111; Miller, *Forging Political Compromise,* 30. On education, see Friedrich Prinz, "Das Schulwesen der Böhmischen Länder von 1848–1939: Ein Überblick," in Karl Bosl, ed., *Aktuelle Foschungsprobleme um die Erste Tschechoslowakische Republik* (Munich: Oldenbourg, 1969), 49–66. On land reform, see Daniel E. Miller, "Colonizing the Hungarian and German Border Areas during the Czechoslovak Land Reform, 1918–1938," *AHY* 34 (2003): 303–317, quotations from 317.

69. Carol Skalnik Leff, *National Conflict in Czechoslovakia: The Making and Remaking of a State* (Princeton, N.J.: Princeton University Press, 1988), 48–49.

70. F. Gregory Campbell, "Empty Pedestals?" *Slavic Review* 44, no.1 (Spring 1985): 12. See also Antonín Klímek, *Boj o Hrad,* 2 vols. (Prague: Panevropa, 1996); and Peter Bugge, "Czech Democracy—Paragon or Parody," in Christianne Brenner, ed., *Phasen und Formen der Transformation in der Tschechoslowake: Vorträge der Tagung des Collegium Carolinum in Bad Wiessee vom 23. bis 26. November 2000* (Munich: R. Oldenbourg, forthcoming), esp. 15. On centralization, see Eduard Táborský, "Local Government in Czechoslovakia, 1918–1948," *American Slavic and East European Review* 10, no. 3 (Oct. 1951): 202–215.

71. For an overview of historians' debates of the "democratic" nature of Czechoslovakia and its relations to national minorities, see the introduction to Václav Kural, *Konflikt místo spolecenství? Češi a Němci v ceskoslovenském státě, 1918–1938* (Prague: Ústav mezinárodních vztahů, 1993); Josef Harna, "Historiography of the First Czechoslovak Republic (1918–1938)," *Historica* 7–8 (2000–2001): 113–143; and T. Mills Kelly, "A Reputation Tarnished: New Perspectives on Interwar Czechoslovakia," *EES News: Woodrow Wilson International Center for Scholars* (Nov.–Dec. 2003): 9–11.

72. Cohen, *Education*, 267.

73. Václav Pavliček, "K ústavním aspectům práv menšin po vzniku Československa," in Jaroslav Valenta, Emil Vorácek, and Josef Harna, eds., *Československo 1918–1938*, vol. 2, *Osudy demokracie ve střední Evropě* (Prague: Historický ústav, 1999), 596.

74. Melissa Feinberg, "Democracy and Its Limits: Gender and Rights in the Czech Lands, 1918–1938," *Nationalities Papers* 30, no.4 (Dec. 2002): 553–570.

75. Jaroslav Kučera, *Minderheit im Nationalstaat: Die Sprachenfrage in den tschechisch-deutschen Beziehungen 1918–1938* (Munich: R. Oldenbourg, 1999), 307.

76. Frommer, *National Cleansing*, 12.

77. On Sokol membership, see *Statistická příručka Československé Republiky* (London: Československé ministerstvo zahraničních věcí, informační oddělení, 194-?), 156–157. On women's participation in civil society, see Jana Burešová, "Společensko-politická aktivita a veřejná činnost žen za první Československé Republiky (1918–1938)," *Československo 1918–1938*, vol. 2, *Osudy demokracie ve střední Evropě* (Prague: Historický ústav, 1999), 393–400. On the few recent works about political and civil society under the First Republic, see Harna, "Historiography," 125.

78. Nancy Meriwether Wingfield, "When Film Became National: 'Talkies' and the Anti-German Demonstrations of 1930 in Prague," *AHY* 29, pt. 1 (1998): 121.

79. Jan Steiner, "Národnost při sčítání lidu v roce 1930 a její zjišťování na Ostravsko," *Slezský sborník* 85, no. 2 (1987): 121.

80. Zahra, "Reclaiming Children," 516–527.

81. Rádl, *Válka*, 213; King, *Budweisers*, 158–159.

82. Jaroslav Bubeník and Jiří Křesťan, "Zjišťování národnosti a židovská otázka," in Helena Krejčová and Jana Svobodová, eds., *Postavení a osudy židovského obyvatelstva v Čechách a na Moravě v letech 1939–1945* (Prague: Ústav pro soudobé dějiny AV ČR, 1998), 11–39. See also Kateřina Čapková, "Uznání židovské národnosti v Československu 1918–1938," *ČČH* 102, no. 1 (2004): 77–103; and Aharon Moshe Rabinowicz, "The Jewish Minority," *The Jews*, 1: 155–266.

83. Bugge, "Czech Democracy," 11, 12.

84. "Nacistická úprava sociálních poměrů," in *Šest let okupace Prahy* (Prague: Orbis, 1946), 244.

85. Alice Teichová, *The Czechoslovak Economy, 1918–1980* (London: Routledge, 1988), 71.

86. Rothschild, *East Central Europe*, 126.

87. Rudolf Jaworski estimates that out of the 846,000 unemployed in Czecho-slovakia in 1935, 525,000 were Germans. "Die Sudetendeutschen als Min-derheit in der Tschechoslowakei 1918–1938," in Wolfgang Benz, ed., *Die Vertreibung der Deutschen aus dem Osten: Ursachen, Ereignisse, Folgen* (Frankfurt: Fischer Taschenbuch, 1985), 35.

88. Hannah Arendt, *The Origins of Totalitarianism* (New York:, Harcourt, Brace & World, 1966), 272. On Spann's *"Teilganzheiten,"* see Hans Schmid-Egger and Ernst Nittner, *Staffelstein: Jugendbewegung und katholische Erneuerung bei den Sudetendeutschen zwischen den Grossen Kriegen* (Munich: Aufstieg-Verlag, 1983), 188.

89. Zimmermann, *Die Sudetendeutschen,* 67.

90. Rothschild, *East Central Europe,* 129.

91. For the November 5, 1937, record, which was transcribed from memory five days after the event by Hitler's Wehrmacht adjutant, Colonel Hoss-bach, see *Documents on German Foreign Policy: From the Archives of the German Foreign Ministry,* ser. D, vol.1 (Washington, D.C.: GPO, 1949), doc. 19, 29–39, quotation from 29.

92. Ronald M. Smelser, *The Sudeten Problem, 1933–1938: Volkstumspolitik and the Formulation of Nazi Foreign Policy* (Middletown, Conn.: Wesleyan Uni-versity Press, 1975), 200–206, quotation from 206.

93. Igor Lukeš, *Czechoslovakia between Stalin and Hitler: The Diplomacy of Ed-vard Beneš in the 1930s* (New York: Oxford University Press, 1996), 139–172, 209–255; Gerhard L. Weinberg, *Hitler's Foreign Policy: The Road to World War II, 1939–1939* (New York: Enigma Books, 2005), 699–777. Hen-lein's comment is quoted from *Documents on German Foreign Policy: From the Archives of the German Foreign Ministry,* ser. D, vol. 2 (Washington, D.C: GPO, 1949), doc. 107, 198. On the number of Sudeten German Freikorps members, see Martin Zückert, "Zur Loyalität deutscher Soldaten in der tschechoslowakischen Armee," in Martin Schulze Wessel, ed., *Loy-alitäten in der Tschechoslowakischen Republik 1918–1938* (Munich: R. Old-enbourg, 2004), 173–174. By October 1, 1939, more than thirty-four thou-sand Sudeten Germans had joined the Freikorps. On the Sudeten German Freikorps, see also Martin Broszat, "Das Sudetendeutsche Freikorps," *Vierteljahrshefte für Zeitgeschichte* 9 (1961): 30–49.

94. Lukeš, *Czechoslovakia,* 255.

95. Zimmermann, *Die Sudetendeutschen,* 71–81.

96. Jörg Osterloh, "Judenverfolgung und 'Arisierung' im Reichsgau Sudeten-land," in Monika Glettler, L'ubomír Lipták, and Alena Mišková, eds., *Geteilt, besetzt, beherrscht: Die Tschechoslowakei 1938–1945: Reichsgau Sudetenland, Protektorat Böhmen und Mähren, Slowakei* (Essen: Klartext, 2004), 218–220.

97. Václav Kural, *Místo společenství—konflikt! Češi a Němci v velkoněmecké říši a cesta k odsunu (1938–1945)* (Prague: Karolinum, 1997), 44. See the comparable figures in Peter Heumos, *Die Emigration aus der Tschechoslowakei nach Westeuropa und dem Nahen Osten 1938–1945: Politisch-soziale Struktur, Organisation, Asylbedingungen der tschechischen, jüdischen, deutschen und slowakischen Flüchtlinge während des Nationalsozialismus: Darstellung und Dokumentation* (Munich: R. Oldenbourg, 1989), 21; Jan Gebhart, "Migrace českého obyvatelstva v letech 1938–1939," *ČČH* 3, no. 96 (1998): 561–573. Livia Rothkirchenová and Eva Schmidtová-Hartmannová, "Osud židů v Čechách a na Moravě v letech 1938–1945," in Livia Rothkirchenová, Eva Schmidtová-Hartmannová, and Avigdor Dagan, eds., *Osud Židů v Protektorátu 1939–1945: Sborník studií* (Prague: Trizonia, 1991), 21. On May 17, 1939, the official German census in the Reichsgau Sudetenland registered only 2,341 Jews, 2,186 "Mischlinge 1. Grad," and 1,301 "Mischlinge 2. Grad," as defined by the Nuremberg Laws. Osterloh, "Judenverfolgung," 220. A treaty signed in 1938 between the successor government in Prague and Germany provided for the transfer of Czechs and Germans between the two countries, ensuring that only Germans would fill "German" lands, but no measures appear to have been enacted to realize these goals. Joseph B. Schechtman, *European Population Transfers, 1939–1945* (New York: Oxford University Press, 1946), 41, 46; Robert L. Koehl, *RKFDV: German Resettlement and Population Policy, 1939–1945* (Cambridge, Mass.: Harvard University Press, 1957), 40–41; Alicia K. Cozine, "A Member of the State: Citizenship Law and Its Application in Czechoslovakia, 1918–1938" (Ph.D. diss., University of Chicago, 1996), 215.

98. Theodor Procházka, *The Second Republic: The Disintegration of Post-Munich Czechoslovakia, October 1938–March 1939* (Boulder,:Colo. East European Monographs, 1981), 58–59, 70; Pavel Maršálak, *Protektorát Čechy a Morava* (Prague: Karolinum, 2002), 58; Mastny, *The Czechs*, 56, 62; Rothkirchenová and Schmidtová-Hartmmanová, "Osud," 19, 26–27; Rabinowicz, "The Jewish Minority," 208; Jan Rataj, *O autoritativní národní stát: Ideologické proměny české politiky v druhé republice 1938–1939* (Prague: Karolinum, 1997), 115–118.

99. Ian Kershaw, *Hitler, 1936–1945: Nemesis* (New York W.W. Norton, 2000), 164–165, 169.

100. SD-PE-15-March-1940, 8.

1. A Hopelessly Mixed People

1. "Protokol o návštěvě dr. E. Háchy u Hitlera," in *Československo a norimberský proces: Hlavní dokumenty norimberského procesu o zločinech*

nacistů Československu (Prague: Ministerstvo informační, 1946), 325–329, quotations from 326 and 328.

2. Dušan Tomášek and Robert Kvaček, *Causa Emil Hácha* (Prague: Themis, 1995), 37. On Hácha's meeting with Hitler, see also Tomáš Pasák, *JUDr. Emil Hácha* (Prague: Horizont, 1997), 44–46; Detlef Brandes, *Die Tschechen unter deutschem Protektorat,* vol. 1 (Munich: R. Oldenbourg, 1969), 15–20; Vojtech Mastny, *The Czechs under Nazi Rule: The Failure of National Resistance, 1939–1942* (New York: Columbia University Press, 1971), 39–42.

3. Tomášek and Kvaček, *Causa,* 38.

4. Mastny, *The Czechs,* 41. Brandes, *Die Tschechen,* 1:19.

5. *DHČSP,* doc. 344, 422.

6. Mastny, *The Czechs,* 45–52.

7. "Protokol," *Československo,* 327.

8. Quotation from *AOP,* doc. 2, 7. See also Hitler's description of the Reich Protector's powers and duties in *DHČSP,* vol. 2, doc. 343, 419. For overviews of the development of the Protectorate's state structure, see *AOP,* x–xiii; Pavel Maršálek, *Protektorát Čechy a Morava* (Prague: Karolinum, 2002); Stanislav Šisler, "Studie o organizaci a působnosti nacistické okupační správy v českých zemích v letech 1939–1945," *Sborník archivních prací* 22 (1972): 46–95; Brandes, *Die Tschechen,* 1:30–37; Mastny, *The Czechs,* 49–51; Norman Rich, *The Establishment of the New Order,* vol. 2 of *Hitler's War Aims* (New York: W. W. Norton, 1974), 30; and Emil Sobota, *Co to byl Protektorát* (Prague: Kvasnička a Hampl, 1946), 89–120. On the Oberlandräte in particular, see Alfred Bohmann, "Die Stellung der Oberlandräte-Inspekteure: Zur deutschen Verwaltungsorganisation im ehemahligen Protektorat Böhmen und Mähren," *Zeitschrift für Ostforschung* 15 (1966): 118–126.

9. John L. Heineman, *Hitler's First Foreign Minister: Constantin Freiherr von Neurath, Diplomat and Statesman* (Berkeley: University of California Press, 1979), esp. 3, 9–16, 86–166. Mastny, *The Czechs,* 60; Richard Overy, *Interrogations: The Nazi Elite in Allied Hands, 1945* (New York: Viking, 2001), 82. Quotation from Albert Speer, *Erinnerungen* (Berlin: Proyläen, 1969), 162; cited in Heineman, *Hitler's First Foreign Minister,* 5.

10. Šisler, "Studie," 188; Brandes, *Die Tschechen,* 1:22, 32; Mastny, *The Czechs,* 94–95; Rich, *The Establishment,* 30. On the jurisdiction of the People's Court, see *RGBl* I, 14.4.1939, 752. For Hitler's order establishing NSDAP jurisdiction in the Protectorate, see *AOP,* doc. 44, 111.

11. "Supplement No. 2 to the Official Czechoslovak Report," 12 Jan. 1945, NARA, RG 238, NG series, Microfilm Publication T988, roll 11 (USA 91–132), 79–83; *AOP,* doc. 25, 76–77. The organization of the Intelligence Ser-

vice in the Protectorate appears to have followed a blueprint designed in the summer before the Munich agreement. See "Einsatz des S. D. im Falle ČSR," June 1938, NARA, RG 238, NG series, Microfilm Publication T988, roll 15 (USA 278–328) and roll 7 (USSR 493–522).

12. Karl Hermann Frank, NARA, RG 242, BDC Microfilm, SSO SS Officer Dossier, A3343, roll SSO-217; *Zpověď K. H. Franka* (Prague: Cíl, 1946), 7–19; Miloslav Moulis and Dušan Tomášek, *K. H. Frank: Vzestup a pád karlovarského knihkupce* (Prague: Epocha, 2003), 12–123; Ralf Gebel, *"Heim ins Reich": Konrad Henlein und der Reichsgau Sudetenland (1938–1945)* (Munich: R. Oldenbourg, 1999), 43–60; Andreas Luh, *Der Deutsche Turnverband in der ersten Tschechoslowakischen Republik: Vom völkischen Vereinsbetrieb zur volkspolitischen Bewegung* (Munich: R. Oldenbourg, 1988), 384-385; Rich, *The Establishment*, 31–32.

13. Eugen Fiechtner, "Das Protektorat Böhmen und Mähren im Deutschen Reich: Erlebnisbericht des Oberlandrats in Iglau über die Zeit vom 15. März bis 15. Juli 1942," 30 Nov. 1979, BB, Ost-Dok 21, 14.

14. Brandes, *Die Tschechen*, 1:29.

15. George Kennan, *From Prague after Munich: Diplomatic Papers, 1938–1940* (Princeton, N.J.: Princeton University Press, 1968), 218.

16. "Supplement No. 2 to the Official Czechoslovak Report," 12.1.1945, NARA, RG 238, NG series, Microfilm Publication T988, roll 11, Prosecution Exhibits Submitted to the International Military Tribunal (USA 91–132), 80–83; *AOP*, doc. 26, 77–79.

17. Brandes, *Die Tschechen*, 1:24; Mastny, *The Czechs*, 56. *AOP*, doc. 28, 83 86. Geheime Staatspolizei, Außendienststelle Deutsch-Brod, arrest reports dated 1 Aug. 1939, 28 July 1939, 18 July 1939, and 29 July 1939, SOAP, OLR Kolín, k. 6.

18. "Schutzvolk, nicht Hilfsvolk: Berlin zum Gesinnungswandel der Tschechen," *Prager Abend* 1, no. 3 (April 1939): 2; Petr Němec, "Český národ a nacistické teorie germanizace prostoru," *ČČH* (1990): 541; *AOP*, x.

19. Speer, *Erinnerungen*, 162, cited in Gebel, *"Heim ins Reich,"* 329. After the war Neurath also recalled that placating the Western powers was one reason why Hitler told him he had been appointed Reich protector. Brandes, *Die Tschechen*, 1:28.

20. Mastny, *The Czechs*, 54.

21. Deutsche Bank, *Das Protektorat Böhmen und Mähren im deutschen Wirtschaftsraum* (Berlin: Deutsche Bank, 1939), 16, 23, 37.

22. Albert Pražák, *Národ se bránil: Obrany národa a jazyka českého od nejstarších dob po přítomnost* (Prague: Sfinz, Bohumil Janda, 1946), 387.

23. "Citoyen," "Poměry v Čechách a na Moravě od německé okupace do

počátku června 1939," 11 June 1939, VHA, fond 37, sign. 91/1, I. díl, 24; Mastny, *The Czechs*, 64; Jan Gebhart and Jan Kuklík, *Dramatické i všední dny protektorátu* (Prague: Themis, 1996), 13.

24. SD-PE-15-March-1940, 23; [anonymous author], "Dozvuky německé sociální a dobročinné péče v Protektorátu," VHA, fond 37, sign. 91/1, 1. díl, 1; Jiří Doležal, *Česká kultura za protektorátu. Školství, písemnictví, kinematografie* (Prague: Národní filmový archiv, 1996), 41, 187–190. Forty-one Czech films were in distribution in 1938 and 1939. Doležal, *Česká kultura*, 238

25. Doležal, *Česká kultura*, 153. SD-PE-15-March-1940, 19–20. Tomáš Pasák has estimated that from March 15, 1939, until the end of the year, 172 Czech newspapers and periodicals were discontinued. Some were discontinued by the government; others merged. He also estimates that by the end of 1940 there were 1,583 legal Czech periodicals in existence. *Soupis legalních novin, časopisů a úředních věstníků v českých zemích z let 1939–1945* (Prague: Univerzita Karlova, 1980), 61, 63. See also Pražak, *Národ*, 387.

26. Dušan Tomášek, "Die nationalsozialistische Zensur im Protektorat Böhmen und Mähren," in Monika Glettler, Ľubomír Lipták, and Alena Mišková, eds., *Geteilt, besetzt, beherrscht: Die Tschechoslowakei 1938–1945: Reichsgau Sudetenland, Protektorat Böhmen und Mähren, Slowakei* (Essen: Klartext, 2004), 71–74; Tomáš Pasák, *Pod ochranou říše* (Prague: Práh, 1998), 129.

27. Ferdinand Peroutka, "Jsme Češi," *Lidové noviny* 23 Apr. 1939, 1; quoted in "citoyen," "Poměry v Čechách a na Moravě od německé okupace do počátku červnů 1939," 11 June 1939, VHA, fond 37, sign. 91/1, I. díl, 2. The title of the article was surely meant to remind readers of Peroutka's 1934 book, *Jací jsme* (How We Are).

28. Pavel Kosatík, *Ferdinand Peroutka: Pozdější život, 1938–1978* (Prague: Paseka, 2000), 24.

29. SD-PE-15-March-1940, 17. See also Ferdinand Peroutka, "Tvář českého čtenáře," *Přítomnost*, 17 May 1939, 297–298.

30. Derek Sayer, *The Coasts of Bohemia: A Czech History* (Princeton, N.J.: Princeton University Press, 1998), 196; Kosatík, *Ferdinand Peroutka*, 25.

31. Sayer, *The Coasts*, 210–211, 217, quotation from 226; Milena Jesenská, "Co očekává Čech od Čecha?" *Přítomnost*, 3 May 1939, 2–4, quotation from 2.

32. Kural, *Vlastenci*, 19–21; Brandes, *Die Tschechen*, 1: 54–78; Pasák, *Český fašismus*, 249–255; Maršálek, *Protektorát*, 116–120. On the seizure of guns and ammunition, see Mastny, *The Czechs*, 65–66.

33. Kural, *Vlastenci*, 21.

34. F. Janáček and B. Pekárek, "Historická zpráva o časopisu V boj (rok 1939)," *V boj* 1, no. 1 (Prague: Historický ústav Čs. Armády, Památník odboje, Vo-

jenský historický archiv, 1992): 837–902; *V boj*, 26 Apr. 1939, 1, no. 1 (Prague: Historický ústav Čs. Armády, Památník odboje, Vojenský historický archiv, 1992): 1–8; *V boj* [shortly after 12 May 1939] 1, no. 2 (Prague: Historický ústav Čs. Armády, Památník odboje, Vojenský historický archiv, 1992): 11–32; Pasák, *Český fašismus*, 255; Sayer, *The Coasts*, 226.

35. Brandes, *Die Tschechen*, 1:74, 75.

36. Jan Šach, "Poválečný stranicko-politický systém v představách domácího odboje v roce 1939," *Historie a vojenství* 6 (1997): 35–56.

37. SD Bericht 1353/39, May 1939, VHA; SDUNO, k. 17, sign. 371, 1; Brandes, *Die Tschechen*, 1:81–82; SD-PE-15-March-1940, VHA, SDNU, k. 7, sbírka č. 74, jednotka 46, 3; [anonymous informant], "Vnitropolitická situace," 14–15 March 1939, VHA, fond 37, sign. 91/1, I. díl, 7; Kennan, *From Prague*, 158–159; Mastny, *The Czechs*, 64; Brandes, *Die Tschechen*, 1:81–82.

38. SD-PE-15-March-1940, 5; Pasák, *Český fašismus*, 257–258.

39. Cynthia J. Paces, "Religious Heroes for a Secular State: Commemorating Jan Hus and Saint Wenceslas in 1920s Czechoslovakia," in Maria Bucur and Nancy M. Wingfield, eds., *Staging the Past: The Politics of Commemoration in Habsburg Central Europe, 1848 to the Present* (West Lafayette, Ind.: Purdue University Press, 2001), 210–216.

40. Cynthia Paces and Nancy M. Wingfield, "The Sacred and the Profane: Religion and Nationalism in the Bohemian Lands, 1880–1920," in Pieter M. Judson and Marsha L. Rozenblit, eds., *Constructing Nationalities in East Central Europe* (New York: Berhahn Books, 2005), 115–119. Paces, "Religious Heroes," 216–221.

41. SD-PE-15-March-1940, 4, 24–36; Mastny, *The Czechs*, 64; Brandes, *Die Tschechen*, 1: 82–83, quotation from 82.

42. OLR Olmütz, Erfassungsbericht August, NA, ÚŘP, k. 280, sign. I-1a 1803 (Kroměříž), 11–12.

43. *DHČSP*, vol. 2, doc. 343, 419.

44. Rich, *The Establishment*, 34; Maršálak, *Protektorát*, 56, 59–60; Brandes, *Die Tschechen*, 1:20; Mastny, *The Czechs*, 62. Quotation from *AOP*, xi.

45. Pasák, *Pod ochranou říše*, 13; Theodor Procházka, *The Second Republic: The Disintegration of Post-Munich Czechoslovakia, October 1938–March 1939* (Boulder, Colo.: East European Monographs, 1981), 69; Sayer, *The Coasts*, 327, n. 30.

46. [Anonymous author], "Ze soukromého dopisu z Moravy," 6 June 1939, VHA, fond 37, sign. 91/1, 1. díl, 1.

47. Pasák, *JUDr. Emil Hácha*, 56.

48. Tomášek and Kvaček, *Causa*, 51; Mastny, *The Czechs*, 58; Pasák, *Pod ochranou říše*, 54. See also Pasák, *JUDr. Emil Hácha*, 138–161.

49. Rich, *The Establishment*, 24; Maršálek, *Protektorát*, 34.

50. On the number of German and Czech officials, see Rich, *The Establishment,* 35. See also Detlef Brandes, "Kolaborace v protektorátu Čechy a Morava," *Dějiny a současnost* 1 (1994): 28; Šisler, "Studie," 60 and 76; and Emil Sobota, *Bodrý byrokrat o svých zkušenostech* (Prague: Václav Petr, 1945).

51. Pasák, *Pod ochranou říše,* 85–88; Maršálak, *Protektorát,* 34–35.

52. Mastny, *The Czechs,* 63; Pasák, *Pod ochranou říše,* 109–118; Jan Rataj, "Obraz Němce a Německa v protektorátní společnosti a československém odboji," in Jan Křen and Eva Broklová, eds., *Obraz Němců, Rakouska a Německa v české společnosti 19. a 20. století* (Prague: Karolinum, 1998), 213. On the Czech fascists' plans for Moravia, see also see also František Mezihorák, *Hry o Moravu: Separatisté, iredentisté a kolaboranti 1938–1945* (Prague: Mladá fronta, 1997).

53. Mastny, *The Czechs,* 59; Pasák, *Pod ochranou říše,* 59–60. On the National Solidarity Movement's exclusion of women, see Melissa Feinberg, "Gender and the Politics of Difference in the Czechlands after Munich," *EEPS* 17, no. 2 (May 2003): 220–228. On the numbers of Czechs registered into the National Solidarity Movement, see SD-PE-15-March-1940, 39; [anonymous author], "Týden 21–28 května—týden těžkého napětí a krize mezi Protektorátem a českou vládou," [no date] VHA, fond 37, sign. 91/1, I. díl, 1; Pasák, *Pod ochranou říše,* 42.

54. SD-PE-15-March-1940, 39; "citoyen," "Poměry v Čechách a na Moravě od německé okupace do počátku června 1939," 11 June 1939, VHA, fond 37, sig. 91/1, I. díl, 1–2; [anonymous author], "Týden 21–28 května—týden těžkého napětí a krize mezi Protektorátem a českou vládou," [no date], VHA, fond 37, sign. 91/1, I. díl, 1; Kennan, *From Prague,* 157–158; Pasák, *Pod ochranou říše,* 63. Quotations from [anonymous informant], "Vnitropolitická situace," 14–15 March 1939, VHA, fond 37, sign. 91/1, I. díl, 6; and Mastny, *The Czechs,* 63.

55. Eugen Fiechtner, "*Das Protektorat Böhmen und Mähren im Deutschen Reich:* Erlebnisbericht des Oberlandrats in Iglau über die Zeit vom 15. März bis 15. Juli 1942," 30 Nov. 1979, BB, Ost-Dok 21, 23, and 1–5a, quotation from 23.

56. Mark Cornwall, "The Struggle on the Czech-German Language Border, 1880–1940," *English Historical Review* 59, no. 433 (Sept. 1994): 914–951, esp. 914, 919, 943, n. 1; also Eugen Fiechtner, "*Das Protektorat Böhmen und Mähren im Deutschen Reich:* Erlebnisbericht des Oberlandrats in Iglau über die Zeit vom 15. März bis 15. Juli 1942," 30 Nov. 1979, BB, Ost-Dok 21, 5.

57. Rich, *The Establishment,* 142. Heinz Lämmel, 16 Sept. 1960, BB, sign. 66, Iglauer Sprachinsel, Ost-Dok 20, 15.

58. Eugen Fiechtner, "*Das Protektorat Böhmen und Mähren im Deutschen Reich:* Erlebnisbericht des Oberlandrats in Iglau über die Zeit vom 15. März bis 15. Juli 1942," 30 Nov. 1979, BB, Ost-Dok 21, 5d.

59. Ibid., 30 Nov. 1979, BB, Ost-Dok 21, 5k, 5g. Quotation from Heinz Lämmel, 16 Sept. 1960, sign. 66, Iglauer Sprachinsel, BB, Ost-Dok 20, 23.

60. SD-PE-15-March-1940, 68; Lagebericht, OLR Prag, September 1939, NA, ÚŘP, k. 279, sign. I-1a 1803 (Praha); "Lagebericht Nr. 4," Der Befehlshaber der Ordnungspolizei beim Reichsprotektor Böhmen und Mähren, 28 Mar. 1940, NA, ÚŘP, sign. 1–1b 1220, 1; [anonymous author], "Dozvuky ně-mecké sociální dobročinné péče v Protektoraátu—Nacional-sozialistische Volkswohlsfahrt—unik svého druhu," [no date], VHA, fond 37, sign. 91/1, 1. díl, 2.

61. SD-PE-15-March-1940, 20; Kreishauptmann in Olmütz, Lagebericht, 7 June 1939, NA, ÚŘP, k. 280, sign. I-1a 1803 (Kroměříž), 2–4; "Monats-bericht. Die politische Entwicklung im Protektorat Böhmen und Mähren," SD report May 1940, VHA, SDNU, k. 7, sbírka č. 74, jednotka 48, 4; "Monatsbericht," SD report June 1940, VHA, SDNU, k. 7, sign. 49, sbírka č. 74, jednotka 71, 17; also [anonymous informant], "Napětí mezi protek-torátem a českou vládou v týdnu 28.V.–4.VI," [no date] VHA, fond 37, sign. 91/1, díl, 1.

62. [Anonymous informant], "Vnitropolitická situace," 14–15 Mar. 1939, VHA, fond 37, 91/1, I. díl, 9; "citoyen," "Obchod, průmysl a finance. Trh práce," 18 June 1939, VHA, fond 37, sign. 91/1, 1. díl, 13–13a. For Baarová's version of events, see Lida Baarová, *Života sladké hořkosti* (Os-trav: Sfinga, 1991).

63. SD-PE-15-March-1940, 11–14, 16; Brandes, *Die Tschechen,* 1:150.

64. SD-PE-15-March-1940, 16.

65. "Zpráva z domova," 18 Dec. 1939, VHA, fond 37, sign. 91/1, 2, 5.

66. The quotation is taken from a Sudeten German woman's letter that was copied and forwarded to London. "Die Verhältnisse im Protektorat," 6 July 1939, VHA, fond 37, sign. 91/1, 2. Verwaltungsbericht, OLR Proßnitz, May 1939, NA, ÚŘP, k. 287, sign. II-b 2000, 1.

67. Lagebericht, Gruppe Mähren, September 1939, NA, ÚŘP, k. 279, sign. I-1a 1803 (Gruppe Mähren), 7; "Zpráva z domova," 18 December 1939, VHA, fond 37, sign. 91/1–2, 5; Mastny, *The Czechs,* 53; Brandes, *Die Tschechen,* 1:31. One notable Protectorate German who did assume a powerful position within the state administration was former professor of history Josef Pfitzner, who became primator of Prague. See Frank Hadler and Vojtěch Šustek, "Josef Pfitzner (1901–1945) Historiker: Geschicht-sprofessor und Geschichtspolitiker," in Monika Glettler and Alena Míšková, eds., *Prager Professoren 1938–1948. Zwischen Wissenschaft und Politik* (Essen: Klartext, 2001), 137–153. On Reich Germans in Prague's German University, see Alena Míšková, *Německá (Karlova) univerzita od Mnichova k 9. květnu 1945* (Prague: Karolinum, 2002), 91–93, esp. 92.

68. Stanislav Biman, "Verführt und machtlos? Der Anteil der Sudetendeutschen an der Verwaltung des Reichsgaus Sudetenland," in Monika Glettler, Ľubomír Lipták, and Alena Míšková, eds., *Geteilt, besetzt, beherrscht: Die Tschechoslowakei 1938–1945: Reichsgau Sudetenland, Protektorat Böhmen und Mähren, Slowakei* (Essen: Klartext, 2004), 155–184; Čeněk Klapal, "Několik poznámek k působení SD v okupovaném Československu," *Odboj a revoluce* 5 (1967): 82–96; Brandes, *Die Tschechen,* 1:159.

69. "Monatsbericht: Die politische Entwicklung im Protektorat Böhmen und Mähren," SD report, May 1940, VHA, SDNU, k. 7, sbírka č. 14; "Die Verhältnisse im Protektorat," 6 July 1939, VHA, fond 37, sign. 91/1, 3. See also Verwaltungsbericht, OLR Deutschbrod, April 1940, NA, ÚŘP, k. 287, sign. I1-b 2000, 3.

70. "Lagebericht Nr. 4," Der Befehlshaber der Ordnungspolizei beim Reichsprotektor Böhmen und Mähren, 28 Mar. 1940, NA, ÚŘP, sign. 1–1b 1220, 1; Oberlandrat Iglau to Reichsprotektor, 24 Apr. 1940, NA, ÚŘP, k. 287, sign. I1-b 1220, 1–2; "Deutsche Geschäftsleute," I1a-549 to Parteiverbindungsstelle beim Reichsprotektor im Böhmen und Mähren, May 1940, NA, ÚŘP, k. 287, sign. I-1b 2000, 1; Heinz Lämmel, 16 Sept. 1960, BB, Ost-Dok 20, sign. 66, Iglauer Sprachinsel, 23.

71. Helena Petrův, *Právní postavení židů v Protektorátu Čechy a Morava (1939– 1941)* (Prague: Sefer, 2000), 22–23; Miroslav Kárný, "Die 'Judenfrage' in der nazistischen Okkupationspolitik," *Historica* 21 (1982): 146–147, 162– 164; and *AOP,* doc. 79, 205–206, doc. 81, 207–212.

72. Petrův, *Právní postavení,* 80–83; Kárný, "Die 'Judenfrage,'" 186.

73. The Jewish religious congregations were reorganized again in 1940 to make the Prague Jewish religious congregations responsible for all of the Protectorate's Jews. Helena Krejčová, "Židovská náboženská obec za války," in Helena Krejčová, Jana Svobodová, and Anna Hyndráková, eds., *Židé v Protektorátu: Hlášení židovské náboženské obce v roce 1942: Dokumenty* (Prague: Ústav pro soudobé dějiny AV ČR, 1997), 12–13; John G. Lexa, "Anti-Jewish Laws and Regulations in the Protectorate of Bohemia and Moravia," in Avigdor Dagan, Gertrude Hirschlers, and Lewis Weiner, eds., *The Jews of Czechoslovakia: Historical Studies and Surveys,* vol. 3 (New York: Jewish Publication Society of America, 1984), 87–88.

74. Kárný, "Die Judenfrage," 171–174. See also Lexa, "Anti-Jewish Laws," 89; and Livia Rothkirchen, "The Jews of Bohemia and Moravia, 1938–1945," in Dagan, Hirschler, and Weiner, *The Jews,* 3: 40–41.

75. Petrův, *Právní postavení,* 61–62, 133–135; Miroslav Kárný, *"Konečné řešení": Genocida českých židů v německé protektorátní politice* (Prague: Academia, 1991), 30–31; *DHČSP,* vol. 2, doc. 343, 419.

76. Alicia K. Cozine, "A Member of the State: Citizenship Law and Its Application in Czechoslovakia, 1918–1938," (Ph.D. diss., University of Chicago, 1996), 215.

77. *DHČSP,* vol. 2, doc. 343, 419; Generalreferent für politische Angelegenheiten to Gruppe I 3, 28 Aug. 1939, NA, ÚŘP, k. 90, sign. I-1b 2020.

78. Reichsprotektor to Oberlandräte, 20 June 1939, NA, ÚŘP, k. 90, sign. I-1b 2020.

79. Verwaltungsbericht, OLR Iglau, January 1939, NA, ÚŘP, k. 280, sign. I-1a 1803 (Jihlava), 5–8; Verwaltungsbericht, OLR Brünn, August 1939, NA, ÚŘP, k. 280, sign. I-1a 1803 (Brno), 2; "Festellung der Protekoratsangehörigkeit für Juden ehemaliger tschechoslowakischer Staatsangehörigkeit," I 3b-6994/40 to Ministerium des Innern in Prag, 7 Sept. 1940, MZAB, B 255, k. 2, sign. 108; "Erfassung der Volksdeutschen im Protektorat Böhmen und Mähren," K. H. Frank to various, 9 Oct. 1939, USHMM, Reichsprotektor in Böhmen und Mähren, osoby fond 1488, opis 1, folder 25, RG 11.001.M 23, reel 91, 2; "Ausstellung von deutschen Staatsangehörigkeitsausweisen an Juden und an Flüchtlinge aus dem Altreich, der Ostmark und dem Sudetengau," I 3 b-2564/40 to Gruppe Mähren and Oberlandräte, 3 Apr. 1940, MZAB, B 255, k. 1, sign. HO 100.

80. Alfred Bohman, "Bevölkerung in Böhmen 1847–1947 mit besonderer Berücksichtigung der Entwicklung der nationalen Verhältnisse," *Wissenschaftliche Materialien zur Landeskunde der Böhmische Länder* 3 (1983): 238; Verwaltungsbericht, OLR Brünn, April 1940, NA, ÚŘP, k. 287, sign. I-1b 2000, 3; "Deutschtumsprogram für das Jahr 1941," OLR Zlin, NA, ÚŘP, k. 290, sign. I-1b 2029, 1.

81. Generalreferent für politische Angelegenheiten to Mokry, 12 Aug. 1939, NA, ÚŘP, k. 90, sign. I-1b 2020, 2.

82. Frank to Oberlandräte, 30 June 1939, NA, ÚŘP, k. 90, sign. I-1b 2020, 1.

83. Generalreferent für politische Angelegenheiten to Mokry, 12 Aug. 1939, NA, ÚŘP, k. 90, sign. I-1b 2020, 2–3; Der Wehrmachtsbevollmächtige im Protektorat Böhmen und Mähren to Reichsprotektor, 27 May 1939, NA, ÚŘP, k. 90, sign. I-1b 2020, 1.

84. Abteilung Reichsversorgung to OLR Prag, 17 Apr. 1940, NA, ÚŘP, k. 279, sign. I-1a 1803 (Praha), 3. See also JUDr. Jan Pavel Pringsheim, "Situační zpráva o poměrech v protektorátě Čechy a Morava se zvláštním přihlédnutím k vnitřní spravě," JS, k. 12, Reports from ČSR, 1942–1943, 18.

85. SD-PE-15-March-1940, 68. Verwaltungsbericht, OLR Prag, [no date], NA, ÚŘP, k. 287, sign. I-1b 2000, 1; Abteilung Reichsversorgung to OLR Prag, 17 Apr. 1940, NA, ÚŘP, k. 279, sign. I-1a 1803 (Praha), 3. Frank's quotation

from Frank to Oberlandräte, 30 June 1939, NA, ÚŘP, k. 90, sign. I-1b 2020, 1.

86. Kreisstabamtsleiter Königgrätz to OLR Kolin, 22 Nov. 1939, SOAP, OLR Kolín, k. 20, inv. č. 14.

87. [Anonymous author], "Milý Grandseigneure," VHA, fond 37, sign. 91/1, 1. díl, 2; Emil Sobota, *Co to byl Protektorát* (Prague: Václav Petr, 1946), 121; Maršálek, *Protektorát,* 60–61.

88. "Bilance dějinného roku 1939," *Hospodářský rozhled,* 21 Dec. 1939, 5. "Monatsbericht," SD report, June 1940, VHA, SDNU, k. 7, sign. 49, sbírka č. 74, jednotka 71, 17; "Die Verhältnisse im Protektorat," 6 July 1939, VHA, fond 37, sign. 91/1, 2.

89. Verwaltungsbericht, OLR Deutschbrod, April 1940, NA, ÚŘP, k. 287, sign. Ia-b 2000, 3; Gebel, *"Heim,"* 226–227.

90. Per thousand, 34.5 Bohemian Germans were killed in battle, compared with 27.7 per thousand in the Austrian half of the dual monarchy and 27.8 per thousand in Germany. S. Harrison Thompson, "The Germans in Bohemia from Maria Theresa to 1918," *Journal of Central European Affairs* 2 (1942): 178. Cited in Joseph Rothschild, *East Central Europe between the Two World Wars* (Seattle: University of Washington Press, 1974), 81; [anonymous author], "Milý Grandseigneure," VHA, fond 37, sign. 91/1, 1. díl, 2.

91. Antonín Ševčík, "Germanizační činnost brněnských nacistických úřadů v letech 1939–1945," *Brno v minulosti a dnes: Sborník příspěvků k dějinám a výstavbě Brna* 7 (1965): 28; Verwaltungsbericht, OLR Brünn, NA, ÚŘP, k. 287, sign. I-1b 2000, 4.

92. Generalreferent für politische Angelegenheiten to Mokry, 12 Aug. 1939, NA, ÚŘP, k. 90, sign. I-1b 2020, 3.

93. Verwaltungsbericht, OLR Brünn, April 1940, NA, ÚŘP, k. 287, sign. I-1b 2000, 3; Lagebericht, OLR Prag, July 1939, NA, ÚŘP, k. 279, sign. I-1a 1803 (Praha), 2–3.

94. SD report 53, 14 Feb. 1940, Heinz Boberach, ed., *Meldungen aus dem Reich 1938–1945: Die geheimen Lageberichte des Sicherheitsdienstes der SS* (Herrsching: Pawlak, 1984), 758.

95. "Monatsbericht: Die politische Entwicklung im Protektorat Böhmen und Mähren," SD report, May 1940, VHA, SDNU, k. 7, sbírka č. 74, jednotka 48, 14, 12, 8.

96. Oberlandrat Pardubitz to Reichsprotektor, NA, ÚŘP, k. 292, sign. I-1b 2140, 1.

97. SD-PE-1940, 8; Verwaltungsbericht, OLR Olmütz, May 1940, ÚŘP, NA, k. 287, sign. I1-b 2000, 5; Abteilung Reichsversorgung to OLR Prag, 17 Apr. 1940, NA, ÚŘP, k. 279, sign. I-1a 1803 (Praha), 3–5; "Monatsbericht," SD

report, June 1940, VHA, SDNU, k. 7, sign. 49, sbírka č. 74, jednotka 71, 16.

98. Lagebericht, Office of the Reich Protector, August 1940, NA, ÚŘP, k. 279, sign. I-1a 1803 (Gruppe Mähren), 7.

99. Mastny, *The Czechs*, 134.

100. The upward trend of marriages in the Protectorate is evidenced by government records: 59,618 in 1933; 56,178 in 1938; 78,169 in 1939; 73,117 in 1940; 65,908 in 1941; and 73, 598 in 1942. See *Statistisches Jahrbuch für das Protektorat Böhmen und Mähren*, 3 (Prague: Melantrich, 1943), 10.

101. SD-PE-15-March-1940, 10. OLR Zlin to Reichsprotektor, 19 July 1939, ÚŘP, NA, sign. I-1b 2140; Petrův, *Právní postavení*, 137. On the importance that Nazi rulers placed on marriage and sexual relations, see Gisela Bock, "Equality and Difference in National Socialist Racism," in Gisela Bock and Susan James, eds., *Beyond Equality and Difference: Citizenship, Feminist Politics, and Female Subjectivity* (London: Routledge, 1992), 94; and Doris L. Bergen, "Sex, Blood, and Vulnerability: Women Outsiders in German-Occupied Europe," in Robert Gellately and Nathan Stoltzfus, eds., *Social Outsiders in Nazi Germany* (Princeton, N.J.: Princeton University Press, 2001), 273–294.

102. Verwaltungsbericht, OLR Brünn, May 1940, NA, ÚŘP, k. 287, sign. I-1b 2000, 1.

103. Verwaltungsbericht, OLR Brünn, April 1940, NA, ÚŘP, k. 287, sign. I-1b 2000, 3–4, 5.

104. Verwaltungsbericht, OLR Pilsen, March 1940, NA, ÚŘP, k. 90, sign. I-1b 2021, 1; "Übersicht über den Geschäftsgang des Standesamtes in der Zeit vom 1. Januar 1940 bis zum 29. February 1940," no date, NA, ÚŘP, k. 279, sign. I-1a 1803 (Praha), 1.

105. "Monatsbericht," SD report, June 1940, VHA, SDNU, k. 7, sign. 49, sbírka č. 74, jednotka 71, 9; "Zpráva z domova," 18 Dec. 1939, VHA, fond 37, sign. 91/1–2, 2.

106. Lagebericht, Office of the Reich Protector, August 1940, NA, ÚŘP, k. 279, sign. I-1a 1803 (Gruppe Mähren), 7.

107. Verwaltungsbericht, OLR Olmütz, April NA, ÚŘP, k. 287, sign. I-1b 2000, 5; also Verwaltungsbericht, OLR Pilsen, March 1940, NA, ÚŘP, k. 90, sign. I-1b 2021, 1.

108. Verwaltungsbericht, OLR Brünn, May 1940, NA, ÚŘP, k. 287, sign. I-1b 2000, 1.

109. Verwaltungsbericht, OLR Pilsen, March 1940, NA, ÚŘP, k. 90, sign. I-1b 2021, 1.

110. Gruppe Mähren, Lagebericht, 5 Sept. 1939, NA, ÚŘP, k. 279, sign. I-1a

1803 (Gruppe Mähren), 1–2; OLR Iglau, Lagebericht, 2 Sept. 1939, NA, ÚŘP, k. 280, sign. I-1a 1803 (Jihlava), 4; SD-Führer und Befehlshaber der Sicherheitspolizei beim Reichsprotektor to OLR Kolín, 19 Sept. 1939, SOAP, OLR Kolín, k. 6; Verwaltungsbericht, OLR Iglau, Sept. 1939, NA, ÚŘP, k. 280, sign. I-1a 1803 (Jihlava), 3–4.

111. Ctibor Nečas, *Holocaust českých Romů* (Prague: Prostor, 1999), 17–18; Michael Zimmermann, *Rassenutopie und Genozid: Die nationalsozialistische "Lösung der Zigeunerfrage"* (Hamburg: Hans Christian, 1996), 218–219; Guenter Lewy, *The Nazi Persecution of the Gypsies* (Oxford: Oxford University Press, 2000), 149–150.

112. Petrův, *Právní povstání*, 83; Lexa, "Anti-Jewish Laws," 79, 76–77; Petr Bednařík, *Arizace české kinematografie* (Prague: Karolinum, 2003), 29; Kárný, *"Konečné řešení,"* 19, 31.

113. Mastny, *The Czechs*, 106; Rothkirchen, "The Jews," 24; Kosatík, *Ferdinand Peroutka*, 26–32; Sayer; *The Coasts*, 226; Doležal, *Česká kultura*, 110; Pasák, *Pod ochranou říše*, 128; Tomášek, "Die nationalsozialistische Zensur," 74–83.

114. Paces, "Religious Heroes," 221–228; Polizeipräsident to OLR Prag, 29 Sept. 1939, NA, ÚŘP, k. 279, I-1a 1803 (Praha), 1939–1943.

115. Lageberichte der Gruppe Mähren, September 1939, NA, ÚŘP, k. 279, sign. I-1a 1803 (Gruppe Mähren); Lageberichte der Gruppe Mähren, October 1939, NA, ÚŘP, k. 279, sign. I-1a 1803 (Gruppe Mähren); Lagebericht, OLR Iglau, 2 Sept. 1939, NA, ÚŘP, k. 280, sign. I-1a 1803 (Jihlava), 1–3; SD-PE-15-March-1940, 6.

116. Elizabeth Wiskemann, "Partitioned Czechoslovakia," in Arnold Toynbee and Veronica M. Toynbee, eds., *Hitler's Europe* (London: Oxford University Press, 1954), 588–589; Mastny, *The Czechs*, 116–117.

117. "Zprávy ze dne 6. ledna 1941," 6 Jan. 1941, JS, K. 11, Reports from Czechoslovakia, 1941, folder 1, 1; Brandes, *Die Tschechen*, 1:82.

118. Verwaltungsbericht, OLR Iglau, November 1939, NA, ÚŘP, k. 280, sign. I-1a 1803 (Jihlava), 4–5; Verwaltungsbericht, OLR Iglau, Dec. 1939, NA, ÚŘP, k. 280, sign. I-1a 1803 (Jihlava), 1–3; Lagebericht, Office of the Reich Protector, March 1940, NA, ÚŘP, k. 279, sign. I-1a 1803 (Gruppe Mähren), 1; Lagebericht, Gruppe Mähren, Jan. 1940, NA, ÚŘP, k. 279, sign. I-1a 1803 (Gruppe Mähren), 1; Brandes, *Die Tschechen*, 1:107.

119. Brandes, *Die Tschechen*, 1:43–44.

120. Tomášek, "Die nationalsozialistische Zensur," 79.

121. SD-PE-15-March-1940, 2; "Einfluss der Intelligenzschicht in der Widerstandsgruppe der tschechischen Geheimorganisationen," SD report, 3 July 1940, VHA, SDNU, k. 8, [no sign.], 3. On the lives of university professors

under the occupation, see John Connelly, *Captive University: The Sovietization of East German, Czech, and Polish Higher Education, 1945–1956* (Chapel Hill: University of North Carolina Press, 2000), 88–91. See also the discussion in Bradley F. Abrams, *The Struggle for the Soul of the Nation: Czech Culture and the Rise of Communism* (Lanham, Md.: Rowman & Littlefield, 2004), 44–47; and the individual biographies in Glettler and Míšková, *Prager Professoren*.

122. Lagebericht, Office of the Reich Protector, Jan. 1940, NA, ÚŘP, k. 279, sign. I-1a 1803 (Gruppe Mähren), 1.

123. Vnitropolitické situace," 14–15 March 1939, VHA, fond 37, sign. 91–1, 1. díl, 6; [anonymous informant], "Zpráva o situaci na železnicích," second half of May, 1939, VHA fond 37, sign. 91/1, 1; [anonymous correspondent], "Zprávy z domova," 12 June 1939, VHA, fond 37, sign. 91/1, 1. díl, 2, 4; Klapal, "Několik poznámek," 91.

124. "Zu der Rede des Staatssekretärs Frank," December 1939, SD report 3336/39, VHA, SDUNO, k. 17, sign. 374.

125. Brandes, *Die Tschechen*, 1:74–77.

126. Lagebericht, Gruppe Mähren, Nov. 1939, NA, ÚŘP, k. 279, sign. I-1a 1803 (Gruppe Mähren), 13–14; Lagebericht, OLR Prößnitz, February 1940, NA, ÚŘP, k. 283, sign. I-1a 1804 (Prostějov), 1; Lagebericht, Office of the Reich Protector, Jan. 1940, NA, ÚŘP, k. 279, sign. I-1a 1803 (Gruppe Mähren), 1; OLR Brünn, Verwaltungsbericht, February 1940, NA, ÚŘP, k. 280, sign. I-1a 1803 (Brno), 2.

127. Gordon Wright, *The Ordeal of Total War, 1939–1945* (New York: Harper & Row, 1968), 29.

128. Gebhart and Kuklík, *Dramatické i všední dny*, 8; Kural, *Vlastenci*, 17.

129. Mastny, *The Czechs*, 58; Pasák, *Pod ochranou říše*, 92; John Connelly, "Nazis and Slavs: From Racial Theory to Racist Practice," *CEH* 32, 1 (1999): 22.

130. SD-PE-15-March-1940, 2–3; also Brandes, *Die Tschechen*, 1:78.

131. Brandes, *Die Tschechen*, 1:78. Sayer, *The Coasts*, 223.

132. Rataj, *O autoritativní národní stát*, 93–96; Pasák, *Pod ochranou říše*, 72.

133. Mastny, *The Czechs*, 90.

134. SD-PE-15-March-1940, 7.

2. The Reich Way of Thinking

1. Jan Gebhart and Jan Kuklík, *Dramatické i všední dny protektorátu* (Prague: Themis, 1996), 12; Josef Gruss, *Jedna paní povídala* (Prague: Alois Hynek, 1945), 102. See also SD-PE-15-March-1940, 2.

2. Verwaltungsbericht, OLR Olmütz, April 1940, NA, ÚŘP, k. 287, sign. I-1b

2000 (Olomouc), 5–8; Zbyněk Válka, *Olomouc pod hákovým křížem: Temná léta okupace 1939–1945* (Olomouc: Votobia, 2001), 9.

3. Verwaltungsbericht, OLR Olmütz, April 1940, NA, ÚŘP, k. 287, sign. I-1b 2000 (Olomouc), 5–8; Petr Němec, "Die Lage der deutschen Nationalität im Protektorat Böhmen und Mähren unter dem Aspekt der 'Eindeutschung' dieses Gebietes," *Boh* 32 (1991): 48.

4. "Zwei Jahre im Protektorat," OLR Olmütz, NA, ÚŘP, k. 281, sign. I-1a 1804 (Olomouc), 5–8. See also "Anlage zum Verwaltungsbericht," OLR Olmütz, 22 Aug. 1941, Oberlandrat Olomouc, Zemský archiv v Opavě, pobočka Olomouc, k. 5, inv. č. 5, 12–15, 29–30; and Josef Bartoš, "Okupace a osvobození," in Josef Bartoš, ed., *Malé dějiny Olomouce* (Olomouc: Profil, 1972), 136.

5. "Zwei Jahre im Protektorat," OLR Olmütz, NA, ÚŘP, k. 281, sign. I-1a 1804 (Olomouc), 9; Válka, *Olomouc,* 61–63. See also "Anlage zum Verwaltungsbericht," OLR Olmütz, 22 Aug. 1941, Oberlandrat Olomouc, Zemský archiv v Opavě, pobočka Olomouc, k. 5, inv. č. 5, 29.

6. "Zwei Jahre im Protektorat," OLR Olmütz, NA, ÚŘP, k. 281, sign. I-1a 1804 (Olomouc), 16–19.

7. SD-PE-1940, 8.

8. Burgsdorff to Staatssekretär, 11 Mar. 1940, NA, ÚŘP, k. 287, sign. I-1b 2000. The main office then shared information gathered from Oberlandräte with administrators from the Reichsgau Sudetenland and the Ministry of the Interior. Fuchs to Regierungspräsident Karlsbad, Aussig, Troppau, Kattowitz, and Regensburg and to Reichsstatthalter in Reichenberg, Wien, and Linz, 1 May 1940, NA, ÚŘP, k. 295, sign. I-1b 2500; and Reichsminister des Innern to Reichsprotektor in Prag and Generalgouverneur in Krakow, 7 June 1940, NA, ÚŘP, k. 295, sign. I-1b 2500, 1.

9. I1a-602, "Wöchentlich wiederkehrende Besprechung über die Volkstumsarbeit im Protektorat," 22 May 1940, NA, ÚŘP, k. 287, sign. I-1b 2000.

10. The official name was the "Fund for the Cultivation of the German Volkstum," (Fond zur Pflege des deutschen Volkstums); Dorer, Gruppe XXI—Vortrag am Herrn Staatssekretärs, 15 May 1940, NA, ÚŘP, k. 292, sign. I-1b 2180. On the fund's budget, see Detlef Brandes, *Die Tschechen unter deutschem Protektorat,* vol. 1 (Munich: R. Oldenbourg, 1969), 162–163.

11. Verwaltungsbericht, OLR Zlin, 21 Nov. 1940, NA, ÚŘP, k. 290, sign. 2090 1940–1941, 6; OLR Iglau to Herrn Deutschen Staatsminister, 8 Oct. 1940, NA, ÚŘP, k. 292, sign. I-1b 2301; SD-PE-1940, 14–15; Tara Zahra, "Your Child Belongs to the Nation: Nationalization, Germanization, and Democracy in the Bohemian Lands, 1900–1945" (Ph.D. diss., University of Michigan, 2005), 481.

12. SD-PE-1940, 12.

13. Jiří Doležal, *Česká kultura za protektorátu: Školství, písemnictví, kinematografie* (Prague: Národní filmový archiv, 1996), 91, n. 16, 52, 84. See also Zahra, "Your Child," 482.

14. Verwaltungsbericht, OLR Tabor, 22 Nov. 1940, NA, ÚŘP, k. 290, sign. 2090, 2; Petr Němec, "Germanizační politika nacistů v Protektorátě Čechy a Morava, 1939–1945" (Ph.D. diss., Masarykova Universita, 1990), 199.

15. Doležal, *Česká kultura*, 91, n. 16, 52, 84. See also Zahra, "Your Child," 482.

16. SD-PE-1940, 13; Němec, "Die Lage," 56.

17. Lagebericht, Office of the Reich Protector, August 1940, NA, ÚŘP, k. 279, sign. I-1a 1803 (Gruppe Mähren), 5; SD-PE-1940, 40; *DHČSP,* doc. 398, 538–539; Brandes, *Die Tschechen,* 1: 164.

18. Verwaltungsbericht, Gruppe Mähren, June 1940, NA, ÚŘP, k. 279, sign. I-1a 1803 (Gruppe Mähren), 20–21; Karel Fremund, "Dokumenty o nacistické vyhlazovací politice," *SAP* 13, no. 2 (1963), doc. 11, 28; Brandes, *Die Tschechen,* 1: 164; [anonymous author], "Germanizace Prahy za okupace," *Šest let okupace Prahy* (Prague: Orbis, 1946), 24; Petr Němec, "Český národ a nacistické teorie germanizace prostoru," *ČČH* (1990): 543; *DHČSP,* doc. 405, 545–546, doc. 425, 576, doc. 404, 543, and doc. 405, 546.

19. SD-PE-1940, 8.

20. "Erfassung der Volksdeutschen im Protektorat Böhmen und Mähren," K. H. Frank to various, 9 Oct. 1940, USHMM, Reichsprotektor in Böhmen und Mähren, osoby fond 1488, opis 1, folder 25, RG 11.001.M 23, reel 91, 3; I3b-5839, "Erfassung der deutschen Volkszugehörigen im Protektorat Böhmen und Mähren," 20 July 1940, NA, ÚŘP, k. 290, sign. I-1b 1627, 2; I3b-9574, "Erfassung der deutschen Volkszugehörigen im Protektorat Böhmen und Mähren," 30 Nov. 1940, USHMM, Reichsprotektor in Böhmen und Mähren, osoby fond 1488, opis 1, folder 25, RG 11.001.M 23, reel 91, 8. See also Lagebericht, Office of the Reich Protector, August 1940, NA, ÚŘP, k. 279, sign. I-1a 1803 (Gruppe Mähren), 6.

21. On the numbers for Brno, see Mokry to Reichsprotektor, 18 May 1940, NA, ÚŘP, k. 90, sign. I-1b 2020; and I3b-9574, "Erfassung der deutschen Volkszugehörigen im Protektorat Böhmen und Mähren," 30 Nov. 1940, USHMM, Reichsprotektor in Böhmen und Mähren, osoby fond 1488, opis 1, folder 25, RG 11.001.M 23, reel 91, 8. On Fiechtner, see OLR Iglau, Verwaltungsbericht, June 1940, NA, ÚŘP, k. 280, sign. I-1a 1803 (Jihlava), 16.

22. Brandes, *Die Tschechen,* 1:320, n. 1167.

23. "Monatsbericht," SD report June 1940, VHA, SDNU, k. 7, sign. 49, sbírka č. 74, jednotka 71, 16, 17.

24. JUDr. Jan Pavel Pringsheim, "Situační zpráva o poměrech v protektorátě Čechy a Morava se zvláštním přihlédnu tím k vnitřní správě," JS, k. 12, Reports from ČSR, 1942–1943, 11.

25. Verwaltungsbericht, OLR Zlin, 21 Nov. 1940, NA, ÚŘP, k. 290, sign. 2090, 5; Antonín Verbík, *Dějiny Žďár nad Sázavou* (Brno: Musejní spolek v Brně a Městský národní výbor ve Žďáře nad Sázavou, 1977), 167.

26. On jobs within the bureaucracy, see Lagebericht Nr. 4, Der Befehlshaber der Ordnungspolizei beim Reichsprotektor Böhmen und Mähren, 28 Mar. 1940, NA, ÚŘP, sign. 1–1b 1220, 1; Gruppe I to Mokry, [no date], NA, UŘP, k. 90, sign. I-1b 2020, 1939–1942, 1; Verwaltungsbericht, OLR Zlin, June 1940, ÚŘP, NA, k. 290, sign. 2090, 1; JUDr. Jan Pavel Pringsheim, "Situační zpráva o poměrech v protektorátě Čechy a Morava se zvláštním přihlédnutím k vnitřní správě," JS, k. 12, Reports from ČSR, 1942–1943, 14; Nr. I3b–3166/41 to Dienst stelle für das Land Mähren, 14 May 1941, MZAB, B 255, k. 1, sign. HO 101, 1–2. On rations and property, see Richard J. Overy, "The Economy of the 'New Order,'" in Richard J. Overy, Gerhard Otto, Johannes Houwink ten Cate, eds., *Die "Neuordnung" Europas: NS-Wirtschaftspolitik in den besetzten Gebieten* (Berlin: Metropol, 1997), 26; Vojtech Mastny, *The Czechs under Nazi Rule: The Failure of National Resistance, 1939–1942* (New York: Columbia University Press, 1971), 83; Dana Musilová, "Zásobování a výživa českého obyvatelstva v podmínkách válečného řízeného hospodářství (1939–1945)," *Slezský sborník* 89, nos. 3–4 (1991): 258; JUDr. Jan Pavel Pringsheim, "Situační zpráva o poměrech v protektorátě Čechy a Morava se zvláštním přihlédnutím k vnitřní správě," JS, k. 12, Reports from ČSR, 1942–1943, 21, 22. On joining Nazi organizations, see "Monatsbericht," SD report, June 1940, VHA, SDNU, k. 7, sign. 49, sbírka č. 74, jednotka 71, 16; Rudolf Niemetz, Stadtgemeinde Holleschau, Mähren, [no date], BB, Ost-Dok 20, Iglauer Sprachinsel, sign. 69, 2.

27. Brandes, *Die Tschechen,* 1:320, n. 1167.

28. Ibid., 1:160–161.

29. Verwaltungsbericht, OLR Olmütz, April 1940, NA, ÚŘP, k. 287, sign. I-1b 2000. On the numbers for Brno, see Mokry to Reichsprotektor, 18 May 1940, NA, ÚŘP, k. 90, sign. I-1b 2020; and I3b-9574, "Erfassung der deutschen Volkszugehörigen im Protektorat Böhmen und Mähren," 30 Nov. 1940, USHMM, Reichsprotektor in Böhmen und Mähren, osoby fond 1488, opis 1, folder 25, RG 11.001.M 23, reel 91, 8.

30. Válka, *Olomouc,* 69; I3b-9574, "Erfassung der deutschen Volkszugehörigen im Protektorat Böhmen und Mähren," 30 Nov. 1940, USHMM, Reichsprotektor in Böhmen und Mähren, osoby fond 1488, opis 1, folder 25, RG 11.001.M 23, reel 91, 8.

31. "Niederschrift eines Tonbandgespräches über die Tätigkeit von Landrat D. Neumann als Landrat des Kreises Reichenberg und Oberlandrat von Königgrätz," Interviewed by Dr. Hopf, Bundesarchiv—Ostdokumentation in Berlin, 31 Jan. 1960, BB, Ost-Dok 21, sign. 44, 11.

32. Gruppe Mähren, Verwaltungsbericht, August 1940, NA, ÚŘP, k. 279, sign. I-1a 1803 (Gruppe Mähren), 10–11; Doležal, *Česká kultura,* 62.

33. Fuchs to Gruppe Mähren and Oberlandräte, 16 Sept. 1940, NA, ÚŘP, k. 90, sign. I-1 2020, 1–2; Lagebericht, Office of the Reich Protector, October 1940, NA, ÚŘP, k. 279, sign. I-1a 1803 (Gruppe Mähren), 7.

34. SD-PE-1940, 8; "Zprávy hospodářské," 10 Feb. 1941, VHA, fond 37, sign. 91/4, 2; and "Zprávy politické," 11 Jan. 1941, VHA, fond 37, sign. 91/4, 3.

35. SD-PE-1940, 11–13, 15.

36. Heinz Lämmel, 16 Sept. 1960, BB, Ost-Dok 20, sign. 66, Iglauer Sprachinsel, 23; "Zprávy z domova," 16 Jan. 1941, JS, k. 11, Reports from Czechoslovakia, 1941, folder 1, 2.

37. *AOP,* doc. 50, 123–126; Heinz Lämmel, 16 Sept. 1960, BB, Ost-Dok 20, Iglauer Sprachinsel, sign. 66, 22; Richard Zimprich, [no date], BB, Ost-Dok 20, Olmütz, sign. 67, 5.

38. On the influx of Reich German civil servants, see Sheila Grant Duff, *A German Protectorate: The Czechs under Nazi Rule* (London: Macmillan, 1942), 164. See also [no author], "Zprávy hospodářské," 10 Feb. 1941, VHA, fond 37, sign. 91/4, 2. Quoted from *Deutschland-Berichte der Sozialdemokratischen Partei Deutschlands (Sopade),* vol. 6 (1939) (Frankfurt: P. Nettelbeck, 1980), 895. On Protectorate German griping, see also Goebbels's *Tagebücher,* 6 Nov. 1940, reprinted in Boris Čelovský, ed., *So oder so: Řešení české otázky podle německých dokumentů, 1933–1945* (Ostrava: Sfinga, 1997), 274.

39. *AOL,* doc. 51, 129.

40. Richard Overy, *Goering: The "Iron Man"* (London: Routledge & Kegan Paul, 1984), 22–108.

41. On the concept of Großraumwirtschaft, see Alan S. Milward, *War, Economy, and Society, 1939–1945* (Berkeley: University of California Press, 1977), 8–9, 153–154; Overy, "The Economy," 20–21; Jean F. Freymond, "Aspects of the Reich's Ministry of Economics Concept of an Economic Reorganisation of Europe (1940)," *Studia Historiae Oeconomicae* 14 (1979): 9–12; Mark Mazower, *Dark Continent: Europe's Twentieth Century* (New York: A. A. Knopf, 1999), 153.

42. Overy, *Goering,* 77.

43. Alfred Kube, *Pour le mérite und Hakenkreuz: Hermann Göring im Dritten Reich* (Munich: R. Oldenbourg, 1986), 232–249, 265–278, 299–312; Stefan Martens, *Hermann Göring: "Erster Paladin des Führers" und "Zweiter*

Mann im Reich" (Paderborn: Schöningh, 1985), 114–171. As one British official reported in December 1938, "a well-authenticated story relates that Herr Hitler remarked angrily, in reference to the September crisis [that led up to the Munich agreement], that all his generals were cowards; Field Marshal Göring asked if he were included. 'Yes, naturally' was Herr Hitler's reply." Martens, *Hermann Göring,* 163.

44. Kube, *Pour le mérite,* 203–206, 359–363; Tatjana Tönsmayer, *Das Dritte Reich und die Slowakei 1939–1945: Politischer Alltag zwischen Kooperation und Eigensinn* (Paderborn: Schöningh, 2003), 48–52. On Mitteleuropa, see Friedrich Naumann, *Mitteleuropa* (Berlin: G. Reimer, 1915); and Henry Cord Meyer, *Mitteleuropa in German Thought and Action, 1815–1945* (The Hague: Nijhoff, 1955).

45. *IMT,* vol. 37, doc. 133-R, 367–368. Figures from Alice Teichová, "The Protectorate of Bohemia and Moravia (1939–1945): The Economic Dimension," in Mikuláš Teich, ed., *Bohemia in History* (Cambridge: Cambridge University Press, 1998), 57; Jana Geršlová, "Die wirtschaftliche Vergangenheit der böhmischen Ländern (1870–1914): Industrie, Handel und Banken," *Vierteljahrschrift für Sozial- und Wirtschaftsgeschichte* 87, no. 3 (2000): 320; and *AOP,* xiii.

46. *AOP,* doc. 53, 131–132.

47. Richard Overy, "Göring's Multi-national Empire," in Alice Teichová and P. L. Cottrel, eds., *International Business and Central Europe* (New York: St. Martin's Press, 1983), 277.

48. Overy, *Goering,* 113–114, quotation on 114.

49. Mastny, *The Czechs,* 75–77.

50. Václav Průcha, "Základní rysy řízeného hospodářství v českých zemích v letech nacistické okupace," *Historie a vojenství* 2 (1967): 224–225; Bartoš, *Olomouc,* 134–135.

51. Mastny, *The Czechs,* 75; Musilová, "Zásobování," 256–258; Průcha, "Základní rysy," 221–222.

52. Teichová, "The Protectorate," 279. See also Overy, "The Economy," 22–23; Ivan T. Berend, *Decades of Crisis: Central and Eastern Europe before World War II* (Berkeley: University of California Press, 1998), 274–275.

53. On German policy in southeastern Europe in the interwar period, see Berend, *Decades,* 273–277.

54. Deutsche Bank, *Das Protektorat Böhmen und Mähren im deutschen Wirtschaftsraum* (Berlin: Deutsche Bank, 1939), 23, 16, 37, 60–61.

55. Overy, *Goering,* 117.

56. Article written by Hans Kehrl for *Der Vierjahresplan,* 20 Apr. 1939, in *TWC,* vol. 13, 654–657, quotation from 655.

57. Mazower, *Dark Continent,* 153–156; Milward, *War,* 148.

58. Milward, *War,* 149.

59. Tönsmayer, *Das Dritte Reich,* 195.

60. *DHČSP,* doc. 393, 529.

61. Alice Teichová and Robert Waller, "Der tschechoslowakische Unternehmer am Vorabend und zu Beginn des Zweiten Weltkriegs," in Wacław Długoborski, ed., *Zweiter Weltkrieg und sozialer Wandel: Achsenmächte und besetzte Länder* (Göttingen: Vandenhoeck & Ruprecht, 1981), 292, 293.

62. Overy, *Goering,* 114.

63. Lagebericht, Office of the Reich Protector, April 1941, NA, ÚŘP, k. 279, sign. I-1a 1803 (Grüppe Mähren), 2.

64. SD-PE-1940, 59.

65. Kube, *Hermann Göring,* 307; John L. Heineman, *Hitler's First Foreign Minister: Constantin Freiherr von Neurath, Diplomat and Statesman* (Berkeley: University of California Press, 1979), 190–191. Mastny, *The Czechs,* 77.

66. *AOP,* doc. 52, 130.

67. *AOP,* doc. 53, 131–132.

68. Although in March 1939 the Reich Ministry of Economics declared that the term "Aryanization" was to be replaced by *"Entjudung"* (de-Jewification), the term stuck, as nearly all the documents relating to the process created in the Protectorate attest. Drahomír Jančik and Eduard Kubů, *"Arizace" and arizátoři. Drobný a střední majetek v úvěrech Kreditanstalt der Deutschen (1939–45)* (Prague: Karolinum, 2005), 13.

69. *AOP,* xxvii; *AOP,* doc. 54, 132–133, doc. 55, 133–134.

70. Livia Rothkirchen, "The Jews of Bohemia and Moravia, 1938–1945," in Avigdor Dagan, Gertrude Hirschler, and Lewis Weiner, eds., *The Jews of Czechoslovakia,* vol. 3 (Philadelphia: The Jewish Publication Society of America, 1984): 60.

71. Kárný, *"Konečné řešení,"* 47–49.

72. Kárný, "Die Judenfrage," 154–159; *AOP,* doc 59, 141–142, doc. 60, 142–144.

73. Helena Krejčová, Jana Svobodová, and Anna Hyndráková, eds., *Židé v Protektorátu: Hlášení Židovské náboženské obce v roce 1942: Dokumenty* (Prague: Ústav pro soudobé dějiny AV ČR, 1997), doc. 15, 238; Kárný, "Die Judenfrage," 158–159, 165–166, 184; Jančík and Kubů, *"Arizace,"* 21.

74. Krejčová, Svobodová, and Hyndráková, *Židé,* doc. 15, 239; Rothkirchen, "The Jews," 27.

75. Rothkirchen, "The Jews," 28; Petr Bednařík, *Arizace české kinematografie* (Prague: Karolinum, 2003), 29; Krejčová, Svobodová, and Hyndráková, *Židé,* doc. 15, 251–252.

76. As of September 1940, for example, 1,084 of the Jewish enterprises that had existed as of March 15, 1939, had been liquidated while another 269 had been transferred to Germans. Fiechtner reported a similar ratio of liq-

uidations to handovers in a report to the Reich Protector's Office in April 1941. Jančík and Kubů, "Arizace," 16–17.

77. Kárný, *"Konečné řešení,"* 61.
78. See, for example, Verwaltungsbericht, OLR Iglau, September 1939, NA, ÚŘP, k. 280, sign. I-1a 1803 (Jihlava), 16–17; Verwaltungsbericht, OLR Iglau, January 1940, NA, ÚŘP, k. 280, sign. I-1a 1803 (Jihlava), 6.
79. Jančík and Kubů, "Arizace," 25–26; Kárný, *"Konečné řešení,"* 63. For an example of disgruntlement among Nazi Party officials, see the protests voiced to Neurath's office by the Gauleiter of Bavarian Ostmark in *AOP,* doc. 70, 165–169. On Aryanization measures in Germany and Austria, see Frank Bajohr, "Arisierung und Rückererstattung: Eine Einschätzung," in Constantin Goschler and Jürgen Lillteicher, eds., *"Arisierung" und Restitution: Die Rückerstattung jüdischen Eigentums in Deutschland und Österreich nach 1945 und 1989* (Göttingen: Wallstein, 2002), 39–60; and Raul Hilberg, *The Destruction of the European Jews,* vol. 1 (New Haven, Conn.: Yale University Press, 2003), 92–131. On Aryanization measures in the Reichsgau Sudetenland, see Jörg Osterloh, "Judenverfolgung und 'Arisierung' im Reichsgau Sudetenland," in Monika Glettler, Ľubomír Lipták, and Alena Mišková, eds., *Geteilt, besetzt, beherrscht: Die Tschechoslowakei 1938–1945: Reichsgau Sudetenland, Protektorat Böhmen und Mähren, Slowakei* (Essen: Klartext, 2004), 220–226.
80. Teichová, "The Protectorate," 290–291.
81. Kennan, *From Prague,* 232.
82. "Zwei Jahre im Protektorat," OLR Olmütz, NA, ÚŘP, k. 281, sign. I-1a 1804 (Olomouc), 17. See also Kárný, *"Konečné řešení,"* 63.
83. Jančík and Kubů, *"Arizace,"* 164–166.
84. "Zwei Jahre im Protektorat," OLR Olmütz, NA, ÚŘP, k. 281, sign. I-1a 1804 (Olomouc), 19.
85. Lagebericht, Office of the Reich Protector, April 1941, NA, ÚŘP, k. 279, sign. I-1a 1803 (Gruppe Mähren), 2.
86. Lagebericht, Gruppe Mähren, January 1940, NA, ÚŘP, k. 279, sign. I-1a 1803 (Gruppe Mähren), 6–7, 10.
87. Kárný, *"Konečné řešení,"* 63–64.
88. Teichová and Waller, "Die tschechoslowakische Unternehmer," 299.
89. Nina Pavelčíková, "Změny v rozmístění a socialní skladbě obyvatel českých zemí za okupace, jejich souvislosti s poválečným vývojem," *Slezský sborník* 90, no. 1 (1992): 3.
90. Kárný, "Die Judenfräge," 167. See also Verwaltungsbericht, OLR Kremsier, Jan. 1940, NA, ÚŘP, k. 280, sign. I-1a 1803 (Kroměříž) 6; Lagebericht, Office of the Reich Protector, January 1940, NA, ÚŘP, k. 279, I-1a 1803 (Gruppe Mähren), 10.

91. Jančík and Kubů, "Arizace," 172
92. Lagebericht, Office of the Reich Protector, February 1940, NA, ÚŘP, k. 279, sign. I-1a 1803 (Gruppe Mähren), 12; Osterloh, "Judenverfolgung," 225.
93. Teichová and Waller, "Die tschechoslowakischen Unternehmer," 289.
94. SD-PE-1940, 75. See also SD-PE-15-March-1940, 84.
95. *Statistisches Jahrbuch für das Protektorat Böhmen und Mähren*, vol. 3 (Prague: Melantrich, 1943), table X 18, 166.
96. Overy, "The Economy," 26; Musilová, "Zásobování," 259–269; Průcha, "Základní rysy," 234.
97. For a description of these activities, see the dispatches dated 31 Oct. 1939, 8 Nov. 1939, and 13 Nov. 1939, in Gustav Bareš, "Depeše mezi Prahou a Moskvou 1939–1941," *Příspěvky k dějinám KSČ* 7 (1967): 397–401.
98. Dispatches dated 1 Dec. 1939, 4 Mar. 1940, 2 Sept. 1940, Bareš, "Depeše," 404–405, 409–410, 419.
99. Albert Kaufmann, "Zprávy z domova," VHA, fond 37, sign. 91/6, 3.
100. *DHČSP*, doc. 424, 575.
101. Dispatch dated 2 Sept. 1940, Bareš, "Depeše," 419.
102. Ctibor Nečas, "Osudy města za nacistické okupace a národně osvobozovacího boje," *Dějiny Ostravy* (Olomouc: Profil, 1967), 516.
103. Mastny, *The Czechs*, 153.
104. Tomáš Pasák, *Pod ochranou říše* (Prague: Práh, 1998), 231.
105. Teichová, "The Protectorate," 283.
106. "Jahres-Bericht für 1938/1940 über das Blechwalzwerk 'Karlhütte' bei Freidrick," 21 Jan. 1941, NA, ÚŘP, k. 291, sign. I-1b 2120.
107. *DHČSP*, doc. 390, 523–524, doc. 394, 532–523; doc. 398, 538; Mastny, *The Czechs*, 156; Dušan Tomášek and Robert Kvaček, *Causa Emil Hácha* (Prague: Themis, 1995), 87.
108. SD-PE-1940, 3; Mastny, *The Czechs*, 157, 99–100.
109. Mastny, *The Czechs*, 158; *DHČSP*, doc. 408, 549, doc. 424, 575.
110. SD-PE-1940, 8; JUDr. Jan Pavel Pringsheim, "Situační zpráva o poměrech v protektorátě Čechy a Morava se zvláštním přihlédnutím k vnitřní správě," JS, k. 12, Reports from ČSR, 1942–1943, 8, 11.
111. SD-PE-1940, 47. Sales numbers are from 19–22. See also František Bauer, "České noviny za války," *Šest let okupace Prahy* (Prague: Orbis, 1946), 74, 76; and Tomáš Pasák, *Soupis legálních novin, časopisů a úředních věstníků v českých zemích z let 1939–1945* (Prague: Univerzita Karlova, 1980), 72.
112. John Connelly, *Captive University: The Sovietization of East German, Czech, and Polish Higher Education, 1945–1956* (Chapel Hill: University of North Carolina Press, 2000), 80–81, 89–91.

113. "Monatsbericht," SD report, June 1940, VHA, SDNU, k. 7, sign. 49, sbírka č. 74, jednotka 71, 2; SD-PE-1940, 17–20.

114. Verwaltungsbericht, Gruppe Mähren, June 1940, NA, ÚŘP, k. 279, sign. I-la 1803 (Gruppe Mähren), 20–21; Lagebericht, Office of the Reich Protector, October 1940, NA, ÚŘP, k. 279, sign. I-la 1803 (Gruppe Mähren), 1.

115. Válka, *Olomouc*, 60.

116. Mastny, *The Czechs*, 147.

117. [No author], "Zprávy z domova z ledna 1941," 20 May 1941, JS, k. 11, Reports from Czechoslovakia, 1941, folder 2, 1; Václav Kural, *Vlastenci proti okupaci: Ústřední vedení odboje domácího 1940–1943* (Prague: Univerzita Karlova and Ústav mezinárodních vztahů, 1997), 129–132. Neither officials from the Reich Protector's Office nor Intelligence Service agents mention Communist broadcasts. London radio, one Czech Communist surmised, was more popular than its Moscow counterpart because the latter contained too much ideological blather and its Czech-language news began at 10:00 P.M.—too late at night for most early rising Czechs. Dispatch dated 16 Feb. 1940, Bareš, "Depeše," 409.

118. Kural, *Vlastenci*, 53–60.

119. Verwaltungsbericht, Gruppe Mähren, June 1940, NA, ÚŘP, k. 279, sign. I-la 1803 (Gruppe Mähren), 2–3. See also Verwaltungsbericht, OLR Iglau, June 1940, NA, ÚŘP, k. 280, sign. I-la 1803 (Jihlava), 14–15.

120. Miloslav Moulis and Dušan Tomášek, *K. H. Frank: Vzestup a pád karlovarského knihkupce* (Prague: Epocha, 2003), 211.

121. Kural, *Vlastenci*, 67.

122. "Monatsbericht. Die politische Entwicklung im Protectorat Böhmen und Mähren," SD report, May 1940, VHA, SDNU, k. 7, sbírka č. 74, jednotka 48, 17; "Mlčící národ," *V boj*, early December 1939, in *V boj: Edice ilegálního časopisu*, vol. 3, *1939–1941* (Prague: Vojenský historický archiv, 1995), 24–25. See also Kural, *Vlastenci*, 67.

123. Kural, *Vlastenci*, 67.

124. Zbyněk Zeman with Antonín Klimek, *The Life of Edvard Beneš, 1884–1948: Czechoslovakia in Peace and War* (Oxford: Clarendon Press, 1997), 14, 15.

125. Mastny, *The Czechs*, 141.

126. In 1917 Beneš recommended transferring the legionnaires to the western front, and "to slaughter," in an attempt to win over France to their cause. "We are responsible, and people at home will want to know this, what we achieved, politically, by sacrificing those 40,000 to 60,000 people," Beneš coolly wrote to Masaryk. Thanks to the Russian Revolution the transfer never happened. Instead the legionnaires, at Allied request, entered the Russian civil war against the Bolsheviks. They did not come home until 1919. Zeman, *The Life*, 35.

127. Ibid., 28.
128. Quotations from Zeman, *The Life*, 141 and 166.
129. Zeman, *The Life*, 174. On Beneš's legal acrobatics and the emergence of the presidential decrees, see Jan Kuklík, *Londýnský exil a obnova československého státu, 1938–1945* (Prague: Karolinum, 1998), 41–70.
130. Mastny, *The Czechs*, 141–142.
131. Letter to Vojta Beneš, 4 Apr. 1940, in Věra Olivová, ed., *Dopisy bratru Vojtovi, 1938–1944* (Prague: Společnost Edvarda Beneše, 1998), 38.
132. Letter to Vojta Beneš, 2 Dec. 1941, *Dopisy*, 49.
133. Lagebericht, Office of the Reich Protector, April 1940, NA, ÚŘP, k. 279, sign. I-1a 1803 (Gruppe Mähren), 8–9. See also Lagebericht, Office of the Reich Protector, February 1940, NA, ÚŘP, k. 279, sign. I-1a 1803 (Gruppe Mähren), 3; Lagebericht, Office of the Reich Protector, March 1940, NA, ÚŘP, k. 279, sign. I-1a 1803 (Gruppe Mähren), 4–5.
134. Peter Heumos, *Die Emigration aus der Tschechoslowakei nach Westeuropa und dem Nahen Osten 1938–1945* (Munich: R. Oldenbourg, 1989), 274; Zeman, *The Life*, 171.
135. Lagebericht, Office of the Reich Protector, April 1940, NA, ÚŘP, k. 279, sign. I-1a 1803 (Gruppe Mahren), 9.
136. Peter Heumos estimates that by 1941 around ten thousand civilians from the former Czechoslovakia had fled to Great Britain, of whom two thousand were Czechs who became directly dependent upon Beneš's government-in-exile. Heumos, *Die Emigration*, 207–208. See also Štefan Osuský, "Autoritativní režim dr. Beneše," in Kúklik, *Londýnský exil*, doc. 4, 164.
137. Lagebericht, Office of the Reich Protector, February 1940, NA, ÚŘP, k. 279, sign. I-1a 1803 (Gruppe Mähren), 3; Lagebericht, Office of the Reich Protector, March 1940, NA, ÚŘP, k. 279, sign. I-1a 1803 (Gruppe Mähren), 4–5; Lagebericht, Office of the Reich Protector, April 1940, NA, ÚŘP, k. 279, sign. I-1a 1803 (Gruppe Mähren), 8; Verwaltungsbericht, OLR Prag, March 1940, NA, ÚŘP, k. 279, sign. I-1a 1803 (Praha), 8; SD Lagebericht 13, 23 Feb. 1940, NA, ÚŘP, k. 286, sign. I-1a 1818 (Hlášení SD), 1–3; and Erfassungsbericht, Befehlshaber der Ordungspolizei, 23 March 1940, NA, ÚŘP, k. 283, sign. 4224 (Zlín), 1.
138. [No author], "Zprávy z domova," 7 Jan. 1941, JS, Reports from ČSR, 1941 (1), 2.
139. [No author], "Zprávy z ČSR," May 1941, JS, Reports from ČSR, 1941 (3), 1.
140. Lagebericht, Office of the Reich Protector, March 1940, NA, ÚŘP, k. 279, sign. I-1a 1803 (Gruppe Mähren), 4. See also "Erfahrungsbericht," Deutsche Gendarmerie-Kommand in Prag, 31 March 1940, NA, ÚŘP, k. 279, sign. I-1a 1803 (Praha), 1.

141. "Zpráva z Prahy přes Istanbul," 3 Oct. 1941, JS, Reports from Czechoslovakia, 1941 (3), 1.

142. *VRBH,* 1 Sept. 1939, 129; Lagebericht, Office of the Reich Protector, January 1940, NA, ÚŘP, k. 279, sign. I-1a 1803 (Gruppe Mähren), 1; Lagebericht, Office of the Reich Protector, February 1940, NA, ÚŘP, k. 279, sign. I-1a 1803 (Gruppe Mähren), 1–2; Lagebericht, Office of the Reich Protector, March 1940, NA, ÚŘP, k. 279, sign. I-1a 1803 (Gruppe Mähren), 4; Lagebericht, Office of the Reich Protector, April 1940, NA, ÚŘP, k. 279, sign. I-1a 1803 (Gruppe Mähren), 5.

143. Albert Kaufmann, "Zpráva z domova," 22 Apr. 1943, VHA, fond 37, sign. 91/6, 8–9; [anonymous informant], "Zprávy o poměrech ve vlasti," 6 Oct. 1943, VHA, fond 37, sign. 91/6, 3; [member of the Protectorate army cross-examined in London], "The Situation in Bohemia and Moravia" [no date], VHA, fond 37, sign. 91/8, 1–2.

144. IV. ŠÍP, "Radiodepeše do Prahy," 22 Feb. 1941, HIWPR, ÚVOD, k. 1, 12; [no author], "Zprávy z domova," 16 Jan. 1941, JS, Reports from ČSR, 1941 (1), 1; [no author], "Zprávy z domova," 22 Jan. 1941, JS, Reports from ČSR, 1941 (1), 1; [no author], "Zprávy z domova," 7 Jan. 1941, JS, Reports from ČSR, 1941 (1), 2; [no title], *V boj* 2, no. 3 (1940): 304; "Naslouchejte spojeneckému rozhlasu," *V boj* 2, no. 3 (1940): 418–419; and "Naslouchejte spojeneckému rozhlasu," *V boj* 2, no. 4 (1940): 541; Adolf F. J. Karlovský, "On the Homefront," in Lewis M. White, ed., *On All Fronts: Czechoslovaks in World War II,* vol. 2 (New York: East European Monographs, 1995), 263.

145. On the Czechoslovak government-in-exile's intelligence network, see Jiří Šolc, *Ve službách prezidenta: Generál František Moravec ve světle achívních dokumentů* (Prague: Vyšehrad, 1994), 160–164; and Jaroslav Kokoška and Stanislav Kokoška, *Spor o Agenta A-54: Kapitoly z dějin československé zpravodajské služby* (Prague: Naše vojsko, 1994).

146. Kural, *Vlastenci,* 91.

147. See, for example, *News Flashes from Czechoslovakia* (Chicago: Czechoslovak National Council in America, 1939–1945).

148. Mastny, *The Czechs,* 153–155.

149. Navrátil, 174–190–28, "Radioprogramy z Sparty I," 29 July 1940, HIWRP, ÚVOD, k. 1.

150. Dora, [no title], 18 Jan. 1941, HIWRP, ÚVOD, k. 1.

151. Lagebericht, Office of the Reich Protector, April 1940, NA, ÚŘP, k. 279, sign. I-1a 1803 (Gruppe Mähren), 5.

152. [No author], "Radioprogramy pro Spartu I," 11 Oct. 1940, HIWRP, ÚVOD, k. 1; Zeman, *The Life,* 181.

153. Navrátil, 174–320–28, "Radioprogramy z Sparty I," 29 July 1940, HIWRP, ÚVOD, k. 1.

154. [No author], "Zprávy z domova," 10 Feb. 1941, JS, Reports from ČSR, 1941 (1), 1.

155. Kural, *Vlastenci,* 68–71; Navrátil, 174–240–28, "Radioprogramy z Sparty I," 29 July 1940, HIWRP, ÚVOD, k. 1. See also [no author], "Zprávy z Prahy," 17 Aug. 1941, JS, Reports from ČSR, 1941 (3), 1–3; and Kural, *Vlastenci,* 110, 113.

156. Zeman, *The Life,* 141.

157. I. Křišťan, "Radiodepeše do Prahy," 11 Feb. 1941, HIWRP, ÚVOD, k. 1, 12.

158. Kural, *Vlastenci,* esp. 74–77. On the role of the domestic resistance pushing Beneš toward increasingly radical transfer plans, see also Václav Vrabec, "Ke genezi transferu Němců v domácím odboji," in Bohumil Černý, Jan Křen, Václav Kural, and Milan Otáhal, eds., *Češi, Němci, odsun: Diskuse nezávislých historiků* (Prague: Academia, 1990), 287–310; Jan Kuklík, "Němci očima Čechů, 1939–1943," in Jan Gebhart and Ivan Šedivý, eds., *Česká společnost za velkých válek 20. století (pokus o komparaci)* (Prague: Karolinum, 2003), 57–76; and Radomír Luža, *The Transfer of the Sudeten Germans: A Study of Czech-German Relations, 1933–1962* (New York: New York University Press, 1964).

159. Hans Lemberg, "'Ethnische Säuberung': Ein Mittel zur Lösung von Nationalitätenproblemen?" *Aus Politik und Zeitgeschichte* 46 (1992): 27–38; Philipp Ther, "A Century of Forced Migration: The Origins and Consequences of 'Ethnic Cleansing,'" in Phillip Ther and Ana Slijak, eds., *Redrawing Nations: Ethnic Cleansing in East-Central Europe, 1944–1948* (Lanham, Md.: Rowman & Littlefield, 2001), 50.

160. Terry Martin, "The Origins of Soviet Ethnic Cleansing," *JMH* 70 (Dec. 1998): 813–861, esp. 815, 858, 859. See also Yuri Slezkine, "The USSR as a Communal Apartment, or How a Socialist State Promoted Ethnic Particularism," *Slavic Review* 53, no. 2 (Summer 1994): 414–452; Amir Weiner, "Nature, Nurture, and Memory in a Socialist Utopia: Delineating the Soviet Socio-Ethnic Body in the Age of Socialism," *American Historical Review* (Oct. 1999): 1114–1155; Norman Naimark, *Fires of Hatred: Ethnic Cleansing in Twentieth-Century Europe* (Cambridge, Mass.: Harvard University Press, 2001), 85–107.

161. Naimark, *Fires,* 123.

162. Ther, "A Century," 47; Naimark, *Fires,* 6–8; Joseph B. Schechtman, *European Population Transfers, 1939–1945* (New York: Oxford University Press, 1946), 16–22.

163. Francis Dostál Raška, *The Czechoslovak Exile Government in London and the Sudeten German Issue* (Prague: Karolinum, 2002), 38.

164. Kuklík, "Němci," 66.
165. Raška, *The Czechoslovak Exile Government,* 42; also Kuklík, "Němci," 68.
166. Raška, *The Czechoslovak Exile Government,* 42; Kuklík, "Němci," 66.
167. Jan Rataj, "Obraz Němce a Německa v protektorátní společnosti a československém odboji," in Jan Křen and Eva Broklová, eds., *Obraz Němců, Rakouska a Německa v české společnosti 19. a 20. století* (Prague: Karolinum, 1998), 225.
168. Zdeněk Suda, *Zealots and Rebels: A History of the Ruling Party of Czechoslovakia* (Stanford, Calif.: Stanford University Press, 1981), 161–162.
169. See, for example, the dispatches dated 14 Sept. 1939, 16 Oct. 1939, 10 Mar. 1940, and 13 Mar. 1940, in Bareš, "Depeše," 392, 396, 411, 412.
170. Raška, *The Czechoslovak Exile Government,* 38–39.
171. Ibid., 36–42, quotation from 42. Also Kural, *Vlastenci,* 75–76.
172. Letter to Votja Beneš, 4 Feb. 1940, *Dopisy,* 34.
173. Quotations from Vondrová, *Češi,* doc. 39, 78; Raška, *The Czechoslovak Exile Government,* 44; and Vondrová, *Češi,* doc 40, 79.
174. Brandes, *Der Weg,* 83–84; Raška, *The Czechoslovak Exile Government,* 44.
175. Vondrová, *Češi,* doc. 45, 82.
176. Kural, *Vlastenci,* 77. See also Brandes, *Der Weg,* 86–87.
177. Raška, *The Czechoslovak Exile Government,* 44, 51.
178. SD-PE-15-March-1940, 7.
179. [No author], *Český kurýr,* 31 Dec. 1940, HIWRP Library, 1.
180. Lagebericht, Office of the Reich Protector, September 1940, NA, ÚŘP, k. 279, sign. I-1a 1803 (Grüppe Mähren), 9.
181. Brandes, *Die Tschechen,* 1:180.
182. Verwaltungsbericht, OLR Proßnitz, February 1940, NA, ÚŘP, k. 283, sign. I-1a 1804 (Prostějov), 7; Verwaltungsbericht, OLR Proßnitz, March 1940, NA, ÚŘP, k. 283, sign. I-1a 1804 (Prostějov), 7.

3. Plans to Make the Czechs German

1. Martin Broszat, "Die völkische Ideologie und der Nationalsozialismus," *Deutsche Rundschau* 1 (Jan. 1958): 58.
2. Cornelia Berning, *Vom "Abstammungsnachweis" zum "Zuchtwart": Vokabular des Nationalsozialismus* (Berlin: De Gruyter, 1964), 191. See also Ulrich Herbert, "'Generation der Sachlichkeit': Die völkische Studetenbewegung der frühen zwanziger Jahre," in *Arbeit, Volkstum, Weltanschauung: Über Fremde und Deutsche im 20. Jahrhundert* (Frankfurt: Fischer, 1995), 42–45.
3. Broszat, "Die völkische Ideologie," 56, 59, 58; Berning, *Vom "Abstam-*

mungsnachweis," 191; Herbert, "'Generation,'" 46. On representations of the Führer, see Ian Kershaw, *The "Hitler Myth": Image and Reality in the Third Reich* (New York: Oxford University Press, 1987).

4. Ernest Gellner, *Nations and Nationalism* (Oxford: Blackwell, 1983). For a discussion of the word "Volksgemeinschaft," see John Connelly, "The Uses of *Volksgemeinschaft:* Letters to the NSDAP Kreisleitung Eisenach, 1939–1940," *JMH* 68, 4 (Dec. 1996): 899–930.

5. Vejas Gabriel Liulevicius, *War Land on the Eastern Front* (Cambridge: Cambridge University Press, 2000), 253–254; Woodruff D. Smith, *The Ideological Origins of Nazi Imperialism* (New York: Oxford University Press, 1986), 83–94, 146–152; Charles Kruszewski, "International Affairs: Germany's Lebensraum," *American Political Science Review* 34, no. 5 (Oct. 1940): 964–975; Werner J. Cahnman, "The Concept of Raum and the Theory of Regionalism," *American Sociological Review* 9, no. 5 (Oct. 1944): 455–462.

6. Liulevicius, *War Land,* 251.

7. First published in 1926, Grimm's novel sold 315,000 copies by 1935. He never used the word "Lebensraum" and, unlike Hitler and most Nazis, believed that overflow space was to be found outside Europe, specifically in the African colonies; Grimm did bring to the public ideas about political space and the vocabulary of geopolitics. Hans Grimm, *Volk ohne Raum* (Munich: A. Langen / G. Müller, 1935, [1926]); Smith, *The Ideological Origins,* 224–230. Quotations from Adolf Hitler in Gerhard L. Weinberg, ed., *Hitler's Second Book,* trans. Krista Smith (New York: Enigma, 2003), 28; Cornelia Schmitz-Berning, *Vokabular des Nationalsozialismus* (Berlin: Walter de Gruyter, 1998), 279; and Ian Kershaw, *Hitler, 1936–45: Nemesis* (New York: W. W. Norton, 2000), 168.

8. Schmitz-Berning, *Vokabular,* 279.

9. On German stereotypes of Poles, including the quotation from Max Weber, see John Connelly, "Nazis and Slavs: From Racial Theory to Racist Practice," *CEH* 32, no. 1 (1999): 23. See also Smith *The Ideological Origins,* 103. On the Pan-German League, see Roger Chickering, *We Men Who Feel Most German: A Cultural Study of the Pan-German League, 1886–1914* (Boston: Allen & Unwin, 1984); and R. W. Tims, *Germanizing Prussian Poland: The H-K-T Society and the Struggle for the Eastern Marches in the German Empire, 1894–1918* (New York: Columbia University Press, 1941). On prewar settlement schemes, see Smith, *The Ideological Origins,* 106–107; Philipp Ther, "A Century of Forced Migration: The Origins and Consequences of 'Ethnic Cleansing,'" in Phillip Ther and Ana Slijak, eds., *Ethnic Cleansing in East-Central Europe, 1944–1948* (Lanham, Md.: Rowman & Littlefield, 2001), 48. On resettlement plans during World War I, see Hans Mommsen, "Der 'Ostraum' in Ideologie und Politik des

Nationalsozialismus," *Von Weimar nach Auschwitz: Zur Geschichte Deutschlands in der Weltkriegsepoche* (Stuttgart: Deutsche Verlags-Anstalt, 1999), 283–294, 286; and R. L. Koehl, "Colonialism inside Germany: 1886–1918," *JMH* 25, no. 3 (Sept. 1953): 255–272.

10. Vahakn N. Dadrian, *German Responsibility in the Armenian Genocide: A Review of the Historical Evidence of German Complicity* (Watertown, Mass.: Blue Crane Books, 1996), esp. 199. Hitler's pronouncement is found in *Akten zur deutschen auswärtigen Politik*, ser. D, vol. 7 (Baden-Baden: Impr. nationale), doc. 193, n. 1, 171. My thanks to Margaret Lavinia Anderson for providing me with this citation. See also Gerhard L. Weinberg, *A World at Arms: A Global History of World War II* (Cambridge: Cambridge University Press, 1994), 59.

11. On Hitler's invocation of the Lausanne Treaty, see Joseph B. Schechtman, *European Population Transfers, 1939–1945* (New York: Oxford University Press, 1946), 16–22. On views of the East and the legacies of World War I, see Liulevicius, *War Land*, 251; and Alexander B. Rossino, *Hitler Strikes Poland: Blitzkrieg, Ideology, and Atrocity* (Lawrence: University Press of Kansas, 2003), 5–8. On the uses of "science," see Michael Burleigh, *Germany Turns Eastwards: A Study of Ostforschung in the Third Reich* (Cambridge: Cambridge University Press, 1988).

12. Herbert, "'Generation der Sachlichkeit,'" 42, 43. See also Michael Wildt, *Generation of the Unbound: The Leadership Corps of the Reich Security Main Office* (Jerusalem: Yad Vashem, 2002). Quotation from Mommsen, "Der 'Ostraum,'" 288.

13. Brigitte Hamann, *Hitler's Vienna: A Dictator's Apprenticeship*, trans. Thomas Thorton (New York: Oxford University Press, 1999), 304–324. For Hitler's views of the Czechs, see also Tönsmayer, *Das Dritte Reich*, 40–41.

14. *Documents on German Foreign Policy: From the Archives of the German Foreign Ministry*, ser. D, vol. 1 (Washington, D.C.: GPO, 1949), doc. 19, 29–39, esp. 36. Or, as Gerhard Weinberg writes: "In his speech of September 26, 1938, Hitler had proclaimed to the world: 'Wir wollen keine Tschechen.' We really don't want any Czechs. As we now know, by that he meant not what most listeners assumed, namely that he wanted only the portion of Czechoslovakia inhabited by Germans, but rather that he expected to seize all of Bohemia and expel its Czech population." *Germany, Hitler, and World War II: Essays in Modern German and World History* (Cambridge: Cambridge University Press, 1995), 120.

15. Schechtman, *European Population Transfers*, 266; Isabel Heinemann, *"Rasse, Siedlung, Blut": Das Rasse- & Siedlungshauptamt der SS und die rassenpolitische Neuordnung Europas* (Göttingen: Wallstein, 2003), 128.

16. Elizabeth Wiskemann, "Partitioned Czechoslovakia," in Arnold Toynbee

and Veronica M. Toynbee, eds., *Hitler's Europe* (London: Oxford University Press, 1954), 585.

17. Ian Kershaw, *Hitler, 1936–1945: Nemesis* (New York: W. W. Norton, 2000), 164.

18. Christopher Browning with Jürgen Matthäus, *The Origins of the Final Solution: The Evolution of Nazi Jewish Policy, September 1939–March 1942* (Lincoln: University of Nebraska Press, 2004), 28. For a thoughtful and concise discussion of Hitler's decision to attack Poland, see Rossino, *Hitler*, 5.

19. Kershaw, *Hitler, 1936–1945*, 172; Wiskemann, "Partitioned Czechoslovakia," 585.

20. Heinemann, *"Rasse,"* 131–140, and Miloš Hořejš, "Pozemkovy Úřad,' in *Encyklopedie českych dějin 1938–1948* (Prague: Libra, forthcoming 2007). During the occupation the Land Office confiscated sixteen thousand holdings totaling 550,000 hectares (1,359,000 acres) for future German settlers. The office appropriated 80,000 hectares (197,680 acres) for military bases whose land would be settled by German settlers after the war. Alice Teichová, "Instruments of Economic Control and Exploitation: The German Occupation of Bohemia and Moravia," in Richard Overy, Gerhard Otto, and Johannes ten Cate, eds., *Die "Neuordnung" Europas: NS-Wirtschaftspolitik in den besetzten Gebieten* (Berlin: Metropol, 1997), 104. On the construction of army bases that would later become German settlements, see Karel Fremund, "Dokumenty o nacistické vyhlazovací politice," *SAP* 13, no. 2 (1963): doc. 9, 24–25.

21. Heinemann, *"Rasse,"* 142, 147–150. Hitler's note to Neurath is reproduced in *AOP*, doc. 22, 72–23.

22. Browning, *The Origins*, 8, 35, 17. See also see also Dieter Schenk, *Hitlers Mann in Danzig: Albert Forster und die NS-Verbrechen in Danzig-Westpreußen* (Bonn: Dietz, 2000), 145–169; and Rossino, *Hitler*, 58–120.

23. Norman Rich, *Hitler's War Aims: Ideology, the Nazi State, and the Course of Expansion* (New York: W. W. Norton, 1973), 73–74.

24. Götz Aly, *"Final Solution": Nazi Population Policy and the Murder of the European Jews* (London: Arnold, 1999). 19.

25. Clifton J. Child, "Germany, 1939–1945," *Hitler's Europe*, 75. The German agency *Reichskommissar für die Festigung deutschen Volkstums*, is described in detail in Robert Koehl, *RKFDV: German Resettlement and Population Policy, 1939–1945* (Cambridge, Mass.: Harvard University Press, 1957). On Heydrich's role in expulsion and resettlement plans, see Aly, *"Final Solution,"* 8.

26. Browning, *The Origins*, 49. On the Reich German exodus to the incorporated Polish territories, see David Bruce Furber, "Going East: Colonialism and German Life in Nazi-Occupied Poland" (Ph.D. diss., State University

of New York at Buffalo, 2003), 144–193; and Elizabeth Harvey, *Women and the Nazi East: Agents and Witnesses of Germanization* (New Haven, Conn.: Yale University Press, 2003), esp. 87–90.

27. Heinemann, *"Rasse,"* 230–232.
28. On the Jihlava incident, see Verwaltungsbericht, OLR Iglau, NA, ÚŘP, k. 280, sign. I-1a 1803 (Jihlava), 16–17. On Eichmann's Nisko operation, see Miroslav Kárný, *"Konečné řešení": Genocida českých židů v německé protektorátní politice* (Prague: Academia, 1991), 39–47; and Browning, *The Origins,* 36–43.
29. Browning, *Origins,* 41–43.
30. German officials deported to the General Government "only" 14,322 people from Upper Silesia and 30,758 people from Danzig–West Prussia. Czesław Madajczyk, *Die Okkupationspolitik Nazideutchlands in Polen 1939–1945* (Berlin: Akademie-Verlag, 1987), table 15. See also Heinemann, *"Rasse,"* 225; Koehl, *RKFDV,* 73.
31. Browning, *The Origins,* 48.
32. Browning, *The Origins,* 49, 50, 54–56; Valdis Lumans, *Himmler's Auxiliaries: The Volksdeutsche Mittelstelle and the German Minorities of Europe, 1933–1945* (Chapel Hill: University of North Carolina Press, 1993), 186–189; Phillip Rutherford, "Race, Space and the 'Polish Question': Nazi Deportation Policy in Reichsgau Wartheland, 1939–1941" (Ph.D diss., Pennsylvania State University, 2001), 143–156; and Richard Overy, *Goering: The "Iron Man"* (London: Routledge & Kegan Paul, 1984), 118–119. Quotation from Aly, *"Final Solution,"* 59.
33. Browing, *The Origins,* 81–89.
34. Ibid., 69–70, 109.
35. Aly, *"Final Solution,"* 99–100; Browning, *The Origins,* 90.
36. Introduction to *AOP,* xxi–xxii.
37. Czesław Madajczyk, "Hiterlovská okupácie vo svetle porovnávacich výskumov," *Historický časopis,* 24, no. 3 (1976): 349; Robert Gies, "Das Einsatzreferat für die Volkstumsarbeit beim Höheren SS- und Polizeiführer," 5 Feb. 1940, in Boris Čelovský, ed., *So oder so: Řešení české otázky podle německých documentů, 1933–1945* (Ostrava: Sfinga, 1997), 246; "Einsatz altreichsdeutscher Hochschüler zur Volkstumsarbeit in den Sprachinseln," Gruppe I 1, I b-3998, NA, ÚŘP, k. 295, sign. I-1b 2304, quotation from 1.
38. SD-PE-1940, 9–10; Verwaltungsbericht, OLR Brünn, 19 Oct. 1940, NA, ÚŘP, k. 292, sign. I-1b 2200, 1; Gruppe I 1 to Gruppe II 4, [no date], NA, ÚŘP, k. 292, sign. I-1b 220, 1. See also *AOP,* doc. 51, 126–128. On proposals for "population bridges," see "Volkstumsarbeit der Oberlandräte," 7 March 1940, NA, ÚŘP, k. 287, sign. 2000, 2–3; Detlef Brandes, *Die*

Tschechen unter deutschem Protektorat, vol. 1 (Munich: R. Oldenbourg, 1969), 169.

39. Petr Němec, "Germanizační politika nacistů v Protektorátě Čechy a Morava, 1939–1945" (Ph.D. diss., Masarykova University, 1990), 187; Fremund, "Dokumenty," doc. 8, 23–24; Shiela Grant Duff, *A German Protectorate: The Czechs under Nazi Rule* (London: Macmillan, 1942), 140, 202–203; *AOP,* doc. 69, 162–165.

40. "Umsiedlungsfürsorge—Unterbringungen von Bessarabisch-Deutschen in den Bezirken Klattau und Budweis," 16 Sept. 1940, NA, ÚŘP, k. 290, sign. I-1b 2110, 1; Oberlandrat Budweis to Reichsprotektor, 19 Sept. 1940, NA, ÚŘP, k. 290, sign. I-1b 2110, 1.

41. Rolf-Dieter Müller, *Hitlers Ostkrieg und die deutsche Siedlungspolitik* (Frankfurt: Fischer, 1991), 86.

42. Schechtman, *European Population Transfers,* 38.

43. Ulrich Herbert, *Hitler's Foreign Workers: Enforced Labor in Germany under the Third Reich,* trans. William Templer (Cambridge: Cambridge University Press, 1997), 298.

44. Wolfgang Benz, "Der Generalplan Ost: Germanisierungspolitik in den besetzten Ostgebieten," *Herrschaft und Gesellschaft im nationalsozialistischen Staat: Studien zur Struktur- und Mentalitatgeschichte* (Frankfurt: Fischer, 1990), 79. Similarly, Phillip Rutherford argues that by 1940 economic necessities, in particular the need for Polish labor, forced Nazi leaders to rethink their expulsion and resettlement plans in incorporated Poland. See especially "Race," 303–327.

45. Hitler's comments from *Mein Kampf* cited in Hamann, *Hitler's Vienna,* 323; and in Weinberg, *Hitler's Second Book,* 49, 53. See also Rossino, *Hitler,* 3–4.

46. Quotation from Browning, *The Origins,* 69. A full version of the document is reprinted in *Vierteljahrshefte für Zeitgeschichte* 5 (1957): 196–198. On Nazi plans for Poland's smaller minorities, which Himmler called "splintered nations," see also the testimony of SS Reich Commissariat for the Strengthening of Germandom officer Ulrich Greifelt, *TWS,* vol. 4, 743–745.

47. Heineman, *"Rasse,"* 283.

48. *IMT,* vol. 31, doc. 2916-PS, 290–294. See also Aly, *"Final Solution,"* 99; and Heinemann, *"Rasse,"* 262.

49. Doc. 3859-PS, *IMT,* vol. 33, 267.

50. Doc. 3859-PS, *IMT,* vol. 33, 255. See also Hitler's December 1939 statement to this effect in *AOP,* doc. 22, 72–73.

51. Petr Němec, "Český národ a nacistická teorie germanizace prostoru," *ČČH* (1990): 538; *AOP,* xxxiv.

52. Václav Král, ed., *Lesson from History: Documents concerning Nazi Policies*

for Germanization and Extermination in Czechoslovakia (Prague: Orbis, 1960), doc. 6, 60.

53. Vojtech Mastny, *The Czechs under Nazi Rule: The Failure of National Resistance, 1939–1942* (New York: Columbia University Press, 1971), 133. Verwaltungsbericht, OLR Pilsen, March 1940, NA, ÚŘP, k. 90, sign. I-1b 2021, 1.

54. See, for example, the memorandum of July 12, 1939, sent to the Reich Protector's Office by General Erich Friderici, the top army official in the Protectorate, which declared that Nazi Germany could "spatially and spiritually" absorb the Czech nation by raising workers' wages and deporting the Czech intelligentsia to the Reich. *AOP*, doc. 13, 49–56.

55. Eduard Kubů, "Die Bedeutung des deutschen Blutes im Tschechentum: Der 'wissenschaftspädagogische' Beitrag des Soziologen Karl Valentin Müller zur Lösung des Problems der Germanisierung Mitteleuropas," *Boh* 45, no. 1 (2004): 93–114; Alena Míšková, *Německá (Karlova) univerzita od Mnichova k 9. květnu 1945* (Prague: Karolinum, 2002), 99–104, 249; Mastny, *The Czechs,* 130; Fremund, "Dokumenty," doc. 5, 18; Karel Fremund, "Heydrichova nadace—důležitý nástroj nacistické vyhlazovací politiky," *SAP* 14, no. 1 (1964): 14. See also Müller's "Zur Rassen- und Gesellschaftsbiologie des Industriearbeiters," *Archiv für Rassen und Gesellschaftsbiologie* 29 (1935); and "Die Bedeutung des deutschen Blutes in Südosteuropa," *Südostdeutsche Forschungen* (1938–1939). For pre-1940 suggestions that Czechs could be made into Germans, see K. Räubler, "Tschechisiertes deutsches Land in Innerböhmen," *Auslandsdeutsche Volksforschung* (1938): 61; and remarks made by the Protectorate's highest-ranking military officer, General Erich Friderici, in 1939, in *AOP,* doc. 13, 53.

56. Karl Valentin Müller, "Zur sozialanthropologischen Bedeutung der Umvolkungsvorgänge im Sudetenraum," *Deutsche Volksforschung in Böhmen und Mähren* 1, no. 1 (1939): 30–51, quotations from 34, 37.

57. Fremund, "Dokumenty," 19. In the May 1940 issue of *Deutsche Volksforschung Böhmen und Mähren,* for example, there were three articles on "national geography": "Volkstumsgeographie in den Sudetenländern," "Volkstumsgeographische Forschungsaufgaben im Kreis Teplitz-Schönau," and "Versuch einer Volksgrenzbeschreibung."

58. Verwaltungsbericht, OLR Proßnitz, May 1940, NA, ÚŘP, k. 287, sign. I-1b 2000; Verwaltungsbericht, OLR Olmütz, April 1940, NA, ÚŘP, k. 287, sign. I-1b 2000, 5.

59. Doc. 3859-PS, *IMT,* vol. 33, 256, 261.

60. Dr. W. Gross, Reichshauptamtsleiter, Leiter des Rassenpolitischen Amtes to Reich Protector's Office, 13 Apr. 1940, NA, ÚŘP, dodatky II, NSDAP, sign. směrnice 1940, 3, 3–4.

61. Otto Reche, "Leitsätze zur bevölkerungspolitischen Sicherung des deutschen Ostens," 24 Sept. 1939, in Mechtild Rössler and Sabine Schleiermacher, eds., *Der "Generalplan Ost": Hauptlinien der nationalsozialistischen Planungs- und Vernichtungspolitik* (Berlin: Akademie, 1993), doc. 10, 270–293.

62. Jan Rataj, *O autoritativní národní stát: Ideologické proměny české politiky v druhé republice, 1938–1939* (Prague, 1997), 149–151.

63. On Spann's influence within Sudeten German circles, see Andreas Luh, *Der Deutsche Turnverband in der Ersten Tschechoslowakischen Republik: Vom völkischen Vereinsbetrieb zur volkspolitischen Bewegung* (Munich: R. Oldenbourg, 1988), esp. 234–235. See also Othmar Spann, *Vom Wesen des Volkstums: Was ist deutsch?* (Eger: Böhmerland-Verlag, 1920).

64. Quotations from SD-PE-1940, 2; and Brandes, *Die Tschechen,* 1:159.

65. "Budweiser Rede," 30 June 1939, NA, ÚŘP, k. 290, sign. I-1b 2020. A condensed version of the speech can be found in *AOP,* doc. 11, 37–38. On Frank wanting to expel the Czech intelligentsia, see Vojtech Mastny, *The Czechs under Nazi Rule: The Failure of National Resistance, 1939–1942* (New York: Columbia University Press, 1971), 112.

66. Josef Čejka et al., eds., *Zločiny nacistů za okupace a osvobozenecký boj našeho lidu* (Prague: Rudé právo, 1961), doc. 2, 157. See also Brandes, *Die Tschechen,* 1:134; and Mastny, *The Czechs,* 127.

67. Němec, "Germanizační politika nacistů," 185; "Deutschtumsprogram für das Jahr 1941," ÚŘP, NA, k. 290, sign. 2090, 1.

68. Brandes, *Die Tschechen,* 1:124–126.

69. Václav Král, *Die Deutschen in der Tschechoslowakei 1933–1947: Dokumentensammlung* (Prague: Československá akademie věd, 1964), doc. 307, 404.

70. Dr. Hugo Jury, NARA, RG 242, BDC Microfilm, SSO SS Officer Dossier, A3343, roll SSO-145A; Petr Němec, "Gauleiter Dr. Hugo Jury and sein Wirken im Protektorat Böhmen und Mähren," in Thomas Winkelbauer, ed., *Kontakte und Konflikte: Böhmen, Mähren und Österreich: Aspekte eines Jahrtausends gemeinsamer Geschichte* (Waidhofen an der Thaya: Waldviertler Heimatbund, 1993), 471.

71. *AOP,* xxiii–xxiv, doc. 2, 12, and doc. 22, 72–72; Brandes, *Die Tschechen,* 1:33; Mastny, *The Czechs,* 125; Volker Zimmermann, *Die Sudetendeutschen im NS-Staat. Politik und Stimmung der Bevölkerung im Reichsgau Sudetenland (1938–1945)* (Essen: Klartext, 1999), 139–142.

72. Němec, "Gauleiter Dr. Hugo Jury," 472; Hugo Jury, "Die NSDAP in Böhmen und Mähren," *Böhmen und Mähren* 9 (Nov. 1940): 286.

73. *AOP,* doc. 95, 251–252.

74. Mastny, *The Czechs,* 126; Němec, "Gauleiter Dr. Hugo Jury," 470. Jury's memorandum is reprinted in *AOP,* doc. 98, 281–285. On Jury's intentions to send his report to Berlin, see "Aus dem Bericht von Kurt Ziemke an die

Abteilung Deutschland im Auswärtigen Amt vom 19. August 1940 über Pläne zur Aufteilung von Böhmen und Mähren unter deutsche 'Reichsgaue,'" in Helma Kaden, ed., *Die faschistische Okkupationspolitik in Österreich und der Tschechoslowakei (1938–1945)* ([East] Berlin: Deutscher Verlag der Wissenschaften, 1998), doc. 74, 149–150. Bormann was a member of Hitler's inner circle and one of the few Nazi officials in Berlin with direct and consistent access to the Führer. He was chief of the Office of the Deputy of the Führer from 1933 to 1941, head of the Party Chancellery from 1941 to 1945, and Hitler's personal secretary from 1943 to 1945. Rich, *Hitler's War Aims,* 436. On warnings about a "Czech reservation," see "Rückwanderung (Ausweisungen) von Tschechen aus dem Sudetengau und der Slowakei in das Protektorat—heutige Grundsätze der Volkstumspolitik im Protektorat," Vermerk by IIa, 12 Apr. 1940, NA, ÚŘP, k. 292, sign. 2210, 3.

75. Doc. 3859-PS, *IMT,* vol. 33, 253, 256–259, 264–266. See also Neurath's comments during the Nuremberg Trials *IMT,* vol. 17, 95.

76. Der Wehrmachtsbevollmächtige beim Reichsprotektor in Böhmen und Mähren, "Grundsätze der Politik in Protektorat," 15 Oct. 1940, NARA, RG 238, NG ser., T988, roll 15. See also Král, *Lesson,* doc. 12, 80–81.

77. Němec, "Gauleiter Dr. Hugo Jury," 471, n. 6.

78. Rich, *Hitler's War Aims,* 29; Werner Jochmann ed., *Monologe im Führerhauptquartier 1941–1944: Adolf Hitler: Die Aufzeichnungen Heinrich Heims* (Hamburg: A. Knaus, 1980), 227–228, 244; Connelly, "Nazis and Slavs," 2.

79. *Zločiny,* doc. 2, after 156. The document, which Heydrich prepared for Lammers, Bormann, and RuSHA chief Otto Hofmann, is also discussed in Charles Sydnor, "Executive Instinct: Reinhard Heydrich and the Planning for the Final Solution," in Michael Berenbaum and Abraham J. Peck, eds., *The Holocaust and History: The Known, the Unknown, the Disputed, and the Reexamined* (Bloomington: Indiana University Press, 1998), 173 and 183, n. 82.

80. Dr. Walter König-Beyer, "Denkschrift über das rassenpolitischen Verhältnis des böhmish-mährischen Raumes und dessen Neugestaltung," 1940, NA, ÚŘP dodatky II, Rassenamt č. 13 (RuSHA).

81. *Zločiny,* doc. 2, 2.

82. Der Wehrmachtsbevollmächtige beim Reichsprotektor in Böhmen und Mähren, "Grundsätze der Politik im Protektorat," 15 Oct. 1940, NARA, RG 238, NG T988, roll 15.

83. "Mitwirkung der Verwaltung bei der Vorbereitung der Germanisierung (Umvolkung) im Protektorat Böhmen und Mähren," December 1940, NA, ÚŘP, k. 287, sign. I-1b 2000, 1, 8.

84. Ibid., 1.

85. I 1b-3881, [no title], 11 June 1941, NA, ÚŘP, k. 292, sign. I-1b 2140, 1, 2. See also I 10 Nr. E I Sch. 1—185/40 to OLR Brünn, 10 Jan. 1941, SOAP, OLR Kolín, k. 3, [no sign.].

86. *AOP,* doc. 73, 174.

87. See, for example, the constant references to "small-scale national work" in Office of the Reich Protector, Lagebericht, November 1940, NA, ÚŘP, k. 279, sign. I-1a 1803 (Gruppe Mähren), 1–3.

88. [No author], Zprávy politické," 11 Jan. 1941, VHA, fond 37, sign. 91/4, 2.

89. Heinemann, *"Rasse,"* 226–227.

90. Browning, *The Origins,* 99–101, quotation from 110. Also Schenk, *Hitlers Mann,* 179.

91. [No author], Zprávy politické," 11 Jan. 1941, VHA, fond 37, sign. 91/4, 2; [no author], "Zprávy politické," 21 Jan. 1941, VHA, fond 37, sign. 91/4, 1.

92. [No author], "Zprávy politické," 11 Jan. 1941, VHA, fond 37, sign. 91/4, 4.

93. Václav Kural, *Vlastenci proti okupaci: Ústřední vedení odboje domácího, 1940–1943* (Prague: Ústav mezinárodních vztahů, 1997), 103, 123, 128–129; Brandes, *Die Tschechen,* 1:200; and Mastny, *The Czechs,* 168. On Thümmel, with a detailed interpretation of his disputed loyalties and his often overstated importance to Czechoslovak intelligence, see Jaroslav Kokoška and Stanislav Kokoška, *Spor o Agenta A-54: Kapitoly z dějin československé zpravodajské služby* (Prague: Naše vojsko, 1994).

94. Mastny, *The Czechs,* 170.

95. On the sharing of intelligence, see Kural, *Vlastenci,* 78–79, 120; Mastny, *The Czechs,* 167, 168; "Zpráva do Prahy," 12 July 1941, HIWRP, ÚVOD, k. 1, 38. On the Soviet and British recognition of Beneš's government, see Kural, *Vlastenci,* 133; Mastny, *The Czechs,* 171.

96. Mastny, *The Czechs,* 171–173, 175–176, quotation from 177; Kural, *Vlastenci,* 134–136.

97. Miroslav Kárný, "Hlavní rysy okupační politiky Reinharda Heydricha," introduction to *PPRH,* 289. Quotations from ONH, doc. 23, 332; and Kural, *Vlastenci,* 144. See also Jiří Doležal and Jan Křen, eds., *Czechoslovakia's Fight: Documents on the Resistance Movement of the Czechoslovak People, 1938–1945* (Prague: Publishing House of the Czechoslovak Academy of Sciences, 1964), doc. 15, 42–44.

98. ONH, doc. 44, 361; Brandes, *Die Tschechen,* 1:205. Kárný, "Hlavní rysy," 291. ONH, doc. 25, 339. See also Tätigkeitsbericht Nr. 31, Der Befehlshaber der Ordnungspolizei in Böhmen und Mähren, 4 Sept. 1941, NA, ÚŘP, k. 286, sign. I-1a 1818, 3–4.

99. ONH, doc. 3, 309.

100. ONH, doc. 22, 360, doc. 41, 357, doc. 23, 237, and doc. 3, 310; Brandes, *Die Tschechen,* 1:204.

101. [No author], "Zpráva z Prahy přes Istanbul," 3 Oct. 1941, JS, k. 11, Reports from Czechoslovakia, 1941, folder 1, 1; ONH, doc. 23, 328; "Zpráva z Prahy," 6 Aug. 1941, JS, k. 11, Reports from Czechoslovakia, 1941, folder 2, 1; Albert Kaufmann, "Zpráva z domova," VHA, fond 37, sign. 91/6, 2; Albert Schmidt, "Pax Germanica: Bohemia and Moravia under Heydrich, 1941–1942" (Ph.D. diss., Brandeis University, 2000), 106, n. 340. On Goebbels's *V* campaign, see Zbyněk Zeman, *Heckling Hitler: Caricatures of the Third Reich* (Hanover, N.H.: University Press of New England, 1987), 112; Josef Gruss, *Jedna paní povídala* (Prague: Alois Hynek, 1945), 40. For Wilhelm Dennler's observation, see *Die böhmische Passion* (Freiburg: Dikreiter Verlagsgesellschaft, 1953), 99. Although related in the present tense, Dennler actually wrote of these events after the war.

102. Tomáš Pasák, *Soupis legálních novin, časopisů a úředních věstníků v českých zemích z let 1939–1945* (Prague: Univerzita Karlova, 1980), 62; Kural, *Vlastenci,* 154; Brandes, *Die Tschechen,* 1:205; Mastny, *The Czechs,* 179.

103. ONH, doc. 53, 381–382.

104. [No author], "Zpráva ze dne 14. září 1941," JS, k. 12, Reports from Czechoslovakia, 1941, folder 2, 1; "Zpráva z Prahy přes Istanbul," 3 Oct. 1941, JS, k. 11, Reports from Czechoslovakia, 1941, folder 1, 1. See also "Zpráva z domova," 17 Sept. 1941, JS, k. 11, Reports from Czechoslovakia, 1941, folder 1, 1.

105. "Zprávy z domova," 16 Jan. 1941, JS, box 11, Reports from Czechoslovakia, 1941, folder 1, 2.

106. Mastny, *The Czechs,* 178.

107. Lagebericht, Office of the Reich Protector, May 1941, NA, ÚŘP, k. 279, sign. I-1a 1803 (Gruppe Mähren), 11–12, 16–18; [no author], Lagebericht, Office of the Reich Protector, June 1941, NA, ÚŘP, k. 279, sign. I-1a 1803 (Gruppe Mähren), 10–13; "Zprávy hospodářské," 21 Jan. 1941, VHA, fond 37, sign. 91/4, 1; [no author], "Zprávy hospodařské," 15 Jan. 1941, VHA, fond 37, sign. 91/4, 1; also [no author], "Zprávy hospodářské," 11 Jan. 1941, VHA, fond 37, sign. 91/4, 1; [no author], "Zprávy z domova z ledna 1941," 20 May 1941, JS, k. 11, Reports from Czechoslovakia, 1941, folder 2, 1; ONH, doc. 8, 314; Brandes, *Die Tschechen,* 1:204–205; Mastny, *The Czechs,* 179.

108. Tätigkeitsbericht Nr. 31, Der Befehlshaber der Ordnungspolizei in Böhmen und Mähren, 4 Sept. 1941, NA, ÚŘP, k. 286, sign. I-1a 1818, 1. On the shortages becoming increasingly acute after the declaration of war with the Soviet Union, see also Tatigkeitsbericht Nr. 31, Der Befehlshaber der Ordnungspolizei in Böhmen und Mähren, 2 Aug. 1941, NA, ÚŘP, k. 286, I-1a 1818; and Tatigkeitsbericht Nr. 31, Der Befehlshaber der Ordnungspolizei in Böhmen und Mähren, 4 Oct. 1941, NA, ÚŘP, k. 286, I-1a

1818, 1929–1942; ONH, doc. 10, 316; doc. 13, 317–318, doc. 52, 381; doc. 46, 366–367; [no author], "Zprávy z Prahy přes Istanbul ze dne 3 října 1941," 3 Oct. 1941, JS, k. 11, Reports from Czechoslovakia, 1941, folder 3, 1; and Kárný, "Hlavní rysy," 289.

109. Peter Heumos, "'Dejte nám brambory, nebo bude revoluce!' Hladové nepokoje, stávky a masové protesty v českých zemích v odbobí 1914–1918," in Hans Mommsen, Dušan Kováč, and Jiří Malíř with Michaela Marková, eds., *První světová válka a vztahy mezi Čechy, Slováky a Němci* (Brno: Matice moravská v Brně, 2000), 207–232; Jan Havránek, "Politické represe a zásobovací potíže v českých zemích v letech 1914–1918," in *První světová válka,* 51; Ivan Šedivý, *Češi, české země a Velká válka 1914–1918* (Prague: Lidové noviny, 2001), 318–321. On shortages, strikes, and protests in Berlin and Vienna, respectively, see Belinda J. Davis, *Home Fires Burning: Food, Politics, and Everyday Life in World War I Berlin* (Chapel Hill: University of North Carolina Press, 2000); and Maureen Healy, *Vienna and the Fall of the Habsburg Empire: Total War and Everyday Life in World War I* (Cambridge: Cambridge University Press, 2004).

110. ONH, doc. 1; 307–308, doc. 5, 312–313, doc. 6, 313, doc. 7, 313–314.

111. [No author], "Zpráva z Prahy," 6 Aug. 1941, JS, k. 11, Reports from Czechoslovakia, 1941, folder 2, 2; [no author], "Zpráva z Prahy," 13 Sept. 1941, JS, k. 11, Reports from Czechoslovakia, 1941, folder 2, 2. On the Gestapo's interest in Czech graffiti, see also Kural, *Vlastenci,* 152.

112. Fuchs to Gruppe Mähren and Oberlandräte, 16 Sept. 1940, NA, ÚŘP, k. 90, sign. I-1 2020, 1–2. Fuchs to Befehlshaber der Sicherheitspolizei und den Leiter der Parteiverbindungsstelle beim Reichsprotektor im B. M., 23 Apr. 1941, NA, ÚŘP, k. 90, sign. I-1 2020, 1–2.

113. ONH, doc. 17, 320–321; also ibid., doc. 42, 357–358, doc. 43, 358–360; *AOP,* doc. 111, 343–344; Verwaltungsbericht, OLR Olmütz, 22 Aug. 1941, Zemský archiv v Opavě, pobočka Olomouc, Oberlandrat Olomouc, k. 5, inv. č. 5, 1.

114. [No author], "Zprávy politické," 10 Feb. 1941, VHA, fond 37, sign. 91/4, 2; Brandes, *Die Tschechen,* 1:207.

115. "*Das Protektorat Böhmen und Mähren im Deutschen Reich:* Erlebnisbericht des Oberlandrats in Iglau über die Zeit vom 15. März 1939 bis 15. Juli 1941," 30 Nov. 1979, BB, Ost-Dok 21, sign. 45, 8; Schmidt, "Pax Germanica," 38.

116. Brandes, *Die Tschechen,* 1:208.

117. ONH, doc. 56, 384–385; Schmidt, "Pax Germanica," 39.

118. ONH, 301–304.

119. Connelly, "Nazis and Slavs," 33.

120. *AOP,* doc. 9, 34.

4. Heydrich Imposes Racial Order

1. *PPRH*, doc. 9, 101, 102–103.
2. Ibid., 109–110, 104–105.
3. Reinhard Heydrich, NARA, RG 242, BDC Microfilm, SSO SS Officer Dossier, A3343, roll SSO-095A; Charles Sydnor, "Reinhard Heydrich: Der 'ideale Nationalsozialist," in Ronald Smelser and Enrico Syring, eds., *Die SS: Elite unter dem Totenkopf: 30 Lebensläufe* (Paderborn: Ferdinand Schöningh, 2000), 208–219; C. A. MacDonald, *The Killing of SS Obergruppenführer Reinhard Heydrich* (New York: Free Press, 1989), 3–44.
4. Quotations from MacDonald, *The Killing*, 19. See also Götz Aly and Karl Heinz Roth, *Die restlose Erfassung: Volkszählen, Identifizieren, Aussondern im Nationalsozialismus* (Berlin: Fischer, 2000), 63.
5. Hannah Arendt, *Eichmann in Jerusalem: A Report on the Banality of Evil* (New York: Penguin, 1994), 80.
6. Sydnor, "Reinhard Heydrich," 218.
7. Václav Kural, *Vlastenci proti okupaci: Ústřední vedení odboje domácího 1940–1943* (Prague: Ústav mezinárodních vztahů, 1997), 158, 156. On the number of people brought before summary courts, see Detlef Brandes, *Die Tschechen unter deutschem Protektorat*, vol. 1 (Munich: R. Oldenbourg, 1969), 212.
8. In addition, 1,487 Czechs accused of political crimes were sent to Auschwitz. Of these accused, 1,187 arrived between January and May 1942. Miroslav Kárný, "Hlavní rysy okupační politiky Reinharda Heydricha," introduction to *PPRH*, 28.
9. On Thümmel and ÚVOD's radio transmitters, see Kural, *Vlastenci*, 164–165; *PPRH*, doc. 33, 168–172, doc. 78, 248. On the fate of the democratic resistance and Sokol, see Brandes, *Die Tschechen*, 1:217. On the fate of the Communist resistance, see Brandes, *Die Tschechen*, 1:244. On strikes and sabotage, see Brandes, *Die Tschechen*, 1:249–250; and Kural, *Vlastenci*, 159.
10. "Zpráva českého učitele A. Merta ze severní Moravy," 6 May 1942, JS, k. 12, Reports from ČSR, 1942–1943, 11; Albert Kaufmann, "Zpráva z domova," 20 Apr. 1943, VHA, fond 37, sign. 91/6, 8.
11. Lib. & Ice, "Zprávy z Prahy ze dne 6. února 1942," JS, k. 12, Reports from ČSR, 1942–1943, 1; "Zpráva českého učitele A. Merta ze severní Moravy," 6 May 1942, JS, k. 12, Reports from ČSR, 1942–1943, 11. For the numbers arrested and Heydrich's "optical effects," see Brandes, *Die Tschechen*, 1:212.
12. On Heydrich's measures for workers, see Dana Severová, "Sociální politika nacistů v takzvaném Protektorátu v letech 1939–1945," *Dějiny socialistického Československa* 7 (1985): 184–190. Vojtech Mastny, *The Czechs*

under Nazi Rule: The Failure of National Resistance, 1939–1942 (New York: Columbia University Press, 1971), 194–195; Brandes, *Die Tschechen*, 1:230–231. For an analysis skeptical of how beneficial these measures actually were for the workers, see Kárný, "Hlavní rysy," 38–47. On grumbling about shortages, see Kárný, *PPRH*, doc. 68, 230–231, doc. 73, 236, and doc. 77, 244. Gross industrial production in constant prices rose by 23 percent from 1941 to 1942 in the Protectorate. It should be kept in mind, however, that this remarkable increase was also a result of the increased employment in heavy industry and shift time in 1942. J. Krejčí, "The Bohemian-Moravian War Economy," in M. C. Kaser and E. A. Radice, eds., *The Economic History of Eastern Europe, 1919–1975* (Oxford: Clarendon Press, 1986), 491, table 19.XXXVII.

13. Brandes, *Die Tschechen*, 1: 213–215; Mastny, *The Czechs*, 187–191; Kárný, "Hlavní rysy," 28–29.
14. Brandes, *Die Tschechen*, 1:224–225. See also Heydrich's letter to Bormann dated 18 May 1942. *PPRH*, doc. 79, 250. On Moravec, see Jiří Pernes, *Až nao dno zrady: Emanuel Moravec* (Prague: Themis, 1997).
15. Mastny, *The Czechs*, 197. See also Kural, *Vlastenci*, 156–157.
16. Mastny, *The Czechs*, 197–198.
17. Brandes, *Die Tschechen*, 1:216.
18. Christopher Browning with Jürgen Matthäus, *The Origins of the Final Solution: The Evolution of Nazi Jewish Policy, September 1939–March 1942* (Lincoln: University of Nebraska Press, 2004), 374.
19. Dieter Pohl, *Nationalsozialistische Judenverfolgung in Ostgalizien 1941–1944: Organisation und Durchführung eines staatlichen Massenverbrechens* (Munich: R. Oldenbourg, 1996), esp. 405. On the role of local actors in committing the atrocities, see Martin Dean, *Collaboration in the Holocaust: Crimes of the Local Police in Belorussia and Ukraine, 1941–44* (New York: St. Martin's Press, 2000); Bernhard Chiari, *Alltag hinter der Front: Besatzung, Kollaboration und Widerstand in Weißrussland 1941–1944* (Düsseldorf: Droste Verlag, 1998), 96–194.
20. Browning, *The Origins*, 309–314, first quotation on 309–310. For Göring's "authorization," which was most likely written by Heydrich, see *IMT*, 26, doc. 710-PS, 266–267; and the discussion in Browing, *Origins*, 315. The number of Jews murdered is from Jürgen Matthäus, "Operation Barbarossa and the Onset of the Holocaust, June-December 1941," in Browning, *The Origins*, 244.
21. Browning, *The Origins*, 327–329; quotations are from Browning, *The Origins*, 327; ibid., 328; *PPRH*, doc. 15, 132, and Browning, *The Origins*, 329; and Matthäus, "Operation Barbarossa," 302.
22. Browning, *The Origins*, 375–377.

23. *PPRH*, doc. 17, 137, doc. 16, 134; H. G. Adler, *Theresienstadt 1941–1945: Das Antlitz einer Zwangsgemeinschaft* (Tübingen: Mohr, 1960); Raul Hilberg, *The Destruction of the European Jews*, vol. 2 (New Haven: Yale University Press, 2003), 447–457. On the number of Jews in the Protectorate in summer 1941, see "Die jüdische Kultusgemeinde in Prag," [no date], HIWRP, folder ID 87026–10.V. On the number of arrivals at Terezín, see Raul Hilberg, *The Destruction*, 455.

24. 'Besprechungsprotokoll' der Wannsee-Konferenz vom 20. Januar 1942, angefertigt von Adolf Eichmann nach Instruktionen Reinhard Heydrichs," in Kurt Pätzold and Erika Schwartz, eds., *Tagesordnung: Judenmord: Die Wannsee Konferenz am 20. Januar 1942: Eine Dokumentation zur Organisation der "Endlösung"* (Berlin: Metropol, 1992), 103, 105.

25. Browning, *The Origins*, 410–414.

26. Ibid., 416–423; Matthäus, "Operation Barbarossa," 304. See also Henry Friedlander, *The Origins of Nazi Genocide: From Euthanasia to the Final Solution* (Chapel Hill: University of North Carolina Press, 1995).

27. Kárný, *"Konečné řešení,"* 153–154.

28. "Evidenz der Juden: Registrierung. Transporte," reproduced in Helena Krejčová, Jana Svobodová, and Anna Hyndráková, eds., *Židé v Protektorátu: Hlášení Židovské náboženské obce v roce 1942: Dokumenty* (Prague: Ústav pro soudobé dějiny AV ČR and Maxdorf, 1997), doc. 10, 167–168; Livia Rothkirchen, *The Jews of Bohemia and Moravia: Facing the Holocaust* (Lincoln: University of Nebraska Press, 2005), 126. For a complex discussion of the role of Jewish religious congregations in the deportations, see Rothkirchen, *The Jews*, 134–137.

29. Benjamin Frommer, "Retribution against Nazi Collaborators in Postwar Czechoslovakia" (Ph.D. diss., Harvard University, 1999), 129; Kárný, *"Konečné řešení,"* 20.

30. Hilberg, *The Destruction*, 2:179–180.

31. Rothkirchen, *The Jews*, 127.

32. Heda Kaufmannová, *Léta 1938–1945: Válečné vzpomínky* (Prague: Ústav pro soudobé dějiny, 1999), 104.

33. Helena Krejčová, "Židovská náboženská obec za války," in Helena Krejčová, Jana Svobodová, and Anna Hyndráková, eds., *Židé v Protektorátu. Hlášení židovské náboženské obce v roce 1942. Dokumenty* (Prague: Ústav pro soudobé dějiny AV ČR, 1997), 14.

34. On the number of Jews who survived in hiding, see Adler, *Theresienstadt*, 15. On Czechs who sheltered Jews, see Rothkirchen, *The Jews*, 216–232. For chilling depictions of life in hiding, see Arnošt Lustig, "The Return," in *Night and Hope*, trans. George Theiner (Evanston, IL.: Northwestern Uni-

versity Press, 1985): 11–59; Jiří Weil, *Life with a Star,* trans. Růžena Ko-vaříková with Roslyn Schloss (New York: Farrar Straus & Giroux, 1989); and Jiří Daníček, ed., *Deník Otta Wolfa 1942–1945* (Prague: Sefer, 1997).

35. Kárný, *"Konečné řešení,"* 30–31; Hilberg, *The Destruction,* 1:72, 434–447.

36. Rothkirchen, *The Jews,* 130.

37. Pätzold and Schwartz, *Tagesordnung,* 108–110; and Hilberg, *The Destruction,* 2:436–439. On the struggle to define Mischlinge, and the debates about their fate, see also Claudia Koonz, *The Nazi Conscience* (Cambridge, Mass.: Belknap Press, 2003), 163–189; and Jeremy Noakes, "The Development of Nazi Policy towards the German-Jewish 'Mischlinge,' 1933–1945," *Leo Baeck Institute Year Book* 34 (1989): 291–354. On the discussion about Mischlinge at Wannsee in particular, see Pätzold and Schwartz, *Tagesordnung,* 71–73; Christian Gerlach, "The Wannsee Conference, the Fate of the German Jews, and Hitler's Decision in Principle to Exterminate All European Jews," *JMH* 70, no. 4 (1998): 777–780; Mark Roseman, *The Wannsee Conference and the Final Solution: A Reconsideration* (New York: Henry Holt and Company, 2002), 143–148.

38. Isabel Heinemann, *"Rasse, Siedlung, Blut": Das Rasse- & Siedlungshauptamt der SS und die rassenpolitische Neuordnung Europas* (Göttingen: Wallstein, 2003), 174.

39. At Wannsee, and later, Heydrich and other Nazi officials struggled with the question of Jews married to "Aryan" Czechs and Germans. In the Protectorate these "close kin of Aryans" had to register with Nazi authorities on October 27, 1942, and were subjected to smaller food rations. Although no concrete numbers are available, Nazi authorities appear to have deported most of the Jewish spouses to Terezín in January and February of 1945. Livia Rothkirchen, "The Jews of Bohemia and Moravia, 1938–1945," in Avigdor Dagan, Gertrude Hirschler, and Lewis Weiner, eds., *The Jews of Czechoslovakia,* vol. 3 (Philadelphia: Jewish Publication Society of America, 1984), 51–52. For a discussion of the confused, and ultimately decentralized, policy toward Jews married to "Aryans" in Germany, see Nathan Stoltzfus, "The Limits of Policy: Social Protection of Intermarried German Jews in Nazi Germany," in Robert Gellately and Nathan Stoltzfus, eds., *Social Outsiders in Nazi Germany* (Princeton, N.J.: Princeton University Press, 2001), 117–144.

40. *PPRH,* doc. 15, 132; *Historikové a kauza Lety* (Prague: Historický ústav AV ČR, 1999), doc. 2, 42–43; Michael Zimmermann, *Rassenutopie und Genozid: Die nationalsozialistische 'Lösung der Zigeunerfrage'* (Hamburg: Hans Christian, 1996), 219–221. On the number of deaths, see Ctibor Nečas, *Holocaust českých Romů* (Prague: Prostor, 1999), 175.

41. Jiří Lipa, "The Fate of the Gypsies in Czechoslovakia under Nazi Domination," in Michael Berenbaum, ed., *A Mosaic of Victims: Non-Jews Persecuted and Murdered by the Nazis* (New York: New York University Press, 1990), 208–209.

42. Zimmermann, *Rassenutopie,* 220.

43. Testimonies of Eduard Holomek and Božena Vladová né Heráková in Ctibor Nečas, *Nemůžeme zapomenout/našt'i bisteras: Nucená táborová koncentrace ve vyprávěních romských pamětníků* (Olomouc: Univerzita Palackého v Olomouci, 1994), 141, 217.

44. Christopher Browning and Jürgen Matthäus, "Preparing for the 'War of Destruction,'" in Browning, *The Origins,* 240, 244. See also Christian Gerlach, *Kalkulierte Morde: Die deutsche Wirtschafts- und Vernichtungspolitik in Weißrussland 1941 bis 1944* (Hamburg: Hamburger Edition, 1999), esp. 26–76 and 1129; Karel C. Berkhoff, *Harvest of Despair: Life and Death in Ukraine under Nazi Rule* (Cambridge, Mass.: Harvard University Press, 2004), 35–54; Dean, *Collaboration,* 110–112.

45. Berkhoff, *Harvest,* 59.

46. Gerlach, *Kalkulierte Morde,* 1.

47. On the genesis of the Generalplan Ost and the RSHA's plans, see Isabel Heinemann, *"Rasse,"* 362–364; and Phillip Terrell Rutherford, "Race, Space, and the 'Polish Question': Nazi Deportation Policy in Reichsgau Wartheland, 1939–1941" (Ph.D. diss., Pennsylvania State University, 2001), 336. On the settlements in the Lublin district of the General Government and in Zhytomyr, in Ukraine, see Rutherford, "Race," 357–358, 376–416, 448–464; Pohl, *Nationalsozialistische Judenverfolgung,* 153–157; Wasser, *Himmlers Raumplanung,* 133–229; and Wendy Lower, *Nazi Empire-Building and the Holocaust in the Ukraine* (Chapel Hill: University of North Carolina Press, 2005), 161–164, quotation from 163.

48. *PPRH,* doc. 9, 103.

49. *PPRH,* doc. 9, 109.

50. John Connelly, "Nazis and Slavs: From Racial Theory to Racist Practice," *CEH* 32, no. 1 (1999): 16–19. Lothar Kettenacker, *Nationalsozialistische Volkstumspolitik im Elsaß* (Stuttgart: Deutsche Verlags-Anstalt, 1973), 232.

51. Similarly, as Doris Bergen writes, "Nazi ideology assumed clear-cut categories. . . . But when Nazi authorities tried to implement policies regarding the Volksdeutsche [ethnic Germans living outside Germany], they found the concept to be full of contradictions, unclarities, and absurdities." "The Nazi Concept of 'Volksdeutsche' and the Exacerbation of Anti-Semitism in Eastern Europe, 1939–1945," *Journal of Contemporary History* 29 (1994): 572.

52. *IMT,* vol. 20, 286; also Josef Ackermann, *Heinrich Himmler als Ideologe* (Göttingen: Musterschmidt, 1970), 115–116; Heinz Höhne, *Der Orden der Totenkopfes: Die Geschichte der SS* (Cambridge: Cambridge University Press, 1967), 137.

53. Matthias Hamann, "Erwünscht und unerwünscht: Die rassenpyschologische Selektion der Ausländer," in Jochen August et al., eds., *Herrenmensch und Arbeitsvölker: Ausländische Arbeiter und Deutsche 1939–1945* (Rothbuch: Berlin, 1986), 144–145.

54. Mechtild Rössler and Sabine Schleiermacher, eds., *Der "Generalplan Ost": Hauptlinien der nationalsozialistischen Planungs- und Vernichtungspolitik* (Berlin: Akademie Verlag, 1993), doc. 44, 285.

55. *Der "Generalplan Ost,"* doc. 16, 65.

56. *IMT,* vol. 13, 462.

57. *IMT,* vol. 31, doc. 2916-PS, 292–294. See also Heinemann, "*Rasse,*" 260–262; Rutherford, "Race," 321–322; Elizabeth Harvey, *Women and the Nazi East: Agents and Witnesses of Germanization* (New Haven, Conn.: Yale University Press, 2003), 83–84. See also Clifton J. Child, "Germany, 1939–1945," in Arnold Toybee and Veronica M. Toynbee, eds., *Hitler's Europe* (London: Oxford University Press, 1954), 90; Robert L. Koehl, *RKFDV: German Resettlement and Population Policy, 1939–1945* (Cambridge, Mass.: Harvard University Press, 1957), 62–63; and Herbert S. Levine, "Local Authority and the SS State: The Conflict over Population Policy in Danzig–West Prussia," *CEH* 2, no. 4 (December 1969): 331–355. My thanks to Catherine Epstein, too, for sharing with me her knowledge about the Volksliste.

58. Quotations from Schenk, *Hitlers Mann,* 174–175; and Rutherford, "Race," 325. Statistics on Danzig-West Prussia's Volksliste from Rutherford, "Race," 325; and Harvey, *Women,* 79.

59. Heinemann, "*Rasse,*" 272–274; Zofia Boda-Krezel, *Sprawa Volkslisty na Górnym Śląsku: Koncepcje likwidacji problemu i ich realizacja* (Opole: Institut Śląski, 1978); Rutherford, "Race," 324–325. Statistics from Harvey, *Women,* 79.

60. Meyer was attached to Himmler's Reich Commissariat for the Strengthening of Germandom. In Cracow, Hans Frank had established his own planning agency for the General Government. Alfred Rosenberg, Reich minister for the occupied eastern territories, had his own planning agency as well. Mechtild Rössler and Sabine Schleiermacher, "Der 'Generalplan Ost' und die 'Modernität' der Großraumordnung: Eine Einführung," in Rössler and Schleiermacher, eds., *Der "Generalplan Ost,"* 9.

61. Schenk, *Hitlers Mann,* 208–210. Bergen, "The Nazi Concept," 575; Berkhoff,

Harvest, 211–212. Volksliste registration was also done in northern France. *TWS*, 719–720.

62. Josef Gruss, *Jedna paní povídala* (Prague: Alois Hynek, 1945), 61–62. The joke also traveled in Germany. See Hans-Jochen Gamm, *Der Flüsterwitz im Dritten Reich* (Munich: Deutscher Taschenbuch, 1979), 50.

63. Martin Zückart, "Edmund Schneeweiß (1886) Slawist und Volkkundler: Anpassung als Wissenschaftsstrategie?" in Monika Glettler and Alena Mišková, eds., *Prager Professoren 1938–1948: Zwischen Wissenschaft und Politik* (Essen: Klartext, 2001), 212; Petr Němec, "Die Lage der deutschen Nationalität im Protektorat Böhmen und Mähren under dem Aspekt der 'Eindeutschung' dieses Gebietes," *Boh* 32 (1991): 42.

64. Mastny, *The Czechs*, 130. Karl Heinz Roth, "Heydrichs Professor: Historiographie des 'Volkstums' und der Massenvernichtungen: Der Fall Hans Joachim Beyer," in Peter Schöttler, ed., *Geschichtsschreibung als Legitimationswissenschaft* (Frankfurt: Surkamp, 1997): 262–342, esp. 307; Alena Mišková, "Rassenforschung und Oststudien an der Deutschen (Karls-) Universität in Prag," in Detlef Brandes, Edita Ivaničková, and Jiří Pešek, eds., *Erzwungene Trennung. Vertreibungen und Aussiedlungen in und aus der Tschechoslowakei 1938–1947 im Vergleich mit Polen, Ungarn und Jugoslawien* (Essen: Klartext, 1999), 51.

65. *PPRH*, doc. 52, 200–204.

66. *PPRH*, doc. 71, 233–234. Or, as one racial expert commented, "In general it is only the worst [racially speaking] who say 'We want to be Germans' while the better ones, racially speaking, continue to side with their Slavic peoples." *IMT*, vol. 39, doc. 060 (9) USSR, 364. Many Nazi leaders in Poland made similar arguments. According to one SS official in Upper Silesia, for example, "Experience has shown that especially the Polish leaders of insurgents or even resistance movements have a considerable portion of Nordic blood, which enables them to be active in contrast to the fatalistic Slavic elements." *TWS*, vol. 4, doc. NO-3076, 767.

67. *PPRH*, doc. 9, 147.

68. *PPRH*, doc. 8, 96; Kárný, "Hlavní rysy," 34; *PPRH*, doc. 9, 112. On Krejčí's patriotism, see Dušan Tomášek and Robert Kvaček, *Obžalována je vláda* (Prague: Themis, 1999), 24.

69. Lucy S. Dawidowicz, *The War against the Jews, 1933–1945* (New York: Holt, Rinehart & Winston, 1975), 58.

70. Detlev J. K. Peukert, *Inside Nazi Germany: Conformity, Opposition, and Racism in Everyday Life*, trans. Richard Deveson (New Haven: Yale University Press, 1987), 208. See also Ann Laura Stoler, "Sexual Affronts and Racial Frontiers: European Identities and the Cultural Politics of Exclusion in Colonial Southeast Asia," in Frederick Cooper and Ann Laura

Stoler, eds., *Tensions of Empire: Colonial Cultures in a Bourgeois World* (Berkeley: University of California Press, 1997), 198–237.

71. On the testing of schoolchildren, see Heinemann, *"Rasse,"* 153–154; and Karel Fremund, "Dokumenty o nacistické vyhlazovací politice," *SAP* 13, no. 2 (1963): 22. On marriage applications, see Heinemann, *"Rasse,"* 171. On training for racial selection, see ONH, doc. 29, 345.

72. On Heydrich's academics and racial experts, see Karl-Heinz Roth, " 'Generalplan Ost'—'Gesamtplan Ost,' " *Der "Generalplan Ost,"* 36; Heinemann, *"Rasse,"* 131; Mišková, "Rassenforschung," 39, 44. On the establishment of the Race and Settlement Office in Prague, see Heinemann, *"Rasse,"* 151, 155–157. On the extension of RKF jurisdiction over the Protectorate, see Henry Buxbaum Brompton, "The Politics of the German Occupation in the Protectorate of Bohemia and Moravia: A Case Study of Totalitarian 'Breakthrough,' " (Ph.D. diss., University of Southern California, 1974), 220.

73. Norman Rich, *Hitler's War Aims: Ideology, the Nazi State, and the Course of Expansion* (New York and London: W. W. Norton, 1973), 106–197; Heinemann, *"Rasse,"* 305–356; Viscount Chilton, "The Occupied Countries in Western Europe," *Hitler's Europe,* 517; Ralf Gebel, *"Heim ins Reich": Konrad Henlein und der Reichsgau Sudetenland (1938–1945)* (Munich: R. Oldenbourg, 1999), 287.

74. Brandes, *Die Tschechen,* 1:223–224. Eugen Fiechtner, *"Das Protektorat Böhmen und Mähren im Deutschen Reich:* Erlebnisbericht des Oberlandrats in Iglau über die Zeit vom 15. März bis 15. Juli 1942," 30 November 1979, BB, Ost-Dok 21, 23. For Heydrich's comment, see *PPRH,* doc. 79, 25. On the number of German civil servants, see Mastny, *The Czechs,* 201.

75. Kárný, "Hlavní rysy," 22–26. Quotation from *PPRH,* doc. 9, 110.

76. SD Tagesbericht 232/41, 12 Nov. 1941, NA, ÚŘP, k. 365, sign. I-3b 5090, 3; "Meldungen zum Deutschtum," Der Befehlshaber der Sicherheitspolizei und des SD, Bö./Nes., 20 Nov. 1941, NA, ÚŘP, k. 365, sign. I-3b, 5090, 1; I-3B, 6469, "Meldungen zum Deutschtum," December 1941, NA, ÚŘP, k. 365, sign. I-3b 5090, 1–3.

77. Fuchs to Oberlandräte, 16 Apr. 1942, NA, ÚŘP, k. 365, sign. I-3b 5090. See also Heinemann, *"Rasse,"* 169–173.

78. In addition, 6,141 citizenship applications had been handed out but had not yet been returned. Fuchs to Oberlandräte, October 1941, NA, ÚŘP, k. 365, sign. I-3b 5090, 1; OLR Iglau to Reichsprotektor, "Erfassung der deutschen Volkszugehörigen in Böhmen und Mähren," 4 June 1941, NA, ÚŘP, k. 365, sign. I-3b 5090; "Nachweisung über die Zahl der deutschen Staatsangehörigen und deutschen Volkszugehörigen nach dem Stande von 31. Dezember 1941," [no date], NA, ÚŘP, k. 365 sign. I-3b 5090; Heinemann, *"Rasse,"* 169.

79. On Plzeň, see OLR Iglau to Reichsprotektor, "Erfassung der deutschen Volkszugehörigen in Böhmen und Mähren," 4 June 1942, NA, ÚŘP, k. 365, sign. I-3b 5090; OLR Pilsen to Reichsprotektor, "Erfassung der deutschen Volkszugehörigen in Böhmen und Mähren," 12 May 1942, NA, ÚŘP, k. 365, sign. I-3b 5090. On Kladno, see Landespräsident in Böhmen to Reichsprotektor, 27 Oct. 1942, NA, ÚŘP, k. 365, sign. I-3b 5090. On confusion because of administrative reorganization, see Jacobi to Reichsprotektor, [no date], NA, ÚŘP, k. 365, sign. I-3b 5090. On the persistent problems with mixed marriages, see OLR Iglau to Reichsprotektor, "Erfassung der deutschen Volkszugehörigen in Böhmen und Mähren," 4 June 1942, NA, ÚŘP, k. 365, sign. I-3b 5090.

80. Schmidt, "Pax Germanica," 64.

81. Verwaltungsbericht, OLR Olmütz, April 1942, Zemský archiv v Opavě, pobočka Olomouc, fond Oberlandrat Olomouc, k. 5, inv. č. 5, 5.

82. Ulrich Herbert, *Hitler's Foreign Workers: Enforced Foreign Labor in Germany under the Third Reich,* trans. William Templar (Cambridge: Cambridge University Press, 1997), 143–150, quotation from 147. Jaroslava Milotová, "'Cizirodí' dělníci a jejich pracovní nasazení v nacistickém Německu v letech 1939–1945," in Jana Havlíková et al., eds., *Museli pracovat pro Říši: Nucené pracovní nasazení českého obyvatelstva v letech 2. světové války* (Prague: Státní ústřední archiv, 2004), 26.

83. Jana Havlíková et al., *Museli pracovat pro Říši: Nucené pracovní nasazení českého obyvatelstva v letech 2. světové války: Doprovodná publikace k výstavě* (Prague: Státní ústřední archiv, 2004), 28. On Göring's fall from grace, see Overy, *Goering,* 205–212.

84. Herbert, *Hitler's Foreign Workers,* 163–167, quotation on 164.

85. *PPRH,* doc. 61, 219–220, doc. 79, 252–253. See also Miroslav Kárný, "Der 'Reichsausgleich' in der deutschen Protektoratspolitik," in *Europa,* 31–32, 39.

86. Herbert, *Hitler's Foreign Workers,* 161–163; *Museli,* 28. On the May decree see *IMT* 26: 485. On the number of Czechs sent to work in the Reich from May to September 1942, see Kárný, "Der 'Reichsausgleich,'" 38. Before Heydrich's arrival Hitler had denied Neurath's suggestions that Czechs be subject to compulsory work duty. *AOP,* doc. 36, 353.

87. Reichsminister des Innern an die Aufsichtsbehörden und an die Oberlandräte im Protektorat Böhmen und Mähren, 3 Apr. 1941, NA, ÚŘP, k. 90, sign. I-1b 2020; Burgsdorff to Oberlandräte, "Ehen von Mitgliedern der NSDAP und ihrer Gliederungen mit Anhörigen fremder Volkgruppen," 9 Sept. 1941, MZAB, B255, k. 2, sign. HO 206. The exact date when the RuSHA became involved is uncertain. See Heinemann, *"Rasse,"* 172.

88. The cards are collected in SOAP, OLR Kolin, k. 7.

89. RuSHA daily report, MZAB, B 255, k. 2, sign. HO. 204/3.

90. "Bekanntmachung zur Verordnung über den Kennkarten," *RGBl*, vol. 1, 100; "Anordnung des Reichprotektors in Böhmen und Mähren über der Kennkartenzwang," 27 Mar. 1942, *VRBM*, 62; *PPRH*, doc. 61, 218; "Zpráva českého učitele A. Merta ze severní Moravy; Unikl z českého zemí dne 6. května 1942," [no date], JS, Reports from ČSR, 1942–1943, k. 12, 15; Aly and Roth, 65–66; Brandes, *Die Tschechen*, 1:238.

91. *PPRH*, doc. 62, 218, doc. 79, 257.

92. Josef Mucha and Karel Petrželka, *O některých současných problémech národnostně smíšených manželství* (Prague: Svoboda, 1946), 6.

93. Kárný, "Der 'Reichsausgleich,'" 38, 45.

94. On the use of identity cards by Nazi authorities, see *PPRH*, doc. 79, 257; "Unikl z českého žemí dne 6. května 1942," JS, Reports from ČSR, 1942–1943, k. 12, 15; "Zprávy z domova," "Došly přes New York, dne 2. června 1941," JS, Reports from ČSR, 1942–1943, k. 12, 3.

95. On the number of Czechs expelled from their homes, see Brandes, *Die Tschechen*, 1:170. Heydrich's plans are in *PPRH*, doc. 61, 218. See also Heinemann, *"Rasse,"* 166–167.

96. MacDonald, *The Killing*, 199.

97. Ibid., 97, 118–120, 142–143; Brandes, *Die Tschechen*, 1:251–253.

98. MacDonald, *The Killing*, 142–143.

99. Brandes, *Die Tschechen*, 1:247–249; MacDonald, *The Killing*, 146–147, 199; [no author], "Zprávy z domova," 2 June 1942, JS, k. 12, Reports from ČSR, 1942–1943, 3; [no author], "Z domova," 21 July 1942, VHA, fond 37, sign. 91/7, 1.

100. MacDonald, *The Killing*, 155.

101. Mastny, *The Czechs*, 156; Brandes, *Die Tschechen*, 1:252. MacDonald, *The Killing*, 156–157, claims that resistance leaders came up with various forms of the last sentence before sending the message.

102. Mastny, *The Czechs*, 209; also Brandes, *Die Tschechen*, 1:253.

103. MacDonald, *The Killing*, 166–167, 171–173.

104. Brandes, *Die Tschechen*, 1:254. Later that evening Himmler telegrammed Frank with a similar order, although he demanded that only one hundred of the ten thousand Czechs arrested should be shot. *PPRH*, doc. 86, 266; Brandes, *Die Tschechen*, 1:255.

105. Mastny, *The Czechs*, 215; Brandes, *Die Tschechen*, 1:256.

106. Brandes, *Die Tschechen*, 1:254, 255; "Erlaß des Reichsprotektors in Böhmen und Mähren über die Meldepflicht," 28 May 1942, *VRBH*, 124.

107. *PPRH*, doc. 87, 271–272; Brandes, *Die Tschechen*, 1:257. Hácha and Moravec quotations are from Mastny, *The Czechs*, 214.

108. Brandes, *Die Tschechen*, 1:261.
109. Brandes, *Die Tschechen*, 1:263–264; Mastny, *The Czechs*, 215–218; Marta Harlasová, "Jed v krvi německé mládeže," *Šest let okupace Prahy* (Prague: Orbis, 1946), 207–208. On the children being sent to Lebensborn, see Georg Lilienthal, *Der "Lebensborn e.V.": Ein Instrument nationalsozialistischer Rassenpolitik* (Frankfurt: Fischer, 1993), 242–245. See also TWS, 679–682; Schmidt, "Pax Germanica," 59–60.
110. Mastny, *The Czechs*, 217–218, quotation from 217; Brandes, *Die Tschechen*, 1:265.
111. MacDonald, *The Killing*, 193–195.
112. Brandes, *Die Tschechen*, 1:254.
113. *DHČSP,* 1: 274; cited in Mastny, *The Czechs*, 217. See also Dr. E. Beneš, "Zpráva z 10. Oct. 1942," HIWRP, ÚVOD, k. 1.
114. Uwe Naumann, ed., *Lidice: Ein böhmisches Dorf* (Frankfurt: Röderberg Verlag, 1983), 51–76, Mann quotation on 54; MacDonald, *The Killing*, 200; Brandes, *Die Tschechen*, 1:266. See also Czechoslovak Ministry of Foreign Affairs, "German Massacres in Occupied Czechoslovakia Following the Attack on Reinhard Heydrich" (London, 1942).
115. Brandes, *Die Tschechen*, 1:265; Mastny, *The Czechs*, 220–221; MacDonald, *The Killing*, 196, 221.
116. Brandes, *Die Tschechen*, 1:266. MacDonald, *The Killing*, 197.
117. JUDr. Jan Pavel Pringsheim, "Situační zpráva o poměrech v protektorátě Čechy a Morava se zvláštním přihledemtím k vnitřní správě," JS, k. 12, "Reports from ČSR, 1942–1943," 22; Kárný, *"Konečné řešení."* 20.
118. Heinemann, *"Rasse,"* 167–168.
119. On Meyer's plan, see "Material zum Generalsiedlungsplan—Flächen- und Bevölkerungsberechnungen, Unterlagen für einen Generalsiedlungsplan—Grundzahlen und Karten," in Czesław Madajczyk, ed., *Vom Generalplan Ost zum Generalsiedlungsplan* (Munich: K. G. Saur, 1994), doc. 71, 238; Heinemann, *"Rasse,"* 168. On plans among party officials in Berlin, see Brandes, *Die Tschechen*, 1:360. Frank's comment is in Volker Zimmermann, *Die Sudetendeutschen im NS-Staat: Politik und Stimmung der Bevölkerung im Reichsgau Sudetenland (1938–1945)* (Essen: Klartext, 1999), 291. See also Brandes, *Die Tschechen*, 2:19. On the number of racial experts in Prague, see Heinemann, *"Rasse,"* 164.
120. "Verwaltungsbericht für das 2. Vierteljahr 1944," 4 July 1944, MZAB, B 252, k. 18, [no sign.]. Der SS-Führer im Rasse- und Siedlungswesen to all Rus-Dienstellen, 25 Jan. 1944, B 245, k. 38 [no sign.]. See also Heinemann, *"Rasse,"* 172; and Andreas Wiedemann, *Die Reinhard-Heydrich Stiftung in Prag, 1942–1945* (Dresden: Hannah-Arendt-Institut für Totalitarismusforschung, 2000), 77–79.

121. Kárný, *"Konečné řešení,"* 153–154.

122. Christopher R. Browning, *The Path to Genocide: Essays on Launching the Final Solution* (Cambridge: Cambridge University Press, 1992), 169.

123. Kárný, *"Konečné řešení,"* 21, 177.

124. "Leiter der Aussenstelle M.d.F.d.G.b to Reichskommissar für die Festigung deutschen Volkstums z.HD SS-Obersturmbannführers Fischer," 2 July 1942, *IMT,* doc. 080(9)-USSR, 365; Heinemann, *"Rasse,"* 157.

125. On the continuing rivalry between Jury and Frank, see Jury to Frank in Karl Hermann Frank, 28 July 1943, NARA, RG 242BDC Microfilm, SSO SS Officer Dossier, A3343, roll SSO-217. On the baptism of Frank's son, see Geschke to Himmler, 18 Dec. 1942, in Karl Hermann Frank, NARA, BDC Microfilm, SSO SS Officer Dossier, A3343, roll SSO-217; and Himmler to Frank, 6 Jan. 1943, in Karl Hermann Frank, NARA, BDC Microfilm, SSO SS Officer Dossier, A3343, roll SSO-217, quotation on 1. On the examination of citizenship applications, see "Report from the Race and Resettlement Main Office SS, Branch Bohemia-Moravia, on a conference with the border county office Lower Danube 19 to 21 June 1942," *IMT,* vol. 39, doc. 060 (9) USSR, 362–364.

126. Nr. 1 3 b—2488 to Landesprasidente-Reichsauftragsverwaltung in Prag und Brünn and others, 22 July 1942, MZAB, B 255, 1939–1945, HO 101, 3.

127. "Letter from the Minister of State for the Protectorate of Bohemia and Moravia to Rudolf Brandt, 13 June 1944, concerning the children of executed Czechs," *TWS,* doc. NO-433, 1031.

128. *Museli,* 28. Statistics from Kárný, "Der 'Reichsausgleich,'" 45.

129. František Mainuš, *Totální nasazení (1939–1945)* (Prague: Mladá fronta, 1974), 54. "Extract from report from Harders to Hofmann, 6 October 1942, concerning results of Germanization program," *TWS,* doc. NO-1600, 773; Kárný, "Der 'Reichsausgleich,'" 39. On Meyer's final version of the Generalplan Ost, see Rutherford, "Race," 337.

130. Heinemann, *"Rasse,"* 359–360, n. 10; Rutherford, "Race," 338; Lower, *Nazi Empire-Building,* 177.

131. Heinemann, *"Rasse,"* 164.

132. Lower, *Nazi Empire-Building,* 162–179, esp. 178.

133. MacDonald, *The Killing,* 166; Brandes, *Die Tschechen,* 1:263.

134. Gerlach, *Kalkulierte Morde,* 26–76, quotation from 1129; Berkhoff, *Harvest of Despair,* 35–54; Dean, *Collaboration,* 110–112.

135. Berkhoff, *Harvest,* 47.

136. Connelly, "Nazis and Slavs," 7.

137. For an insightful discussion of the tensions created by the demands of the wartime economy and Nazi leaders' determination to realize their

ideological goals, foremost among them being the annihilation of the Jews, see Ulrich Herbert, "Labour and Extermination: Economic Interest and the Primacy of Weltanschauung in National Socialism," *Past and Present* 138 (Feb. 1993): 144–195. On the fate of the Mischlinge in the last years of the war, see Annegret Ehmann, "From Colonial Racism to Nazi Population Policy: The Role of the So-Called Mischlinge," in Michael Berenbaum and Abraham J. Peck, eds., *The History of the Holocaust: The Known, the Unknown, the Disputed, and the Reexamined* (Bloomington: Indiana University Press, 1998), 128–129; and Noakes, "The Development," 348-352. In her case study of Nazi rule in Zhytomyr, Wendy Lower makes a similar argument concerning Germanization measures and the Holocaust. Although local officials could all agree on killing the Jews, there was very little consensus when it came to resettlement plans for Himmler's Hegewald colony there. Lower, *Nazi Empire-Building,* 179.

138. Aly and Roth, *Die restlose Erfassung;* Omer Bartov, "Defining Enemies, Making Victims: Germans, Jews, and the Holocaust," in Amir Weiner, ed., *Landscaping the Human Garden: Twentieth-Century Population Management in a Comparative Framework* (Stanford, Calif.: Stanford University Press, 2003): 135–147; Eric D. Weitz, *A Century of Genocide: Utopias of Race and Nation* (Princeton, N.J.: Princeton University Press, 2003), 113–119.

139. Hans Joachim Beyer, *Umvolkung: Studien zur Frage der Assimilation und Amalgamation in Ostmitteleuropa und Übersee* (Brno: Rudolf M. Rohrer, 1945).

140. Connelly, "Nazis and Slavs," 33.

5. Surrounded by War, Living in Peace

1. Toman Brod, *Ceskoslovensko a sovetsky svaz, 1939–1945* (Prague: Prace, 1992), 241; [anonymous informant], "Poměry v Protektorátě," 23 May 1944, VHA, fond 37, sign. 91/7, 1.

2. Gordon Wright, *The Ordeal of Total War, 1939–1945* (New York: Harper & Row, 1968), 175, 179.

3. Ulrich Herbert, *Hitler's Foreign Workers: Enforced Foreign Labor in Germany under the Third Reich,* trans. William Templer (Cambridge: Cambridge University Press, 1997), 257–261, quotation on 258.

4. Miloslav Moulis and Dušan Tomášek, *K. H. Frank: Vzestup a pád karlovarského knihkupce* (Prague: Epocha, 2003), 298.

5. [Anonymous author], [untitled], 28 July 1944, VHA fond 37, sign. 91/7, 8, 5, 9.

6. On Frank's consolidation of power, see *PPRH*, doc. 87, 267–276; Vojtech Mastny, *The Czechs under Nazi Rule: The Failure of National Resistance* (New York: Columbia University Press, 1971), 211–212; Detlef Brandes, *Die Tschechen unter deutschem Protektorat*, vol.1 (Munich: R. Oldenbourg, 1969), 274–275; Moulis and Tomášek, *K. H. Frank*, 303–309.

7. Václav Průcha, "Základní rysy válečného řízeného hospodářství v českých zemích v letech nacistické okupace," *HV* 2 (1967): 238.

8. Ibid., 237.

9. Alice Teichová and Robert Waller, "Der tschechoslowakische Unternehmer am Vorabend und zu Beginn des Zweiten Weltkriegs," in Waclaw Długoborski, ed., *Zweiter Weltkrieg und sozialer Wandel: Achsenmächte und besetzte Länder* (Göttingen: Vandenhoeck & Ruprecht, 1981, 289.

10. František Mainuš, *Totálne nasazení (1939–1945)* (Prague: Mladá fronta, 1974); Nina Pavelčíková, "Změny v rozmístění a sociální skladbě obyvatel českých zemí za okupace, jejich souvislosti s poválečným vývojem," *Slezský sborník* 90, no. 1 (1992): 6; and Jana Havlíková et al., *Museli pracovat pro Říši: Nucené pracovní nasazení českého obyvatelstva v letech 2. světové války: Doprovodná publikace k výstavě* (Prague: Státní ústřední archiv, 2004), esp. 29–48. The number of Czechs mobilized is from Miroslav Kárný, "Der 'Reichsausgleich' in der deutschen Protektoratspolitik," in Ulrich Herbert, ed., *Europa und der 'Reichseinsatz': Ausländische Zivilarbeiter, Kriegsgefangene und KZ-Häftlinge in Deutschland, 1938–1945* (Essen: Klartext, 1991), 45.

11. Edvard Beneš, *Šest let exilu a druhé světové války* (Prague: Orbis, 1946), 159. See also ibid., 212–213.

12. Jaroslav Stránský, *Hovory k domovu* (Prague: Fr. Borový, 1946), 407. See also Jan Masaryk, *Volá Londýn* (Prague: Práce, 1948), 260.

13. Brandes, *Die Tschechen*, 2: 88, 89.

14. Brandes, *Die Tschechen*, 2: 101–106.

15. Writing during the political thaw of the 1960s, Václav Průcha estimated that industrial production in the Protectorate rose by 12 percent from 1939 to 1945. Průcha, "Základní rysy," 237. See also Teichová and Waller, "Die tschechoslowakische Unternehmer," 289.

16. [Anonymous informant], "Zpravy z domova," 13 July 1944, VHA, fond 37, sign. 91/7, 3. Kraftové skupiny, "Pro Dr. Beneše," 22 Jan. 1944, VHA, fond 37, sign. 91/7, 2. Also [no author], "Zpráva z domova ze začátku února 1943," February. 1943, JS, k. 12, Reports from ČSR, 1942–1943, 3.

17. Teichová and Waller, "Der tschechoslowakische Unternehmer," 289; SD Tagesbericht, 12 Sept. 1944, VHA, SDNU, k. 8, no. 79, 1.

18. [Anonymous correspondent], [no title] 13 Sept. 1943, VHA, fond 37, sign. 91/6, 1; [anonymous correspondent], "Zprávy z domova," 10 July 1944,

VHA, fond 37, sign. 91/7, 6; "Kaviár-Muzeum," "Zprávy z domova," 14 Aug. 1944, VHA, fond 37, sign. 91/7, 2; [no author], "Zpráva ze dne 15, 18 dubna," 15–18 Apr. 1943; JS, k. 12, Reports from ČSR, 1942–1943, 1.

19. Marek, "Zprávy z domova," 2 Oct. 1944, VHA, fond 37, sign. 91/7, 2.

20. A. Merta, "Zpráva českého učitele A. Merta ze severní Moravy," 6 May 1942, JS, k. 12, Reports from ČSR, 1942–1943, 15. Also [no author], "Zprávy z domova," 2 June 1942, JS, k. 12, Reports from HSR, 1942–1943, 3; Lib. & Ice, "Zprävy z Prahy ze dne 22 ledna 1942," 22 Jan. 1942, JS, box 12, Reports from ČSR, 1942–1943, 1; Vilém Beneš, "Zprávy z Protektorátu," 28 Mar. 1944, VHA, fond 37, sign. 91/7, 8.

21. Václav Buben, "Hrůzovláda i mrtvého R. Heydricha," *Šest let okupace Prahy* (Prague: Orbis, 1946), 158.

22. Moulis and Tomášek, *K. H. Frank,* 308–308; also 310.

23. Heda Margolius Kovály, *Under a Cruel Star: A Life in Prague, 1941–1968,* trans. Franci Epstein, Helen Epstein, and the author (Cambridge, Mass.: Plunkett Lake Press, 1986), 29. Shortly after Heydrich's assassination the Reich Protector's Office issued the decree promising the death penalty for hiding a person without proper document. *VRBH,* 3 July 1942, 182.

24. [Anonymous informant], "Zpráva o domově," 24 Jan. 1944, VHA, fond 37, sign. 91/7, 5; [no author], "Zprávy z Protektorátu," 30 Aug. 1943, VHA, fond 37, sign. 91/6, 3. See also [anonymous informant], "Zprávy z ČSR," 23 Sept. 1943, VHA, fond 37, sign. 91/6, 1. On the randomness of violence in the General Government and the "irrationality" of collaborating with the Nazi regime there see Jan Tomasz Gross, *Polish Society under German Occupation: The Generalgouvernement, 1939–1944* (Princeton, N.J.: Princeton University Press, 1979). See also John Connelly, "Nazis and Slavs: From Racial Theory to Racist Practice," *CEH* 32, no. 1 (1999): 9–10; and John Connelly, "Why the Poles Collaborated So Little—And Why That Is No Reason for Nationalist Hubris," *Slavic Review* 64, no.4 (Winter 2005): 771–781.

25. Karel Přikryl, "Zprávy z domova," 23 Sept. 1943, VHA, fond 37, sign. 91/6, 5; Moulis and Tomášek, *K. H. Frank,* 296–297.

26. [No author], "Zpráva z domova," 5–8 Feb. 1944, VHA, fond 37, sign. 91/6, 5.

27. Masaryk, *Volá Londýn,* 278–280. SD Tagesbericht, 8 Aug. 1944, VHA, SDNU, k. 8, no. 68, 4.

28. Beneš, *Šest let,* 106, 152, and 159. Emphasis in the original.

29. Quotation from Masaryk, *Volá Londýn,* 260. See also Beneš, *Šest let,* 199. On Czechs promising that collaborators have been identified see, for example, Vilém Beneš, "Zprávy z Protektorátu," 28 Mar. 1944, VHA, fond 37, sign. 91/7, 7.

30. Benjamin Frommer, "Retribution against Nazi Collaborators in Postwar Czechoslovakia" (Ph.D. diss., Harvard University, 1999), 59–61.

31. Zbyněk Zeman with Antonín Klimek, *The Life of Edvard Beneš, 1884–1948: Czechoslovakia in Peace and War* (Oxford: Clarendon Press, 1997), 199, quoted in Frommer, "Retribution," 56–57.

32. Masaryk, *Volá Londýn,* 228.

33. [Anonymous informant], "Zprávy z domova," 5 May 1944, VHA, fond 37, sign. 91/7, 4; [anonymous informant], "Zprávy o poměrech ve vlasti," 6 Aug. 1943, VHA, fond 37, sign. 91/7, 2; [anonymous informant], "Zprávy hospodářské," 10 Feb. 1944, VHA, fond 37, sign. 91/7, 2.

34. [Anonymous informant], "Situace býv. vlád. vojáků," 12 Dec. 1944, VHA, fond 37, sign. 91/7, 1; Josef Měkýš, Frant. Štěpánek, Frant. Fajek, and Josef Mach, [no title], VHA, fond 37, sign. 91/7, 1. The Protectorate employed seven thousand government troops. Half served in Hácha's presidential offices, and the other half were stationed in towns without German garrisons. The number of Czech gendarmes was five thousand, and the number of policemen was even higher. Tomášek and Kvaček, *Causa,* 59; Tomáš Pasák, *Pod ochranou říše* (Prague: Práh, 1998), 136–139. On the varied judgments, see [anonymous informant], "Zprávy z domova," 5 May 1944, VHA, fond 37, sign. 91/7, 1; [anonymous informant], "Zprávy z domova," 2 Sept. 1944, VHA, fond 37, sign. 91/7, 3; [anonymous informant], "Zprávy z domova," 14 Sept. 1944, VHA, fond 37, sign. 91/7, 2; [anonymous informant], "Zprávy z domova," 24 Jan. 1944, VHA, fond 37, sign. 91/7, 3.

35. [No author], "Zpráva ze dne 24. dubna 1943," JS, k. 12, Reports from ČSR, 1942–1943, 1.

36. Beneš, *Šest let,* 158. Every one of London's major personality figures joined in the attacks on Hácha. See Masaryk, *Volá Londýn,* 257–258; Prokop Drtina, *A nyní promluví Pavel Svatý: Londýnské rozhlasové epištoly z let 1940–1945* (Prague: Melantrich, 1947), 295–298; Stránský, *Hovory,* 417–420.

37. [Anonymous informant], "Zprávy z domova," 7 Sept. 1944, VHA, fond 37, sign. 91/7, 2. For a sample of the wide-ranging opinions about Hácha among Czechs, see Netík, "Zprávy z domova," 5 Aug. 1944, VHA, fond 37, sign. 91/7, 1; [no author], "Zpráva došla přes Washington ze dne 12. června 1942," 12 June 1942, JS, k. 12, Reports from ČSR, 1942–1943, 1; and Dr. Feuter, "Zpráva z domova za začátku února 1943," JS, k. 12, Reports from ČSR, 1942–1943, 2.

38. "Dopis K. H. Franka dr. Lammerovi v Říšském kancléřství, 1. IX. 1940" and "Memorandum říšského ministra pro vědu, školství, a osvětu z 1. V. 1942," in Boris Čelovský, ed., *Řešení české otázky podle německých dokumentů 1933–1945* (Ostrava: Tilia, 1997), 272, 336.

39. ONH, doc. 55, 383. Brandes, *Die Tschechen,* 2:37.

40. Doležal, *Česká kultura,* 41; [no author], "Zprávy z ČSR," 23 Sept. 1943, VHA, fond 37, sign. 91/7, 1; "Výroční zpráva státního akademického gymansium v Praze II za školní rok 1947/48" (Prague: Státní nakladatelsví, 1948), 5–6. Both sides agreed that older children, who remembered the First Republic and were less "malleable," were less enthusiastic about Kuratorium events and speaking German. SD Tagesbericht, 5 May 1944, VHA, SDNU, k. 8, sbírka č. 35, 7; "Zpráva z domova," 2 Sept. 1944, VHA, fond 37, sign. 91/7, 5; Doležal, *Česká kultura,* 71.

41. Doležal, *Česká kultura,* 69–70, 71.

42. Antonín Juppa, "Byl to soumrak české výchovy," *Šest let,* 6.

43. [No author], "Zprávy o školských," 16 Oct. 1944, VHA, fond 37, sign. 91/7, 2. See also Doležal, *Česká kultura,* 72; Vyroční zpráva," *Šest let,* 17; and Václav Buben, "Dějepis na školách v době okupace," *Šest let,* 56.

44. "Zpráva šeského učitele A. Merta ze severní Moravy," 6 May 1942, JS, k. 12, Reports from ČSR, 1942–1943, 8; [no author], [no title], 17 Apr. 1944, VHA, fond 37, sign. 91/7, 3; [no author], "Zprávy o školských," 16 Oct. 1944, VHA, fond 37, sign. 91/7, 3; Josef Mrázek, "Střední školy v Praze za okupace," *Šest let,* 42. On teacher "reeducation," see Tara Zahra, "Reclaiming Children for the Nation: Germanization, Nationl Ascription, and Democracy in the Bohemian Lands, 1900–1050," *CEH* 37, no. 40 (Winter 2004): 534.

45. Jar. P. Blašek, "Národní školy za okupace," *Šest let,* 47.

46. Quotation from Inz. Barton, "Zpráva o domově," 14 Aug. 1944, VHA, fond 37, sign. 91/7, 3. See also "Zpráva českého učitele A. Merta ze severní Moravy," 6 May 1942, JS, k. 12, Reports from ČSR, 1942–1943, 7–8; SD Tagesbericht, 8 June 1944, VHA, SDNU, k. 8, sbírka č. 47, 1; SD Tagesbericht, 8 Aug. 1944, VHA, SDNU, k. 8, sbírka č. 68, 5; and Zdeněk David, "The War, the Nazi Protectorate, and Victory: Recollections," *Kosmos* 12, no. 1 (Summer 1996): 7.

47. For a sampling of Heydrich's views on teachers, see *PPRH,* doc. 61, 221; Doležal, *Česká kultura,* 51. As usual, Heydrich seemed to be mimicking ideas found within Intelligence Service reports. See, for example, "Monatsbericht: Die politische Entwicklung im Protektorat Böhmen und Mähren," SD report, May 1940, VHA, SDNU, k. 7, sbírka č. 74, jednotka 48, 17. On Nazi views about teachers being "conservative" and "effeminate," see Peter Diehl-Thiele, *Partei und Staat im Dritten Reich: Untersuchungen zum Verhältnis von NSDAP und allgemeiner innerer Staatsverwaltung 1933–1945* (Munich: C. H. Beck, 1969), 2–3.

48. Doležal, *Česká kultura,* 51; M. Charfreitag, "Totální nasazení pražského učitelstva," *Šest let,* 52. See also no. 10. 418/d/44 [no date or title], VHA, fond 37, sign. 91/7, 1.

49. *PPRH*, doc. 61, 221.

50. Zahra, "Reclaiming Children," 535; Bosák, *Česká škola*, 52–53; Jan Gebhart and Jan Kuklík, *Dramatické i všední dny Protektorátu* (Prague: Themis, 1996), 229.

51. SD Tagesbericht, 23 May 1944, VHA, SDNU, k. 8, č. 40, 3. See also Albert Kaufmann, "Zpráva z domova," April 1943, VHA, fond 37, sign. 91/7, 7; "Zprávy z domova," 24 Jan. 1944, VHA, fond 37, sign. 91/7, 3; and Brandes, *Die Tschechen*, 2:38.

52. On views from the Intelligence Service, see SD Tagesbericht, 9 May 1944, VHA, SDNU, k. 8, sbírka č. 36, 6; SD Tagesbericht, 23 May 1944, VHA, SDNU, k. 8, sbírka č. 40, 7.

53. [Anonymous correspondent], "Zpráva z domova," [no date], VHA, fond 37, sign. 91/7, 1. Also Inž. Barton, "Zpráva o domově," 14 Aug. 1944, VHA, fond 37, sign. 91/7, 3; Richard Kluger, [no place], [no date], BB, Ost-Dok 20, Olmütz, sign. 67, 2; [anonymous informant], "Fuertera a zprávy z domova," 2 Oct. 1944, VHA, fond 37, sign. 91/7, 2.

54. Radomír Luža with Christiane Vella, *The Hitler Kiss: A Memoir of the Czech Resistance* (Baton Rouge: Louisiana State University Press, 2002), 40.

55. Dana Musilová "Zásobování a výživa českého obyvatelstva v podmínkách valečného řízeného hospodářství (1939–1945)," *Slezský sborník* 89, nos. 3–4 (1991): 258–261. Quotation from [no author], "Zpráva z domova," 7 Oct. 1944, VHA, fond 37, sign. 91/7, 2.

56. 42-ka, [no title], 6 Feb. 1945, HIWPR, ÚVOD, k. 1, 3. On the demands for political, social, and national unity after the war, see Karel Přikryl, "Zprávy z domova," 23 Sept. 1944, VHA, fond 37, sign. 91/6, 2; SD Tagesbericht, 9 May 1944, VHA, SNDU, k. 8, no. 36, 1.

57. On working hours, see Ctibor Nečas, "Osudy města za nacistické okupace národně osvobozovacího boje," in Miroslav Havrlat et al., eds., *Dějiny Ostravy* (Ostrava: Profil, 1967), 518. On deaths in Germany, see Mainuš, *Totálně nasazení*, 209. In 1943, 10,808 factory workers died of tuberculosis. Musilová "Zásobováni, 263.

58. [Anonymous author], "Zprávy z Protektorátu," 28 Mar. 1944, VHA, fond 37, sign. 91/6, 3.

59. On agricultural production, the quality of goods, and average calorie intake in the last years of the war, see Musilová, "Zásobování," 261–263. E. Šedivý, "Zpráva a domova," 19 May 1944, VHA, fond 37, sign. 91/7, 1–2, quotation from 2. See also "Zpráva ceského ucitele A. Merta ze severní Moravy," 6 May 1942, JS, k. 12, Reports from ČSR, 1942–1943, 8–9; [anonymous informant], 17 Aug. 1943, VHA, fond 37, sign. 91/6, 1; Inž. Barton, "Zpráva o domově," 14 Aug. 1944, VHA, fond 37, sign. 91/7, 2.

60. Frommer, "Retribution," 112. See also "Zpráva v poměrech ve vlasti," 6

Oct. 1943, VHA, fond 37, sign. 91/6, 3; "Zprávy o školských," 16 Oct. 1944, VHA, fond 37, sign. 91/7, 2; [no title], 17 Apr. 1944, VHA, fond 37, sign. 91/7, 3; "Zprávy hospodářské," 10 Feb. 1944, VHA, fond 37, sign. 91/4, 2.

61. Frommer, "Retribution," 113–119.

62. František Bauer, "Materiály k odboji," personal papers, AV ČR, 1, 2.

63. Quotation from [anonymous informant], "Zprávy z domova," 21 Feb. 1944, VHA, fond 37, sign. 91/7, 1. See also Netík, "Zpráva z domova," 5 Feb. 1944, VHA, fond 37, sign. 91/7, 2.

64. Václav Černý, *Křik koruny české: Paměti 1938–1945: Náš kulturní odboj za války* (Prague: Atlantis, 1992), 227–228.

65. "Ze soukromého dopisu z Moravy," 6 June 1939, VHA, fond 37, sign. 91/1, 1. díl, 2, 1.

66. Inž. Barton, "Zpráva o domově," 14 Aug. 1944, VHA, fond 37, sign. 91/7, 6.

67. [Anonymous informant], "Spojenecký nálet na Most a zprávy z domova," 5 June 1944, VHA, fond 37, sign. 91/7, 2. See also Zahra, "Reclaiming Children," 535.

68. "Zprávy z Prahy z konce června 1942," JS, k. 12, Reports from ČSR, 1942–1943, 1.

69. Zdeněk Sládek, "Vliv nacistické nadvlády na politický vývoj v Čechách a na Moravě," *Soudobé dějiny* 1, nos. 4–5 (1995): 535; Tomáš Pasák and Milan Drápala, "Čeští vysokoškolští studenti v Sachsenhausenu a postoj protektorátní správy," *Soudobé dějiny* 2, no. 4 (1996): 509, 512.

70. Inž. Šrajbera, "Zpráva z domova," 2 Sept. 1944, VHA, fond 37, sign 91/7, 2. Similar claims were made before and during the Heydrich era. See, for example, [anonymous informant], "Vnitropolitická situace," 14–15 Mar. 1939, VHA, fond 37, sign. 91/1, 1 díl, 1, 6; and Lib. & Ice, "Zprávy z Prahy ze dne 6. února 1942," JS, k. 12, Reports from ČSR, 1942–1943, 3.

71. On views about London radio, see [anonymous informant], [no title], 17 Apr. 1944, VHA, fond 37, sign. 91/7, 3. Also Netík, "Zpráva z domova," 5–8 Feb. 1944, VHA, fond 37, sign. 91/7, 5; Albert Kaufmann, "Zpráva z domova," 22 Apr. 1943, VHA, fond 37, sign. 91/6, 8–9. On rumors, see Albert Kaufmann, "Zpráva z domova," 22 Apr. 1943, VHA, fond 37, sign. 91/6, 1; [anonymous informant], "Zprávy o sabotážích, politické a hospodářské situaci v Protektorátě," 27 Aug. 1943, VHA, fond 37, sign. 91/6, 1. Also [anonymous informant], "Zprávy z vlasti a Maďarska," 16 Nov. 1943, VHA, fond 37, sign. 91/6, 1.

72. Gross, *Polish Society,* 178, 180. For a literary account, see Jurek Becker, *Jacob the Liar,* trans. Melvin Kornfeld (New York: Harcourt Brace Jo-

vanovich, 1975). Flem's observation quoted in Alain Corbin, *The Village of Cannibals: Rage and Murder in France, 1870*, trans. Arthur Goldhammer (Cambridge, Mass.: Harvard University Press, 1992), 7–8.

73. [Anonymous informant], "Zprávy o poměrech ve vlasti," 6 Oct. 1943, VHA, fond 37, sign. 91/6, 3. See also Marek, "Feutera a zprávy z domova," 2 Oct. 1944, VHA, fond 37, sign. 91/7, 1.

74. People have little appetite for satire from London radio, one informant reported: "The nation today finds itself in a serious situation, [surrounded by] great events, and we cannot bear frivolous jokes [from you]." [Anonymous informant], "Zpráva z Čech," 13 May 1944, VHA, fond 37, sign. 91/7, 1.

75. Czech sources cite both *vtipy* and *anekdoty*. The former refer to a crisp, short form of humor often involving wordplay that ends with a distinct punch line. The latter usually comes in the form of a very short story, although it, too, usually ends with a punch line. In the interest of word economy I refer to both as "jokes."

76. [Escaped Protectorate soldier], "Zprávy z domova," 10 Sept. 1944, VHA, fond 37, sign. 91/7, 1; [anonymous informant], "Zpráva z domova," 24 Jan. 1944, VHA, fond 37, sign. 91/7, 8.

77. [Anonymous informant], "Zprávy z domova," 10 July 1944, VHA, fond 37, sign. 91/7, 10.

78. Albert Kaufmann, "Zpráva z domova," VHA, fond 37, sign. 91/6, 2.

79. Stanislav Michalec, [no title], February 1944, VHA, fond 37, sign. 91/7, 1.

80. *VRBM*, 1 Sept. 1939, 129.

81. Oskar Krejčí, *Země úsměvů, 1939–1945* (Prague: Gustav Peter, 1945), 22.

82. Dagmar A. interviewed by Pavla Frýdlová, in Pavla Frýdlová, ed., *Všechny naše včerejšky* (Prague: Nadace Gender Studies, 1998), 47; see also David, "The War," 7.

83. "Zprávy z Prahy," 24–32 Mar. 1942, JS, k. 12, Reports from ČSR, 1942–1943, 6; *Šest let*, 83–105.

84. Vladimír Macura, "Tak vlast si tvoří," *Masarykovy boty a jiné semi(o)fejetony* (Prague: Pražská imaginace 1993), 11–13.

85. Richard Rorty, *Contingency, Irony, and Solidarity* (Cambridge: Cambridge University Press, 1989), 185.

86. Michel de Certeau, *The Practice of Everyday Life*, trans. Steven Rendall (Berkeley: University of California Press, 1984), xix.

87. "Supplement No. 2 to the Official Czechoslovak Report," Dec. 1945, NARA, RG 238, Microfilm Publication T988, roll 11 (USA 91–132), 95–96.

88. Gruss, *Jedna paní*, 10.

89. Sigmund Freud, *The Joke and Its Relation to the Unconscious* (New York: Penguin Books, 2003); Henri Bergson, *Laughter: An Essay on the Meaning of the Comic*, trans. Cloudesley Brereton and Fred Rothwell (New York: Macmillan, 1911); Mary Douglas, "The Social Control of Cognition: Some Factors in Joke Perception," *Man* 3, no. 1 (Sept. 1968): 361–376. Of course, not all jokes are destabilizing. Ethnic jokes, for example, can reinforce rather than question debilitating stereotypes and, hence, reinforce existing orders and hierarchies.

90. Detlev Peukert, *Inside Nazi Germany: Conformity, Opposition, and Racism in Everyday Life*, trans. Richard Deveson (New Haven, Cann.: Yale University Press, 1987), 63–64.

91. Corbin, *The Village*, 7; SD Tagesbericht, 6 June 1944, VHA, SDNU, k. 8, sign. 74/5, no. 44, 8; [anonymous informant], "Z domova," 21 July 1942, VHA, fond 37, sign. 91/5, 3; Moulis and Tomášek, *K. H. Frank*, 437; Dr. Feuter, "Zpráva z domova ze začátku února 1943," JS, box 12, Reports from ČSR, 1942–1943, 6.

92. Karel Kosík, "Švejk and Bugulma, or, The Birth of Great Humor," *The Crisis of Modernity: Essays and Observations from the 1968 Era*, trans. James H. Satterwhite (Boston: Rowman & Littlefield, 1995), 98–99.

93. Aleš Dubovský, *Kroměříž ve stínu hákového kříže* (Kroměříž: Muzeum kroměřížská, 1995), 128, 129. The second joke is also in Gruss, *Jedna paní*, 97.

94. De Certeau, *The Practice of Everyday Life*, xix.

95. The Belgian Information Center, *Belgian Humor under the German Heel* (New York: Belgian Information Center, 1943); Otto Ramfjord, *Ockupationshumor: Historier från ockupationstidens Norge och Danmark och andra länder* (Stockholm: Folket i bilds förlag, 1944); *Wien wehrt sich mit dem Witz: Flüsterwitze aus dem Jahren 1938–1945* (Vienna: Im Weltweiten Verlag, 1946); Sait Orahovac, *Partizani u anegdotama* (Sarajevo: Svjetlost, 1964); Hans-Jochen Gamm, *Der Flüsterwitz im Dritten Reich* (Munich: List, 1979); Franz Danimann, *Flüsterwitze und Spottgedichte unterm Hakenkreuz* (Vienna: Böhlau, 1983); Fritz Karl Michael Hillenbrand, *Underground Humour in Nazi Germany, 1933–1945* (London: Routledge, 1995).

96. Dubovský, *Kroměříž*, 130–131; *Wien wehrt sich*, 18; similar jokes can also be found in Danimann, *Flüsterwitze*, 24.

97. One joke from summer 1939, for example, went: Hitler, when he gave Poles their ultimatum, said at the end: *"Entweder-oder"* (either-or). The Poles answered: OK as far as the Oder. (The Oder is a river that now marks the border between Germany and Poland.) "Ze soukromého dopisu z Moravy," 6 June 1939, VHA, fond 37, sign. 91/1, 1. díl, 2, 1.

98. Krejčí, *Země*, 22–23. See also [anonymous informant], [no title], 17 Apr. 1944, VHA, fond 37, sign. 91/7, 3.

99. Tomáš Staněk, *Odsun Němců z Československa, 1945–1947* (Prague: Naše vojsko, 1991), 53.

100. "Miroslav," "Zprávy z vlasti a Maďarska," VHA, fond 37, sign. 91/6, 1; Volker Zimmermann, *Die Sudetendeutschen im NS-Staat: Politik und Stimmung der Bevölkerung im Reichsgau Sudetenland (1938–1945)* (Essen: Klartext, 1999), 433.

101. [No author], "Zpráva ze dne 15 dubna," 15–18 Apr. 1943, JS, k. 12, Reports from ČSR, 1942–1943, 5.

102. Mastny, *The Czechs*, 21.

103. Jiří Pernes, *Až na dno zrady: Emanuel Moravec* (Prague: Themis, 1997), 163. See also František Bauer, "České noviny za války," *Šest let*, 71–76; "Novinářský odboj," personal papers of František Bauer, AV ČR, esp. 8; Tomáš Pasák, *Soupis legálních novin, časopisů a úředních věstníků v českých zemích z let 1939–1945* (Prague: Univerzita Karlova, 1980).

104. Dr. Feuter, "Zpráva z domova ze začatku února 1943," JS, k. 12, Reports from ČSR 1942–1943, 6.

105. Zahra, "Reclaiming Children," 333–338, quotations from *Rudé právo* and the author on 535. Intelligence Service quotation from SD Tagesbericht, 23 May 1944, VHA, SDNU, k. 8, sbírka č. 40, 6. See also A. Krejčí, "Sokolstvo," *Šest let*, 238; Brandes, *Die Tschechen*, 2: 241; "Zprávy z domova," 24 Jan. 1944, VHA fond 37, sign. 91/7, 3. Václav Černý called the Kuratorium a "Czech caricature" of the Hitler Youth. Černý, *Křik koruny české*, 226.

106. Numerous reports to the London government take note of the influx of German refugees, and especially children, into the Protectorate. Given the nature of the sources, however, it is difficult to determine exactly how many arrived. Albert Kaufmann, 22 Apr. 1943, VHA, fond 37, sign. 91/6, 6; [no author] "Czechoslovakia," March 1943, VHA, fond 37, sign. 91/6, 7; [no author], "Zprávy hospodářské," 10 Feb. 1944, VHA fond 37, sign. 91/4, 2; and [no title], 6 Feb. 1945, HIWPR, ÚVOD, 9.

107. Joanna K.M. Hanson, *The Civilian Population and the Warsaw Uprising* (Cambridge: Cambridge University Press, 1982), esp. 202. My thanks to Mary Kathryn Werden for this citation.

108. Norman Rich, *Hitler's War Aims: The Establishment of the New Order* (New York: W. W. Norton, 1974), 64–65. On the number of Slovak dead, see Pavel Škropil, "Probleme bei der Berechnung der Zahl der tschechoslowakischen Todesopfer des nationalsozialistischen Deutschlands," in Detlef Brandes and Václav Kural, eds., *Der Weg in die Katastrophe: Deutsch-tschechoslowakische Beziehungen 1938–1947* (Essen: Klartext, 1994): 161–164.

109. SD Tagesbericht, 6 Oct. 1944, VHA, SDNU, k. 8, no. 86, 3. Also SD Tages-bericht, 26 Sept. 1944, VHA, SDNU, k. 8, no. 83, 1; [anonymous in-formant], "Fuertera a zprávy z domova," 2 Oct. 1944, VHA, fond 37, sign. 91/7, 2.

110. First quotation from Brandes, *Die Tschechen*, 2: 100. Second quotation from SD Tagesbericht, 26 Sept. 1944, VHA, SDNU, k. 8, no. 83, 2. Third quotation from SD Tagesbericht, 15 Aug. 1944, VHA, SDNU, k. 8, no. 79, 5.

111. Tony Judt, "The Past Is Another Country: Myth and Memory in Postwar Europe," in István Deák, Jan T. Gross, and Tony Judt, eds., *The Politics of Retribution in Europe: World War II and Its Aftermath* (Princeton, N.J.: Princeton University Press, 2000), 298–299.

112. Gruss, *Jedna paní*, 10, Dubovský, *Kroměříž*, 127.

113. Krejčí, *Země*, 22.

6. All the Germans Must Go

1. Edvard Beneš, *Šest let exilu a druhé světové války* (Prague: Orbis, 1946), 215–222, quotations from 221, 220, 221.

2. On the number of Germans expelled from Eastern Europe, see Robert Paul Magosci, *Historical Atlas of Central Europe* (Seattle: University of Wash-ington Press, 2002), 192. On the number of expellees in West Germany, see Wolfgang Benz, "Vierzig Jahre nach der Vertreibung: Einleitende Be-merkungen," in Wolfgang Benz, ed., *Die Vertreibung der Deutschen aus dem Osten: Ursachen, Ereignisse, Folgen* (Frankfurt: Fischer, 1985), 8.

3. Norman M. Naimark, *Fires of Hatred: Ethnic Cleansing in Twentieth-Century Europe* (Cambridge, Mass.: Harvard University Press, 2001), 122–123; Klaus-Dietmar Henke, "Der Weg nach Potsdam—Die Allierten und die Vertreibung," in *Die Vertreibung*, 61.

4. Eduard [*sic*] Beneš, "The Organization of Postwar Europe," *Foreign Affairs* 20, no. 2 (Jan. 1942): 226–242, quotations from 237, 238, and 239.

5. Eva Schmidt-Hartmann, "Menschen oder Nationen? Die Vertreibung der Deutschen aus tschechischer Sicht," in *Die Vertriebung*, 143.

6. Masaryk's two quotations are from Jan Masaryk, *Volá Londýn* (Prague: Práce, 1948), 195–196 and 218. For Drtina's radio address following the Lidice massacres, see Jan Kuklík, "Němci očima Čechů, 1939–1943," in Jan Gebhart and Ivan Šedivý, eds., *Česká společnost za velkých válek 20. sto-letí (pokus o komparaci)* (Prague: Karolinum, 2003), 71–72, quotation on 72. Beneš, *Šest let*, 233. See also Prokop Drtina, *A nyní promluví Pavel Svatý: Londýnské rozhlasové epištoly z let 1940–1945* (Prague: Melantrich, 1947), 367–368. On the salience of the language of "guilt" surrounding

the expulsions, see Tomáš Staněk, *Verfolgung 1945: Die Stellung des Deutschen in Böhmen, Mähren und Schlesien (außerhalb der Lager und Gefängnisse)*, trans. Otfrid Pustejovsky (Vienna: Böhlau, 2002), esp. 10. On the St. James agreement, see Benjamin Frommer, *National Cleansing: Retribution against Nazi Collaborators in Postwar Czechoslovakia* (Cambridge: Cambridge University Press, 2005), 66. On the linkages between retribution and the transfer, and the effects that each had on the other, see Benjamin Frommer, "To Prosecute or Expel? Czechoslovak Retribution and the 'Transfer' of the Sudeten Germans," in Phillip Ther and Ana Siljak, eds., *Redrawing Nations: Ethnic Cleansing in East-Central Europe, 1944–1948* (Lanham, Md.: Rowman & Littlefield, 2001), 221–240.

7. Detlef Brandes, *Der Weg zur Vertreibung 1938–1945: Pläne und Entscheidungen zum "Transfer" der Deutschen aus der Tschechoslowakei und aus Polen* (Munich: R. Oldenbourg, 2001), 291.

8. Eagle Glassheim, "The Mechanics of Ethnic Cleansing: The Expulsion of the Germans from Czechoslovakia, 1945–1947," in *Redrawing Nations*, 200–201.

9. Francis Dostál Raška, *The Czechoslovak Exile Government in London and the Sudeten German Issue* (Prague: Karolinum, 2002), 61.

10. Vojtech Mastny, *Russia's Road to the Cold War: Diplomacy, Warfare, and the Politics of Communism, 1911–1945* (New York: Columbia University Press, 1979), 139.

11. Gottwald's quotation is from Zbyněk Zeman with Antonín Klimek, *The Life of Edvard Beneš, 1884–1948: Czechoslovakia in Peace and War* (Oxford: Clarendon Press Oxford, 1997), 197. Beneš's comment to the Communists is from Igor Lukeš, "The Czech Road to Communism," in Norman Naimark and Leonid Gibianskii, eds., *The Establishment of Communist Regimes in Eastern Europe, 1944–1949* (Boulder, Colo.: Westview Press, 1997), 248.

12. Brandes, *Der Weg*, 290. For a thoughtful treatment of Stalin's various attitudes toward postwar expulsions in Eastern Europe, as well as their relationship to nationalities policy in the Soviet Union before 1945, see Timothy Snyder, *The Reconstruction of Nations: Poland, Ukraine, Lithuania, Belarus, 1569–1999* (New Haven, Conn.: Yale University Press, 2003), 182–187.

13. Igor Lukeš, *Czechoslovakia between Stalin and Hitler: The Diplomacy of Edvard Beneš in the 1930s* (Oxford: Oxford University Press, 1996), 68–78.

14. Emilia Hrabovec, *Vertreibung und Abschub: Deutsche in Mähren 1945–1947* (Frankfurt: Peter Lang, 1995), 43–48, quotation on 46.

15. On Czechoslovak Communist broadcasts from London, see Zdeněk Suda, *Zealots and Rebels: A History of the Ruling Party of Czechoslovakia* (Stanford,

Calif.: Stanford University Press, 1981), 161–162; Klement Gottwald, *Selected Speeches and Articles, 1929–1953* (Prague: Orbis, 1954), 113, 119–121. On *Rudé právo,* see Jan Rataj, "Obraz Němce a Německa v protektorátní společnosti a československém odboji," in Jan Křen and Eva Broklová, eds., *Obraz Němců, Rakouska a Německa v české společnosti 19. a 20. století* (Prague: Karolinum, 1998), 227.

16. For the 1944 memorandum, see Jitka Vondrová, ed., *Češi a sudetoněmecká otázka 1939–1945: Dokumenty* (Prague: Ústav mezinárodních vztahů, 1994), doc. 148, 308. Brandes, *Der Weg,* 299–302. On the Allied responses to the 1944 memorandums, see Brandes, *Der Weg,* 305–306; Raška, *The Czechoslovak Exile Government,* 72–73.

17. On the exchange between Stránský and Gottwald, see Hrabovec, *Vertreibung,* 54. For Beneš's quotation, see Brandes, *Der Weg,* 308.

18. Beneš, *Šest let,* 225–226; [anonymous informant], "Zprávy z domova," 10 July 1944, VHA, fond 37, sign. 91/7, 1–2. This portion of the document has been reprinted in Vondrová, *Češi,* doc. 135, 279.

19. Brandes, *Der Weg,* 291–292.

20. Vilém Beneš, "Zprávy z Protektorátu," 28 Mar. 1944, VHA, fond 37, sign. 91/7, 8.

21. See, for example, [anonymous informant], "Zpráva z domova," 19 May 1944, VHA, fond 37 sign. 91/7, 2. See also Abrams, *The Struggle,* 53–61; Abrams's term, "revolutionary élan," is on 56.

22. SD Tagesbericht, 9 May 1944, VHA, SDNU, k. 8, no. 36, 1.

23. Glassheim, "The Mechanics," 213–214.

24. [Anonymous informant], [no title], 22 June 1944, fond 37, sign. 91/7, 6.

25. Netíka, "Zpráva z domova," 5–8 Feb. 1944, VHA, fond 37, sign. 91/7, 2; [Anonymous informant], "Pro doktora Beneše," 22 Jan. 1944, VHA, fond 37, sign. 91/7, 2.

26. A. Merta, "Zpráva českého učitele A. Merta ze severní Moravy," 6 May 1942, 6 Feb. 1942, JS, k. 12, Reports from ČSR, 1942–1943, 18; [anonymous informant], "Zprávy z domova," 18 Jan. 1945, VHA, fond 37, sign. 91/8, 1.

27. Vondrová, *Češi,* doc. 39, 77; and doc. 40, 79. See also "Jak to bude se sudetskými Němci?" *V boj* 3, no. 47 (1940): 372; and Brandes, *Die Tschechen,* 1:179.

28. "Monatsbericht: Die politische Entwicklung im Protektorat Böhmen und Mähren," SD report, May 1940, VHA, SDNU, k. 7, sbírka č. 74, jednotka 48, 1, 46; "Zprávy politické," 20 Feb. 1940, VHA, fond 37, 91/4, 2; [no author], "Zprávy politické," 21 Jan. 1941, VHA, fond 37, sign. 91/4, 2; Brandes, *Die Tschechen,* 1:170.

29. ONH, doc. 27, 342–344. See Neurath's angry response to this indiscretion

in a letter to Martin Bormann in ONH, doc. 28, 344; Mastny, *The Czechs,* 133; Jaroslava Milotová, "Die NS-Pläne zur Lösung der 'tschechische Frage,'" *Erzwungene Trennung,* 24–25.

30. [Anonymous informant], "Zprávy z domova," 10 July 1944, VÚA, fond 37, sign. 91/7, 2. See also Kuklík, "Němci," 67, 70; Raška, *The Czechoslovak Exile Government,* 43; and, more generally, Václav Vrabec, "Ke genezi transferu Němců v domácím odboji," in Bohumil Černý, Jan Křen, Václav Kural, and Milan Otáhal, eds., *Češi, Němci, odsun. Diskuse nezávislých historiků* (Prague: Academia, 1990): 289–291.

31. Roger D. Petersen, *Understanding Ethnic Violence: Fear, Hatred, and Resentment in Twentieth-Century Eastern Europe* (Cambridge: Cambridge University Press, 2002), 3. The emotions described in the preceding and following paragraph draw heavily on Petersen's four "emotion narratives"—Fear, Hatred, Resentment, and Rage. I have not, however, restricted myself to Petersen's definitions of these emotions or the mechanisms discussed in his study. See also Beth Wilner, "Czechoslovakia, 1848–1998," in Petersen, *Understanding Ethnic Violence,* 175–207.

32. Albert Kaufmann, "Zpráva z domova," April 1943, VHA, fond 37, sign. 91/6, 2; [no author], "Zprávy z domova," 2 June 1942, JS, k. 12, Reports from ČSR, 1942–1943, 4. See also SD Tagesbericht, 25 Aug. 1944, VHA, SDNU, k. 8, no. 73, 3.

33. Vilém Beneš, "Zprávy z Protektorátu," 28 Mar. 1944, VHA, fond 37, sign. 91/7, 8.

34. JUDr. Pavel Pringsheim, "Situační zpráva," August [?] 1942, JS, k. 12, Reports from ČSR, 1942–1943, 14; Inž. Barton, "Zpráva o domově," 14 Aug. 1944, VHA, fond 37, sign. 91/7, 5; Vilém Beneš, "Zprávy z Protektorátu," 28 Mar. 1944, VHA, fond 37, sign. 91/7, 4; [anonymous author], "Vyživování—všeobecné," 1944, VHA, fond 37, sign. 91/6, 11–15. Quotation from Vilém Beneš, "Zprávy z Protektorátu," 28 Mar. 1944, VHA, fond 37, sign. 91/7, 4.

35. Aleš Dubovský, *Kroměříž ve stínu hákového kříže* (Kroměříž: Muzeum kroměřížská, 1995), 128. A collection of jokes that leave the punch lines to Jews is in Josef Gruss, *Jedna paní povídala* (Prague: Alois Hynek, 1945), 21–28.

36. [Anonymous informant], "Zprávy z domova," 10 July 1944, VHA, fond 37, sign. 91/7, 1. This portion of the document has been reprinted in Vondrová, *Češi,* doc. 135, 279; [anonymous informant], "Pro doktora Beneše," 22 Jan. 1944, VHA, fond 37, sign. 91/7, 2. Also see Rudolf Niemetz, "Stadtgemeinde Hollegschau," [no date], BB, Ost-Dok 20, Zlin, sign. 69, 3. Members of the resistance and the intelligentsia might have been projecting

their experiences on their countrymen, laying the groundwork for a postwar resistance myth. Although the number of arrests and internments during the occupation is difficult to tabulate, it appears that less than one hundred thousand gentile Czechs and Slovaks perished at the hands of the Nazis from 1939 to 1945. The majority of these gentiles died during the Slovak uprising. The total number of gentile Czech and Slovak dead comes from Derek Sayer, *The Coasts of Bohemia: A Czech History* (Princeton, N.J.: Princeton University Press, 1998), 221. Norman Rich estimates that seventy thousand Slovaks died during the 1944 uprising. *Hitler's War Aims: Ideology, the Nazi State, and the Course of Expansion* (New York: W. W. Norton, 1973), 64.

37. Josef and Jindřich, "Zprávy z domova," 11 Apr. 1945, VHA, fond 37, sign. 91/8, 1. See also Ronald M. Smelser, "The Expulsion of the Sudeten Germans, 1945–1952," *Nationalities Papers* 24, no. 1 (Mar. 1996): 83.

38. Bohumil Hrabal, *I Served the King of England,* trans. Paul Wilson (London: Picador, 1989), 139–140.

39. On ethnic German settlers, see Vilém Beneš, "Zprávy z Protektorátu," 28 Mar. 1944, VHA, fond 37, sign. 91/7, 8. Also [no author], "Zpráva z Prahy," 30 Aug. 1943, JS, k. 12, Reports from ČSR, 1942–1943, 5. On the differences among Reich Germans, see [anonymous informant], 17 Apr. 1944, VHA, fond 37, sign. 91/7, 1. Also Inž. Šrajbera, "Zpráva z domova," 2 Oct. 1944, VHA, fond 37, sign. 91/7, 2; Dr. Feuter, "Zpráva ze začátku února 1943," Feb. 1943, JS, k. 12, Reports from ČSR, 1942–1943, 5.

40. [Anonymous informant], "Zprávy z domova," 5 May 1944, VHA, fond 37, sign. 91/7, 3, 1. See also SD Tagesbericht, 25 Aug. 1944, VHA, SDNU, k. 8, no. 73, 7.

41. Vojtěch Žampach, "The Expulsion of the Germans from Brno and the Immediate Consequences, 30 May to 7 July 1945," in Derek Paton, ed., *The Prague Yearbook of Contemporary History* (Prague: Institute of Contemporary History, 1999), 89. Inž. Barton, "Zpráva o domově," 14 Aug. 1944, VHA, fond 37, sign. 91/7, 2; Vondrová, *Češi,* doc. 137, 281. On the number of Protectorate Germans in low- to mid-level bureaucratic posts, see Rataj, "Obraz," 222.

42. Helena Krejčová and Anna Hyndráková, "Postoj Čechů k židům: Z politického zpravodajství okupační zprávy a protektorátního tisku v letech 1939–1941," *Soudobé dějiny* 2, no. 4. (1995): 593; Frommer, *National Cleansing,* 164–174.

43. [Anonymous informant], "Zpráva z domova," 5 May 1944, VHA, fond 37, sign. 91/7, 3, 4.

44. A. Merta, "Zpráva českého učitele A. Merta ze severní Moravy," 6 May 1942, JS, k. 12, Reports from ČSR, 1942–1943, 17; [anonymous in-

formant], [no title], 17 Apr. 1944, VHA, fond 37, sign. 91/7, 2. See also [anonymous informant], "Zpráva z domova," 5 May 1944, VHA, fond 37, sign. 91/7, 3, 4.

45. Netíka, "Zpráva z domova," 5–8 Feb. 1944, VHA, fond 37, sign. 91/7, 7. See also Livia Rothkirchen, *The Jews of Bohemia and Moravia: Facing the Holocaust* (Lincoln: University of Nebraska Press, 2005), 206–207.

46. Masaryk, *Volá Londýn*, 262; also ibid., 211. For a discussion of the London government's conflicting attitudes toward the "Jewish question," see Rothkirchen, *The Jews*, 160–186.

47. "Zpráva ze dne 15, 18 dubna," 15–18 Apr. 1943, JS, k. 12, Reports from ČSR, 1942–1943, 1. See also Staněk, *Verfolgung*, 27. On German fears of parachutists, see [no author], "Z domova," 21 June 1942, VHA, fond 37, sign. 91/7, 1.

48. [Anonymous informant], "Zprávy z Protektorátu a ze Slovenska," 28 Apr. 1943, VHA, fond 37, sign. 91/6, 1; "Zpráva ze dne 24. dubna 1943," 24 Apr. 1943, JS, k. 12, Reports from ČSR, 1942–1943, 1; [anonymous informant], "Zprávy z Protektorátu a ze Slovenska," 28 Apr. 1943, VHA, fond 37, sign. 91/6, 2; [anonymous informant], "Zpráva z domova," 20 Apr. 1944, VHA, fond 37, sign. 91/7, 3; [anonymous informant], "Zpráva z domova," 3 May 1944, VHA, fond 37, sign. 91/7, 5; SD Tagesbericht, 15 Sept. 1944, VHA, SDNU, k. 8, no. 80, 7; SD Tagesbericht, 29 Sept. 1944, VHA, SDNU, k. 8, no. 84, 6; SD Tagesbericht, 8 June 1944, VHA, SDNU, k. 8, no. 47, 1; SD Tagesbericht, 12 Sept. 1944, VHA, SDNU, k. 8, no. 79, 8.

49. Brandes, "Die Exilpolitik," 158. SD Tagesbericht, 29 Sept. 1944, SDNU, k. 8, no. 84, 3.

50. Rudolf Niemetz, "Stadtgemeinde Hollegschau," [no date], BB, Ost-Dok 20, Zlín, sign. 69, 4; Jan Kajfoš, "Zprav. příloha výslechovaného listu," VHA, fond 37, sign. 91/7, 1.

51. Miloslav Moulis and Dušan Tomášek, *K. H. Frank: Vzestup a pád karlovarského knihkupce* (Prague: Epocha, 2003), 299, 437.

52. [Anonymous informant], "Zpráva o domově," 24 Sept. 1944, VHA, fond 37, sign. 91/7, 2; [anonymous informant] "Situace v Čechách a na Moravě," 14 Sept. 1944; reprinted in Vondrová, *Češi*, doc. 143, 293. Quotation from [anonymous informant], "Zprávy z domova," 10 Oct. 1944, VHA, fond 37, sign. 91/7, 2.

53. Naimark, *Fires*, 124.

54. Žampach, "The Expulsion," 93. Nr. 60- Tgb.Nr. 891/44g. to Landespräsident in Brünn, 28 Dec. 1944, MZAB, B 252, k. 18, 2. Nr. 60—Tgb.Nr. 779/44g to Landespräsident in Brünn, 25 Oct. 1944, MZAB, B 252, k. 18, 1.

55. Nr. 60—Tgb.Nr. 998/45g. to Landespräsident in Brünn, 22 Feb. 1945, MZAB, B 252, k. 18, 1–2.

56. J. Charvát, "Deníky," 10 Feb. 1945, 11 Jan. 1945, 20 Jan. 1945, personal papers, AV ČR.

57. Staněk, *Verfolgung,* 28.

58. Brandes, *Der Weg,* 377. Also Staněk, *Verfolgung,* 28. On the local population's reaction to the refugees' stories, see Nr. 60—Tgb.Nr. 625/44g. to Landespräsident in Brünn, 25 Aug. 1944, MZAB, B 252, k. 18, 1.

59. Marek, "Fuetera a zprávy z domova," 2 Aug. 1944, VHA, fond 37, sign. 91/7, 4; [anonymous informant], "Zprávy z domova," 26 June 1944, VHA, fond 37, sign. 91/8, 1; [no author], "Zpráva ze dne 15., 18. dubna," 15–18 Apr. 1943, JS, k. 12, Reports from ČSR, 1942–1943, 1.

60. Jan Musekamp, "Brno/Brünn 1938–1945: Eine Stadt in einem Jahrzehnt erzwungener Wanderungen," *Zeitschrift für Ostmitteleuropa-Forschung* 53 (2004): 14. Brandes, *Der Weg,* 377. Quotation from Heinz Lämmel, 16 Sept. 1960, Iglau, BB, Ost-Dok 20, Iglauer Sprachinsel, sign. 66, 27. On Protectorate German expectations about Czech behavior, see also Staněk, *Verfolgung,* 68. On the feeling of hopelessness, see also Der Polizeidirektor in Olmütz to Landespräsident in Brünn, 4 Apr. 1945, MZAB, B 252, k. 18, 1.

61. On the Czechoslovak soldiers abroad, see the articles and recollections in Lewis M. White, ed., *On All Fronts: Czechoslovaks in World War II,* vols. 1–3 (Boulder, Colo.: East European Monographs, 1991, 1995, 2000), and especially the introduction by Lewis M. White in vol. 2, 1–14. Quotations from Rataj, "Obraz," 227; and Brandes, *Der Weg,* 299.

62. On the Red Army's atrocities in Slovakia, see Zeman, *The Life,* 222–223. On atrocities committed by the SS, see Frommer, *National Cleansing,* 41.

63. Mark Mazower, *Dark Continent: Europe's Twentieth Century* (London: Penguin Books, 1998), 235; John Lampe, *Yugoslavia as History: Twice There Was a Country* (Cambridge: Cambridge University Press, 2000), 228–229.

64. Beneš, *Šest let,* 212.

65. Zeman, *The Life,* 226; Raška, *The Czechoslovak Exile Government,* 69.

66. Vondrová, *Češi,* doc. 140, 288 and n. 2, 286. Drtina, in fact, had been urging similar actions as early as December 1940. Vondrová, *Češi,* doc. 42, 80.

67. Beneš, *Šest let,* 223. Italics in the original.

68. Masaryk, *Volá Londýn,* 302.

69. Jan Gronský, ed., *Dokumenty k ústavnímu vývoji Československa (1945–1968)* (Prague: Karolinum, 1999), doc. 2, 14–26, quotation on 14. See also Bradley Abrams, *The Struggle for the Soul of the Nation: Czech Culture and the Rise of Communism* (Lanham, Md.: Rowman & Littlefield, 2004), 55; and Frommer, *National Cleansing,* 45–49, 72–75

70. Frommer, *National Cleansing,* 73–74, n. 35.

71. Glassheim, "The Mechanics," 204.

72. Jech, *Dokumenty,* doc. 2, 19–21, quotations on 20 and 21. See also Glassheim, "The Mechanics," 203.

73. Brandes, *Der Weg,* 313.

74. Stanislav Kokoška, *Praha v květnu 1945. Historie jednoho povstání* (Prague: Lidové noviny, 2005), 75–77; Zeman, *The Life,* 242; Moulis and Tomášek, *K. H. Frank,* 378–379.

75. Kokoška, *Praha,* 106–108, 113–127, quotation on 113; Brandes, *Die Tschechen,* 2:122–124; Zeman, *The Life,* 240–241.

76. Brandes, *Die Tschechen,* 2:136. On the underground's decision to accept Vlasov's aid, see Kokoška, *Praha,* 156–184.

77. Brandes, *Die Tschechen,* 2:135–136, quotations on 135, 136.

78. Staněk, *Verfolgung,* 91–92; Glassheim, "The Mechanics," 206.

79. Zdeněk David, "The War, The Nazi Protectorate, and Victory: Recollections," *Kosmos* 12, no. 1 (Summer 1996): 23. This was not the only case of people being burned alive. See Staněk, *Verfolgung,* 95.

80. Glassheim, "The Mechanics," 206; Staněk, *Verfolgung,* 94–97. On Czech casualties, see ibid., 92.

81. Staněk, *Verfolgung,* 98; Zeman, *The Life,* 242.

82. Naimark, *Fires,* 118–119; Staněk, *Verfolgung,* 146. Quotation from Staněk, *Verfolgung,* 161. See also ibid., 34.

83. Frommer, *National Cleansing,* 57–60.

84. Staněk, *Verfolgung,* 225.

85. Glassheim, "The Mechanics," 203–204, quotation from 204; Staněk, *Verfolgung,* 32, 57–59, 71.

86. Staněk, *Verfolgung,* 90.

87. Franz Koupil, Iglau, 9 Nov. 1955, BB, Ost-Dok 21, Iglauer Sprachinsel, sign. 66, 2; J. D., Iglau, [no date], BB, Ost-Dok 21, Iglauer Sprachinsel, sign. 66, 2; Staněk, *Verfolgung,* 34, 114.

88. Musekamp, "Brno/Brünn 1938–1945," 16.

89. Žampach, "The Expulsion," 94.

90. Glassheim, "The Mechanics," 206. See also Staněk, *Verfolgung,* 115–121.

91. Staněk, *Verfolgung,* 108–109; quotation from 125.

92. Alois Harasko, "Die Vertreibung der Sudetendeutschen: Sechs Erlebnisberichte," in *Die Vertreibung,* 105–117, here 111–112.

93. Eagle Glassheim, "National Mythologies and Ethnic Cleansing: The Expulsion of the Czechoslovak Germans in 1945," *CEH* 33, no. 4 (Winter 2000): 474.

94. Frommer, *National Cleansing,* 42; Staněk, *Verfolgung,* 161.

95. Frommer, *National Cleansing,* 42.

96. Staněk, *Verfolgung,* 16.

97. Ida Weidenhofferová, ed., *Konfliktní společenství, katastrofa, uvolnění: Náčrt výkladu německo-českých dějin od 19. století* (Prague: Ústav mezinárodních vztahů, 1996), 29–30. Many respected historians consider this number too low. Czech and German historians have spent much effort and time disputing the number, but, given that they lack proper documentation, the true number will likely never be known. See Naimark, *Fires*, 121. The number of Germans expelled before July (660,000) is Karel Kaplan's estimate. *Poválečné Československo: Národy a hranice* (Munich: Národní politika, 1985), 136; cited in Frommer, *National Cleansing*, 34. Theodor Schieder and a number of historians working with the West German Ministry of Expellees in the late 1950s calculated that approximately 870,000 Germans had been expelled during this time. Theodor Schieder, ed., *Documents on the Expulsion of the Germans from Eastern-Central Europe*, vol. 4, *The Expulsion of the German Population from Czechoslovakia* (Bonn: Ministry for Expellees, Refugees, and War Victims, 1960), 127.

98. Staněk, *Verfolgung*, 43, 50.

99. Henke, "Der Weg," 66.

100. Glassheim, "National Mythologies," 481–482; Staněk, *Verfolgung*, 169–175.

101. Glassheim, "The Mechanics," 208; Staněk, *Verfolung*, 44–45.

102. Mastny, *Russia's Road*, 295.

103. The phrase "channeling" is from Hans Lemberg, "Die Entwicklung der Pläne für die Aussiedlung der Deutschen aus der Tschechoslowakei," in Detlef Brandes and Václav Kural, eds., *Der Weg in die Katastrophe: Deutsch-tschechoslowakische Beziehungen 1938–1947* (Essen: Klartext, 1994), 89.

104. Brandes, *Der Weg*, 401–417; Churchill's quotation on 406; quotation from the text of the agreement and the member of the British delegation on 416. See also Naimark, *Fires*, 109–110.

105. Tomáš Staněk, *Tábory v českých zemích 1945–1948* (Opava: Tilia, 1996), 193–194.

106. Karel Jech, ed., *Němci a Maďaři v dekretech prezidenta republiky: Studie a dokumenty 1940–1945*, trans. Jan Hon and Wilfrid Antusch (Brno: Ústav pro soudobé dějiny AV ČR and Doplněk, 2003), doc. 9, 350–353. For details, see Tomáš Staněk, *Tábory*, 59–65.

107. Jech, *Němci*, doc. 10, 356–358; Staněk, *Verfolgung*, 78.

108. Gronský, *Dokumenty*, doc. 18, 81–90. See also Tomáš Staněk, *Odsun Němců z Československa 1945–1947* (Prague: Naše vojsko, 1991), 346–357.

109. *Dokumentation der Vertreibung*, 79–80.

110. Glassheim, "National Mythologies," 473–474, 478.

111. Jech, *Dokumenty*, doc. 4, 29–34, esp. 30–31. See also Jeremy King, *Budweisers into Czechs and Germans: A Local History of Bohemian Politics, 1848–1948* (Princeton, N.J.: Princeton University Press, 2002), 194.

112. Oldřich Sládek, "Vliv ARLZ na dochovanost archiválií v odtržených českých oblastech," *SAP* 30 (1980): 18–60; Josef Zahradniczek, Nebotein, BB, Ost-Dok 21, Olmütz, sign. 67, 11.

113. Vilém Beneš, "Zprávy z Protektorátu," 28 Mar. 1944, VHA, fond 37, sign. 91/7, 4.

114. Eva Hartmannová, "'My' a 'oni': hledání české národní identity na stránkách *Dneška* z roku 1946," in Karel Jech, ed., *Stránkami soudobých dějin: Sborník statí k pětašedesátinám historika Karla Kaplana* (Prague: Ústav pro soudobé dějiny, 1993), 101.

115. Jech, *Dokumenty,* doc. 14, 68–71, quotation on 69.

116. Benjamin Frommer, "Expulsion or Integration: Unmixing Interethnic Marriages in Postwar Czechoslovakia," *EEPS* 14 (Spring 2000): 387; Musekamp, "Brno/Brünn," 24. King, *Budweisers,* 195, 200–202, quotation on 202.

117. Toman Brod, *Československo a Sovětský svaz, 1939–1945* (Prague: Práce, 1992), 431.

118. A 1944 memorandum sent to the European Advisory Commission promised that "Germans for whom linguistic and cultural allegiance does not imply a political allegiance to Germany" would be allowed to remain, as would "most of the nationally indifferent elements who considered themselves German because of some fortuitous [sic] circumstances." The memorandum also stated that the transfers should be "planned so as to keep to a minimum the economic injury to the Republic, which might result from a sudden and indiscriminate removal of skilled man-power." Vondrová, *Češi,* doc. 148, 305–306, 304. See also Brandes, *Der Weg,* 294, 295. On postwar requests for German labor, see Staněk, *Verfolgung,* 47; Frommer, "To Prosecute," 234.

119. Andrei Villen Bell, "The Expulsion of the Sudeten Germans: A Breakdown in the Ethnic Boundary Maintenance Mechanisms" (Ph.D. diss., Boston University, 1997), 294–295.

120. Frommer, "Expulsion," 402–403, quotation on 402.

121. V. Brož, "Rozvody a rozluky za okupace," *Statistický zpravodaj* 9, no. 6 (June 1946): 183.

122. Frommer, "Expulsion," 387–88, 390–1, 406; Staněk, *Odsun,* 167.

123. Hrabovec, *Vertreibung,* 371–419, esp. 373–374, 377, 417.

124. Frommer, *National Cleansing,* 2.

125. Benjamin Frommer, "To Prosecute," esp. 225–227; Tomáš Staněk, *Retribuční vězni v českých zemích 1945–1955* (Opava: Slezský ústav Slezského zemského muzea, 2002), 40.

126. Frommer, "To Prosecute," 222–225, 229–231; quotation from 224–225.

127. Staněk, *Verfolgung,* 37, 41, 48–50, 77.

128. Hrabovec, *Vertreibung,* 384, 388, 418; Frommer, "Expulsion," 390–395; King, *Budweisers,* 200.

129. Šárka Nepalová, "Židé v českých zemích v letech 1945–1948," *Dějiny a současnost* 21, no. 21 (1999); statistics from 54, quotation from 55.

130. *Němci,* doc. 3, 235–236, doc. 5, 271, doc. 12, 363–364; Nepalová, "Židé," 54–55; Helena Krejčová, "Český a slovenský antisemitismus 1945–1948," *Stránkami soudobých dějin,* 159–162.

131. Karel Kaplan, *Pravda o Československu 1945–1948* (Prague: Panorama, 1990), 135–137, quotation on 137.

132. On political rhetoric, see Glassheim, "National Mythologies," 479. On offenses against national honor, see Frommer, *National Cleansing,* 204–206. On Pitter, see Tomáš Pasák, "Přemysl Pitters Protest: Eine unbekannte tschechische Stimme gegen die Greuel in den Internierungslagern, 1945," *Boh* 35, no. 1 (1994): 90–104. On the protest by Catholic writers, see Nancy Wingfield, *Flag Wars and Stone Saints: How the Bohemian Lands Became Czech* (Cambridge, Mass.: Harvard University Press, forthcoming, 2007), 385–386. On the debates surrounding mixed marriages, see Benjamin Frommer, "Expulsion," 381–410.

133. Staněk, *Odsun,* 227, 317; Staněk, *Německá menšina v českých zemích 1948–1989* (Klatovy: Dragon Press, 1993), 86–87.

134. Naimark, *Fires,* 122.

135. On the collapse of institutions as providing the conditions for ethnic cleansing, see Rogers Brubaker, "Aftermaths of Empire and the Unmixing of Peoples," *Nationalism Reframed: Nationhood and the National Question in the New Europe* (New York: Cambridge University Press, 1996), 148–78.

136. Henke, "Der Weg," 53–64.

137. For a discussion of how political leaders can establish a context for mass violence and population displacements to occur, see Mark Mazower, "Violence and the State in the Twentieth Century," *American Historical Review* 107 (Oct. 2002): 1164. See also Frommer, *National Cleansing,* 60–61.

138. 21 Sept. 1940, *Šest let,* 85, 86. Beneš's determination to draw upon Masaryk's legacy while pursuing a "revolution" continued after the war. For a discussion, see Christianne Brennerová, "Mezi tradicí a revolucí: Kontinuita a změny v myšlení Edvarda Beneše po druhé světové válce," *DaS* 24, no. 6 (2004): 40–44.

Conclusion

1. The new arrivals to West Germany included refugees from the Soviet zone in Germany as well as from Eastern Europe. Rainer Schulze, "The German Refugees from the East and the Creation of a Western German Identity

after World War II," in Phillip Ther and Ana Siljak, eds., *Redrawing Nations: Ethnic Cleansing in East-Central Europe, 1944–1948* (Lanham, Md.: Rowman & Littlefield, 2001), 308.

2. Norman M. Naimark, "Revolution and Counterrevolution in Eastern Europe," in Christiane Lemke and Gary Marks, eds., *The Crisis of Socialism in Europe* (Durham, N.C.: Duke University Press, 1992), 78.

3. Alice Teichová, *The Czechoslovak Economy, 1918–1980* (London: Routledge, 1988), 102.

4. Zbyněk Zeman with Antonín Klimek, *The Life of Edvard Beneš, 1884–1948: Czechoslovakia in Peace and War* (Oxford: Clarendon Press, 1997), 247–248; Zdeněk Radvanovský, "The Social and Economic Consequences of Resettling Czechs into Northwestern Bohemia," in *Redrawing Nations*, 245, 248.

5. Teichová, *The Czechoslovak Economy*, 92.

6. Radvanovský, "The Social and Economic Consequences," 252; Teichová, *The Czechoslovak Economy*, 99.

7. Naimark, "Revolution," 68.

8. Teichová, *The Czechoslovak Economy*, 103, 109.

9. Jon Bloomfield, *Passive Revolution. Politics and the Czechoslovak Working Class, 1945–1948* (New York: St. Martin's Press, 1979), 91–105; Naimark, "Revolution," 67–68; Zdeněk Sládek, "Vliv nacistické nadvlády na politický vývoj v Čechách a na Moravě," *Soudobé dějiny* 1, nos. 4–5 (1994): 534–535.

10. Karel Kaplan, *The Short March. The Communist Takeover in Czechoslovakia, 1945–1948* (London: C. Hurst, 1987), 44, 45; Peter Heumos, "Arbeiterschaft und kommunistische Machtübernähme in der Tschechoslowakei und in Polen," in Peter Heumos, ed., *Polen und die böhmischen Länder im 19. und 20. Jahrhundert: Politik und Gesellschaft im Vergleich* (Munich: R. Oldenbourg, 1997), 301–309. For an excellent overview on the fate of clubs and associations after the war, see *Průvodce po archivních fondech a sbírkách* 2, no. 3 (Prague: Archivní správa ministerstva vnitra ČR, 1990): 5–144. On the political exclusion of resistance fighters, see Zeman, *The Life of Edvard Beneš*, 244. Indeed, as early as 1945 leaders of the London government had dismissed as "naïve" calls by the domestic resistance for even more revolutionary economic and political measures, including the establishment of political parties. Stanislav Kokoška, *Praha v květnu 1945: Historie jednoho povstání* (Prague: Lidové noviny, 2005), 18–20. Communist leaders also managed to exclude from political power many resistance fighters loyal to Moscow. See Radomír Luža, "The Communist Party of Czechoslovakia and the Czech Resistance," 1939–1945," *Slavic Review* 28, no. 4 (Dec. 1969): 574–575.

11. M. R. Myant, *Socialism and Democracy in Czechoslovakia, 1945–1948* (Cambridge: Cambridge University Press, 1981), 56–57, 73.

12. Ibid., 86.

13. Karel Přikryl, "Zprávy z domova," 23 Sept. 1944, VHA fond 37, sign. 91/6, 2.

14. Adrian von Arburg, "Tak či onak: Nucené přesídlení v komplexním pojetí poválečné sídelní politiky v českých zemích," *Soudobé dějiny* 10, no. 3 (2003): 271–290, quotation 253.

15. Radvanovský, "The Social and Economic Consequences," esp. 248, 252–253; Jan Musekamp, "Brno/Brünn 1938–1945: Eine Stadt in einem Jahrzehnt erzwungener Wanderungen," *Zeitschrift für Ostmitteleuropa-Forschung* 53 (2004): 44.

16. Jiří Pešek, *The Revolution in Prague* (Prague: Orbis, 1946), 4–5. See also, for example, the pictures of decomposed bodies that accompanied *Šest let okupace Prahy* (Prague: Orbis, 1946).

17. Paul E. Zinner, *Communist Strategy and Tactics in Czechoslovakia, 1918–1948* (New York: Frederick A. Praeger, 1963), 180.

18. Karel Kaplan, *Pravda o Československu 1945–1948* (Prague: Panorama, 1990), 135–137, quotation on 137.

19. Eagle Glassheim, "National Mythologies and Ethnic Cleansing: The Expulsion of Czechoslovak Germans in 1945," *CEH* 33, no. 4 (2000): 463–486.

20. Antonín Kostlán, *Druhý sjezd československých historiků (5.–11 října 1947) a jeho místo ve vývoji českého dějepisectví v letech 1935–1948* (Prague: Archiv akademie věd České Republiky, 1993), esp. 143–151.

21. Jan T. Gross, "Themes for a Social History of War Experience and Collaboration," in István Deák, Jan T. Gross, and Tony Judt, eds., *The Politics of Retribution in Europe: World War II and Its Aftermath* (Princeton, N.J.: Princeton University Press, 2000), 23; Mark Mazower, *Dark Continent: Europe's Twentieth Century* (New York: Vintage Books, 2000), 214–225.

22. Tomáš Staněk, *Verfolgung 1945: Die Stellung der Deutschen in Böhmen, Mähren, und Schlesien (außerhalb der Lager und Gefängnisse)*, trans. Otfrid Pustejovsky (Vienna: Böhlau, 2002), 17.

23. Teichová, *The Czechoslovak Economy*, 106.

24. On the turn away from the West, see Abrams, *Struggle*, 104–117.

25. Joseph Rothschild and Nancy M. Wingfield, *Return to Diversity: A Political History of East Central Europe since World War II* (New York: Oxford University Press, 2000), 91.

26. Milan Kundera, *The Book of Laughter and Forgetting*, trans. Michael Henry Heim (New York: Penguin Books, 1981), 8.

27. Bradley Abrams, *The Struggle for the Soul of the Nation: Czech Culture and*

the *Rise of Communism* (Lanham, Md.: Rowman & Littlefield, 2004), 6, 281.

28. Ibid., 33. According to statistics compiled by Jan Gebhart and Ján Šimovček, almost a quarter of all partisans operating in the Protectorate in late August 1944 were twenty-four years of age or younger. Most partisans, however (just over 40 percent in August 1944), were between twenty-nine and thirty-eight years of age and had been officers in the Czechoslovak army before 1938–1939. In December 1943 the twenty-four-year-old and younger age group made up only 14 percent of the total. *Partyzáni v Československu 1941–1945* (Prague: Naše vojsko, 1984), 168.

29. Mazower, *Dark Continent*, 256.

30. Myant, *Socialism*, 136.

31. Benjamin Frommer, *National Cleansing: Retribution against Nazi Collaborators in Postwar Czechoslovakia* (Cambridge: Cambridge University Press, 2005), 180–185, quotation on 182.

32. Kaplan, *Pravda*, 137. Radvanovský, "Resettling," 251; Benjamin Frommer, "Retribution against Nazi Collaborators in Postwar Czechoslovakia" (Ph.D. diss., Harvard University, 1999), 31.

33. Rothschild and Wingfield, *Return*, 91; Bradley Abrams, "The Politics of Retribution: The Trial of Jozef Tiso in the Czechoslovak Environment," in Deák, Gross, and Judt, *The Politics*, 260–261.

34. John Connelly, *Captive University: The Sovietization of East German, Czech, and Polish Higher Education, 1945–1956* (Chapel Hill: University of North Carolina Press, 2000), 40, 101.

35. Naimark, "Revolution," 73.

36. Martin Conway, "Justice in Postwar Belgium: Popular Passions and Political Realities," in Deák, Gross, and Judt, *The Politics*, 134; Luc Huyse, "The Criminal Justice System as a Political Actor in Regime Transitions: The Case of Belgium, 1944–1950," in Deák, Gross, and Judt, *The Politics*, 161.

37. David Childs, *The Two Red Flags: European Social Democracy and Soviet Communism since 1945* (London: Routledge, 2000), 25, 29–36.

38. Gross, "Themes," 15–23; Naimark, "Revolution," 70–72; Abrams, *The Struggle*, 14–36.

39. Rothschild and Wingfield, *Return*, 88–89, 98.

40. Abrams, *The Struggle*, 10–12.

41. Rothschild and Wingfield, *Return*, 92.

42. Abrams, *The Stuggle*, 276.

43. Ibid., 277; Zeman, *The Life*, 266.

44. Abrams, *The Struggle*, 113–115.

45. Mazower, *Dark Continent*, 222.

46. Teichová, *The Czechoslovak Economy*, 102, 107.
47. Rothschild and Wingfield, *Return*, 95; Connelly, *Captive University*, 31–70. "Zákon č. 52/1949 Sb. ze dne 23. února 1949, o hlášení obyvatelstva a o povolování pobytu cizincům," in Jan Gronský, ed., *Dokumenty k ústavnímu vývoji Československa* (Prague: Karolinum, 1999), doc. 13, 332–339; Tomáš Staněk, *Retribuční vězni v českých zemích 1945–1955* (Opava: Slezský ústav Slezského zemského muzea, 2001), 142–149. For a full treatment of the camp systems in postwar Czechoslovakia, see Tomáš Staněk, *Tábory v českých zemích 1945–1948* (Opava: Tilia, 1996); and Mečislav Borák and Dušan Janák, *Tábory nucené práce v ČSR 1948–1954* (Opava: Tilia, 1996).
48. David Čaněk, "Tschechische Schulbücher für Geschichte: Ist die Zeit reif für einen Wandel?" *Bohemia* 39, no. 1 (1998): 52–70.
49. *Statistická ročenka České Republiky 1993* (Prague: Český statistický úřad, 1993), 412; "Obyvatelstvo podle věku, národnosti a podle pohlaví k 1. 3. 2001," *www.czso.cz* (accessed 12/16/05). A little more than 380,000 respondents in the 2001 census marked "Moravian" as their nationality.
50. Barbara Crossette, "Europe Stares at a Future Built by Immigrants," *New York Times*, Sunday, 2 Jan. 2000, D1, D4. Demographically speaking, the Czech Republic already has much in common with its Western neighbors. Fewer people are getting married, and the death rate has outstripped the birth rate, meaning that fewer people live in the Czech Republic now than in 1994. On average, each woman has 1.15 children, down from 2.07 in 1980. In order to maintain current population levels (without immigration), this number must be 2.1. Vladimír Dubský, "Česko má jednu z nejnižších porodností na světě," *Lidové noviny*, 12 July 2000, 3; see also Miroslava Mašková and Leona Stašová, "Population Development in the Czech Republic in the 1990s," in T. Kučera, O. V. Kučerová, O. B. Opara, and E. Schaich, eds., *New Demographic Faces of Europe: The Changing Population Dynamics in the Countries of Central and Eastern Europe* (Heidelberg: Springer, 2000), 79–102.
51. See, for example, the comments made during and after the historians' conference at Hradec Králové in 2000 at "Diskuse: Qverela historiae bohemicae (VIII. sjezd historiků ČR)," *www.clavmon.cz/archiv/polemily/index.html* (accessed 11/14/06); "Vážení čtenáři," *Kuděj* 2 (2000): 2.
52. George Orwell, "Politics and the English Language," *A Collection of Essays* (Garden City, N.Y.: Doubleday Anchor Books, 1954), 173–174.
53. E. Šedivý, "Zpráva z domova," 19 May 1944, VHA fond 37, sign. 91/7, 2.
54. 2 KLs 217/44, Sondergericht, SOAP.

Archival Sources

Czech Republic

Archiv Akademie věd České Republiky v Praze
  František Bauer papers
  Jan Charvát papers
Moravský zemský archiv v Brně
  B 252 Zemský president Brno
  B 254 Vrchní zemský rada v Brně a okresní hejtman v Brně
  B 255 Vrchní zemský rada v Jihlavě
Národní archiv (formerly the Státní ústřední archiv)
  Úřad říšského Protektora
  Úřad říšského Protektora-dodatky II
Státní oblastní archiv v Praze
  Oberlandrat Kolín
  Sondergericht
Vojenský historický archiv v Praze
  Fond 37 (zprávy z domova)
  Sbírka dokumentů nacistických úřadů a institucí na
  území okupovaných českých zemí
  Sbírka dokumentů ústředních nacistických orgánů
  politické policie
Zemský archiv v Opavě, pobočka Olomouc
  Oberlandrat Olomouc

Germany

Bundesarchiv Bayreuth, Bayreuth
  Ost-Dokumentation 20: Dokumentation der Sudetendeutschen
  Volksgruppe 1918–1945. Erlebnisberichte
  Ost-Dokumentation 21: Dokumentation der Sudetendeutschen
  Volksgruppe 1918–1945. Berichte über die Tätigkeit der

deutschen Verwaltung des Sudetenlandes 1938–1945 und
des Protektorates Böhmen und Mähren 1939–1945

United States

Columbia University Rare Book and Manuscript Library, New York City
    Jaromír Smutný collection
Hoover Institution on War, Revolution, and Peace, Stanford University
    Český kurýr
    Folder ID: 85037–8.16—Ústřední vedení odboje domácího
    Folder ID: 87026–10.V.—Die jüdische Kultusgemeinde in Prag
    Verordnungsblatt des Reichsprotektors in Böhmen und Mähren, 1939–1945
National Archives and Records Administration, College Park, Maryland
    RG 238 Records of the International Military Tribunal at Nuremberg
    NG Series
    RG 242 Collection of Foreign Records Seized
    Berlin Document Center microfilm, SS Officer Personnel Files
    Rasse-und Siedlungs hauptamt (RuSHA), Ordner
United States Holocaust Memorial Museum, Washington, D.C.
    RG 11.001 M reel 91—Reichsprotektor in Böhmen und Mähren

Published Document Collections

Bareš, Gustav. "Depeše mezi Prahou a Moskvou, 1939–1941." *Příspěvky k dějinám KSČ* 7 (1967).

Beneš, Edvard. *Šest let exilu a druhé světové války.* Prague: Orbis, 1946.

Boberach, Heinz, ed. *Meldungen aus dem Reich 1938–1945: Die geheimen Lageberichte des Sicherheitsdienstes der SS.* Herrsching: Pawlak, 1984.

Čelovský, Boris, ed. *So oder so: Řešení české otázky podle německých dokumentů, 1933–1945.* Ostrava: Sfinga, 1997.

Danimann, Franz. *Flüsterwitze und Spottgedichte unterm Hakenkreuz.* Vienna: Böhlau, 1983.

Deutschland-Berichte der Sozialdemokratischen Partei Deutschlands (Sopade). seven vols. Frankfurt: P. Nettelbeck, 1980.

Doležal, Jiří, and Jan Křen, eds. *Czechoslovakia's Fight: Documents on the Resistance Movement of the Czechoslovak People, 1938–1945.* Prague: Czechoslovak Academy of Sciences, 1964.

Drtina, Prokop. *A nyní promluví Pavel Svatý: Londýnské rozhlasové epištoly z let 1940–1945.* Prague: Melantrich, 1947.

Fremund, Karel. "Dokumenty o nacistické vyhlazovací politice." *SAP* 13, no. 2 (1963): 2–41.

——. "Heydrichova nadace—důležitý nástroj nacistické vyhlazovací politiky." *SAP* 14, no. 1 (1964): 3–16.

Gamm, Hans-Jochen. *Der Flüsterwitz im Dritten Reich.* Munich: Deutscher Taschenbuch, 1979.

Gottwald, Klement. *Selected Speeches and Articles, 1929–1953.* Prague: Orbis, 1954.

Gronský, Jan, ed. *Dokumenty k ústavnímu vývoji Československa.* Prague: Karolinum, 1999.

Gruss, Josef. *Jedna paní povídala.* Prague: Alois Hynek, 1945.

Hillenbrand, Fritz Karl Michael. *Underground Humour in Nazi Germany, 1933–1945.* London: Routledge, 1995.

Jochmann, Werner, ed. *Monologe im Führerhauptquartier 1941–1944: Adolf Hitler: Die Aufzeichnungen Heinrich Heims.* Hamburg, A. Knaus, 1980.

Kaden, Helma, ed. *Die faschistische Okkupationspolitik in Österreich und der Tschechoslowakei (1938–1945)*. [East] Berlin: Deutscher Verlag der Wissenschaften, 1988.

Kárný, Miroslav, and Jaroslava Milotová, eds. *Anatomie okupační politiky hitlerovského Německa v "Protektorátu Čechy a Morava": Dokumenty z období říšského protektora Konstantina von Neuratha*. Prague: Ústav československých a světových dějin ČSAV, 1987.

————, eds. *Protektorátní politika Reinharda Heydricha*. Prague: Archivní správa MV ČR, 1991.

Král, Vaclav, ed. *Die Deutschen in der Tschechoslowakei 1933–1947: Dokumentensammlung*. Prague: Československá akademie věd, 1964.

————, ed. *Lesson from History: Documents concerning Nazi Policies for Germanization and Extermination in Czechoslovakia*. Prague: Orbis, 1960.

Krejčí, Oskar. *Země úsměvů, 1939–1945*. Prague: Gustav Peter, 1945.

Masaryk, Jan. *Volá Londýn*. Prague: Práce, 1948.

Milotová, Jaroslava, and Miroslav Kárný, eds. "Od Neuratha k Heydrichovi: Na rozhraní politiky hitlerovského Německa v 'Protektorátu Čechy a Morava.'" *SAP* 39, no. 2 (1989): 281–394.

Olivová, Věra, ed. *Dopisy bratru Vojtovi, 1938–1944*. Prague: Společnost Edvarda Beneše, 1998.

Otáhalová, Libuše, and Milada Červinková, eds. *Dokumenty z historie československé politiky, 1939–1943*. 2 vols. Prague: Academia, 1966.

Overy, Richard. *Interrogations: The Nazi Elite in Allied Hands, 1945*. New York: Viking, 2001.

Pätzold, Kurt, and Erika Schwartz, eds. *Tagesordnung: Judenmord: Die Wannsee Konferenz am 20. Januar 1942: Eine Dokumentation zur Organisation der "Endlösung."* Berlin: Metropol, 1992.

Schieder, Theodor, ed. *The Expulsion of the German Population from Czechoslovakia*. Bonn: Federal Ministry for Expellees, Refugees, and War Victims, 1960.

Stránský, Jaroslav. *Hovory k domovu*. Prague: Fr. Borový, 1946.

Trial of the Major War Criminals before the International Military Tribunal: Proceedings and Documents. 42 vols. Nuremberg: International Military Tribunal, 1947–1949.

Trials of the War Criminals before the Nuremberg Military Tribunals under Control of Council Law No. 10. 15 vols. Nuremberg: Nuremberg Military Tribunals, 1946–1949.

V boj: Edice ilegálního časopisu. 3 vols. Prague: Vojenský historický archiv, 1995.

Vondrová, Jitka, ed. *Češi a sudetoněmecká otázka 1939–1945: Dokumenty*. Prague: Ústav mezinárodních vztahů, 1994.

Wien wehrt sich mit dem Witz: Flüsterwitze aus den Jahren 1938–1945. Vienna: Im Weltweiten Verlag, 1946.

Acknowledgments

"No, I didn't recognize you!" Jaroslav Seifert says to his beloved city in "Prague in Black," a poem published shortly after the Munich agreement. Previously innocent and loving, Prague in late 1938 seemed to the poet dressed in clothes "mournful and somber." After the creation of the Protectorate, Seifert, like so many Czech artists of his generation, turned to writing poems meant to encourage national solidarity. Yet sadness runs through many of his poems written during the occupation years. Like his city, Seifert's poetry often remained mournful and somber.

Before I wrote this book, I expected to be confronted with events and situations that could only be described as immensely sad. My expectations proved correct, even to the point that while reading my primary sources I, too, barely recognized a culture and country that I had first encountered while an English-language teacher in Moravia shortly after the fall of Communism. Before I wrote this book, I also imagined the process to be a lonely, solitary affair. Here, my expectations were happily proven incorrect, for nothing could have been further from the truth. Thanks to this book I have had the pleasure of meeting, and getting to know, a long list of first-rate scholars. I have had the opportunity to learn from a wide array of individuals; friends and colleagues have graciously offered their time and advice. It is a pleasure to thank at least some of these people here.

Many people have read portions of the manuscript, offering valuable comments and criticisms: Julian Bourg, Christopher R. Browning, Peter Bugge, Kathleen Duval, Catherine Epstein, David Frey, Benjamin Frommer, Eagle Glassheim, Miloš Hořejš, Jeremy King, Katherine Lebow, Damani Partridge, Peter Holquist, Edith Replogle Scheffer, Lisa Fetheringill Swartout, Sarah Willerty, and Daniel Ziblatt. The two anonymous readers for Harvard University Press approached their task with integrity, care, and intelligence. The manuscript is immensely improved thanks to their comments. James Patrick Daughton, Kaarin Michaelsen, and Jason Scott Smith read every word of the manuscript in its earliest stages. Their good humor and good sense made them great editors. Those same qualities still make them great friends. Before I wrote a book, I also puzzled at the tendency among authors to beg forgiveness for inconveniences caused to family and friends. This, too, I now understand. Milada Anna Vachudova read every page of the manuscript, taking her, briefly, away from our otherwise pleasant lives together. My father, the late William A. Bryant, revealed himself to be a talented editor.

I began my archival research in Prague thanks to generous funding from IREX. Without additional federal funding through the ACLS, FLAS, and the National Council for Eurasian and East European Research, this book would not have been realized in its present form. I also benefited greatly from generous funding from the American Historical Association, the Mabelle McLeod Lewis Memorial Fund, the Spray Foundation and the Randleigh Foundation Trust, and numerous institutions at the University of North Carolina at Chapel Hill—the Center for European Studies; the Center for Slavic, Eurasian, and East European Studies; the University Center for International Studies; and the University Research Council, as well as the Committee on Faculty and Research Study Leaves. None of these institutions or the people associated with them is responsible for the views expressed. At the University of North Carolina at Chapel Hill, Josef Anderle, Angela Graf, John Rutledge, and Nadia Zilper have created a library collection that made excellent research at home possible. Jaroslava Severová and Viera Žižková kindly helped in locating many of the book's photographs. Philip Schwartzberg, in addition to introducing me to the art of cartography, drew the book's maps. Krystyna Budd, Andrea Franzius, Barbara Goodhouse, and Lenka Siroká-Buštíková provided invaluable editorial assistance. At Harvard University Press, Kathleen McDermott guided me through the book production process.

In the Czech Republic, Katherine David-Fox, the late Jan Havránek, Stanislav Kokoška, Alena Miškova, and Oldřich Tůma generously offered their time and sage advice, helping me, among other things, to navigate the country's archives. Radovan "Koala" Bouman, David Čaněk, Marek Čaněk, Matt Christopher, Jiří "Marta" Dvořák, Sonja Dvořáková, Kateřina Horničková, Pepa, Ondřej Šnadr, Daša Sotonová, and Veronika Zajaková made, and still make, every return trip enjoyable. The Sonderforschungsbereich "Kriegserfahrungen, Krieg und Gesellschaft in der Neuzeit" at the University of Tübingen in Germany and the Woodrow Wilson Center for Scholars in Washington, D.C., kindly invited me to spend time at their institutions as a visiting scholar. In Tübingen, Dietrich Beyrau, Christoph Mick, Jan Plamper, and Ingrid Schierle also requested my presence at a conference on Eastern European historiographies. I am grateful to them and the following people for inviting me to speak about my research for this book at their respective institutions: Gary Cohen and Eric Weitz; Olga Fejtová; Isabel Heinemann and Ulrich Herbert; Rainer Ohliger; Egbert Klautke and Martin Rady; Jindřich Toman; Dominique Arel; and the many organizers of the German Historical Institute Transatlantic Doctoral Seminar and the Woodrow Wilson Center's Junior Scholars Seminar for East-Central Europe. The book was completed at my new institutional home in Chapel Hill, where the faculty and staff of the History Department well deserve their reputation for collegiality and for supporting young scholars. In this respect Donald J. Raleigh stands out. He not only commented on the whole manuscript but also showed me how to be a professional historian.

It has been a long journey to this point. Wherever my academic life has taken me, I have been blessed with intelligent and caring teachers and mentors. At Middlebury College Marjorie Lamberti and Paul Monod introduced me to the joys of learning history while providing early tutoring in the art of writing. While a graduate student at Berkeley I benefited from the intellectual dynamism of many people—too many to be named here. Some of my earliest ideas worked themselves out during my many afternoon conversations with Eleanor Alexander. Perhaps more than he realizes, James J. Sheehan offered, at exactly the right moment, helpful insights on how to construct a book. David Frick provided much early inspiration for the project, and his comments on an early draft proved invaluable. From my first day at Berkeley, Margaret Lavinia Anderson took a keen interest in my career, playing the role of mentor and guardian angel. Her meticulous editing made me a better writer. Her challenging comments, combined with confident encouragement, spurred me to take on questions I might otherwise have avoided. John Connelly has been a kind friend and my toughest critic. In him I see the scholar that I strive to be: extraordinarily learned, wide-ranging, creative, modest, and dedicated to our craft. My father and my mother, Janet Bryant, have been my most cherished teachers. Without them little that I have accomplished, including this book, would have been possible or worthwhile. After a long and courageous struggle with cancer, William A. Bryant died just months before these pages went to print. Only now do I realize that in many ways I had always been writing this book for him.

Index

Page numbers in italics refer to figures.

"Acting nationally" defined, 4

Agrarian Party, 231, 258

Allied Control Council, 241

"Amphibians" defined, 3–4

Anti-Semitism, 4; Habsburg monarchy and, 17; Czecho-Slovakia (Second Republic) and, 25; "transfer issue" and, 224–225; postwar period and, 249; Nazis and, 268–269. *See also* Aryanization; Jews

Arburg, Adrian von, 256–257

Árijský boj (Aryan Struggle), 149

Aryanization, 82–84; Göring and, 82; Neurath and, 82–83; Oberlandräte and, 82–83; Gestapo and, 83; Nazi Party and, 83; beneficiaries of, 83–85

Auschwitz, 148

Baarová, Lida, 47, 247

Bartoš, Alfred, 168, 172

Belarus, 153–154

Beneš, Edvard, 7, 24–25, 38–39, 62, 67, 89–93, *90*; Munich agreement and, 89, 91–92, 172; as foreign minister, 91; as president, 91–92; Tomáš Masaryk and, 91, 252; political standing and, 93–94, 218–219; propaganda and, 93–94, 171–172; resistance and, 95, 130, 183–184, 188–189; ÚVOD and, 95–103, 130–131; Hácha and, 95, 145; "transfer" issue and, 97–103, 209–215; Stalin and, 130, 208, 209–210, 214; Heydrich assassination and, 167, 171; collaboration and, 189–191; guilt and, 209–210, 212–213; "wild transfer" and, 239; postwar period and, 253–254, 263–264

Beran, Rudolf, 28

Berning, Cornelia, 105–106

Bertsch, Walter, 78, 81, 102, 163

Bormann, Martin, 123

Boycotts, 15, 17, 36, 39, 47, 53, 60, 132

Brandes, Detlef: *Die Tschechen unter deutschem Protektorat*, 7

British Broadcasting Company (BBC), 93–94

Broszat, Martin, 105–106

Browning, Christopher, 146

Burgsdorff, Kurt von, 127

Čas (Time), 91

Censorship, 36–37, 58–59, 264

Censuses, 14, 16, 17, 21–22, 45

Central Association of Industry, 78

Central Office for Jewish Emigration, 50–51

Černý, Václav, 196, 200

Certeau, Michel de, 201

Český kurýr (Czech Courier), 98, 101

Český svaz pro spolupráci s Němci (Czech League for Cooperation with the Germans), 44, 68–69

Chamberlain, Neville, 24

Churchill, Winston, 89, 208, 209, 217, 240–241, 261

Citizenship: interwar Czechoslovakia (First Republic) and, 20; Reich German, 51–57, 71–74, 135–136, 152, 157, 160–162, 174, 226; "organized transfer" and, 232, 242–246

Civil society and political society: effects of Nazi rule on, 5, 38, 39, 75, 87; Habsburg monarchy and, 13–15; Czechoslovakia

Civil society (*continued*)
  (First Republic) and, 18, 20–21; postwar
  Czechoslovakia and, 256, 257–258;
  Communist rule and final destruction of,
  264; defined, 277, n.12
Collaboration (*kolaborace*), 5–6, 189–191
Communist underground, 38, 39, 62, 86, 88,
  98, 130–131, 143, 172, 184, 260; and "wild
  transfer," 226, 229, 234, 237, 238. *See also*
  Czechoslovak Communist Party; *Rudé právo*
Connelly, John, 136–137
Corbain, Alain, 202
Council of Three, 184
Čurda, Karel, 171
Czech Armaments Works, 78
Czech Republic, 256–266
Czechs under Nazi Rule (Mastny), 7
Czechoslovak Army, radicalization of,
  228–229
Czechoslovak Communist Party, 38, 86,
  130–131, 214, 253, 259–261; Gestapo
  and, 196; "transfer" issue and, 215–216
Czechoslovakia (First Republic) and
  interwar period, 17–25; population
  according to nationality, *19*
Czecho-Slovakia (Second Republic),
  25–26
Czechoslovakia and postwar period:
  Czechoslovak Communist Party and, 253;
  Edvard Beneš and, 253–254, 263–264;
  economy, 254–256; National Front
  government and, 254; Two-Year Plan and,
  255; civil and political society and, 256,
  257–258; borderlands and, 256–257, old
  beliefs and, 258–259; Soviet Union and,
  259–260; Western Europe and, 261–262;
  Communist coup and, 263–264

Daladier, Édouard, 24
Daniel, Ignatz, 53
David, Zdeněk, 235
Dennler, Wilhelm, 131–132
Deutsche Bank, 81, 83
Deutsche Kulturverband, 48
Devětsil avant-gardists, 38
Dnešek (Today), 244, 249
Dresdner Bank, 81, 83
Drtina, Prokop, 212, 217, 230
Dubovský, Aleš, 206–207

Eden, Anthony, 241
Eichmann, Adolf, 50, 149; Heydrich and, 142
Eliáš, Alois, 43–44, 95, 130, 172; Heydrich
  and, 144–145
European Union, Czech Republic and,
  265–266

Fascists, Czech, 44
Feierabend, Ladislav, 258
Ferdinand, Franz, 17
Fiechtner, Eugen, 45–46, 49, 70, 160; Nazi
  plans for Germanization and, 122
Fierlinger, Zdeněk, 231, 240; "organized
  transfer" and, 245
Foreign Affairs, 211, 213–214
Forster, Albert, 112–113
France, 65, 101–102. *See also under* World
  War II
Frank, Karl Hermann, 23–24, 33–34, *35*, 48,
  52–53, 60, 65; Volkstumsarbeit and, 74;
  Nazi Germanization plans in the
  Protectorate and, 104–105, 114, 117, 121,
  125, 128, 159, 173; Hitler and, 117, 121;
  Heydrich and, 141; "total war" and, 182;
  "transfer" issue and, 219–220; trial of,
  247–248, 253
Frommer, Benjamin, 247
Führer, Der. *See* Hitler, Adolf

Gabčík, Jozef, 167–168
Gellner, Ernest, 2, 106
General Government, 111, 154, 155, 188,
  198. *See also* Poland
Generalplan Ost (General Plan East), 154, 174
German University in Prague, 49, 118
Germanizability, testing for, 154–159
Germanization, Nazi plans in the
  Protectorate for, 3, 114–128, 159–163,
  166, 173–175; economic and military
  considerations and, 10, 116–117, 127,
  140, 162–163, 174–175, 176; Neurath
  and, 23, 104–105, 108–109, 117, 119,
  122, 125, 128; Hitler and, 23, 108–109,
  116, 125; Frank and, 104–105, 114, 117,
  121, 125, 128, 159, 173; Oberlandräte
  and, 114–115, 122, 128; Protectorate
  Germans, Intelligence Service, and,
  121–122; Nazi Party and, 122–123, 125;
  Heydrich and, 125–126, 159–163, 166

Gestapo, 1, 33–35, 66–69; "enemies of the Reich" and, 1, 25; informants, 44, 62, 72, 89, 195–196, 198, 220; censorship and, 58–59, 143; Göring Works and, 78; Aryanization and, 83, 88–89; Heydrich assassination and, 169–172; schools and, 193; Czechoslovak Communist Party and, 196

Glassheim, Eagle, 237

Globocnik, Odilo

Goebbels, Hermann, 47, 131; "total war" and, 180–181

"Good Czechs," 38–40, 179–180, 197–198, 250–251

Göring, Hermann, 33, 162; Großraumwirtschaft and, 76–77; Aryanization and, 82; Poland and, 111; "final solution" and, 146

Göring Works, 78, 81, 101–102

Gottberg, Curt von, 110

Gottwald, Klement, 214–215, 217, 263

Great Depression, 22–23

Gross, Jan, 9, 258

Großraumwirtschaft, 76–77, 101; Göring and, 76–77; price controls and, 78–79; foreign trade and, 79–80; Reich Customs Union and, 80; foreign investment and, 81; Neurath and, 82

Gypsies, 3, 57, 177–178; Nazi definitions of, 152–153

Habsburg monarchy, 11–17

Hácha, Emil, 28–30, 41–45, *43*, 63, 87, 130; Munich agreement and, 42; Beneš and, 95, 145; Heydrich and, 144–145; collaboration and, 191; death of, 253

Heinemann, Isabel, 175

Henke, Klaus-Dietmar, 251

Henlein, Konrad, 23–24, 34, *35*, 49, 253

Herder, Johann Gottfried, 11–12

Heydrich, Reinhard, 108, 137, 139–140; Intelligence Service and, 33, 141; goals and ideology, 108, 130–140; Himmler and, 111, 141; Poland and, 111–112; Nazi Germanization plans in the Protectorate and, 125–126, 159–163, 166; resistance and, 136, 142–145; arrival in Prague, 139, *142*, 143; Germanizability, notions about, and, 139, 154, 158; background, 141–143;

Eichmann and, 142; terror and, 142–145; "optical effects" and, 144–145; "final solution" and, 146–152; Nazi Party and, 160; assassination of, 163–170; schools and, 193

Himmler, Heinrich, 34, 108, Heydrich and 111, 141; Poland and, 111–113, 115–116; "final solution" and, 112; "Some Thoughts on the Treatment of Alien Populations," 113; Generalplan Ost and, 154, 174; Ukraine and, 154, 174–175

Hitler, Adolf, 2, 23; Nazi Germanization plans in the Protectorate and, 23, 108–109, 116, 125; Neurath and, 36, 125; creation of Protectorate and, 28–30; *Mein Kampf*, 107, 108–109; Poland and, 111; Frank and, 117, 121; "Garden of Eden" declaration, 146

Horký, Karel, 41–42

Hrabal, Bohumil: *I Served the King of England*, 223

Hus, Jan, 40

I Served the King of England (Hrabal), 223

Industrial workers, 255–256; Great Depression and, 22; unemployment and, 85; German war effort and, 85–86, 175–176, 182–183; resistance, strikes, and, 85, 132–135, 185, 188; food shortages and, 133–135; Heydrich and, 144; Czechoslovak Communist Party and, 255–256, 264

Ingr, Sergej, 96

Intelligence Service (Sicherheitsdienst), 10; "enemies of the Reich" and, 25; organization and powers of, 33–34; Heydrich and, 33; repression and, 37; Protectorate Germans and, 49; amphibians and, 75; Jews and, 82–83; Nazi Germanization plans in the Protectorate and, 121–222

Iron Curtain, 263

Jaksch, Wenzel, 99, 204

Jesenská, Milena, 38, 39, 58

Jews, 1, 3, 4; Habsburg monarchy and, 17; Czechoslovakia (First Republic) and, 21–22; Czecho-Slovakia (Second Republic) and, 25; early Protectorate measures against, 50–52, 58; Nazi

Jews (continued)
  definitions of, 51, 149–152; Nuremberg
  Laws and, 51, 151; Mischlinge and, 52,
  151–152, 173; Reich Citizenship Law and,
  151; Heydrich and, 146–147; "final
  solution" and, 146–152, 173, 176;
  "organized transfer" and, 248–249. See
  also Anti-Semitism; Aryanization
Jokes and rumors, 198–203
Judt, Tony, 206
Jury, Hugo, 34, 122–123, 125, 157, 253

Kaplan, Karel, 249
Kennan, George, 1, 34
Kershaw, Ian, 109
King, Jeremy, 244
Klapka, Otokar, 144–145
Klecanda, Vojtěch Vladimír, 232
Klofáč, Václav, 91
König-Beyer, Walter, 126
Kopecký, Václav, 232
Košice Program, 231–232, 246–247
Kramář, Karel, 91
Krejčí, Jaroslav, 44, 158
Krofta, Kamil, 118
Kubiš, Jan, 167–169
Kundera, Milan, 259
Künzel, Erwin, 159
Kural, Václav, 97
Kuratorium, 193–194, 205

Lammers, Heinrich, 114
League of North Moravian Germans, 15
"Lebensraum," Nazi ideology and, 107,
  108, 109
Lewis, Cecil Day, 172
Lidice, destruction of, 168–169, 172, 179
Lidové noviny (The People's News), 37
Lockart, Bruce, 213–214
London Times, 91
Luža, Radomír, 194

Mácha, Karel Hynek, 39
Macura, Vladimír, 200
Mann, Thomas, 172
Marshall Plan, 263
Masaryk, Jan, 188, 190; "transfer issue" and,
  212, 250; Czech Anti-Semitism and, 225;
  postwar period and, 253–254

Masaryk, Tomáš, 22, 37, 40, Beneš and,
  91, 252
Mastny, Vojtech, 214; Czechs under Nazi
  Rule, 7
Mauthausen concentration camp, 142
Mein Kampf (Hitler), 107, 108–109, 116
Meyer, Konrad, 154, 173
Military draft, 53–54
Millay, Edna St. Vincent, 172
Moravec, Emanuel, 145, 181–182, 191,
  204, 253
Moravec, František, 96
Müller, Karl Valentin, 118–119
Munich agreement, 2, 26; Hácha and, 42;
  Beneš and, 89, 91–92, 172
Mussolini, Benito, 24
Mylnář, Zdeněk, 260

Naimark, Norman, 9, 209, 254
National Front government, 254
National movements: Czech, 11–14;
  German, 12–14, 18; civil and political
  society and, 13–15, 18, 20–21;
  combativeness and, 14; industrialization
  and, 14–16; "professional nationalists"
  and, 15; schools and, 15–16; boycotts and,
  15, 17; religion and, 15, 40–41
National Socialist Party of Czechoslovakia,
  91, 256, 258, 260, 262
National Solidarity Movement, 44–45, 54,
  61; Protectorate of Bohemia and Moravia
  and, 86–87
National Union of Employees, 144
Nationality: amphibians, choice of, and, 3–4,
  16–17, 21–22; collaboration and, 5; Nazis
  and, 5; resistance and, 5; myths of, 6; Jews
  and, 17, 21–22. See also Citizenship;
  Germanizability, testing for; "Good Czechs";
  Gypsies; Jews; "Organized transfer"; Race
"Nationality politics," defined, 5
Nazi Party (Nationalsozialistische Deutsche
  Arbeiterpartei, or National Socialist
  German Workers' Party): organization and
  powers of, 33, 49, 123, 124; Reich German
  citizenship and, 52, 53, 57, 74, 157, 174;
  Aryanization and, 83; Nazi Germanization
  plans in the Protectorate and, 122–123,
  125: Heydrich and, 160
Nečas, Jaromír, 98

Nejedlý, Zdeněk, 231
Neurath, Konstantin von, 23, 31–36, *35*,
    41–42, 48–49; Nazi Germanization plans
    in the Protectorate and, 23, 104–105,
    108–109, 117, 119, 122, 125, 128;
    Großraumwirtschaft and, 82; Hitler and,
    36, 125; racial mixing and, 119; ousting,
    135–136; trial of, 253
Nicholai, Helmut, 158
Nisko Project, 112
Nuremberg Laws, 3, 25, 51, 55–56, 58

Oberlandräte: organization and powers of,
    31, *32*; Reich German citizenship and, 31,
    52–53, 54–57, 71–74, 135–136, 157,
    160–162, 174; Protectorate Germans
    versus Reich Germans and, 45–50;
    Volkstumsarbeit and, 67–71; Aryanization
    and, 82–83; Nazi Germanization plans in
    the Protectorate and, 114–115, 122, 128;
    reduced powers under Heydrich, 160
Obrana národa, 38–39
Opletal, Jan, 60
"Organized transfer," 240–252; Potsdam
    Conference and, 3, 209, 241–242, 268;
    questions of guilt and, 209, 211–213, 214,
    216, 247–249; citizenship and, 232,
    242–246; restoration of order and, 242;
    Czech economy and, 245; Fierlinger and,
    245; Czech population and, 245–246;
    "antifascists" and, 246–247; Jews and,
    248–249; Settlement Office in Prague and,
    256–257. *See also* "Transfer" issue
Orwell, George, 269

Pan-German League, 107
Pekař, Josef, 119
Peroutka, Ferdinand, 37–38, 45, 58, 119,
    253; "apolitical politics" and, 63; hatred
    of Germans and, 258
Poland, 57; Nazi ideology and, 107–109;
    Adolf Hitler and, 109; Nazi population
    politics and, 110–114, 116, 128, 139–140,
    154, 156–157
Poldina huť Iron and Steel Works, 78
Politické ústředí (Political Central), 38–39
Population bridges, 114–115, 122
Potsdam Conference, 1, 3, 209, 240–242, 268
Prager Abend (Prague Evening), 35

Prague Jewish Congregation, 50, 58, 149,
    150–151
Prague Uprising, 233–235, 257–258
Přítomnost (Presence), 38, 58
"Protectorate Germans" defined, 6
Protectorate Germans versus Reich Germans,
    6, 45–50, 75–76, 86, 121, 174, 203–204
Protectorate of Bohemia and Moravia, 2, 29;
    organization of, 31–36, 123–124; Czech
    government and, 41–45. *See also specific
    people, organizations, and subjects*

Race: Nazi definitions of, 158–159, 177–178;
    testing for, 159–166, 175–176
Race and Settlement Office, SS, 114, 126,
    155; Frank and, 159; Heydrich and, 161
Racial mixing, 117–119
Raeder, Erich, 141
Reich Citizenship Law, 51
Reich Commissariat for the Strengthening of
    Germandom, 111, 159–169
Reich Protector's Office, 29, 31, 36. *See also*
    Frank, Karl Hermann; Heydrich,
    Reinhard; Neurath, Konstantin von
Reichsgau Sudetenland, 25, 33, 41, 75, 83,
    123, 160, 204, 228
Resistance (*odboj*), 5–6, 59–61, 88–89,
    184–189; Beneš and, 95, 130, 183–184,
    188–189; Soviet Union, German invasion
    of, and, 129–135; boycott of official
    newspapers, 132–133; Neurath and,
    135–136; Heydrich and, 136, 142–145
Röhm, Ernst, 141
Roma, 3, 7, 57
Roosevelt, Franklin Delano, 93, 214
Rorty, Richard, 200–201
Rosenberg, Alfred, 109, 120
Roštiková, Milena, 269
Rudé právo (Red Truth), 39, 98, 131, 205
Rumors and jokes, 198–199, 201–203

St. James Declaration, 189, 212
St. Wenceslas, 59, 88
Sauckel, Fritz, 163, 174
Schönerer, Georg von, 122
Schools, 15–16, 18, 21, 48, 49, 50, 68, 70,
    73, 127, 192–193
Schörner, Ferdinand, 232
Seyss-Inquart, Arthur, 46

Škoda Works, 78, 168, 185
Slovakia, 25, 26, 81, 205, 229, 257, 261
Social Democratic Party of Czechoslovakia, 39, 254, 256, 263
Sokol, 13, 47, 143
"Some Thoughts on the Treatment of Alien Populations" (Himmler), 113
Soviet Union, 63, 128–129; Czech resistance following the German invasion of, 129–135; Treaty of Friendship and Cooperation (Czechoslovakia-Soviet Union), 208; postwar period and, 259–260
Spann, Othmar, 23
Speer, Albert, 162
Stránský, Jaroslav, 184, 217; resistance and, 184
Stuckart, Wilhelm, 31–33, 48–49
Stürmer, Der (One Who Storms), 120
Sudeten German Party, 23, 24, 34, 49, 52
Sudetenland, 2, 25. *See also* Reichsgau Sudetenland
Svoboda, Ludvík, 231

Teichová, Alice, 255
Terezín concentration camp, 147, 148, 232
Thümmel, Paul, 129, 143
"Total war," 180–181; Protectorate economy and, 182–183
Toussaint, Rudolf, 233
"Transfer" issue: ÚVOD and initial debates about, 97–103; Beneš and, 97–103, 209–215; Czechoslovak Communist Party and, 215–216; Czech hatred of the Germans and, 219–224. *See also* "Organized transfer"; "Wild transfer"
Treaty of Friendship and Cooperation (Czechoslovakia-Soviet Union), 208
Truman Doctrine, 262–263
Tschechen unter deutschem Protektorat, Die (Brandes), 7
Turnverein, 13

Ukraine, 153, 154, 174–175
Unemployment, 85

Ústřední vedení odboje domácího (Central Leadership of the Home Resistance) (ÚVOD), 87–88; initial debates about "transfer" issue and, 97–103; Heydrich and, 143; Heydrich assassination and, 168–169

V boj (In Battle), 39, 60, 131
Vítkovice Mining and Iron Works, 78, 79, 81, 185
Vlasov, Andrej Andrejovič, 234
"Volk," Nazi ideology and, 105–106, 108, 109
Volksliste (List of Germans), 156–157
Volkstumsarbeit (nationality work), 69–76; Oberlandräte and, 67–71; funding for, 69–70; "new Germans" and, 71–72; amphibians and, 72–73; Reich German citizenship and, 73–74; Frank and, 74
Volkstumsfond (nationality fund), 69–70, 136, 160

Wannsee Conference, 148, 151–152
Weber, Max, 107
"Werewolves," 240
"Wild transfer," 10, 230–240; results of, 239. *See also* "Transfer" issue
Wolff, Karl Hermann, 122
World War II, 11, 225–226; Poland, invasion of, 2, 57, 225–226; France, defeat of, 66, 125; Soviet Union, invasion of, 129; during 1942–1943, 180–181; during 1943–1944, 205; Potsdam Conference, 209, 240–242; Yalta Conference, 217; final months of, 225–227
Wright, Gordon, 62

Yalta Conference, 217
Yugoslavia, 185, 229, 262

Zahra, Tara, 205
Zeman, Zbyněk, 190
Židovské listy (The Jewish Pages), 149
Žižka, Jan, 120